Modern Socialism

A volume
in
THE DOCUMENTARY HISTORY
of
WESTERN CIVILIZATION

MODERN SOCIALISM

edited by
MASSIMO SALVADORI

WALKER AND COMPANY
New York

Published in the United States of America in
1968 by Walker and Company, a division of the
Walker Publishing Company, Inc.

Published simultaneously in Canada by
The Ryerson Press, Toronto.

Volumes in this series are published in association
with Harper & Row, Publishers, Inc., from
whom paperback editions are available in Harper
Torchbooks.

Contents

I

Introduction

Summary: A few data—Definition—Anti-capitalism—Equality—Fraternity—Other facets—The dual soul of socialism—The role of the
intelligentsia—A continuing thread—The libertarian phase—Socialdemocracy and laborism—Marxism—The debate on democracy—Marxism-Leninism or communism—Democratic Socialism—Nationalcommunism and other recent socialist variations.

A FEW DATA: The term socialist, particularly if spelled with a capital S, is conventionally applied to tendencies, parties, governments,
groups, and individuals who belong to the democratic, or liberal,
wing of the socialist movement. Some are, or consider themselves
to be, Marxists. Most are not. The term communist is mostly
applied to the authoritarian and totalitarian wing of socialism, the
bulk of it formed by Marxist communists. Although this distinction is an oversimplification, it can be useful in making an approximate estimate of the present extent of world socialism.

In the late 1960's there was enough political liberty to make
democracy (however limited and imperfect) meaningful in fewer
than fifty independent states with about one and a quarter billion
inhabitants. Authoritarian or dictatorial régimes of various kinds,
from traditional monarchies to military and radical dictatorships of
the left and of the right, were in control of the other ninety-odd
independent countries and several territories on the threshold of
independence, with just over two billion inhabitants. In seven
democracies majority or minority socialist governments were in
power or had recently been in power for some time. In another
seven, socialists were senior or junior partners of coalition governments. In fourteen, socialists formed the opposition or were a
significant element in it. Forty-nine democratic socialist, social-
democratic, and labor parties with a membership close to 15 million
and an electoral strength in democratic countries of around 80

million, were affiliated with the Socialist International. Eleven democratic socialist parties were affiliated with the Asian Socialist Conference, and other kindred parties were unaffiliated with any international organization. Politically close to the Socialist International were most of about 120 labor organizations with a membership close to 65 million, affiliated with the International Confederation of Free Trade Unions; also many of the 200 million members of half a million cooperatives affiliated with the International Co-Operative Alliance. In twenty-eight dictatorships with combined populations of over 1.4 billion, power was in the hands of communists, socialnationalists, and other authoritarian socialists. Communist parties and Workers' parties of Marxist persuasion were nearly one hundred, and had a membership of about 55 million. Many of the organizations that joined the Tri-Continent Solidarity Conference, established in Havana early in 1966, were communist oriented or communist supported. Forty-one labor organizations with a membership close to 140 million were affiliated with the communist-controlled World Federation of Trade Unions.

There is some overlapping in these figures. Also, not all members of a socialist-led organization are socialists; certainly many or most citizens in countries governed democratically or dictatorially by socialists are not. On the other hand, there are many socialists who do not belong to any organization and do not vote for democratic or authoritarian socialist parties in countries where voting is meaningful. But all in all, the above figures give an idea of the size of the socialist movement, which had its beginnings in western Europe during the first half of the nineteenth century and later spread among most nations to become a major force in mankind today. Of particular significance is the fact that socialism in its various forms appeals more than any other ideology to large sections of the intelligentsia, mankind's dynamic element.

DEFINITION: There is no denying the varieties of socialism. The names socialists give themselves, and the adjectives they use to distinguish themselves from other socialists, correspond to different tendencies, currents, schools of thought, political organizations. Today, besides socialists without qualification there are Social-democrats, Laborites, Communists of several persuasions. It is a peculiarity of socialism that currents have often been called after a prominent individual, from Babouvism, Marxism, Blanquism, to Castroism, Nasserism, Maoism. Adjectives characterizing a specific socialist tendency have included revisionist, reformist, meliorist, possibilist, democratic, libertarian, revolutionary, dogmatist, authoritarian, totalitarian; also Christian, Fabian, and more recently African. In the wide socialist stream were currents that have now disappeared or are disappearing: Syndicalism, Anarchism, Anarcosyndicalism, (East European) Populism. New tendencies have emerged in recent decades: Nationalcommunism, "Arab" socialnationalism, the New Left in European and North American democracies. It may be noted here that by majority consent of both socialists and nonsocialists, European National Socialism (Nazism) and kindred movements in all continents are not considered to be socialist, despite their labels.

The variations seem to bear out the commonplace that a comprehensive definition of socialism—as of most isms—is difficult, even impossible. Actually, it presents no difficulty provided one takes into account what has been and what is, not, as is done by socialist thinkers whose subjective definitions are derived from *a priori* principles, just what should be. What *should be* represents the goal on the ideal plane, and has the support of an ideology that is often a logically integrated web of rationalizations rather than of principles. Goals and rationalizations act as motivating force, are part of the socialist scene, and must be included in the definition. But they are only a part of it. What *is* includes the few simple concepts and values shared by millions, the common denominator of those who belong to the socialist movement. There is a relationship between the complex ideas formulated by thinkers and the simpler ideas that form the consensus of the many; but it is the simpler that matter most for understanding the socialist movement. What *is* also includes what socialists have done and do, and this differs from the ideology as much as the practice of a religion differs from holy writ. All influential socialists, and hordes of uninfluential ones, have given their definitions of socialism. Through empirical analysis the historian finds what makes for agreement among those who call themselves socialists. Without that agreement there would be no socialist movement.

Analysis of what *is* tells us how the practice diverges from the ideas. It also tells us which of several meanings socialists give to terms describing concepts important as guides to action: equality, class struggle, collectivism, fraternity, peace, justice, democracy, etc. It tells us their order of priority: if civil war is necessary to achieve classlessness, and dictatorship is required to organize collectivism, what takes precedence, classlessness and collectivism or peace and democracy? Socialists have been divided both on meanings and priorities. Taking as a base the consensus among socialists —or, more accurately, among the majority of those who have called and call themselves socialists—socialism during the formative period, from the origins to the crisis of 1917 and the succeeding years, which compelled socialists to clarify and modify their position, can be briefly described as follows: a movement centered on uncompromising opposition to capitalism, giving pre-eminence to the economic aspect of life, convinced that the end of capitalism will usher in an era of permanent prosperity, peace, and progress; aimed at achieving an egalitarian and brotherly society through the abolition of most or all individual ownership of property; strengthened by the certainty of possessing the truth and the key to happiness for all. From critical revision of these convictions and beliefs, in some cases (particularly after 1917) reaching the point of rejection, came contemporary democratic socialism. From dogmatic application of the same convictions and beliefs came Marxist communism and other variations of authoritarian socialism.

ANTI-CAPITALISM: During the formative period three elements were outstanding in socialism: anti-capitalism, equality, and fraternity. Some, exaggeratedly, maintain that anti-capitalism has perhaps been the only element common to all socialists. Certainly it took first place, at least emotionally, over the others. A few observations on what was implicit in anti-capitalism, or closely linked to it, are pertinent to today's developments:

Socialists were clearer about what they were against than about what they were for. Their energies were focused on discussion of capitalism and agitation against it. On the formulation of socialism there was, in contrast, vagueness.

Socialists differed in what they intended by capitalism. For most, it was a vague general term including practically everything nonsocialist. Every economic system in which enterprises were owned privately they described as capitalist, lumping under the same heading free enterprise economies functioning in a free market under the stimulus of profit-making, domestic exchange economies in which the role of capital was minimal, corporative and welfare economies in which free enterprise was severely restricted, neomercantilistic economies in which the free market had been suppressed, and mixed economies in which the public sector played a greater role than the private. Profit epitomized the evils of capitalism. Its share of the economy was usually exaggerated.

Attributing all evil to capitalism, socialists (at first following a Manichaean way of thinking, later refined into a dialectical one) attributed all virtue to what they considered its antithesis, overlooking the fact that an antithesis can be as defective as its thesis. For most socialists the antithesis meant collectivism, an economic system in which all or most means of production, distribution, and exchange are owned and managed by the state, or whatever agency the organized community operates through. For other socialists (sometimes many, sometimes few), the antithesis was cooperativism, a system in which enterprises are owned and managed not by the state or some other public body but collectively by private individuals; or syndicalism, a system in which the workers manage the enterprises.

In total rejection of capitalism was implicit the will to destroy the so-called bourgeois classes. In socialist terminology bourgeoisie meant the owners and managers of big business, petty bourgeoisie meant small business. To the bourgeoisie as evil was opposed the proletariat as goodness. Definitions of the proletariat were many: it might include all who worked or only manual workers, all wage-earners or only industrial wage-earners.

Individualism, supposedly the key value in a capitalistic society, was rejected and replaced by communalism, postulating the priority of the group over the individual. The group that mattered was the socioeconomic, not the geographic, ethnic, or cultural. Taking a leaf from the book of nineteenth-century European sociologists, most socialists maintained that classes and society have a life of their own, independent of the individuals composing it. Society, for instance, thinks, wills, and acts. It is also responsible for the welfare of the individual. Competition in economic activities or, better, in all activities, is replaced by cooperation, preferably voluntary but compulsory if need be.

Because of their concern with the economic aspect of life, most socialists stressed materialism, subscribing at the level of intellectual speculation to the tenets of a philosophical school that originated in ancient Greece; revived in the eigthteenth century, particularly among the French intelligentsia, in the wake of the emancipation of minds brought about by the intellectual revolution of the previous century; became, under the name of Marxism, a major dogmatic school of thought by the last quarter of the nineteenth century; and is today the conceptual framework of large, possibly the largest, sectors of the world intelligentsia.

EQUALITY: For most socialists, equality came second only to anti-capitalism as an idea and a powerful emotion. There have been small socialist schools of thought rejecting equality, advocating instead rule by the best. More important, equality has been absent in all régimes established since 1917 by authoritarian socialists, founded rather on the separation between a closed oligarchy of party leaders and organizers, and the masses of the people. Whatever the ideological exceptions and the practice, however, equality was, and has remained, a basic article in the creed of most socialists. It was identified with justice. As with other general concepts, the translation of equality into concrete terms was not easy. For run-of-the-mill socialists, who count in the socialist movement more than sophisticated intellectuals, equality simply meant uniformity; uniformity in economic standards at the level of practical activities, uniformity in ways of thinking at the level of intellectual activities. Democrats—convinced that diversity is the natural outcome of conditions of freedom enabling citizens to formulate their own position on any problem, and that diversity, being the source of progress, is good—saw in equal rights and equality before the law the formula for peaceful coexistence of diverse groups. Maintaining that differences of opinion, the main cause of tensions, derive from divergent economic interests, socialists were not concerned—in relation to their own society—about problems of diversity and the relationships between groups with diverse opinions. Since, according to them, divergent economic interests result from private ownership of property, when this is abolished all citizens think alike.

FRATERNITY: Socialists of the formative period shared the ultimate aim of the affluent society without divisions and hence without tensions; composed of happy and contented individuals cooperating voluntarily for the common weal, particularly in what matters

most, the production of material goods; taking (because of affluence, without quarreling or depriving anyone else) from the common pool what each needs or (during a transitional period, until
affluence is achieved) what would be assigned to each as compensation for his labor. From each according to his abilities and to each
according to his needs has been a simple and appealing slogan for
four generations of socialists. To achieve harmony in the society all
that was needed was affluence: this could be obtained through the
elimination of capitalism, in socialist eyes a wasteful and inefficient
system, and especially of profit, the source of greed and cause of
scarcity. With affluence, there would no longer be any motives for
quarrels, divisions, conflicts, because these are due to scarcity and
to the greed of the strong exploiting the weak. Peace would reign,
within and between nations, until such time as there would be just
one brotherly world society. Pacifism has been a dominant socialist
theme, even if there have been great divergences on how to achieve
peace—views ranging, since the beginning, from the immediate
renunciation of violence in any form (which made of Tolstoi and
Gandhi heroes in the eyes of socialists of past generations) to the
extreme use of violence aimed at destroying all enemies of peace, as
advocated by generations of terrorists. Whatever the means, peace
was sincerely a major aim.

Beyond the immediate concerns stemming from revulsion against
suffering of all kinds, and beyond action geared to a determination
to end suffering, was the vision of a society (eventually to embrace
all mankind, it was hoped) without corruption, ambition, or greed,
without insanity, crime, or war, without repression or suppression,
without any of the pathological manifestations socialists attributed
to private ownership of property. This vision was shared by early
socialist thinkers as different as Owen, Fourier, Herzen, and Marx;
three or four generations later it was shared by socialists no less
different, such as Cole, Browder, Nehru, and Mao. The City of
God of heavenly love, which gave inspiration and courage to
Christians during the difficult formative centuries of Christianity,
was replaced by the City of Man of brotherly love. One need only
scrape the crust formed by rationalizations of all kinds, to find
underneath the simple and generous vision that is the source of
socialism's strength and of its appeal—and that matters more than
any rationalization. From Léon Blum in France to Chou En-lai in
China, to Norman Thomas in the United States, intellectuals of the

first rank have been motivated by this vision of prosperity and peace no less powerfully than nonintellectuals.

Firmly and sincerely convinced that socialism would usher in the triumph of equality, brotherhood, and peace, socialists saw in the abolition of capitalism the most radical step ever taken in the progressive transformation of mankind. For them it was a step more important than the replacement of fetishist paganism with spiritual monotheism; more important than the replacement of absolutism with régimes founded on liberty; more important in the modern Western context than Reformation and Counter-Reformation, than the intellectual revolution, scientific discoveries, technological inventions and the Industrial Revolution, than the British, American, and French Revolutions of the seventeenth and eighteenth centuries. Socialists saw in their movement the embodiment of genuine progressive revolutionarism.

OTHER FACETS: The development of socialism has been tied to those aspects that socialists were particularly aware of—the opposition to capitalism, the search for equality, the vision of a society founded on brotherly love. It has also been tied to those elements which socialists ignored but which existed; or dismissed as irrelevant when they were not; or were unconscious of in their thinking, but which were still manifest when problems were met in the course of action —whatever the kind of action, from the organization of communist settlements in the United States in the 1820's and of semi-clandestine societies in France in the 1830's, to the consolidation of power in China after 1949. What socialists left unsaid was as important for their movement as what they said. It explains the contradictions, the gap between the idea and the practice, and the failures.

More than anything else, the vision outlined above made for the utopianism that nonsocialists considered a basic feature of socialism. Socialists have accused one another of utopianism: actually the utopian element was present in all schools of socialist thought during the first hundred years of the movement, and in most during the last half century. Besides the ultimate vision of happiness, several convictions shared by most socialists contributed to utopianism: that human behavior can be reduced to a function of the economic environment; that those who share identical economic status think alike; that workers are socialists, *qua* workers;

that the socialist state (or whatever organizational structure replaces it) lacks the defects of nonsocialist states; that economic affluence makes for happiness. Each conviction contains a small or large element of truth. Each becomes error when one conceives it, as socialists did, as total truth.

Oversimplification of everything pertaining to man was another major facet of the socialist position. Socialism sprang from the awareness (made possible by freedom of expression) of grievous socioeconomic problems, and socialists saw all problems solely in the light of the economic ones. Ignoring the evidence that, for instance, identical ways of thinking and values are to be found in different economic structures, they were genuinely convinced that a change in the economic structure would affect everything, from politics to ideas. From this kind of simplification derived their impatience with the debates, fundamental for nonsocialist modern revolutionaries, on political systems. (Impatience did not prevent socialists from quarreling among themselves more about political problems than economic ones.) The discussion on the organization of power among conservatives, liberals, democrats, was dismissed as futile. Most socialists thought of themselves as democrats, but their democracy had little or nothing to do with constitutionalism, free representative institutions, rule of law, bills of rights, and the rest of the position painfully elaborated through generations-long efforts by nonsocialist democrats on both sides of the Atlantic and beyond.

Convinced that differences of opinion would not exist in their society, socialists replaced the democrats' intellectual and political pluralism with monism. The socialists did not face the problem of diversity, present even under the most egalitarian conditions in any society that has gone beyond the most primitive level. They did not face the problem of finding a formula for the coexistence of a multiplicity of tendencies. No socialist thinker was concerned with the problem of "others," those who for any reason might choose not to be socialists. The question of means, again fundamental for democrats, was glossed over as meaningful only from the angle of expediency until the time came in the twentieth century (and specifically in relation to the events following the success of Marxist socialists in Russia in 1917) when it suddenly acquired the importance as an ethical problem that it should have had from the beginning.

Utopianism, simplification, monism, all were manifestations of dogmatism, another of socialism's major facets in the formative period. Most socialists prided themselves on being rationalists. In making reason the guide to their action, they saw themselves as heirs to the Enlightenment. In effect, they postulated the priority of reason over nonreason. However, unlike the followers of Locke, Voltaire, and Kant, they also postulated the omnipotence of reason and did not face the problem of its limitations, which is the problem of error and of the need for a procedure to uncover and correct it. The conviction that they possessed the truth made for intolerance of other views, noticeable even in such otherwise moderate socialists as the Fabians in Great Britain. For many socialists, socialism was a secular faith with all the attributes of religion. As believers often do, socialists tended to live among themselves and to alienate themselves from the rest of the community. In nonsocialists they saw enemies with whom no reconciliation was possible, or else future converts who could be emancipated from ignorance with whom contacts took the form of missionary activities.

THE DUAL SOUL OF SOCIALISM: Because of the role played by anti-capitalism, early socialism is best understood when seen against the background of the system whose major manifestation was capitalism. In the countries of western Europe where socialism was born, the system was known as liberalism in the post-Napoleonic period, and as liberal democracy a few generations later. Ideologically, even if not always institutionally (for instance on the question of the head of state), European liberalism roughly corresponded to American constitutional republicanism, and liberal democracy to republican democracy. In Great Britain first, next in France and a few smaller nations of northwestern Europe, then in other Continental countries, through a series of revolutionary upheavals lasting several generations liberalism replaced absolutism and destroyed some of its pillars—state-enforced intellectual conformity and restrictive economic mercantilism among them.

European liberalism was founded on individualism, derived from the postulate that man, endowed with reason, is responsible for his self-determined actions. Opposing rational and nonrational dogmatism, liberals stressed reasonableness, derived from recognition of the limitations of reason as much as from its priority over nonreason. Parliamentarianism was the liberal political formula. Bills of rights were an essential part of constitutions. Economically, liberals stressed private ownership of property, free enterprise, free contract, and the free market; from these, in an environment characterized by availability of capital, technological inventions, and entrepreneurial willingness to work hard for profits, came capitalism. The liberals' goal was a loose-knit society in which individuals would enjoy a maximum of autonomy. Since liberty enables individuals to make choices, the liberal society was bound to be diversified.

The liberals' political success in much of Europe in the nineteenth century made for intellectual and economic progress. It also made for the exploitation of the economically weak, particularly the wage-earners, by the economically strong, the capitalists; for more economic insecurity than most people could stand; for speculation and corruption; for the suffering of large sections of the population; and for the revulsion felt by many who did not share the suffering but saw it, together with filth and growing criminality, in the slums of industrial cities. European liberals stressed the many advantages of the capitalistic organization of the economy. Socialists saw only its defects, which also were many.

Between these two antagonistic concepts of the economy was that of the reform liberals, in Europe often called radicals, sometimes democrats or progressives. Anticipating the position of the American New Dealers, European radicals aimed at correcting capitalism's worst defects while maintaining private ownership of property, free enterprise, and a market economy. (This, in later decades, would also be the economic program of Christian Democratic movements.) The European radicals failed, but in their heyday, just before 1914, they were a major force in many nations.

Once the socialists became politically organized and entered the electoral arena, they were deeply split on the question of their relationship with radical parties and liberal parties with a strong radical wing (for instance, the British Liberal Party). But underlying the political debate among socialists was a more fundamental division concerning the ideology of liberalism, which was also largely the ideology of radicalism. Some socialists saw their movement as the fulfillment of liberal aspirations: elimination of privilege and emancipation of repressed groups, individual autonomy, intellectual freedom, tolerance of dissent, self-government through representative institutions. They reasoned that the destruction of capitalism would enable intellectual and political liberalism to flourish. Other socialists rejected, together with capitalism, everything connected with liberalism. Since fulfillment and rejection of liberalism often existed in the same individuals and in the same sector of the socialist movement, this made for ambivalence and a good deal of vacillation. In this dualism was the root of the post-1917 polarization of socialist tendencies in the antagonistic positions of democratic socialism, liberalism's heir, and Marxist communism, liberalism's enemy. Ever since the ideological debates of the 1840's, liberty and the institutions through which the idea of liberty becomes part of a way of life have, more than economic programs, been at the center of what has divided socialists.

THE ROLE OF THE INTELLIGENTSIA: From authoritarian *ancien régimes* Europeans had inherited divisions in classes, and the idea that each class formed a homogenous whole politically. In the freer societies replacing the *ancien régimes*, class cohesion weakened and homogeneity disappeared, members of the same class pursuing different goals and forming different tendencies. But the idea that a class is politically homogeneous survived, and from it was derived the corollary that classes are also homogeneous ideologically. Socialists and nonsocialists alike fell into the common error of equating the part (e.g., some members of a class support a certain tendency) with the whole (all members of a class support a certain tendency). In socialist intellectual circles it was fashionable to identify the upper middle classes, and progressive sections of the upper classes, with liberalism; the lower middle classes of very small entrepreneurs and white-collar employees with democracy or radicalism; the lower or working classes with socialism. One wonders who, once universal suffrage had been achieved and free elections were held, supported conservatism, confessionalism, or nationalism (just to name three examples), which at times received a plurality or even a majority of the votes.

Socialists thought themselves the voice of the proletariat. Actually, socialism originated as a movement of the intelligentsia—like most other significant new isms of the nineteenth and twentieth centuries. It was a movement for the workers, but not necessarily of the workers. Even counting the proletariat as limited to urban wage-earners, their response to socialism varied in different sections of the proletariat, in different countries, at different times. As long as there was an efficient authoritarian régime, as in France under Napoleon III and in Russia under Alexander III, the response was minimal. As soon as political liberty replaced absolutism, however, some workers would make common cause with the socialist members of the intelligentsia; sometimes a majority of them, but never all. Large sections of the wage-earners remained indifferent to socialism, even when actively involved in labor agitation aimed at immediate gains within the capitalistic system. Other large sections aimed at joining the ranks of the middle classes, both economically and culturally. But the myth that all wage-earners are for socialism was a powerful myth, and it played its role in the political activities of socialists.

Less limited than the correlation of socialism with social classes was the correlation with educational levels, which are only partly related to social ones. Socialism appealed mostly to those who, newcomers to the ranks of the intelligentsia, were unaware of the effort involved in winning the struggle against absolutism, and of the difference between an authoritarian and a free society; those whose thinking was at a dogmatic level, who were unfamiliar with criticism, with the mind looking at itself and conscious of its operation, its limitations, and its defects; those of generous heart but of intellectual vision bounded by immediate concerns. The flourishing of socialism was related more to the size of new sectors of the intelligentsia than to the size and poverty of the proletariat. What happened in the nineteenth century within the ranks of the expanding Western intelligentsia happens today within the ranks of the expanding world intelligentsia.

A CONTINUING THREAD: Socialists were convinced that their formula for the organization of society was new. Those acquainted with history denied any relationship between their formula and any previous systems. The word socialism was, in fact, new (it was used first in Great Britain in the 1820's), but what it designated was old. Institutions that embodied the subordination of the individual to the group, the socialization of property, and egalitarianism as uniformity of views, in fact characterized many primitive societies and early civilizations. And residues of these institutions

were present on all continents when modern times began. In
relation to thousands of years of history and somewhat docu-
mented prehistory, it was capitalism, not socialism, that was new.

It is no literary accident that in Western civilization most fic-
tional utopias have identified the ideal society (if happiness was the
paramount goal) or the necessary society (if survival and efficiency were the main concern) with variations on modern socialism. The formulas of Plato in the fourth century B.C., of Thomas
More early in the sixteenth century, and of a host of others down
to British and American writers of the twentieth century varied,
but not some of the basic ideas: community of goods, uniformity
of views, complete merging of the individual in the group. Variations of socialism have been present, not just as ideas but in
practical implementation, in Christian and non-Christian religions,
in Western and Eastern monastic religious orders, and nonreligious
brotherhoods. But most early socialist thinkers were not aware of
this heritage; if they had been, they might have tried to see the
future in the light of the experience of the past. As it was, they
were enthusiastic as only discoverers of a promised land can be.

THE LIBERTARIAN PHASE: The first phase of modern socialism
begins in Great Britain early in the nineteenth century while war
was still being waged against Napoleon, and in France shortly after
the end of Napoleon's despotism. It fades away in the 1860's and
early 1870's. That was the age of Robert Owen, William Thompson, Frederick Maurice, Charles Kingsley in Great Britain; of
Robert Dale Owen, George Ripley, Albert Brisbane in the United
States; of Claude-Henri de Saint-Simon, Charles Fourier, Philippe
Buchez, Louis Cabet, Louis Auguste Blanqui, Louis Blanc, Pierre-
Joseph Proudhon in France; of exiles from Italy, Germany, and
Russia, who spent part of their lives in Great Britain, France, and
other countries of western Europe where the liberals' success
enabled people to express new ideas and to work for their realiza-
tion: Filippo Buonarroti, Giuseppe Mazzini, Carlo Pisacane,
Wilhelm Weitling, Moses Hess, Karl Marx, Friedrich Engels,
Alexander Herzen, and Mikhail Bakunin. That was the age of New
Lanark, New Harmony, the North American Phalanx, familistères,
phalanstères, Icarian colonies, of the establishment of a few experimental socialist communities in western Europe and of scores in
the United States. Great Britain and France were the cradle of

socialism, intellectually and politically; the United States was the country where more socialists worked actively for the realization of their ideals: because industrialization was more advanced, maintained all socialists; because there was greater liberty, dissent was legitimate and new paths could be explored, maintained European liberals. During this phase political action began with semi-clandestine societies in France stimulated by the freer atmosphere created by the Revolution of 1830; had its baptism of fire in Paris in June, 1848; and ended in the bloodbath of the Paris Commune in 1871.

Of the men mentioned above, not all thought of themselves as socialists; not all were thought of by others as socialists. They were, however, ideologically related. What they and their disciples had in common was their opposition to capitalism; the preference accorded to communalism over individualism; and the conviction that cooperation, solidarity, any manifestation of fraternity, was preferable to competition. That phase has been labelled "utopian" by socialists and nonsocialists. So far as utopianism is concerned, there has in fact, as already noted, been little to choose between one socialist school and another. Still, the phase did have a distinctive character. It can be described as libertarian chiefly because most socialists of the period (with the notable exception of some of the younger ones, the Frenchman Blanc and the Germans Marx and Engels) either relied on the efforts of citizens acting in their private capacity to bring about socialism, rather than on state action; or, going further, advocated the total elimination of the state.

The Englishman Owen—a successful businessman who turned social reformer when he saw the appalling conditions in which many British wage-earners were living—and Saint-Simon—a revolutionary French aristocrat who had failed as a businessman—are usually mentioned as the first socialists. There had been immediate forerunners: writers in both countries, and, as man of action, Babeuf in France.

Robert Owen saw the passage from capitalism to socialism as a relatively simple problem. One only needed to organize a community based on the principles he had formulated; its success would induce more and more people to imitate it. New Lanark was the community he organized in Scotland, New Harmony was organized by him and his son in the United States. Owen and his

disciples took an active interest in the labor organizations that
developed in Great Britain after the repeal of the Combination
Acts in 1824 that were temporarily united in 1834 and were a
major component in the Chartist movement of 1839 to 1848. It is a
moot question whether Chartism can be considered a manifestation
of socialism. Radicals, not socialists, formed the main driving force
of Chartism, whose chief emphasis was on democratizing representative institutions. British laborism itself was concerned with the
immediate improvement of the wage-earners' lot, not with the
abolition of capitalism. Whatever their written and oral statements,
Owenite socialists, and the smaller group of British Christian Socialists active for a few years after 1848, reflected the empiricism
then prevailing among the dynamic sectors of the English-speaking
nations. They laid the foundation of twentieth-century democratic
socialism.

The organizer of a conspiracy in 1796 aimed at resurrecting an
improved, more egalitarian, version of Jacobinism, Babeuf was
typical of thousands of revolutionaries, first in Europe, now in all
continents: his mind full of generous ideals, deeply resenting the
defects of the existing system, convinced that it needed only a
show of force to usher in a new social order. His friend and
disciple, the Italian Buonarroti, was the link between the conspirators of 1796 and the socialists who organized themselves and
began to conspire in France in the early 1830's. At that time the
best-known names among Continental socialists were Saint-Simon
and Fourier, whose enthusiastic disciples were trying to put their
ideas into practice. The writings of Fourier circulated among
progressive intellectuals from Russia to the United States.

There were other influential French socialists. Buchez fused
socialism and Catholicism. Blanqui became the prototype of the
pure revolutionary: little concerned with the future, totally dedicated to the destruction of the existing order. Blanc, as a member
of the provisional government of the French Second Republic,
tried to put into practice ideas he had formulated for solving
unemployment. The influence of Proudhon, spokesman for the
anarchist wing of French socialism, was paramount among the
socialists who cooperated with heirs to the Jacobin tradition in
setting up the Paris Commune of 1871, misleadingly the prototype
of the Russian Soviet of 1905. The first collectivist settlement
based on Cabet's ideas was founded in the United States in 1848,

the last was disbanded in 1895. By the middle of the nineteenth century what socialism existed on the Continent outside France received its inspiration from French socialism.

SOCIALDEMOCRACY AND LABORISM: Until the 1860's, French and other Continental socialists who considered themselves democrats gave to democracy the Jacobin meaning: the dictatorship of those supposedly representing the general will, or, more accurately, of those strong enough to seize power, the general will being simply their own will. A revolutionary step was taken on the Continent in 1863 when Ferdinand Lassalle (or Lasal), of a wealthy German business family, founded a Workers' Association advocating constitutional democracy. Thus Lassallean socialists accepted the liberal political system with the all-important proviso that suffrage would be universal. At first, their democraticism was mere expediency. Owenites, Fourierists and others had counted on the success of socialism through imitation of a successful experiment; but no experiment had been successful and there had been no imitation, except on a small scale in the United States. Blanquists had counted on revolutionary action; Lassalleans discounted the possibility of successful socialist revolutionarism. Liberals were in the ascendant; even their opponents, such as Napoleon III in France and Bismarck in Prussia, accepted important features of political liberalism. If suffrage were universal, not limited as advocated by European liberals fearful of mob rule, then representative institutions might provide the easiest road to socialist success.

The Lassalleans' idea of establishing socialism through representative institutions was based on two misconceptions: that all industrial wage-earners were socialists, and that industrial wage-earners were, or would one day be, the majority of the citizens. Aware of the difference between democracy and socialism, German socialists called the movement using democratic procedure *socialdemocratic*, and considered it a transitional phase. In the freer climate created by the formation of the constitutional North German Confederation in 1867 (German Empire in 1871) a Social Democratic Workers' Party was organized in 1869. Disputes between advocates and opponents of constitutional democracy over the means to achieve socialism were settled with the success of the advocates, whose Gotha Program of 1875 became the party's charter.

Political laborism, a slightly younger contemporary of social-democracy, was more frankly democratic. It resulted largely from the alliance of socialists with reform liberals (radicals in Europe), whose democraticism was a conviction and not expediency. As the political expression of the labor movement (in Europe, trade unionism), it aimed at improving workers' conditions through the legislative process. Political laborism had appeared briefly in the United States with a Workers' Party in 1828. It reappeared in 1872 with the National Reform Party and in 1873 with the Social Democratic Party, replaced in 1877 by the Socialist Labor Party. The agreement in 1900 between a new Social Democratic Party led by Eugene V. Debs and splinter groups from the Socialist Labor Party led to the formation of the American Socialist Party. Despite some electoral successes just before and after World War I, political laborism remained a minor element on the American scene. Besides other factors, certain widespread features of the American way of life, akin to socialist ones, cut the ground from under laborism, as from under socialism and European-style socialdemocracy: high level of voluntary cooperation, sense of the community, teamwork, class mobility, governmental economic role. Political laborism became instead a major force in the Commonwealth. In Great Britain, in Australia, and in New Zealand, laborites co-operated for a considerable time, as junior partners, with the radical wing of liberalism. Not until 1893 did British laborites, dissatisfied with the Liberal Party, found the Independent Labour Party, which however achieved only a limited electoral success. More successful was the Labour Party organized in 1900. The first Labour government ever to take governmental power was that of Australian Queensland in 1903. In Canada the Liberal Party included many labor demands in its platforms. In India, laborism attached itself to the Congress Party founded in 1886.

MARXISM: Among the opponents of the Gotha Program of the German Social Democratic Party had been Karl Marx and Friedrich Engels who, despite that setback and others, were becoming the most influential socialist thinkers outside the English-speaking nations; a position they still hold. Clear ideas help effective engagement in action. The two friends provided at first a few socialists, then more and more, with a clear and cogent set of ideas that explained the present, interpreted the past, and provided a guideline for the future, thus fulfilling for the dissatisfied the function Christianity had fulfilled fourteen centuries earlier. For the Communist League, formed in London in 1847 by a few German exiles in touch with the French Society of the Just, Marx and Engels had written a Manifesto printed early in 1848. The two friends' influence among socialists spread after the 1860's. In 1867 appeared the first volume of Marx's major work *Capital*. More important, in 1864 British labor leaders who for a couple of years had had frequent contacts with French socialists and were in touch with many Continental exiles then living in London, including Marx, had called an international conference of socialists and labor representatives. The well-known Italian exile Mazzini was asked to draft a statement. But Mazzini, a republican nationalist, though sympathetic to socialism was not a genuine socialist. His draft was rejected and Marx was invited to prepare another. This was accepted by the organization created by the conference, the (First) International. The antagonism between authoritarian socialists led by Marx and the libertarian faction, then larger, led by Bakunin caused a split in 1872. The Marxist rump of the International moved its headquarters to New York, and formed branches in Chicago and San Francisco, but ceased to function in 1876.

As in other movements linked to influential thinkers, there is a distinction between the position formulated by its founders, and the simpler one, soon known as Marxism, of the followers. Historically, it is the simpler that counts. Marxism can be summarized sketchily in a few major propositions. Only matter is reality, there is neither spirit nor transcendence. Ideas and emotions are induced by the economic conditions in which men live. Mankind's unit is the economic class, formed by those who share the same relationship with the means of production and exchange. There is no such thing as individual autonomy (therefore no individual responsibility). The dialectical process is the law of the universe; the law is inexorable; men cannot modify it, but they can accelerate or slow it where it affects them, according to their level of comprehension. (This makes for limited voluntarism within a general frame of determinism.) The class struggle is the manifestation of the dialectical process in human affairs; it is the outcome of the forcible appropriation by parasites (aristocrats once, later capitalists) of the wealth created by workers, to whom is left what is barely sufficient for their survival. The next step in the social dialectical process will be the replacement of capitalism first with socialism and then with communism, of private with collective ownership of property, of competition with cooperation, of production for profit with production for service. The step is inevitable because of the capitalists' concentration of wealth, the proletariat's increasing poverty, and the growing tension, which will erupt into violence. Having seized power by force, the proletariat will set up its dictatorship and will use the state for the realization of socialism. Once production, rationally conducted, has reached the level enabling all to satisfy their needs (communism), the state will wither away, liberty will be total, and—the dialectical process having come to an end—peace will be total.

Democritus and materialists of the Enlightenment, the philosophers Hegel and Feuerbach, the economists Ricardo, de Sismondi, and Rodbertus, and the socialists Owen, Thompson, Blanc, and Proudhon provided the elements of Marxism. The synthesis, product of the intellectual effort testifying to the power of the two friends' minds, was original. It was on a par with other syntheses produced in a climate of intellectual freedom by nineteenth-century European thinkers convinced that they possessed the truth, syntheses that appealed to large sections of the intelligentsia: Benthamism, Comtianism, Hegelianism, Neo-Thomism, Spencerianism, Freudianism. Each had its share of unproven postulates, of unprovable extrapolations about the future, of corollaries deduced from *a priori* principles, of selective historical evidence. Postulates and extrapolations were working hypotheses, not certainties.

Marx and Engels had deduced universal laws from the incomplete analysis of a short period of British and French economic developments; had used limited statistical evidence; knew little outside the field of recent Western civilization; and were only dimly aware of what was going on in the field of science. Too much concerned with their own theories, they were not as widely read as other contemporary thinkers and scientists. They called their socialism scientific, but besides ignoring in their writings the canons of the scientific method (observation, classification, formulation of an hypothesis, verification) and using the dialectical method instead, they lacked the objectivity and balanced judgment that make for the scientific approach. Apart from what was said, written, and meant by Marx and Engels (the topic of endless discussions), Marxists compounded in their minds the related elements of utopianism, simplification, monism, dogmatism, extremism, and intolerance, to the detriment of the humanitarianism, pacifism, and genuine sense of brotherhood of other socialists. Marxists were not aware that the truth or nontruth of materialism, and atheism, is as much beyond the grasp of reason as the truth or nontruth of idealism and God's presence; that dialectics and the class struggle were the misleading simplifications of a complex diversity; that the defects of an economic system (capitalism) are no ground from which to jump to the conclusion that another system (collectivism) is good when it may be even more defective; that capitalism and democracy (in Marxist terms, the dictatorship of the bourgeoisie) were not developing according to the Marxist scheme.

Truth and untruth have little to do with influence. Marxism provided large sections of the intelligentsia, and of those newly becoming educated, with easily assimilable formulas. It contributed to an awareness of the problems related to industrialization. It transformed a few concepts into powerful social forces: the class struggle, the evil of capitalistic monopoly, bourgeois selfishness, surplus value, contradictions (everything affecting uniformity), dictatorship by the proletariat, the inevitability of socialism, the internationalism of the proletariat, the imperialism of capitalism, violence as the midwife of progress, man's ability to solve all his problems. Marxism strengthened certain attitudes: intransigence, contempt for democracy, crusading spirit. What Marxists did in the twentieth century may not have been implicit in what Marx and Engels wrote, but it was implicit in the Marxism of the late nineteenth century.

THE DEBATE ON DEMOCRACY: During the last quarter of the nineteenth century, the formation of socialist parties followed economic growth in countries where free institutions made political action possible. Soon there were socialist, socialdemocratic, or labor parties not only in Germany, Great Britain, and the United States, but in more than a score of independent states of Europe, the Commonwealth, the Americas. Many of these parties—some prevalently democratic, most prevalently Marxist—cooperated in establishing another socialist international in 1889, the Second International. From small clandestine movements with at most a few thousand adherents organized in the late 1870's and again, more efficiently, in the 1890's, sprang socialist parties electorally

active in Russia after the granting of the constitution of 1905.
Before 1914, socialism had the greatest electoral strength in Germany and France, while the largest organized labor movement
linked to socialism was in Great Britain. European socialists had
carried their ideas to some of the overseas territories then held in
Asia and Africa by eight European powers.

The possibility of action emphasized the question of means.
Most socialists, contemptuous of free representative institutions as
unimportant bourgeois devices, aiming instead at authoritarian
Jacobin democracy or frankly at the dictatorship of the proletariat,
agreed that the end justifies the means. What, then, would give the
best results? The sharpest differences concerned the use of democratic procedure versus the use of violence.

Through universal suffrage the liberals' constitutionalism was
becoming liberal democracy. During the forty years preceding
World War II, a majority of socialists, under different labels, acted
as Lassallean socialdemocrats. They rejected the use of violence
and participated in elections. On the other hand, they refused to
play the democratic game at the level of governmental responsibility. Convinced that they would soon have the majority of the votes
and would legally form socialist governments that would legislate
the end of capitalism, they refused to have anything to do with
nonsocialist parties. All these, differences notwithstanding, were
branded bourgeois by the socialists. By sitting in parliament while
remaining aloof from parliamentary responsibilities, socialdemocrats weakened the parliamentary system in the major Continental
states, and discredited it. A majority of Marxists, postponing to
some future date the establishment of the dictatorship of the
proletariat, acted as socialdemocrats. Before 1914 their main intellectual spokesmen were the German Kautsky, the Frenchman
Guesde, and the Russian Plekhanov. Influential too were the Austrian Adler, the Russian Martov, the Italian Turati, the Swede
Branting, and the Belgian Vandervelde.

The second largest group of socialists refused to see, then or
ever, the road to socialism in free elections held in competition with
other parties. Called revolutionaries, they included a minority of
Marxists, among whose spokesmen were the German Karl Liebknecht, the Pole Rosa Luxemburg active first in Russia and then in
Germany, and the Russian exile in Switzerland Lenin; Social Revolutionaries of eastern Europe, heirs to the Populists of the late

1870's, whose goal was to replace the state with a loose federation of democratic agrarian communities, who ignored industrialization and its problems, admired Bakunin, and whose major intellectual voice had recently been Lavrov; Syndicalists who wanted to replace the state immediately with workers' democratic associations or syndicates, and who had an effective spokesman in the Frenchman Georges Sorel (among his disciples was the Italian revolutionary socialist Benito Mussolini); and Anarchosyndicalists and Anarchists, numerous in Latin Europe and among recent European immigrants to the United States. When participating in elections, as this Marxist wing did at times, as likewise the Social Revolutionaries and (more rarely) the Syndicalists did, it was with the aim of destroying free representative institutions.

From the 1890's on, a third, smaller group of socialists veered toward democracy. This meant renouncing pure socialism except as a very distant ideal. It meant working democratically for the partial modification of capitalism in a socialist sense through the socialization of sectors of the economy, social-welfare measures, labor legislation, government planning, redistribution of incomes. It meant seeing in the political laborism that was developing in the Commonwealth not a temporary uneasy alliance with reform liberalism (whose immediate goals were similar but more limited), but socialism itself. It meant renouncing extremism for moderation, dogmatism for empiricism, uniformity for the equality of diverse groups (and so monism for pluralism), parliamentarian aloofness for cooperation with progressive nonsocialist parties (in Europe, then, particularly the Radical parties). By 1914 this was not yet a clear-cut ideological position, but toward it groped many of the several thousand members of the Fabian Society in Great Britain, German revisionists following Bernstein, Jean Jaurès and possibilists in France, the Italian followers of Bissolati, and many American socialists.

It was difficult, in 1914, to see where socialism was going. Ultimate goals were theoretically common to all socialists; not common were the immediate goals and the means to achieve them, and these were more important than anything else in shaping socialist practice and therefore future socialist societies. The bitterness of the antagonisms between different tendencies was a major feature of the movement. This bitterness was related to the nature of socialism as a secular faith; the intense hatred of one faction against others, often greater than the hatred against nonsocialist or anti-socialist tendencies, explains much of what happened to socialism after World War I. These antagonisms had as their central element not the economy but, as already noted, liberty and the problems to which it gives rise.

MARXISM-LENINISM OR COMMUNISM: The seizure of power in Russia in November, 1917, by the Bolsheviks, numerically the smallest of the three main organized tendencies within Russian socialism, caused a major crisis. Varieties of socialism became polarized on support for, or opposition to, the Bolsheviks. Bolshevism was the name for Russian revolutionary Marxism, since then ideologically described as Marxism-Leninism, politically as communism. It owed some of its fundamental characteristics to Russian civilization. It owed others to its leader, for two decades Vladimir Ilyich Ulyanov, known in exile and now universally as Lenin. He was an intellectual of great stature, as shown by his vast knowledge, by his interpretation of Marx's and Engels's ideas, by the way, for instance, in which, convincingly for many intellectuals, he identified imperialism with the final phase of capitalism —as if imperialism had not been a common occurrence in man's history! Lenin's main concern, however, was action. Whatever he thought of Marxist determinism, Lenin acted as a voluntarist, as if man's will can change the course of history. His clarifications and modifications of Marxism dealt mainly with problems related to method and organization: violence is indispensable to achieve socialism; not the accidental violence of impersonal forces, but the deliberate violence of revolutionaries; violence must be directed against a whole class, not just individuals, and should aim at the obliteration of that class; successful revolutionary action requires a cohesive group of disciplined professional revolutionaries who guide the masses and among whom no dissent is to be tolerated. Marx's vague dictatorship of the proletariat became concretely Lenin's dictatorship of the vanguard of the proletariat (the party of professional revolutionaries). This dictatorship is necessary to create socialism. It will disappear once it has fulfilled its function. Lenin was the creator of the one-party system, the successful twentieth-century formula for old-fashioned political absolutism. All activities, including the intellectual and economic, being subordinated to the dictatorship, this is totalitarianism. Total rejection of compromise (except on the basis of expediency), total stress on groups and not on individuals, total devotion to the socialist cause, flexibility in action combined with intransigence in thought and justified by conscious acceptance of the unethical principle that the end justifies the means, the double standard (what is right for me is wrong for others) that is the corollary of the principle, were other major contributions on Lenin's part to his variation of socialism. Terrorism and war against internal and external opposition, and conformity through the monopoly of education and communications media were implicit in Marxism-Leninism, as were the considerable—sometimes spectacular—achievements made possible by discipline, enthusiasm, coercion, and centralization.

Since 1903 Lenin had led the Bolsheviks, that faction of the Marxist Party formed clandestinely in Russia in 1898. Later, he organized the faction as a separate party. Membership was small when revolution began in March, 1917, but cohesion, determination, and firm leadership compensated for lack of numbers. Leninism acted as a catalyst upon socialism: at first a few Russian exiles; then thousands of the Russian intelligentsia, and those among European socialists who were determined to make of World War I a series of civil wars; later hundreds of thousands from all walks of life during the turmoil following the March, 1917, revolution in Russia and the November, 1918, defeat of Austria-Hungary and Germany by the western Allies; and, today, tens of millions in the world. Leninism appealed primarily to a certain type of mind—integralist, perfectionist, dogmatic. It appealed to those who besides being motivated by socialist aspirations rejected with greater awareness and more definitely than other socialists the legitimacy of differences, to those for whom the good society was the ideologically uniform one.

After the 1924 to 1927 interlude due to rivalries between Lenin's chief lieutenants (Trotsky, Zinoviev, Bukharin, Stalin), the mantle of Marxism-Leninism fell on Stalin, for a quarter of a century ruler of the Soviet Union and leader of world communism. Stalin's major contributions to world socialism were the application of Lenin's principles to the organization of the economy, the elimination from the communist movement of tendencies at variance with Leninism, and the help given to communists who seized power in eastern Europe and the Far East. Starting in 1948, rivalries between leaders who had their own armed forces broke the unity of communism, but each segment kept the intellectual features of Marxism-Leninism and the institutional features of Lenin's one-party state.

Many socialists were repelled by the cruelty of the 1918 to 1921 Red Terror in Russia, of Soviet collectivization in 1930, of the Stalinist purges of 1936 to 1938, of the constant liquidation of uncomfortable minorities; by tyranny labelled as democratic centralism; by the suppression of freedom of expression; and by the seizure of foreign territories. Czarist crimes against which socialists had inveighed—executions, deportations, censorship, violation of mail, arbitrariness—were minor compared with those of the Marxist-Leninists. There were socialists who approved of the crimes, justifying them on the basis of historical necessity, Russian national character, capitalist animosity. Others found that the crimes had their origin in the Marxist-Leninist ideology. Thus, the socialists split. In France a majority sided with communism; in Germany a majority decidedly opposed it. In the socialist movement as a whole, only a minority (though a large one) chose communism. Debates were furious and bitter: on the socialist historical scheme, concerning for instance the correct sequence of economic systems; on the proper relationship between socialists of different persuasions; on the meaning and practice of the dictatorship of the proletariat; on the organization of collectivism; on democracy within a socialist party; on the use of violence. Emotions were exacerbated by the execution in Russia of socialists who refused to cooperate with Bolsheviks, and attacks between 1918 and 1921 against newly established national states governed by anti-Bolshevik socialists. Passions ran high, hatreds were intense, but basic points became clarified. Communists organized their (Third) International, known as the Comintern, in 1919. They took the wind from the sails of non-Marxist revolutionaries, who declined fast, lasting only in Spain until the late 1930's as a major political force. Backed by Soviet resources, communist agents—actually dedicated missionaries—were active not only in industrial nations but also in underdeveloped countries, where organized socialism until then had been weak: first in Mexico and China, soon after in southeastern Asia, the Middle East and South America (reaching Negro Africa after World War II). By 1939 communism was the worldwide movement that pre-1914 socialism had failed to become.

Major World War II and postwar communist developments

have been territorial expansion (most of it from 1944 to 1949) and (starting in 1948) the breaking up of the movement into several currents. The political vacuum created in vast areas of Europe and Asia by the collapse of the wartime German and Japanese empires enabled the Soviet Union to annex or re-annex large border territories, and to put communists in control of seven countries occupied by Soviet troops. (Soviet-supported local communists had already been in power for many years in an eighth country, Mongolia.) A Partisan movement organized by communists led by Josip Broz (Tito) established itself in power in Yugoslavia with little Soviet help, and aided communists to seize power in Albania. Their own ability and Soviet military aid enabled Chinese Communists, led by a pentarchy in which Mao Tse-tung was the major figure, to defeat their opponents in mainland China by October, 1949. Communist insurgents led by Ho Chi Minh achieved control with Chinese help in North Vietnam in 1954. Shortly after the 1959 victory of an insurgency led by Fidel Castro, communists acquired considerable influence in the new Cuban régime.

The breaking up of the communist movement into several currents was made possible by internal Soviet developments and by the autonomy a few non-Soviet communist leaders enjoyed as heads of powerful armed forces. Stalin died in 1953. Five years before, he had been defied by the Yugoslav Communist leader Tito, who had his own army and was in a position to be helped by the United States should Yugoslavia be attacked by the Soviet Union. Stalin's death was followed by a power struggle, which at first involved seven top leaders. Later, there came to the fore a few figures who had been in only secondary positions during Stalin's rule. The power struggle had its justification in divergences over the related problems of internal economic policies and external affairs. It did not lead to relevant institutional changes. So-called democratic centralism (political absolutism), bureaucratic over-all collectivist planning, and conformity through censorship and control of education, remained the basic features of Soviet communism. The power struggle did, however, cause governmental paralysis enough to weaken the hold of the Soviet Union over other communist countries, and the hold of Soviet communist leaders over the world communist movement. The outcome of this situation was the anti-communist agitation (which failed) in East Germany, Poland, and Hungary, and the successful revolt of Chinese,

Albanian, and, later, Rumanian Communists against Soviet leadership. The monolithism of the Lenin and Stalin era was replaced with what in the late 1950's was called polycentrism. Internal and external policies varied, but, with the possible exception of Yugoslavia, the institutional frame, keyed to absolutism, collectivism, and state-enforced conformity, was identical in all communist states.

Yugoslav and Chinese Communist leaders controlled their own armed forces. Albanian and Cuban leaders ruled countries geographically isolated from the rest of what communists referred to as the socialist camp. Rumanian leaders played on the dissensions within the Soviet communist leadership and between rulers of antagonistic communist states. These factors gave them an autonomy that other communists had not enjoyed. Where the dissident communists of the 1920's had failed, Titoists and Maoists succeeded, creating their own distinctive currents, labelled respectively "revisionist" and "dogmatist" by other Marxist-Leninists. Yugoslav Communists distinguished themselves from orthodox or Soviet Communists on two main counts: whatever their theory, in practice they replaced internationalism as a basic article of faith with nationalism; in the late 1960's they were considering an institutional structure providing room for different Marxist-Leninist factions. If this were to be effected, Yugoslav nationalcommunism would represent a revolutionary departure from traditional Marxism and Marxism-Leninism. Chinese Communist leaders, bent on achieving total conformity within China and on making China the main base for radical revolutions everywhere, took over the mantle of Stalinism internally, and acted externally with the dynamism Trotsky had advocated in the 1920's. The so-called Great Proletarian Cultural Revolution of 1966 and 1967 aimed at achieving in China the total conformity to Marxism-Leninism that had been achieved in the Soviet Union with the terror of 1918 to 1921 and the purges of 1936 to 1938. In Cuba, Marxism-Leninism was just one element in an agrarian nationalcommunist experiment modified by Latin American caudillismo and geared specifically to making Cuba the base for militant communist-supported insurgencies in Central and South America.

Whatever the polycentrism, leadership squabbles in Moscow and Peking, and occasional failures (as for instance in Indonesia in 1965), the post-World War II communist movement was in a process of expansion. Marxism-Leninism appealed more than democratic socialism to larger and larger sections of the fast-growing world intelligentsia.

DEMOCRATIC SOCIALISM: Anti-communist socialists reorganized the Second International, disrupted in 1914 by the antagonism between pacifist socialists and socialists who had supported the war effort of the respective countries. It became the Labor and Socialist International in 1923, when it merged with the so-called Vienna International formed in 1920 by socialists who had tried to stop the split between communists and anti-communists from becoming final. By the time World War II began, socialists who objected to communism had, except for small groups, abandoned the Lassallean position of rejecting governmental responsibility within the limitations imposed by constitutional democracy, while using universal suffrage as the road to power. They had, instead, accepted the view held by the 1914 minority of laborites, revisionists and possibilists, that democracy is valuable *per se*, that socialists should stand for it unequivocally, and that socialist ideas should be modified in terms of what is compatible with democracy. This meant abandoning the goals of an ideologically uniform society and of complete collectivism; renouncing a future dictatorship of the proletariat; advocating class mobility and the narrowing of class differences instead of classlessness; and working for the gradual modification rather than the immediate destruction of existing economic systems. In terms of elements common to all socialists, anti-capitalism was limited by the recognition that private ownership of property, individual initiative, private enterprise, free market, and the profit motive, besides guaranteeing fundamental liberties, exercise partially a useful role in stimulating and regulating economic activities, and therefore in helping the economy to fulfill its major function (the satisfaction of material needs); that moreover there is no monopoly of economic truth. Equality was no longer uniformity but the equal rights of diverse groups, each entitled to have its say politically; brotherhood was not the inevitable outcome of changes in the mode of production but the result of attitudes linked to convictions having little or nothing to do with economic conditions.

It had been said of the pre-1914 majority of socialists, politically Lassallean even when intellectually Marxist, that they were evolutionary and not revolutionary, but that their goals and those of revolutionary socialists were identical. There was no more identity of goals than of means between post–World War I democratic socialists and communists or Marxist revolutionaries. For democratic socialists, communism was not a variation of socialism but, because of its political and intellectual coercion, its negation. Similarly for communists, democratic socialism was not a variation but, because of the recognition of the rights of nonsocialists and the self-imposed limitation on socialist goals, its betrayal.

A fundamental step in the genuine democratization of large sectors of the socialist movement was taken during the crisis in Germany following the military defeat of 1918. The majority of the German Social Democratic Party—still the most authoritative party in the socialist movement—cooperated with nonsocialist parties in putting through a liberal democratic constitution and in governing the country. Other socialists, particularly of course the Marxist-Leninists who had seceded from the Social Democratic Party, accused the majority socialists of having betrayed the cause of socialism. There had been no betrayal: majority socialists had simply acted democratically. They were actually the most trustworthy supporters of German democracy, practically the only ones when Nazism seized power in 1933. There had been no betrayal, but there had been a failure: between the two world wars German democratic socialists had not reformulated their ideology and their long-range programs in terms of what they did.

Something similar happened on the other side of the Rhine. French democratic socialists briefly exercised governmental power as the senior partners of a Popular Front that won the election in 1936, and included reform liberals (the Radical Socialist Party) and communists. But they failed to reformulate their ideology, which remained largely Marxist. On both sides of the Rhine, democratic socialists acted as if they recognized the priority of democracy over socialism, and they adjusted their immediate policies accordingly. But not until after World War II did they adjust ideologically, or modify long-range goals. As a result, there was a confusing and damaging disparity between the ideas and practice of German and French democratic socialism. The same disparity existed in the case of Austrian, Italian, Spanish, and other Continental democratic socialists, and outside Europe in the case of the fairly substantial democratic socialist movements of Japan and Argentina.

The adjustment of ideology and ultimate goals to the requirements of democracy, the abandonment therefore of the Lassallean position, was made instead by other democratic socialists, particularly those of Great Britain, other Commonwealth countries, and several British dependent territories in which there was a substantial democratic socialist movement: Australia, New Zealand, India, Ceylon, Jamaica and Trinidad in the Caribbean, and Palestine. It was made also in Scandinavia and the Low Countries and in the United States.

The Labour Party was briefly in power in Great Britain in 1924 and again, with a larger plurality, from 1929 to 1931. It had adopted the position formulated by socialists of the Fabian Society, who stood firmly for democratic procedure and advocated as immediate goals a mixed economy instead of collectivism, the nationalization of some basic industries and of transportation and banking, flexible planning, considerable increase in public services, comprehensive social and labor legislation, redistribution of incomes through governmental action, and the break-up of large fortunes through taxation. After the electoral success of 1945, following concepts formulated and plans drafted by the reform liberal economists Beveridge and Keynes, the Labour Party, in power first for six years and then again after 1964, introduced a fullfledged guided welfare economy in which the state played a greater role than in the liberal New Deal of the United States, and a lesser one than in the collectivist economies of countries ruled by Marxist-Leninists. Elsewhere in the Commonwealth nations and in what were then self-governing territories of the British Empire, democratic socialists patterned their programs largely on those of the British Labour Party. The collectivist element was at times so diluted that there was little or no difference between the position of democratic socialists and that of reform, or progressive, liberals. A major feature of Commonwealth democratic socialism was the role played by cooperativism, in which, contrary to collectivism, democracy is implicit. Another major feature, and also an economic weakness, was the emphasis on distribution to the detriment of production and its problems. This contrasted unfavorably with the emphasis on production characteristic of the Marxist-Leninists.

Universal suffrage and the rules of political democracy put democratic socialists in power first in Sweden (from 1920 to 1924 and again in the thirties), then in Norway and Denmark, and in coalition with other parties in Finland. Scandinavian democratic socialists did relatively little nationalizing of enterprises. The public sector of the economy competed with the private, cooperativism was encouraged, allocation of resources was regulated, public services expanded, labor and social legislation improved. Democratic socialist parties in Belgium, the Netherlands, and Switzerland adopted programs similar to those of the Scandinavian parties. In the United States, democratic socialism, organized in the American Socialist Party, reached its maximum electoral strength in 1920, when its Presidential candidate, Eugene V. Debs, received nearly one million votes. After the death of Debs in 1926, Norman Thomas became the standard-bearer of the party. American democratic socialism was even closer than the British to reform, or progressive, liberalism; it was no wonder that the implementation of the economic, social, and labor programs of the New and Fair Deals first, and of the New Frontier and the Great Society later, undermined the electoral strength of the Socialist Party, which finally decided not to run its own Presidential candidate. In Congressional, state, and local elections American socialists supported the more liberal candidates.

In Canada the situation did not differ essentially from that in the United States. The Canadian Liberal Party's progressiveness deprived democratic socialists of much of the appeal they might otherwise have had for the electorate. Weakness of socialist parties in North America does not mean absence of socialist tendencies and aspirations. Large sections of the American and Canadian intelligentsia are socialist-inclined. At the same time they realize that, together with the emphasis on individualism, free enterprise, competition, and anything else that horrifies socialists, there is, in the American and Canadian way of life—as already noted—a good deal of socialism in the sense of community feeling, solidarity, concern for others, willingness to give high priority to the social good. Not only is there a great deal of ethical—as distinct from ideological and political—socialism, but it increases in the measure in which the democratic process improves.

In countries governed by socialists or by coalitions in which socialists have been the senior partners, the results of socialist action have varied. In the mid-1960's Sweden had the highest per capita income of any European nation; in terms of equivalent purchasing power, perhaps the highest in the world. In view of Swedish backwardness only two or three generations earlier, the economic performance was astounding. However, contrary to the socialists' expectations, pathological social phenomena did not disappear. Under socialist leadership Finland recovered from the economic ravages caused by Soviet aggression during World War II. Norway, a country remarkable for lack of natural resources, prospered. Democratic socialists governed Israel since independence in 1948, in coalition with other parties: if there has been an economic miracle in man's history it has been Israel. Egalitarianism and a fairly even increase in personal incomes gained ground in Great Britain, but in terms of total economic expansion the country lagged behind many socialist and nonsocialist nations. In Australia and New Zealand, policies of democratic socialist parties led to a high level of welfare for all, and also tended after a while to weaken the dynamism of the economy. The socialist component in the policies followed by the government of India since independence in 1947 has not been particularly successful; but India's problems are such that lack of success is no indictment against any economic system. In Jamaica and Trinidad, governed by democratic socialists even before independence in 1962, the economic performance was inferior to that of Puerto Rico but better than in collectivist Cuba.

In 1951, at a congress held at Frankfurt in Western Germany, representatives of democratic socialist parties re-established, under the name of the Socialist International, the organization known in prewar years as the Second International. In view of the recent successes of democratic socialists in several European nations, of what seemed to be favorable prospects in Asian nations like India, Japan, and Indonesia as well as in several smaller ones, of the adherence of most Latin American labor organizations to the International Confederation of Free Trade Unions, and of the friendly cooperation between European democratic socialists and Negro African nationalists, hopes were high. They did not materialize. Disenchantment with democratic socialism prevailed over confidence among European voters. In India the Socialist Party did not play the role it had counted on, although the Prime Minister and leader of the ruling Congress Party, Jawaharlal Nehru, was an avowed socialist. Japanese socialism was in the throes of dissensions similar to those of pre-1914 European socialism. A nationalist dictatorship supported by Marxist-Leninists nearly obliterated democratic socialism in Indonesia. Christian Democrats took the place democratic socialists had hoped to occupy in Chile and other Latin American republics. Shortly after independence, most Negro African nationalists turned to authoritarianism.

In the half century since the crisis that accompanied the Bolshevik success in Russia, the relationship between democratic and authoritarian socialism became inverted. Only a minority of socialists had sided with the Marxist-Leninist Third International. There were then other anti-democratic socialist currents, but the majority of socialists had chosen democracy. In the late 1960's, instead, Marxist-Leninists and kindred authoritarian socialists formed the bulk of the world socialist movement. In spite of violent dissensions and occasional failures, they had the support of more and more people everywhere, with the exception of a score or so of democratic or semi-democratic nations. On the world scene, often seen dimly by Western eyes, democratic socialists were not only a minority, they were also gradually losing ground. As liberalism's heir and democracy's genuine supporter, democratic socialism was affected by the growing indifference and antagonism toward basic liberal and democratic concepts and values on the part of mankind's most dynamic element, the intelligentsia.

NATIONALCOMMUNISM AND OTHER RECENT SOCIALIST VARIATIONS: Internationalism, practiced or not, remains a fundamental article in the creed of Marxist-Leninists, convinced that the full realization of the promises implicit in their system requires the establishment in all nations of their brand of authoritarian socialism, or communism. Only when this is universal will there be peace, orderly progress, equality among all human beings, the disintegration or withering away of the state. In the 1960's an increasing number of revolutionary socialists, although ideologically close to Marxism-Leninism, departed from it through the advocacy of communism within a national frame only, and the admission that communism should be molded by national characteristics. While from East Germany to Bulgaria communism was patterned on the Soviet model, Titoism—as Yugoslav national communism was called—put considerable emphasis on the peculiarities of the Yugoslav situation and the features of Yugoslav culture. Titoism stressed decentralization instead of centralization, and so diversity instead of uniformity, even power from below instead of power from above. Later, Titoism reached the point of envisaging the possibility of a free expression of divergent Marxist positions. This would mean the end of democratic centralism or absolutism. Titoism, dating from the break between Stalin and Tito in 1948, failed to have a major impact on the Marxist-Leninist movement and remained for a while a small-scale heresy. But later, the ideas and practice of Titoism attracted the attention of many socialists, particularly those in the newly independent countries of Asia and Africa, who rejected the dogmatism of Soviet and Chinese Marxist-Leninists as much as the liberalism of democratic socialists.

Castroism was another major manifestation of nationalism with a deep influence on socialism. Socialism had not been particularly evident in the Cuban insurgency led by Fidel Castro, which triumphed in 1959. The small group of Cuban Marxist-Leninists provided the insurgents, after their victory, with a program and with the people who could implement it. In Cuba, however, Marxism-Leninism was checked by traditional Latin American caudillismo and by an agrarianism reminiscent of that of Russian Populists and their successors the Social Revolutionaries; reminiscent too of the Mexican revolutionarism of the 1930's.

The "Arab" socialism that came to the fore in the 1960's had its beginnings in the program of the Ba'th Party, established during World War II and in recent years influential in Syria and Iraq. In spite of personal contrasts with Ba'thist spokesmen, "Arab" socialism became the ideology of Nasserism, a movement that took its name from its charismatic leader, Egypt's dictator Nasser. It was also the ideology of the faction of Arab Algerian nationalists, which in the struggle for power at the time of independence triumphed over the older confessional and democratic factions. In Ba'thism, Nasserism, and Algerian socialism, the nationalist component prevailed over the socialist. Because of fervent nationalism, the acceptance of traditional elements, and tendencies toward territorial expansion, "Arab" socialism (more correctly, socialnationalism) has more affinities with European National Socialism than with Titoism and other authoritarian and nonauthoritarian socialist currents. The political convergence in the late 1960's of "Arab" socialnationalism and Marxism-Leninism justifies the inclusion of the former among the varieties of today's socialism.

Leaders in a majority of the nearly thirty independent Negro African states call themselves socialists. A few, like Senghor of Senegal, veer toward democratic socialism, as did prominent African intellectuals before their countries became independent. Most, however, stand frankly for an authoritarian, even totalitarian, socialism, looking admiringly at the Soviet Union, China, and Cuba. Because of their nationalism, they can also be described as socialnationalists. Their main spokesmen have been Nkrumah of Ghana and, after his downfall in 1966, Touré of Guinea. African Negro political and intellectual leaders insist on the distinctiveness of African socialism, rooted in traditional communalism, and differentiate it from both democratic and Marxist socialism. However, unlike "Arab" socialnationalism, the African variation is more a vague aspiration susceptible of several meanings than a clearly formulated ideology. In its concrete application, during its brief existence, African socialism has meant absolutism politically, partial collectivism economically, state-enforced cultural conformity: with a new name, an old formula aimed at strengthening the cohesion of the national community.

The 1960's saw, first in North America and shortly after in some nations of Continental western Europe, the development of a small dynamic movement, socialist-oriented, using the arguments of nineteenth-century European socialists against democracy, distrustful at times of Marxism and especially of Marxism-Leninism. The New Left is one of the names by which it is known. It is confined to democratic countries and would not be tolerated in any state ruled by Marxist-Leninists, nationalcommunists, or other authoritarian socialists. Anarchism and collectivism are major elements in the socialism of the New Left, ideologically close to the socialism that prevailed among Continental socialists of the mid-nineteenth century, particularly that of the followers of Proudhon and Blanqui. Support for the New Left comes from the intelligentsia of the generation reaching maturity in the 1960's, little or not at all aware of debates during previous generations between socialists and nonsocialists, and among the socialists themselves. Although still groping for a clear formulation of its position, the

New Left has its distinctive place next to democratic socialism and to Marxism.

In view of space limitations, it is not easy to screen the material for an anthology on modern socialism. It has been found preferable to include comparatively few, but fairly long excerpts, rather than a multiplicity of passages too short to be meaningful. In Part II, excerpts from the writings of three authors indicate the persistence of a socialist current in Western thought. Part III has excerpts from the writings of only a few among the many distinguished socialist thinkers of the nineteenth century. Owen was the earliest main spokesman for what became the democratic socialism of the twentieth century. Outside the English-speaking world, socialism in its authoritarian and libertarian wings had its fountainhead in French thinkers of the first half of the nineteenth century. The works of Marx and Engels are the basic text for today's largest and most influential socialist current, Marxism. The extreme libertarianism called anarchism has faded away, but the anarchist component is still present in socialism. This explains the inclusion of excerpts from the works of Bakunin and Sorel. In Part IV are excerpts from the works of the founder of Marxism-Leninism, and of some of his collaborators and disciples including the Chinese Mao Tse-tung, the most prominent Marxist-Leninist of the 1960's. In Part V, two Englishmen, a German, and an American speak out for democratic socialism, whose main charter is the Frankfurt Declaration of 1951. Post–World War II nationalcommunism and socialnationalism, the former more socialist and the latter more nationalist, are explained through excerpts in Part VI.

II

The Continuing Thread

Excerpts from the works of three authors appear in this section. They were highly different men. Plato (427–347 B.C.), probably the West's most influential thinker, was a conservative upper-class Athenian. Thomas More (1478–1535), an English commoner who rose to high position in public service, was held in a vice: close in spirit to the progressives of his times, he was unable to give up his loyalty to the traditional faith in which he had been brought up. For this loyalty he died on the scaffold. François-Noël Babeuf (1760–1797), a fiery revolutionary, was an intellectual bent on setting straight the course of the French Revolution. Revolutionaries of another school of thought put him to death. Starting from different positions, the three aimed at man's happiness. The conviction that communalism and its economic counterpart collectivism is the road to happiness made of them, if not actual socialists, forerunners of modern socialism.

Collectivist communalism is the proper way of living for the ruling class: so wrote Plato when early in the fourth century B.C. he described the ideal commonwealth in *The Republic*. Its words and concepts he attributed to his teacher Socrates (sentenced to death in 399 B.C., when the democratic party governed Athens), but there is little doubt that the Socrates of Books II–IV was none other than Plato himself. Like countless modern intellectuals, Plato had been repelled by the conflicts, the divisions, and the tensions in the city-state of which he was a citizen. In Athens, liberty (at least the relative liberty of the free citizens) had emancipated energies and stimulated creativity. The outcome was the astounding progress, in all areas, of classical Athens; it was also wealth and power. On the other side of the coin were dissension, antagonism, and mob emotionalism. These contributed to a crushing military defeat from which Athens never recovered. As will be the case 2,200 years later with the British Southey and the German Rodbertus, conservatism made Plato the advocate of a well-ordered and disciplined society, founded on partial collectivism—basically an idealized version of authoritarian, proud, and culturally backward Sparta. One may smile at some details of Plato's ideal commonwealth, for instance the community of women and children. But the details are unimportant; what makes Plato a forerunner of modern socialism is his central concept of the total merging of the individual in the community.

Sir Thomas More's little book, *Utopia* (or No-Place), belongs to the literature of escapism. It was written in 1516. No-Place is an island, England as it should be. In the real England there had been much recent bloodshed and suffering, and bloody wars were being waged on the Continent. Europe was on the threshold of the Reformation. More dreamed of the well-ordered and happy society: a collectivist one. Minds were alert in Utopia. There was tolerance. Good people took charge of public affairs. No one was tied to his job. Through emigration overseas, there was plenty of elbow room for all. The Utopian society was the antithesis of dynamic but chaotic Renaissance Italy, then in the throes of agony. Yet, somehow, it was supposed to attain the high level of intellectual and economic achievement that parts of Italy, particularly republican commonwealths like Florence and Venice, had reached when More was a young man.

With Babeuf we are on the threshold of modern socialism. His friend, fellow conspirator, and disciple, the Italian Filippo Buonarroti (1767–1837), was the link between Babeuf and the semi-clandestine socialist groups formed in France after the Revolution of 1830. Babeuf had lived through the upheavals of 1789–1794. In the revolutionary trinity of liberty, equality, and fraternity, his god was equality. Thermidor and the end of Jacobin terror in 1794 had for him been the betrayal of the Revolution. He organized a conspiracy against the members of the Directory, which was trying to govern republican France in the midst of enormous internal and external difficulties. The *Manifesto of the Equals* was the conspirators' declaration of faith. Arrested, Babeuf was sentenced to death. During the trial he wrote his own eloquent defense. Babeuf and his conspiracy were, at the time, a small episode in the convulsions from which a new French nation was born. With the present spread of socialism the episode looms larger and larger, and attracts more and more attention.

Plato's Ideal Community

"THE ORIGIN of a city," I said, "is, in my opinion, due to the fact that no one of us is sufficient for himself, but each is in need of many things. Or do you think there is any other cause for the founding of cities?"

"No," he said, "none."

"Then men, being in want of many things, gather into one settlement many partners and helpers; one taking to himself one man, and another another, to satisfy their diverse needs, and to this common settlement we give the name of city. Is not that so?"

SOURCE: Plato, *The Republic*, trans. A. D. Lindsay (Dent, London, 1935), passim Books II–IV.

"Certainly."

"And when they exchange with one another, giving or receiving as the case may be, does not each man think that such exchange is to his own good?"

"Certainly."

"Come, then," I said. "Let us in our argument construct the city from the beginning. Apparently it will be the outcome of our need?"

"Surely."

"But the first and greatest of our needs is the provision of food to support existence and life?"

"Yes, assuredly."

"The second the provision of a dwelling-place, and the third of clothing, and so on?"

"That is so."

"Come, then," I said, "how will our city be able to supply a sufficiency of all those things? Will it not be by having one man a farmer, another a builder, and a third a weaver? Shall we add a shoemaker, and perhaps another provider of bodily needs?"

[Continuing the dialogue, the speaker—Socrates—adds to the people of the city carpenters, smiths, merchants, experts in sea-trading, hired laborers, servants, swineherds, makers of all kinds of articles, poets, artists, doctors, and finally guardians, including the rulers and the auxiliaries or warriors.]

"Then," I said, "because the work of our guardians is the most important of all, it will demand the most exclusive attention and the greatest skill and practice."

"I certainly think so," he said.

"And will it not need also a nature fitted for this profession?"

"Surely."

"Then it will be our business to do our best to select the proper persons and to determine the proper character required for the guardians of the city?"

"Yes, we shall have to do that."

"Well, certainly it is no trivial task we have undertaken, but we must be brave and do all in our power."

[Education is discussed by Socrates at considerable length. Education in the ideal community is rigidly enforced selective indoctrination, as shown by the following two passages:]

" . . . We have settled . . . which of [the stories of the gods] our young children may hear and which they may not, if they are to grow up to honour the gods and their parents, and to hold friendship dear."

" . . . The founders [of a city] ought to know the canons in accordance with which the poets should tell their stories, and which they are not allowed to trangress. . . ."

"But besides this education, any man of sense will tell us that their houses and their other arrangements must be so regulated as in no way to discourage them from being the best of guardians, or to incite them to maltreat the rest of the citizens."

"And he will tell us rightly," he said.

"Consider, then," I said, "whether their manner of life and their dwelling-places must be of some such fashion as this if they are to answer our description. In the first place, no one shall have any private property, unless it is absolutely necessary. Secondly, no one shall have dwelling-place or storehouse which any one who pleases may not freely enter. To supply the proper necessities of men who are warrior athletes, and both prudent and courageous, they shall receive from the other citizens a fixed reward for their guardian-ship, large enough to support them for a year and leave nothing over. They shall live in common, taking their meals at the public tables, as in an army. As for silver and gold, we shall tell them that they have the divine metals always in their hearts, given them by the gods, and have no need of men's silver and gold; nay, that it is an act of impiety to pollute their possession of the divine gold by conjoining it with the mortal; for many unholy deeds are done for the common currency, but the coinage in their souls is unsullied. They alone in all the city are not allowed to handle or touch silver and gold, or to be under the same roof with it, or hold it in their hands, or drink out of gold and silver vessels; this will be their salvation, and the salvation of the city. But if at any time they acquire land or houses or money of their own, and are men of business and farmers instead of guardians, they will become the hated masters instead of the allies of the other citizens. They will live their life, hating and being hated, plotting and being plotted against, always in greater and more intense fear of the citizens within than of the enemies without, rushing to the very brink of destruction, and the city with them. For all those reasons," I said, "shall we not say that this is the manner in which our guardians must be provided with houses and other necessaries, and shall we legislate accordingly?"

"Certainly," said Glaucon.

" . . . We . . . have to consider whether in establishing the guardians we are to aim at giving them as much happiness as possible, or whether we ought rather to turn our attention to giving happiness to the whole city, in which case we must compel the auxiliaries and guardians to second our efforts, and we must persuade them to be as skilful at their own business as lies in their power, and similarly with all the others. And when the whole city is thus increasing and prosperous, we may allow each class to partake of such happiness as their nature allows."

"Your words," he said, "seem to me excellent."

"Then," I said, "will you equally approve of the companion remark I make to that?"

"What is that?"

"Consider whether this is what corrupts the other craftsmen, so that they become not only corrupt, but bad workmen."

"To what do you refer?"

"Riches and poverty," I said.

"In what way?"

"In this way. Do you think that a potter who has come into money will want to go on with his craft?"

"Certainly not."

"Will he not become more idle and careless than he was before?"

"Yes, much more."

"And that will make him a worse potter?"

"Yes; a much worse potter too."

"Then, to take the other case, if poverty prevents him from buying tools or anything else required for his craft his work will be inferior, and he will make worse craftsmen of his sons or apprentices?"

"Surely."

"Then both poverty and riches produce worse handicraft and worse craftsmen?"

"Evidently."

"Then it seems we have found some other things against whose secret entrance into the city the guardians must take every precaution."

"What are they?"

"Riches and poverty," I answered; "for the one produces luxury and idleness and revolution, the other revolution and meanness and villainy besides."

[Guardians will have "community of wives and children."]

" . . . we must make the wives of our guardians strip, for they will clothe themselves with excellence instead of garments, and we must make them take their share in war and the other duties of guarding the city, and let them do nothing else. Only of these we must assign the lighter to the women, because of the weakness of the sex."

" . . . our men and women guardians must follow all pursuits in common: rather the argument somehow comes to an agreement with itself that its proposals are practical and advantageous."

"Certainly," he said; "it is a small wave that you are surmounting."

"You will say that it is no great one," I said, "when you see the next."

"Say on, and let me see it," he answered.

"This new law," I said, "follows, I fancy, the one we have just had, and all those that went before."

"What is it?"

"That these women should be all of them wives in common of all these men, and that no woman should live with any man privately, and that their children too should be common, and the parent should not know his own offspring nor the child its parent."

"I imagine," I said, "that if our rulers are worthy of the name, and if their auxiliaries are the same, that the latter will be willing to carry out their orders, and the former in giving their orders will themselves obey the laws, or where we leave them discretion, will be faithful to their spirit."

"Naturally," he said.

"Then you, the lawgiver, as you have selected the men, will select the women, choosing as far as possible those of a similar nature, and place them together. Both sexes will live together, with common houses and common meals, no one possessing any private property; and associating with one another in the gymnasia and in the rest of their daily life, they will be led, I imagine, by an inherent necessity to form alliances. Do you not think that this will be inevitable?"

"Yes," he said; "not by geometric but by lovers' necessity, which, perhaps, is stronger than the other in its power to persuade and constrain the mass of men."

" . . . the best of both sexes ought to be brought together as often as possible, the worst as seldom as possible, and . . . we should rear the offspring of the first, but not the offspring of the second, if our herd is to reach the highest perfection, and all these arrangements must be secret from all save the rulers if the herd of guardians is to be as free as possible from dissension."

"You are perfectly right," he said.

"We must then have statutory festivals, at which we shall bring together the brides and bridegrooms. There should be accompanying sacrifices, and our poets must compose strains in honour of the marriages which take place. But the number of marriages we shall place under the control of the rulers, that they may as far as possible keep the population at the same level, having regard to wars and disease and all such ravages, and also taking care to the best of their power that our city become neither great nor small."

" . . . to our young men who acquit themselves well in war or other duties we may give, along with other rewards and prizes, a more unrestricted right of cohabitation in order that there may be a colourable excuse for such fathers having as many children as possible."

"You are right."

"Then the children as they are born will be taken in charge by the officers appointed for the purpose, whether these are men or women, or both. For of course offices also are common to men and women."

"Yes."

"The children of good parents, I suppose, they will put into the rearing pen, handing them over to nurses who will live apart in a particular portion of the city; but the children of inferior parents and all defective children that are born to the others, they will be put out of sight in secrecy and mystery, as is befitting."

"Yes, they must," he said, "if the race of guardians is to be pure."

"And will not these officers also superintend the rearing of the children, bringing the mothers to the nursery when their breasts are full, and taking every precaution to prevent any woman knowing her own child, and providing wet-nurses if the mothers are not enough; and will they not take care that the mothers do not give too much time to suckling the children, and assign night watchers and all troublesome duties to nurses and attendants?"

"As you describe it," he said, "child-bearing will be a very easy matter for the wives of the guardians."

Thomas More's Utopia

. . . The island is broadest in the middle, where it measures about two hundred miles across. It's never much narrower than that, except towards the very ends, which gradually taper away and curve right round, just as if they'd been drawn with a pair of compasses, until they almost form a circle five hundred miles in circumference. So you can picture the island as a sort of crescent, with its tips divided by a strait approximately eleven miles wide.

There are fifty-four splendid big towns on the island, all with the same language, laws, customs, and institutions. They're all built on the same plan, and, so far as the sites will allow, they all look exactly alike. The minimum distance between towns is twenty-four miles, and maximum, no more than a day's walk.

Each town sends three of its older and more experienced citizens to an annual meeting at Aircastle, to discuss the general affairs of the island. Aircastle is regarded as the capital, because of its central position, which makes it easy to get at from every part of the country. The distribution of land is so arranged that the territory of each town stretches for at least twenty miles in every direction, and in one direction much farther—that is, where the distance between towns reaches its maximum. No town has the slightest wish to extend its boundaries, for they don't regard their land as property but as soil that they've got to cultivate.

At regular intervals all over the countryside there are houses supplied with agricultural equipment, and town dwellers take it in turns to go and live in them. Each house accommodates at least forty adults, plus two slaves who are permanently attached to it, and is run by a reliable, elderly married couple, under the supervision of a District Controller, who's responsible for thirty such houses. Each year twenty people from each house go back to

SOURCE: Sir Thomas More, *Utopia*, trans. Paul Turner (Penguin Books, Harmondsworth, Middlesex, 1965), passim pp. 69–102.

town, having done two years in the country, and are replaced by twenty others. These new recruits are then taught farming by the ones who've had a year on the land already, and so know more about the job. Twelve months later the trainees become the instructors, and so on. This system reduces the risk of food shortages, which might occur if the whole agricultural population were equally inexperienced.

Two years is the normal period of work on the land, so that no one's forced to rough it for too long, but those who enjoy country life—and many people do—can get special permission to stay there longer.

. . . each [group of thirty households] elects an official called a Styward every year. Styward is the Old Utopian title—the modern one is District Controller. For every ten Stywards and the households they represent there is a Bencheater, or Senior District Controller.

Each town has two hundred Stywards, who are responsible for electing the Mayor. They do it by secret ballot, after solemnly swearing to vote for the man that they consider best qualified. He has to be one of four candidates nominated by the whole electorate —for each quarter of the town chooses its own candidate and submits his name to the Council of Bencheaters. The Mayor remains in office for life, unless he's suspected of wanting to establish a dictatorship. Bencheaters are elected annually, but they're not normally changed. All other municipal appointments are for one year only.

Every three days, or more if necessary, the Bencheaters have a meeting with the Mayor, at which they discuss public affairs, and promptly settle any private disputes—though these are very rare. They always invite two Stywards, a different pair each day, to attend their meetings, and there's a rule that no question affecting the general public may be finally decided until it has been debated for three days . . . any major issue is referred to the Assembly of Stywards, who explain it to all their households, talk it over among themselves, and then report their views to the Council. Occasionally the matter is referred to Parliament.

And now for their working conditions. Well, there's one job they all do, irrespective of sex, and that's farming. It's part of every child's education. They learn the principles of agriculture at school, and they're taken for regular outings into the fields near the town, where they not only watch farm-work being done, but also do some themselves, as a form of exercise.

Besides farming which, as I say, is everybody's job, each person is taught a special trade of his own. He may be trained to process wool or flax, or he may become a stonemason, a blacksmith, or a carpenter. Those are the only trades that employ any considerable quantity of labour. They have no tailors or dressmakers, since everyone on the island wears the same sort of clothes—except that they vary slightly according to sex and marital status. These clothes last for a lifetime, they're quite pleasant to look at, they allow free movement of the limbs, they're equally suitable for hot and cold weather—and the great thing is, they're all home-made. So everybody learns one of the other trades I mentioned, and by everybody I mean the women as well as the men—though the weaker sex are given the lighter jobs, like spinning and weaving, while the men do the heavier ones.

Most children are brought up to do the same work as their parents, since they tend to have a natural feeling for it. But if a child fancies some other trade, he's adopted into a family that practises it. Of course, great care is taken, not only by the father, but also by the local authorities, to see that the foster-father is a decent, respectable type. When you've learned one trade properly, you can, if you like, get permission to learn another—and when you're an expert in both, you can practise whichever you prefer, unless the other one is more essential to the public.

The chief business of the Stywards—in fact, practically their only business—is to see that nobody sits around doing nothing, but that everyone gets on with his job. They don't wear people out, though, by keeping them hard at work from early morning till late at night, like cart-horses. That's just slavery—and yet that's what life is like for the working classes nearly everywhere else in the world. In Utopia they have a six-hour working day—three hours in the morning, then lunch—then a two-hour break—then three more hours in the afternoon, followed by supper. They go to bed at 8 P.M., and sleep for eight hours. All the rest of the time of the twenty-four they're free to do what they like—not to waste their time in idleness or self-indulgence, but to make good use of it in some congenial activity. Most people spend these free periods on further education, for there are public lectures first thing every morning. Attendance is quite voluntary, except for those picked out for academic training, but men and women of all classes go crowding in to hear them—I mean, different people go to different lectures, just as the spirit moves them. However, there's nothing to stop you from spending this extra time on your trade, if you want to. Lots of people do, if they haven't the capacity for intellectual work, and are much admired for such public-spirited behaviour.

. . . out of all the able-bodied men and women who live in a town, or in the country round it, five hundred at the most are exempted from ordinary work. This includes the Stywards, who, though legally exempt, go on working voluntarily to set a good example. It also includes those who are permanently relieved of other duties so that they can concentrate on their studies. This privilege is only granted on the recommendation of the priests, confirmed by the Stywards in a secret ballot—and, if such a student produces disappointing results, he's sent back to the working class. On the other hand, it's not at all unusual for a manual worker to study so hard in his spare time, and make such good progress, that he's excused from practising his trade, and promoted to the intelligentsia.

This is the class from which the diplomats, priests, Bencheaters, and of course mayors are recruited.

With everybody doing useful work, and with such work reduced to a minimum, they build up such large reserves of everything that from time to time they can release a huge labour force to mend any roads which are in bad condition. And quite often, if there's nothing of that sort to be done, the authorities announce a shorter working day. They never force people to work unnecessarily, for the main purpose of their whole economy is to give each person as much time free from physical drudgery as the needs of the community will allow, so that he can cultivate his mind—which they regard as the secret of a happy life.

. . . the smallest social unit is the household, which is virtually synonymous with the family. When a girl grows up and gets married, she joins her husband's household, but the boys of each generation stay at home, under the control of their oldest male relative—unless he becomes senile, in which case the next oldest takes over.

Each town consists of six thousand households, not counting the country ones, and to keep the population fairly steady there's a law that no household shall contain less than ten or more than sixteen adults—as they can't very well fix a figure for children. This law is observed by simply moving supernumerary adults to smaller households. If the town as a whole gets too full, the surplus population is transferred to a town that's comparatively empty. If the whole island becomes overpopulated, they tell off a certain number of people from each town to go and start a colony at the nearest point on the mainland where there's a large area that hasn't been cultivated by the local inhabitants. Such colonies are governed by the Utopians, but the natives are allowed to join in if they want to. When this happens, natives and colonists soon combine to form a single community with a single way of life, to the great advantage of both parties—for, under Utopian management, land which used to be thought incapable of producing anything for one lot of people produces plenty for two.

If the natives won't do what they're told, they're expelled from the area marked out for annexation. If they try to resist, the Utopians declare war—for they consider war perfectly justifiable, when one country denies another its natural right to derive nourishment from any soil which the original owners are not using themselves, but are merely holding on to as a worthless piece of property.

Should any town become so depopulated that it can't be brought up to strength by transfers from elsewhere on the island, without reducing the population of some other town below the prescribed minimum—a thing which is said to have happened only twice in their history, each time as the result of a violent epidemic—they recall colonists to fill the gap, on the principle that it's better to lose a colony than to weaken any part of Utopia itself.

. . . Each household . . . comes under the authority of the oldest male. Wives are subordinate to their husbands, children to their parents, and younger people generally to their elders. Every town is divided into four districts of equal size, each with its own shopping centre in the middle of it. There the products of every household are collected in warehouses, and then distributed according to type among various shops. When the head of a household needs anything for himself or his family, he just goes to one of these shops and asks for it. And whatever he asks for, he's allowed to take away without any sort of payment, either in money or in kind. After all, why shouldn't he? There's more than enough of everything to go round, so there's no risk of his asking for more than he needs—for why should anyone want to start hoarding, when he knows he'll never have to go short of anything? No living creature is naturally greedy, except from fear of want—or in the case of human beings, from vanity, the notion that you're better than people if you can display more superfluous property than they can. But there's no scope for that sort of thing in Utopia.

. . . Whatever you may think of their doctrines, you won't find a more prosperous country or a more splendid lot of people anywhere on earth. Physically, they're very active, full of energy, and stronger than their height would suggest—though you couldn't call them exactly short. Their land isn't always very fertile, and their climate's not too good, but by a well-balanced diet they build up their resistance to bad weather conditions, and by careful cultivation they correct the deficiencies of the soil. The result is that they've beaten all records for the production of corn and livestock, their expectation of life is the highest in the world, and their disease-rate the lowest. Thus, by scientific methods, they've done wonders with a country that's naturally rather barren. Not that their talents are confined to ordinary farming. You'll also find them uprooting whole forests and replanting them elsewhere, not to increase the yield, but to facilitate the transport of timber, by bringing it nearer to the sea, or to a river, or to a town—for it's not so easy to carry timber long distances by roads as corn. The people themselves are friendly and intelligent, with a good sense of humour. Though fond of relaxation, they're capable of hard physical work when necessary. Otherwise they don't much care for it—but they never get tired of using their brains.

By applying their trained intelligence to scientific research, they've become amazingly good at inventing things that are useful in everyday life. Two inventions, however, they owe to us—though even there much of the credit should go to them. For the moment we showed them some books that Aldus had printed, and talked a bit about printing and paper-making—we couldn't explain them properly, as none of us knew much about either process—they immediately made a shrewd guess how the things were done. Up till then they'd only produced skin, bark, or papyrus manuscripts, but now they instantly started to manufacture paper, and print from type. At first they weren't too successful, but after repeated experiments they soon mastered both techniques so thoroughly that, if it weren't for the shortage of original texts, they could have all the Greek books they wanted. As it is, they have only the works I mentioned, but of these they've already printed and published several thousand copies.

. . . the slaves that I've occasionally referred to are not, as you might imagine, non-combatant prisoners-of-war, slaves by birth, or purchases from foreign slave markets. They're either Utopian convicts or, much more often, condemned criminals from other countries, who are acquired in large numbers, sometimes for a small payment, but usually for nothing. Both types of slaves are kept hard at work in chain-gangs, though Utopians are treated worse than foreigners. The idea is that it's all the more deplorable if a person who has had the advantage of a first-rate education and a thoroughly moral upbringing still insists on becoming a criminal—so the punishment should be all the more severe.

Another type of slave is the working-class foreigner who, rather than live in wretched poverty at home, volunteers for slavery in Utopia. Such people are treated with respect, and with almost as much kindness as Utopian citizens, except that they're made to work harder, because they're used to it. If they want to leave the country, which doesn't often happen, they're perfectly free to do so, and receive a small gratuity.

François-Noël Babeuf on a Communal Régime

Man's condition ought not to have deteriorated in passing from a state of nature to a state of social organization. In the beginning the soil belonged to none, its fruits to all. The introduction of private property was a piece of trickery put over on the simple and un-suspecting masses. The laws that buttressed property operated inevitably to create social classes—privileged and oppressed, masters and slaves.

The law of inheritance is a sovereign wrong. It breeds misery even from the second generation. Two sons of a rich man receive equal shares of their father's fortune. One son has but one child,

SOURCE: F.-N. Babeuf, *The Defense of Gracchus Babeuf*, trans. and ed. by Dr. John Anthony Scott (Gehenna Press, Northampton, Mass., 1964), pp. 28–33.

the other, twelve. Of these twelve each receives only a twelfth part of the fortune of his uncle and the twenty-fourth part of the fortune of his grandfather. This portion is not enough to live on; and so twelve poor men must work for one rich one. Hence we find masters and servants among the grandchildren of a single man.

The law of alienability is no less unjust. This one man, already master over all the other grandchildren in the same line, pays what he will for the work that they must do for him. Their wages are insufficient to maintain life and they are obliged to sell their meager inheritance to their master. They become landless men; and if they have children of their own, these inherit nothing.

The gulf between rich and poor, rulers and ruled, proceeds from yet another cause, the difference in value and in price that arbitrary opinion attaches to the diverse products of toil and manufacture. Thus a watchmaker's working day has been valued twenty times higher than a ploughman's or laborer's. The wages of the watchmaker enable him to get possession of the inheritance of twenty ploughmen whom he is thus in a position to expropriate, and enhance his own condition.

These three roots of our public woes—heredity, alienability, and the differing values which arbitrary opinion assigns to different types of social product—proceed from the institution of private property. All the evils of society flow from them. They isolate the people from each other; they convert every family into a private commonwealth, pit it against society at large, and dedicate it with an ever growing emphasis to inequality in all its vicious, suicidal forms.

If the earth belongs to none and its fruits to all; if private ownership of public wealth is only the result of certain institutions that violate fundamental human rights; then it follows that this private ownership is a usurpation; and it further follows that all that a man takes of the land and its fruits beyond what is necessary for sustenance is theft from society.

All that a citizen lacks for the satisfaction of his various daily needs, he lacks because he has been deprived of a natural property right by the engrossers of the public domain. All that a citizen enjoys beyond what is necessary for the satisfaction of his daily needs he enjoys as a result of a theft from the other members of society. In this way a more or less numerous group of people is deprived of its rightful share in the public domain.

Inheritance and alienability are institutions destructive of basic human rights.

The plea of superior ability and industry is an empty rationalization to mask the machinations of those who conspire against human equality and happiness. It is ridiculous and unfair to lay claim to a higher wage for the man whose work requires more concentrated thought and more mental effort. Such effort in no way expands the capacity of the stomach. No wage can be defended over and above what is necessary for the satisfaction of a person's needs.

The worth of intelligence is only a matter of opinion, and it still remains to be determined if natural, physical strength is not of equal worth. Clever people have set a high value upon the creations of their minds; if the toilers had also had a hand in the ordering of things, they would doubtless have insisted that brawn is entitled to equal consideration with brain and that physical fatigue is no less real than mental fatigue.

If wages are not equalized, the clever and persevering are given a licence to rob and despoil with impunity those less fortunately endowed with natural gifts. In this way the economic equilibrium of society is upset, for nothing has been more conclusively proven than the maxim: *a man succeeds in becoming rich only through the spoliation of others.*

All our civic institutions, our social relationships, are nothing else but the expression of legalized barbarism and piracy, in which every man cheats and robs his neighbor. In its festering swamp our dwindling society generates vice, crime, and misery of every kind. A handful of well-intentioned people band together and wage war on these evils, but their efforts are futile. They can make no headway because they do not tackle the problem at its roots, but apply palliatives based upon the distorted thinking of a sick society.

It is clear from the foregoing that whatever a man possesses over and above his rightful share of the social product has been stolen. It is therefore right and proper to take this wealth back again from those who have wrongfully appropriated it. Even a man who shows that he can do the work of four, and who consequently demands the wages of four, will still be an enemy of society; he is using criminal means to shake the social order and to obliterate its sacred quality. Common sense tells us, with no small emphasis, that we should curb a man of this type and drive him out as if he had the plague. At the very least he should be allowed to perform no more than one man's work and to lay claim to no more than one man's pay. The human species alone has made insane value distinctions between one of its members and another. As a result, the human species alone has been obliged to experience misery and want. There is no need for men to lack those things which nature has provided for all, though, of course, if want should arise as a result of the unavoidable calamities of wind, storm, flood or famine, such privation must be borne and shared equally by all.

The creations of the human mind become the property of society, part of the nation's capital, from the very moment that thinkers and workers bring these creations into being. Invention is the fruit of prior investigation and effort. The most recent workers in the field reap their reward as a result of the social labors of their predecessors in a society that nurtures invention and that aids the scientific worker in his task. It is clear that if knowledge is a social product it must be shared by all alike.

It is a truth, which only ignorant or prejudiced people are likely to contest, that if knowledge were made available to all alike, it would serve to make men roughly equal in ability and even in talent. Education is a monstrosity when it is unequally shared, since then it becomes the exclusive patrimony of a section of society; it becomes, in the hands of this section, a set of tools, an ideological armory, with the help of which the privileged make war upon the defenseless masses. In this way the rich succeed, with little difficulty, in stifling and deceiving and robbing the people, thus subjecting them to a shameful servitude.

One thinker expressed a profound truth when he wrote: "Talk as long as you will of the forms of government; it will all be idle speculation until you destroy the seeds of human greed and acquisitiveness." Society must be made to operate in such a way that it eradicates once and for all the desire of a man to become richer, or wiser, or more powerful than others.

Putting this more exactly, we must try to *bring our fate under control*, try to make the lot of every member of society independent of accidental circumstances, happy or unhappy. We must try to guarantee to each man and his posterity, however numerous, a sufficiency of the means of existence, and nothing more. We must try and close all possible avenues by which a man may acquire more than his fair share of the fruits of toil and the gifts of nature.

The only way to do this is to organize a communal regime which will suppress private property, set each to work at the skill or job he understands, require each to deposit the fruits of his labor in kind at the common store, and establish an agency for the distribution of basic necessities. This agency will maintain a complete list of people and of supplies, will distribute the latter with scrupulous fairness, and will deliver them to the home of each worker.

A system such as this has been proven practicable by actual experience, for it is used by our twelve armies with their 1,200,000 men. And what is possible on a small scale can also be done on a large one. A regime of this type alone can ensure the general welfare, or, in other words, the permanent happiness of the people —the true and proper object of organized society.

Such a regime . . . will sweep away iron bars, dungeon walls, and bolted doors, trials and disputations, murders, thefts and crimes of every kind; it will sweep away the judges and the judged, the jails and the gibbets—all the torments of body and agony of soul that the injustice of life engenders; it will sweep away enviousness and gnawing greed, pride and deceit, the very catalogue of sins that Man is heir to; it will remove—and how important that is!—the brooding, omnipresent fear that gnaws always and each of us concerning our fate tomorrow, next month, next year, and in our old age; concerning the fate of our children and of our children's children.

Manifesto of the Equals (Pierre Sylvain Maréchal)

PEOPLE OF FRANCE!

For fifteen hundred years you have lived in slavery and in misery. And for the last six years you have existed in the hourly expectation of independence, happiness, and equality.

Equality is the first principle of nature, the most elementary need of man, the prime bond of any decent association among human beings. But in this you, the French people, have fared no better than the rest of mankind. Humanity, the world over, has always been in the grip of more or less clever cannibals—creatures who have batten on men in order to advance their own selfish

SOURCE: Sylvain Maréchal, *Manifeste des Egaux* (in *The Defense of Gracchus Babeuf*, trans. and ed. by Dr. John Anthony Scott, Gehenna Press, Northampton, Mass., 1964), pp. 61–64.

ambitions and to nourish their own selfish lust for power. Throughout man's history he has been gulled with fine words, he has received only the shadow of a promise, not its substance. Hypocrites, from time immemorial, have told us that *men are equal;* and yet monstrous and degrading inequality has, from time immemorial, ground humanity into the dust. Since the dawn of human history man has understood that equality is the finest ornament of the human condition, yet not once has he been successful in his struggles to bring his vision to life. Equality has remained a legal fiction, beautiful but baseless. And today, when we demand it with a new insistence, our rulers reply: "Silence! Real equality is an idle dream. Be content with equality before the law. Ignorant and lowborn herd, what else do you need?"

Men of high degree—lawmakers, rulers, the rich—now it is your turn to listen to us.

Men are equal. This is a self-evident truth. As soon say that it is night when the sun shines, as deny this.

Henceforth we shall live and die as we have been born—equal. Equality or death: that is what we want. And that is what we shall have, no matter what the price to be paid. Woe to you who stand in our way or try to thwart the realization of our dearest wish!

The French Revolution is only the forerunner of another, even greater, that shall finally put an end to the era of revolutions. The people have swept away the kings and priests who have been leagued against them. Next they will sweep away the modern upstarts, the tyrants and tricksters who have usurped the ancient seats of power.

What else do we need other than equality before the law?

We need not only this equality as it is written down in the Declaration of the Rights of Man and of the Citizen; we need it in life, in our very midst, in our homes. For the true and living equality we will give up everything. Let the arts perish, if need be! But let us have real equality.

Men of high degree—lawmakers, rulers, the rich—strangers as you are to the love of man, to good faith, to compassion: it is no good to say that we are only "bringing up again the old cry of *loi agraire.*" It is our turn to speak. Listen to our just demands and to the law of nature which sanctions them.

The *loi agraire*—the division of the land—has been the instinctive demand of a handful of soldiers of fortune, of peoples here and

there governed by passion, not by reason. We intend something far
better and far more just: the COMMON GOOD, or the COMMUNITY OF
GOODS. There must be an end to individual ownership of the land,
for *the land is nobody's personal property*. Our demand is for the
communal ownership of the earth's resources. *These resources are
the property of mankind*.

We say that an end must be put to the situation in which the
overwhelming majority of mankind, living under the thumb of a
tiny minority, sweats and toils for the sole benefit of a few. In
France fewer than a million persons own and dispose of wealth that
rightfully belongs to twenty millions of their fellow men, to their
fellow citizens.

There must be an end to this outrage! Will people in times to
come even be able to conceive that such a situation ever existed?
There must be an end to this unnatural division of society into rich
and poor, into strong and weak, into masters and servants, into
rulers and ruled.

Age and sex are the sole natural distinctions existing between
men. All men have the same needs, all are endowed with the same
faculties, all are warmed by the same sun, and all breathe the same
air. Why then should not all receive an equal share of food and
clothing—equal both in that quantity and quality to which all shall
be entitled?

But a howl arises from the sworn enemies of a truly natural
order of things. "Anarchists! Demagogues!" they shriek. "You are
nothing more than instigators of mob violence. That's what you
are."

PEOPLE OF FRANCE,
We shall not waste time dignifying such charges with an answer.
But to you we say: the high enterprise which we are engaged upon
has a single purpose—to put an end to civil strife and to the
sufferings of the masses.

No vaster plan than ours has ever been conceived or put into
execution. Once in a long while men of vision have discussed it,
cautiously and in whispers; none of them has had the boldness to
speak out and to tell the whole truth.

The hour for decisive action has now struck. The people's
suffering has reached its peak; it darkens the face of the earth. For
centuries chaos has reigned under the name of "order." Now the
time has come to mend matters. We, who love justice and who seek

happiness—let us enter the struggle for the sake of equality. The time has come to establish THE REPUBLIC OF EQUALITY, to prepare an asylum for mankind. The time has come to set the earth to rights. You, who are oppressed, join us: come and partake of the feast which nature has provided for all her sons and daughters.

PEOPLE OF FRANCE,

A glorious and historic destiny has been reserved for you.

Hidebound tradition and blind prejudice will set barriers, as they always have, in the way of the establishment of the Republic of Equality. True equality—that alone provides for all human needs without sacrificing some men to the selfish interests of others—will not be welcome to everyone. Selfish and ambitious people will curse us. Men who have grown rich by thieving from their fellows will be the first to cry "thief." Proud men, living in privilege or in idleness, who have grown callous to the sufferings of others, will do battle with us. Men who wield arbitrary power, or who are its creatures, will not unprotesting bow their stiff necks beneath the yoke. The shape of things to come, the common good, their blind eyes cannot see. But how can a handful of such people prevail against a whole nation that has at last found the rapturous happiness it sought so long?

The day after the revolution for true equality has taken place people will be amazed. They will say: "The common good was so easy to attain! We only had to will it! Why on earth didn't we realize that sooner—why did we have to be told so often? It's absolutely true: when one man is richer and more powerful than the rest of us, everything is spoiled; crime and misery flourish."

PEOPLE OF FRANCE,

What is the hallmark of excellence in a constitution? Only true equality can serve as a foundation on which to base your Republic and satisfy all your needs. The aristocratic charters of 1791 and 1795 did not break your chains: they riveted them upon you more firmly. The Constitution of 1793 was a giant step toward true equality, the greatest that we have yet taken. It was dedicated to the goal of the common good, but did not, even so, fully provide the basis for organizing it.

PEOPLE OF FRANCE,

Open your eyes and hearts to full happiness: recognize the REPUBLIC OF EQUALITY. Join with us in working for it.

III

Some Nineteenth-Century Socialist Thinkers

Two sets of conditions favored the development of thought along socialist lines in nineteenth-century Europe. Starting with the establishment in 1803 of a British-type factory at Liège in the Low Countries, industrialization spread eastward from its original home in Great Britain. This was the work of "capitalists," owners and managers of capital. It made for rapid economic progress; it also brought with it the proletarianization of industrial wage-earners, urbanization, class antagonism, economic insecurity, what by the end of the century will be called the social problem. Following the defeat of Napoleonic despotism in 1814 and 1815 and the weakening of political authoritarianism through a succession of liberal and democratic revolutions, freedom of expression and of action increased in most of Europe. Even in Russia, shortly after the accession of Alexander II, censorship became lenient for a while. Capitalistic industrialization made for new problems; freedom of expression made it possible to discuss them, and political liberty made it possible to launch new movements.

It was natural for many who, for a variety of motives, rejected capitalism, to stress ideas that seemed to be antithetical to those held by capitalism's advocates: communalism instead of individualism, collective instead of private ownership, solidarity and cooperation instead of competition, state guidance instead of laissez-faire. When opposition to capitalism was linked to emphasis on equality and on the brotherhood of man, when collectivism was held to be the road to the social good, there was socialism.

The list of nineteenth-century European and American thinkers who formulated their personal socialist position and who influenced their contemporaries or their successors is long. The excerpts in this section are from the works of eight authors. Three of them live on in today's socialism: the Welshman Robert Owen and the Germans Karl Marx and Friedrich Engels. The other five, four Frenchmen (Saint-Simon, Fourier, Proudhon, Sorel) and a Russian (Bakunin), played a role in shaping contemporary socialism that cannot be ignored. Among the omitted authors with whom the student should become acquainted are the Frenchmen Cabet, inspirer of the "Icarian" settlements in the United States, Blanqui, inspirer of the socialist revolts in Paris of 1848 and 1871, and Blanc, who tried to introduce reforms along socialist lines in France in 1848; the British Christian socialist Kingsley; the Russian humanitarian socialist Herzen and agrarian socialist Lavrov; the German advocate of socialism as traditional paternalism, Rodbertus, and his fellow countryman Lassalle, who saw in democratic universal suffrage the road to a peaceful socialist revolution.

A. ROBERT OWEN: PRACTICAL IDEALIST

Robert Owen was born in Wales in 1771 and died in 1858. Son of an artisan (in Europe, a member of the lower middle class), he started in business on his own before he was twenty. At forty he was a wealthy manufacturer. For over two decades, until around 1834, he was indefatigable in writing about and preaching his plan for social reform. He was no less indefatigable in action, creating the industrial community of New Lanark in Scotland, coming to the United States in 1824 and starting the collectivist settlement of New Harmony, stimulating labor organization in Great Britain. When he was well into his sixties, the problems of the afterlife held greater interest for him than those of this life.

Owen, largely self-educated and entirely self-made, was a highly intelligent man who had acquired a vast store of knowledge. He was a very good man, animated by a deep and sympathetic understanding for his fellow men. He belonged, as a man of thought and of action, to that vast current of British humanitarianism that did more for the improvement of mankind than any government. He launched on their successful careers British democratic socialism, British trade unionism, and British cooperativism. Not so much because of what he actually wrote but because of the values and principles inspiring his writings, and because of the way he acted, he is the founder of today's democratic socialism. Not only in Great Britain but also everywhere in the old and in much of the new Commonwealth and in the English-speaking nations outside the Commonwealth, such as the United States and Ireland, socialism bears Owen's mark. He was a man of his times, a believer in the British experiment in liberty then only a few generations old, a follower of the Enlightenment, a believer in progress. He appreciated what had been achieved by nearly three hundred years of progressive transformation in Great Britain. He did not reject what the British had; he wanted more of it. His socialism was the fulfillment of what in his lifetime began to be known as liberalism.

Owen's ideas were put forth clearly and cogently in a series of essays, papers, and reports published between 1812 and 1821. The year 1813, when the first two essays on "A New View of Society" appeared, saw the birth of British socialism. Two other essays on the same topic appeared in 1814, and all four were published as one work in 1816. His ideas on human nature, on the influence of environment, on the role of education, are typically ideas of the progressive sector of the Enlightenment. Owen accepted them; but unlike the foremost synthesis builders of the nineteenth century, Owen was also willing to learn, i.e., to modify his convictions on the basis of new evidence.

New Lanark

IN THE year 1784 the late Mr. Dale, of Glascow, founded a manufactory for spinning of cotton, near the falls of the Clyde, in the county of Lanark, in Scotland; and about that period cotton mills were first introduced into the northern part of the kingdom.

It was the power which could be obtained from the falls of water that induced Mr. Dale to erect his mills in this situation; for in other respects it was not well chosen. The country around was uncultivated; the inhabitants were poor and few in number; and the roads in the neighbourhood were so bad, that the Falls, now so celebrated, were then unknown to strangers.

It was therefore necessary to collect a new population to supply the infant establishment with labourers. This, however, was no light task; for all the regularly trained Scotch peasantry disdained the idea of working early and late, day after day, within cotton mills. Two modes then only remained of obtaining these labourers; the one, to procure children from the various public charities of the country; and the other, to induce families to settle around the works.

To accommodate the first, a large house was erected, which ultimately contained about five hundred children, who were procured chiefly from workhouses and charities in Edinburgh. These children were to be fed, clothed, and educated; and these duties Mr. Dale performed with the unwearied benevolence which it is well known he possessed.

To obtain the second, a village was built; and the houses were let at a low rent to such families as could be induced to accept employment in the mills; but such was the general dislike to that occupation at the time, that, with a few exceptions, only persons destitute of friends, employment, and character, were found willing to try the experiment; and of these a sufficient number to supply a constant increase of the manufactory could not be obtained. It was therefore deemed a favour on the part even of such individuals to reside at the village, and, when taught the business,

SOURCE: R. Owen, *A New View of Society and Other Writings* (Dutton, New York, 1949), passim pp. 26–60.

they grew so valuable to the establishment, that they became agents not to be governed contrary to their own inclinations.

Mr. Dale's principal avocations were at a distance from the works, which he seldom visited more than once for a few hours in three or four months; he was therefore under the necessity of committing the management of the establishment to various servants with more or less power.

Those who have a practical knowledge of mankind will readily anticipate the character which a population so collected and constituted would acquire. It is therefore scarcely necessary to state, that the community by degrees was formed under these circumstances into a very wretched society: every man did that which was right in his own eyes, and vice and immorality prevailed to a monstrous extent. The population lived in idleness, in poverty, in almost every kind of crime; consequently, in debt, out of health, and in misery. Yet to make matters still worse,—although the cause proceeded from the best possible motive, a conscientious adherence to principle,—the whole was under a strong sectarian influence, which gave a marked and decided preference to one set of religious opinions over all others, and the professors of the favoured opinions were the privileged of the community.

The boarding-house containing the children presented a very different scene. The benevolent proprietor spared no expense to give comfort to the poor children. The rooms provided for them were spacious, always clean, and well ventilated; the food was abundant, and of the best quality; the clothes were neat and useful; a surgeon was kept in constant pay, to direct how to prevent or cure disease; and the best instructors which the country afforded were appointed to teach such branches of education as were deemed likely to be useful to children in their situation. Kind and well-disposed persons were appointed to superintend all their proceedings. Nothing, in short, at first sight seemed wanting to render it a most complete charity.

But to defray the expense of these well-devised arrangements, and to support the establishment generally, it was absolutely necessary that the children should be employed within the mills from six o'clock in the morning till seven in the evening, summer and winter; and after these hours their education commenced. The directors of the public charities, from mistaken economy, would not consent to send the children under their care to cotton mills, unless the children were received by the proprietors at the ages of six, seven, and eight.

Mr. Dale was advancing in years: he had no son to succeed him; and, finding the consequences just described to be the result of all his strenuous exertions for the improvement and happiness of his fellow-creatures, it is not surprising that he became disposed to retire from the cares of the establishment. He accordingly sold it to some English merchants and manufacturers; one of whom, under the circumstances just narrated, undertook the management of the concern, and fixed his residence in the midst of the population. This individual had been previously in the management of large establishments, employing a number of work-people, in the neighbourhood of Manchester; and, in every case, by the steady application of certain general principles, he succeeded in reforming the habits of those under his care, and who always, among their associates in similar employment, appeared conspicuous for their good conduct. With this previous success in remodelling English character, but ignorant of the local ideas, manners, and customs, of those now committed to his management, the stranger commenced his task.

At that time the lower classes in Scotland, like those of other countries, had strong prejudices against strangers having any authority over them, and particularly against the English, few of whom had then settled in Scotland, and not one in the neighbourhood of the scenes under description. It is also well known that even the Scotch peasantry and working classes possess the habit of making observations and reasoning thereon with great acuteness; and in the present case those employed naturally concluded that the new purchasers intended merely to make the utmost profit by the establishment, from the abuses of which many of themselves were then deriving support. The persons employed at these works were therefore strongly prejudiced against the new director of the establishment—prejudiced, because he was a stranger, and from England,—because he succeeded Mr. Dale, under whose proprietorship they acted almost as they liked,—because his religious creed was not theirs—and because they concluded that the works would be governed by new laws and regulations, calculated to squeeze, as they often termed it, the greatest sum of gain out of their labour.

In consequence, from the day he arrived amongst them every means which ingenuity could devise was set to work to counteract the plan which he attempted to introduce; and for two years it was a regular attack and defence of prejudices and malpractices between the manager and the population of the place, without the former being able to make much progress, or to convince the latter of the sincerity of his good intentions for their welfare. He, however, did not lose his patience, his temper, or his confidence in the certain success of the principles on which he founded his conduct.

These principles ultimately prevailed: the population could not continue to resist a firm well-directed kindness, administering justice to all. They therefore slowly and cautiously began to give him some portion of their confidence; and as this increased, he was enabled more and more to develop his plans for their amelioration. It may with truth be said, that at this period they possessed almost all the vices and very few of the virtues of a social community. Theft and the receipt of stolen goods was their trade, idleness and drunkenness their habit, falsehood and deception their garb, dissensions, civil and religious, their daily practice; they united only in a zealous systematic opposition to their employers.

Here then was a fair field on which to try the efficacy in practice of principles supposed capable of altering any characters. The manager formed his plans accordingly. He spent some time in finding out the full extent of the evil against which he had to contend, and in tracing the true causes which had produced and were continuing those effects. He found that all was distrust, disorder, and disunion; and he wished to introduce confidence, regularity, and harmony. He therefore began to bring forward his various expedients to withdraw the unfavourable circumstances by which they had hitherto been surrounded, and to replace them by others calculated to produce a more happy result. He soon discovered that theft was extended through almost all the ramifications of the community, and the receipt of stolen goods through all the country around. To remedy this evil, not one legal punishment was inflicted, not one individual imprisoned, even for an hour; but checks and other regulations of prevention were introduced; a short plain explanation of the immediate benefits they would derive from a different conduct was inculcated by those instructed for the purpose, who had the best powers of reasoning among themselves.

They were at the same time instructed how to direct their industry in legal and useful occupations, by which, without danger or disgrace, they could really earn more than they had previously obtained by dishonest practices. Thus the difficulty of committing the crime was increased, the detection afterwards rendered more easy, the habit of honest industry formed, and the pleasure of good conduct experienced.

Drunkenness was attacked in the same manner; it was discountenanced on every occasion by those who had charge of any department: its destructive and pernicious effects were frequently stated by his own more prudent comrades, at the proper moment when the individual was soberly suffering from the effects of his previous excess; pot and public houses were gradually removed from the immediate vicinity of their dwellings; the health and comfort of temperance were made familiar to them: by degrees drunkenness disappeared, and many who were habitual bacchanalians are now conspicuous for undeviating sobriety.

Falsehood and deception met with a similar fate: they were held in disgrace: their practical evils were shortly explained; and every countenance was given to truth and open conduct. The pleasure and substantial advantages derived from the latter soon overcame the impolicy, error, and consequent misery, which the former mode of acting had created.

Dissensions and quarrels were undermined by analogous expedients. When they could not be readily adjusted between the parties themselves, they were stated to the manager; and as in such cases both disputants were usually more or less in the wrong, that wrong was in as few words as possible explained, forgiveness and friendship recommended, and one simple and easily remembered precept inculcated, as the most valuable rule for their whole conduct, and the advantages of which they would experience every moment of their lives; viz.:—"That in future they should endeavour to use the same active exertions to make each other happy and comfortable, as they had hitherto done to make each other miserable; and by carrying this short memorandum in their mind, and applying it on all occasions, they would soon render that place a paradise, which, from the most mistaken principle of action, they now made the abode of misery." The experiment was tried: the parties enjoyed the gratification of this new mode of conduct; references rapidly subsided; and now serious differences are scarcely known.

Considerable jealousies also existed on account of one religious sect possessing a decided preference over the others. This was corrected by discontinuing that preference, and by giving an uniform encouragement to those who conducted themselves well among all the various religious persuasions; by recommending the same consideration to be shown to the conscientious opinions of each sect, on the ground that all must believe the particular doctrines which they had been taught, and consequently that all were in that respect upon an equal footing, nor was it possible yet to say which was right or wrong. It was likewise inculcated that all should attend to the essence of religion, and not act as the world was now taught and trained to do; that is, to overlook the substance and essence of religion, and devote their talents, time, and money, to that which is far worse than its shadow, sectarianism; another term for something very injurious to society, and very absurd, which one or other well-meaning enthusiast has added to *true religion*, which, without these defects, would soon form those characters which every wise and good man is anxious to see.

Such statements and conduct arrested sectarian animosity and ignorant intolerance; each retains full liberty of conscience, and in consequence each partakes of the sincere friendship of many sects instead of one. They act with cordiality together in the same department and pursuits, and associate as though the whole community were not of different sectarian persuasions; and not one evil ensues.

The same principles were applied to correct the irregular intercourse of the sexes:—such conduct was discountenanced and held in disgrace; fines were levied upon both parties for the use of the support fund of the community. (This fund arose from each individual contributing one-sixtieth part of their wages, which, under their management, was applied to support the sick, the injured by accident, and the aged.) But because they had once unfortunately offended against the established laws and customs of society, they were not forced to become vicious, abandoned, and miserable; the door was left open for them to return to the comforts of kind friends and respected acquaintances; and, beyond any previous expectation, the evil became greatly diminished.

The system of receiving apprentices from public charities was abolished; permanent settlers with large families were encouraged, and comfortable houses were built for their accommodation.

The practice of employing children in the mills of six, seven, and eight years of age, was discontinued, and their parents advised to allow them to acquire health and education until they were ten years old. (It may be remarked, that even this age is too early to keep them at constant employment in manufactories, from six in the morning to seven in the evening. Far better would it be for the children, their parents, and for society, that the first should not commence employment until they attain the age of twelve, when their education might be finished, and their bodies would be more competent to undergo the fatigue and exertions required of them. When parents can be trained to afford this additional time to their children without inconvenience, they will, of course, adopt the practice now recommended.)

The children were taught reading, writing, and arithmetic, during five years, that is, from five to ten, in the village school, without expense to their parents. All the modern improvements in education have been adopted, or are in process of adoption. (To avoid the inconveniences which must ever arise from the introduction of a particular creed into a school, the children are taught to read in such books as inculcate those precepts of the Christian religion which are common to all denominations.) They may therefore be taught and well-trained before they engage in any regular employment. Another important consideration is, that all their instruction is rendered a pleasure and delight to them; they are much more anxious for the hour of school-time to arrive than to end; they therefore make a rapid progress; and it may be safely asserted, that if they shall not be trained to form such characters as may be most desired, the fault will not proceed from the children; the cause will be in the want of a true knowledge of human nature in those who have the management of them and their parents.

During the period that these changes were going forward, attention was given to the domestic arrangements of the community.

Their houses were rendered more comfortable, their streets were improved, the best provisions were purchased, and sold to them at low rates, yet covering the original expense, and under such regulations as taught them how to proportion their expenditure to their income. Fuel and clothes were obtained for them in the same manner; and no advantage was attempted to be taken of them, or means used to deceive them.

In consequence, their animosity and opposition to the stranger subsided, their full confidence was obtained, and they became satisfied that no evil was intended them; they were convinced that a real desire existed to increase their happiness upon those grounds alone on which it could be permanently increased. All difficulties in the way of future improvement vanished. They were taught to be rational, and they acted rationally. Thus both parties experienced the incalculable advantages of the systems which had been adopted. Those employed became industrious, temperate, healthy, faithful to their employers, and kind to each other; while the proprietors were deriving services from their attachment, almost without inspection, far beyond those which could be obtained by any other means than those of mutual confidence and kindness.

. . . a building, which may be termed the "New Institution," was erected in the centre of the establishment, with an enclosed area before it. The area is intended for a playground for the children of the villagers, from the time they can walk alone until they enter the school.

It must be evident to those who have been in the practice of observing children with attention, that much of good or evil is taught to or acquired by a child at a very early period of its life; that much of temper or disposition is correctly or incorrectly formed before he attains his second year; and that many durable impressions are made at the termination of the first twelve or even six months of his existence. The children, therefore, of the uninstructed and ill-instructed, suffer material injury in the formation of their characters during these and the subsequent years of childhood and of youth.

It was to prevent, or as much as possible to counteract, these primary evils, to which the poor and working classes are exposed when infants, that the area became part of the New Institution.

Into this playground the children are to be received as soon as they can freely walk alone; to be superintended by persons instructed to take charge of them.

As the happiness of man chiefly, if not altogether, depends on his own sentiments and habits, as well as those of the individuals around him; and as any sentiments and habits may be given to all infants, it becomes of primary importance that those alone should be given to them which can contribute to their happiness. Each child, therefore, on his entrance into the playground, is to be told in language which he can understand, that "he is never to injure his playfellows; but that, on the contrary, he is to contribute all in his power to make them happy." This simple precept, when comprehended in all its bearings, and the habits which will arise from its early adoption into practice, *if no counteracting principle be forced upon the young mind*, will effectually supersede all the errors which have hitherto kept the world in ignorance and misery. So simple a precept, too, will be easily taught, and as easily acquired; for the chief employment of the superintendents will be to prevent any deviation from it in practice. The older children, when they shall have experienced the endless advantages from acting on this principle, will, by their example, soon enforce the practice of it on the young strangers: and the happiness which the little groups will enjoy from this rational conduct, will ensure its speedy and general and willing adoption. The habit also which they will acquire at this early period of life by continually acting on the principle, will fix it firmly; it will become easy and familiar to them, or, as it is often termed, natural.

Thus, by merely attending to the evidence of our senses respecting human nature, and disregarding the wild, inconsistent, and absurd theories in which man has been hitherto trained in all parts of the earth, we shall accomplish with ease and certainty the supposed Herculean labour of forming a rational character in man, and that, too, chiefly before the child commences the ordinary course of education.

The character thus early formed will be as durable as it will be advantageous to the individual and to the community; for by the constitution of our nature, when once the mind fully understands that which is true, the impression of that truth cannot be erased except by mental disease or death; while error must be relinquished at every period of life, whenever it can be made manifest to the mind in which it has been received. This part of the arrangement, therefore, will effect the following purposes:

The child will be removed, so far as is at present practicable, from the erroneous treatment of the yet untrained and untaught parents.

The parents will be relieved from the loss of time and from the care and anxiety which are now occasioned by attendance on their children from the period when they can go alone to that at which they enter the school.

The child will be placed in a situation of safety, where, with its future school-fellows and companions, it will acquire the best habits and principles, while at meal times and at night it will return to the caresses of its parents; and the affections of each are likely to be increased by the separation.

The area is also to be a place of meeting for the children from five to ten years of age, previous to and after school hours, and to serve for a drill ground, the object of which will be hereafter explained; and a shade will be formed, under which in stormy weather the children may retire for shelter.

These are the important purposes to which a playground attached to a school may be applied.

Those who have derived a knowledge of human nature from observation, know, that man in every situation requires relaxation from his constant and regular occupations, whatever they be: and that if he shall not be provided with or permitted to enjoy innocent and uninjurious amusements, he must and will partake of those which he can obtain, to give him temporary relief from his exertions, although the means of gaining that relief should be most pernicious. For man, irrationally instructed, is ever influenced far more by immediate feelings than by remote considerations.

Those, then, who desire to give mankind the character which it would be for the happiness of all that they should possess, will not fail to make careful provision for their amusement and recreation.

It has been and ever will be found more easy to lead mankind to virtue, or to rational conduct, by providing them with well-regulated innocent amusements and recreations, than by forcing them to submit to useless restraints, which tend only to create disgust, and often to connect such feelings even with that which is excellent in itself, merely because it has been judiciously associated.

Hitherto, indeed, in all ages and in all countries, man seems to have blindly conspired against the happiness of man, and to have remained as ignorant of himself as he was of the solar system prior to the days of Copernicus and Galileo.

Many of the learned and wise among our ancestors were conscious of this ignorance, and deeply lamented its effects; and some of them recommended the partial adoption of those principles which can alone relieve the world from the miserable effects of ignorance.

The time, however, for the emancipation of the human mind had not then arrived: the world was not prepared to receive it. The history of humanity shows it to be an undeviating law of nature, that man shall not prematurely break the shell of ignorance; that he must patiently wait until the principle of knowledge has pervaded the whole mass of the interior, to give it life and strength sufficient to bear the light of day.

Those who have duly reflected on the nature and extent of the mental movements of the world for the last half-century, must be conscious that great changes are in progress; that man is about to advance another important step towards that degree of intelligence which his natural powers seem capable of attaining. Observe the transactions of the passing hours; see the whole mass of mind in full motion; behold it momentarily increasing in vigour, and preparing ere long to burst its confinement. But what is to be the nature of this change? A due attention to the facts around us, and to those transmitted by the invention of printing from former ages, will afford a satisfactory reply.

From the earliest ages it has been the practice of the world to act on the supposition that each individual man forms his own character, and that therefore he is accountable for all his sentiments and habits, and consequently merits reward for some and punishment for others. Every system which has been established among men has been founded on these erroneous principles. When, however, they shall be brought to the test of fair examination, they will be found not only unsupported, but in direct opposition to all experience, and to the evidence of our senses.

This is not a slight mistake, which involves only trivial consequences; it is a fundamental error of the highest possible magnitude; it enters into all our proceedings regarding man from his infancy; and it will be found to be the true and sole origin of evil. It generates and perpetuates ignorance, hatred, and revenge, where, without such error, only intelligence, confidence, and kindness would exist. It has hitherto been the Evil Genius of the world. It severs man from man throughout the various regions of the earth; and makes enemies of those who, but for this gross error, would have enjoyed each other's kind offices and sincere friendship. It is, in short, an error which carries misery in all its consequences.

This error cannot much longer exist; for every day will make it more and more evident *that the character of man is, without a single exception, always formed for him; that it may be, and is, chiefly, created by his predecessors: that they give him, or may give him, his ideas and habits, which are the powers that govern and direct his conduct. Man, therefore, never did, nor is it possible he ever can, form his own character.*

The principle . . . on which the doctrines taught in the New Institution are proposed to be founded, is, that they shall be in unison with universally revealed facts, which cannot but be true.

The following are some of the facts, which, with a view to this part of the undertaking, may be deemed fundamental:

That man is born with a desire to obtain happiness, which desire is the primary cause of all his actions, continues through life, and, in popular language, is called self-interest.

That he is also born with the germs of animal propensities, or the desire to sustain, enjoy, and propagate life; and which desires, as they grow and develop themselves, are termed his natural inclinations.

That he is born likewise with faculties, which, in their growth, receive, convey, compare, and become conscious of receiving and comparing ideas.

That the ideas so received, conveyed, compared, and understood, constitute human knowledge, or mind, which acquires strength and maturity with the growth of the individual.

That the desire of happiness in man, the germs of his natural inclinations, and the faculties by which he acquires knowledge, are formed unknown to himself in the womb; and whether perfect or imperfect, they are alone the immediate work of the Creator, and over which the infant and future man have no control.

That these inclinations and faculties are not formed exactly alike in any two individuals; hence the diversity of talents, and the varied impressions called liking and disliking which the same external objects make on different persons, and the lesser varieties which exist among men whose characters have been formed apparently under similar circumstances.

That the knowledge which man receives is derived from the objects around him, and chiefly from the example and instruction of his immediate predecessors.

That this knowledge may be limited or extended, erroneous or true; limited, when the individual receives few, and extended when he receives many, ideas; erroneous, when those ideas are inconsistent with the facts which exist around him, and true when they are uniformly consistent with them.

That the misery which he experiences, and the happiness which he enjoys, depend on the kind and degree of knowledge which he receives, and on that which is possessed by those around him.

That when the knowledge which he receives is true and unmixed with error, although it be limited, if the community in which he lives possesses the same kind and degree of knowledge, he will enjoy happiness in proportion to the extent of that knowledge. On the contrary, when the opinions which he receives are erroneous, and the opinions possessed by the community in which he resides are equally erroneous, his misery will be in proportion to the extent of those erroneous opinions.

That when the knowledge which man receives shall be extended to its utmost limit, and true without any mixture of error, then he may and will enjoy all the happiness of which his nature will be capable.

That it consequently becomes of the first and highest importance that man should be taught to distinguish truth from error.

That man has no other means of discovering what is false, except by his faculty of reason, or the power of acquiring and comparing the ideas which he receives.

That when this faculty is properly cultivated or trained from infancy, and the child is rationally instructed to retain no impressions or ideas which by his powers of comparing them appear to be inconsistent, then the individual will acquire real knowledge, or those ideas only which will leave an impression of their consistency or truth on all minds which have not been rendered irrational by an opposite procedure.

That the reasoning faculty may be injured and destroyed during its growth, by reiterated impressions being made upon it of notions not derived from realities, and which it therefore cannot compare with the ideas previously received from the objects around it. And when the mind receives these notions which it cannot comprehend, along with those ideas which it is conscious are true and which yet are inconsistent with such notions, then the reasoning faculties become injured, the individual is taught or forced to believe, and not to think or reason, and partial insanity or defective powers of judging ensue.

That all men are thus irrationally trained at present, and hence the inconsistencies and miseries of the world.

That the fundamental errors now impressed from infancy on the minds of all men, and from whence all their other errors proceed, are, that they form their own individual characters and possess merit or demerit for the peculiar notions impressed on the mind during its early growth, before they have acquired strength and experience to judge of or resist the impression of those notions or opinions, which, on investigation, appear contradictions to facts existing around them, and which are therefore false.

That these false notions have ever produced evil and misery in the world; and that they still disseminate them in every direction.

That the sole cause of their existence hitherto has been man's ignorance of human nature; while their consequences have been all the evil and misery, except those of accidents, disease, and death, with which man has been and is afflicted: and that the evil and misery which arise from accidents, disease, and death, are also greatly increased and extended by man's ignorance of himself.

That, in proportion as man's desire of self-happiness or his self-love, is directed by true knowledge, those actions will abound which are virtuous and beneficial to man; that in proportion as it is influenced by false notions, or the absence of true knowledge, those actions will prevail which generate crimes, from whence arises an endless variety of misery; and, consequently, that every rational means should be now adopted to detect error, and to increase true knowledge among men.

That when these truths are made evident, every individual will necessarily endeavour to promote the happiness of every other individual within his sphere of action; because he must clearly, and without any doubt, comprehend such conduct to be the essence of self-interest, or the true cause of self-happiness.

There is still another arrangement in contemplation for the community at New Lanark, and without which the establishment will remain incomplete.

It is an expedient to enable the individuals, by their own foresight, prudence, and industry, to secure to themselves in old age a comfortable provision and asylum.

Those now employed at the establishment contribute to a fund which supports them when too ill to work, or superannuated. This fund, however, is not calculated to give them more than a bare existence; and it is surely desirable that, after they have spent nearly half a century in unremitting industry, they should, if possible, enjoy a comfortable independence.

To effect this object, it is intended that in the most pleasant situation near the present village, neat and convenient dwellings should be erected, with gardens attached; that they should be surrounded and sheltered by plantations, through which public walks should be formed; and the whole arranged to give the occupiers the most substantial comforts.

That these dwellings, with the privileges of the public walks, &c., shall become the property of those individuals who, without compulsion, shall subscribe each equitable sums monthly, as, in a given number of years will be equal to the purchase, and to create a fund from which, when these individuals become occupiers of their new residences, they may receive weekly, monthly, or quarterly payments, sufficient for their support; the expenses of which may be reduced to a very low rate individually, by arrangements which may be easily formed to supply all their wants with little trouble to themselves; and by their previous instruction they will be enabled to afford the small additional subscription which will be required for these purposes.

This part of the arrangement would always present a prospect of rest, comfort, and happiness to those employed; in consequence, their daily occupations would be performed with more spirit and cheerfulness, and their labour would appear comparatively light and easy. Those still engaged in active operations would, of course, frequently visit their former companions and friends, who, after having spent their years of toil, were in the actual enjoyment of this simple retreat; and from this intercourse each party would naturally derive pleasure. The reflections of each would be most gratifying. The old would rejoice that they had been trained in habits of industry, temperance, and foresight, to enable them to receive and enjoy in their declining years every reasonable comfort which the present state of society will admit; the young and middle-aged, that they were pursuing the same course, and that they had not been trained to waste their money, time, and health in idleness and intemperance. These and many similar reflections could not fail often to arise in their minds; and those who could look forward with confident hopes to such certain comfort and independence would, in part, enjoy by anticipation these advantages. In short, when this part of the arrangement is well considered, it will be found to be the most important to the community and to the proprietors; indeed, the extensively good effects of it will be experienced in such a variety of ways, that to describe them even below the truth would appear an extravagant exaggeration. They will not, however, prove the less true because mankind are yet ignorant of the practice, and of the principles on which it has been founded.

These, then, are the plans which are in progress or intended for the further improvement of the inhabitants of New Lanark.

B. FRENCH FOUNDING FATHERS OF SOCIALISM

Singly, no French socialist thinker exercised as much influence on the socialist movement as Owen, or the two Germans Marx and Engels, or the Russian Lenin. Collectively, however, French socialist thinkers, from Saint-Simon early in the nineteenth century to Sorel nearly one hundred years later, exercised the most influence. Great Britain and France were the birthplace of socialism, but there is a sharp distinction between British socialism, which was rooted philosophically in critical reasonableness, ethically in progressive reformed Christianity, politically in free representative institutions, and French socialism, rooted in variations of dogmatic rationalism, in non-Christian values, in Jacobin authoritarianism or a loose federalism calling for the death of the state. At the center of the distinction is acceptance or rejection of democracy, particularly of intellectual and political liberty, and of the principles and values that go with it. Even when the founder of a French socialist school of thought did not reject democracy, his disciples soon did; or if they did not reject it, they held it in contempt. There have been democrats among French socialists, particularly since the 1890's; among their spokesmen have been Jean Jaurès, Léon Blum, Guy Mollet. There is a democratic socialist party in France. But the majority of French socialists have rejected democracy, because they wanted either an authoritarian state or abolition of the state. Authoritarian socialism, four-fifths or so (as noted in the Introduction) of world socialism today, had its origin in France.

This selection gives excerpts from the writings of three French socialist thinkers: Saint-Simon, Fourier, and Proudhon. Excerpts from the writings of a fourth, Sorel, who belongs to a later generation, appear in selection D. Claude-Henri de Saint-Simon (1760–1825) belonged to one of France's first families. His was a varied and adventurous career. He reached maturity at a time when French intellectuals were drafting blueprints for a new and, it was hoped, perfect society. Saint-Simon had probably formulated the main lines of his position by 1800, but to publish his views on social affairs he had to wait for the defeat of Napoleonic despotism on the battle-field and for a measure of constitutional liberty brought by invading armies in 1814. His *Social Organization* appeared in 1825 and was one of his last efforts. Saint-Simon's concern for the industrial workers justifies his inclusion among socialists. His motivating ideas were industrialization and state action to carry it out. His formula may have sounded new but was in fact old—a hierarchical social structure, the best people at the top with plenty of power, use of state force. By the time he died he had a circle of disciples, several of whom had remark-able careers. Among them was Saint-Amand Bazard (1791–1832), the author of *The Doctrine of Saint-Simon*, published in 1829, from which excerpts appear in this selection. The names of Comte, Carlyle, and Marx, all deeply influenced by Saint-Simon, suffice to indicate the extent of the latter's role.

Charles Fourier (1772–1837), who came from a modestly well-to-do family and was a white-collar worker most of his life, wrote copiously but unsystematically. In the freer climate created by the Revolution of 1830, a circle of young people gathered around him and tried to implement his ideas. His works, though little known during his life-time, circulated after his death from Russia to the United States, young intellectuals in Moscow and the founders of Brook Farm being equally attracted by Fourierism. Fourier was convinced that a better system than capitalism could be organized for the production and distribution of goods and services, if only human nature were allowed to follow its course. If men's passions (of which he listed thirteen) were freed from constraints, men would cooperate in working efficiently. Individual efforts would be naturally integrated, and harmony would reign. (The French economist Bastiat, 1801–1850, a strong advocate of laissez-faire capitalism, was equally convinced that harmony was the end result of laissez-faire.) All that was needed for the transformation of mankind was to create one community in which passions operated freely; its success, thought Fourier, would rapidly lead to universal imitation.

Pierre-Joseph Proudhon (1809–1865), of yeoman origin, was largely self-made and self-taught. The book *What is Property?*, pub-lished in 1840, made him known. The phrase "property is theft" soon became a household slogan for all socialists. Proudhon felt distaste for industry and belonged in the long list of prominent socialists who refused to face the problems of industrialization. His attacks against capitalism were serious and well-documented; his concern for indus-trial wage-earners was deep and sincere. In him the anarchist com-ponent of socialism prevailed over the collectivist. He was convinced that once capitalistic property (in practice, big business) had been abolished, the state could be replaced by a system in which people voluntarily help one another, a kind of universal fraternal association. In his condemnation of the state, the condemnation of democracy was implicit. Because of his intelligence and his moral rectitude, Proudhon became, and remained for many years after his death, a major figure in French socialism. The 1871 Paris Commune, the prototype for the soviets established briefly in Russian industrial centers in 1905, was largely the work of Proudhon's disciples.

Saint-Simon on Social Organization

THE MECHANISM of social organization was inevitably very complicated so long as the majority of individuals remained in a state of ignorance and improvidence which rendered them incapable of administering their own affairs. In this state of incomplete intellectual development they were swayed by brutal passions which urged them to revolt and every kind of anarchy.

In such a situation, which was the necessary prelude to a better social order, it was necessary for the minority to be organized on military lines, to obtain a monopoly of legislation, and so to keep all power to itself, in order to hold the majority in tutelage and subject the nation to strong discipline. Thus the main energies of the community have till now been directed to maintaining itself as a community, and any efforts directed to improving the moral and physical welfare of the nation have necessarily been regarded as secondary.

Today this state of affairs can and should be completely altered. The main effort should be directed to the improvement of our moral and physical welfare; only a small amount of force is now required to maintain public order, since the majority have become used to work (which eliminates disorder) and now consists of men who have recently proved that they are capable of administering property, whether in land or money.

As the minority no longer has need of force to keep the proletarian class in subordination, the course which it should adopt is as follows:

(1) A policy by which the proletariat will have the strongest interest in maintaining public order.

(2) A policy which aims at making the inheritance of landed property as easy as possible.

(3) A policy which aims at giving the highest political importance to the workers.

SOURCE: H. de Saint-Simon, *Social Organization, The Science of Man and Other Writings*, trans. Felix Markham (Harper Torchbooks, Harper & Row, New York, 1964), pp. 76–80.

Such a policy is quite simple and obvious, if one takes the trouble to judge the situation by one's own intelligence, and to shake off the yoke enforced on our minds by the political principles of our ancestors—principles which were sound and useful in their own day, but are no longer applicable to present circumstances. The mass of the population is now composed of men (apart from exceptions which occur more or less equally in every class) who are capable of administering property whether in land or in money, and therefore we can and must work directly for the improvement of the moral and physical welfare of the community.

The most direct method of improving the moral and physical welfare of the majority of the population is to give priority in State expenditure to ensuring work for all fit men, to secure their physical existence; spreading throughout the proletarian class a knowledge of positive science; ensuring for this class forms of recreation and interests which will develop their intelligence.

We must add to this the measures necessary to ensure that the national wealth is administered by men most fitted for it, and most concerned in its administration, that is to say the most important industrialists.

Thus the community, by means of these fundamental arrangements, will be organized in a way which will completely satisfy reasonable men of every class.

There will no longer be a fear of insurrection, and consequently no longer a need to maintain large standing armies to suppress it; no longer a need to spend enormous sums on a police force; no longer a fear of foreign danger, for a body of thirty millions of men who are a contented community would easily repel attack, even if the whole human race combined against them.

We might add that neither princes nor people would be so mad as to attack a nation of thirty millions who displayed no aggressive intentions against their neighbours, and were united internally by mutual interests.

Furthermore, there would no longer be a need for a system of police-spying in a community in which the vast majority had an interest in maintaining the established order.

The men who brought about the Revolution, the men who directed it, and the men who, since 1789 and up to the present day, have guided the nation, have committed a great political mistake. They have all sought to improve the governmental machine, whereas they should have subordinated it and put administration in the first place.

They should have begun by asking a question the solution of which is simple and obvious. They should have asked who, in the present state of morals and enlightenment, are the men most fitted to manage the affairs of the nation. They would have been forced to recognize the fact that the scientists, artists and industrialists, and the heads of industrial concerns are the men who possess the most eminent, varied, and most positively useful ability, for the guidance of men's minds at the present time. They would have recognized the fact that the work of the scientists, artists, and industrialists is that which, in discovery and application, contributes most to national prosperity.

They would have reached the conclusion that the scientists, artists and leaders of industrial enterprises are the men who should be entrusted with administrative power, that is to say, with the responsibility for managing the national interests; and that the functions of government should be limited to maintaining public order.

The reformers of 1789 should have said to themselves as follows:

The kings of England have given a good example to monarchy by agreeing to give no order without the approval and signature of a minister. The magnanimity of the kings of France demands that they shew still greater generosity to their people, and that they should agree to make no decision without the approval of the men most fitted to judge their decisions—that is to say, without the approval of the scientists and the most eminent artists, without the approval of the most important industrialists.

The community has often been compared to a pyramid. I admit that the nation should be composed as a pyramid; I am profoundly convinced that the national pyramid should be crowned by the monarchy, but I assert that from the base of the pyramid to its summit the layers should be composed of more and more precious materials. If we consider the present pyramid, it appears that the base is made of granite, that up to a certain height the layers are composed of valuable materials, but that the upper part, supporting a magnificent diamond, is composed of nothing but plaster and gilt.

The base of the present national pyramid consists of workers in their routine occupations; the first layers above this base are the leaders of industrial enterprises, the scientists who improve the methods of manufacture and widen their application, the artists who give the stamp of good taste to all their products. The upper layers, which I assert to be composed of nothing but plaster, which is easily recognizable despite the gilding, are the courtiers, the mass of nobles whether of ancient or recent creation, the idle rich, the governing class from the prime minister to the humblest clerk. The monarchy is the magnificent diamond which crowns the pyramid.

Saint-Simonians on Industry

The wonders of *industry* have perhaps been even more extolled than those of science: let us endeavor to appreciate the efforts made in this direction.

Here, as in the sciences, we do not seek to gainsay any of the advances that have been made. Obviously, the sciences, recently directed towards practical application, were bound to illuminate several branches of technology; it is no less clear that, profiting from all the efforts of our predecessors, we were bound to surpass them. The question, then, is not whether industry has made conquests—no one could appreciate its conquests more than we do; but what we are concerned with is to find out if its progress along the path of amelioration might not have been much more rapid than it was. We are therefore led to observe industry in its three major aspects: (1) the technological aspect; (2) the organization of labor, or, in other words, the division of the tasks of *production* with respect to the needs of *consumption;* and (3) the relationship between the *laborers* and the *owners of the instruments of labor.*

In the present advanced state of science and industry, industry is, in its technological aspect, a derivation of science, a direct application of its data to material production, rather than a simple collection of routine procedures more or less confirmed by experience. Meanwhile, nothing is organized in such a way as to enable industry to escape the narrow confines within which we see it still ensnared, to enable industrial *practice* to rise to the level of scientific *theory*. Everything here is still at the mercy of chance and scattered individual insight. The method of trial and error, often extremely time-consuming, often giving rise to unwarranted pre-

SOURCE: Saint-Amand Bazard, *The Doctrine of Saint-Simon* (in A. Fried and R. Sanders, *Socialist Thought,* Doubleday, Garden City, New York, 1964), pp. 113–117.

dilections, is virtually the only method those engaged in industry employ for the improvement of their techniques; furthermore, each industrialist is obliged to go through this method from start to finish for himself, since, thanks to the competitive system, each considers it to be in his interest to shroud his discoveries in mystery, so as to preserve his monopoly of them. When, as happens every now and then, a rapprochement between *theory* and *practice* does take place, it occurs fortuitously, in isolated instances, and always incompletely.

Undoubtedly various improvements have seen the light of day in spite of these obstacles; but would it be possible to ascertain how much they have cost? How many futile efforts, how many wasted investments, how many emotional agonies there have been, the fruits of which have not been reaped by the founders of the most worthy enterprises! In industry, as in science, we find only isolated efforts; the sole sentiment that dominates all its thinking is *selfishness*. The industrialist troubles himself very little about the interests of society. His family, his instruments of labor, and the personal fortune he is striving to attain—these, respectively, are his *humanity*, his *universe* and his *God*. In those who are pursuing the same career as he, he sees only enemies; he hovers over them in expectation, spying upon them, and the prospect of ruining them is his glory and happiness. Into what kind of hands, then, have most of the workshops and instruments of industry fallen? Have they been turned over to the men who would make the best possible use of them, in the interest of society? Certainly not. They are managed, in general, by incompetent directors, who have been guided in the choice of what they feel they must learn by *personal interest*—a fact that has not generally been noticed until now.

Faults no less grave are to be seen in the *organization of labor*. Industry is in possession of a theory, as we have said; one might therefore be led to believe that this theory would show how *production* and *consumption* can and must be harmonized in every instance. Now, it happens that this very theory is the principal source of disorder, and the economists seem to have set themselves the following problem:

"Given leaders who are more ignorant than those whom they govern; supposing, furthermore, that these leaders, far from favoring the advancement of industry, want to place obstacles in its way, and that their delegates are the born enemies of the producers; what, then, is the most suitable form of industrial organization for society?"

Laissez faire, laissez passer! such has been the solution that has necessarily followed, the sole general principle that they have proclaimed. It is well enough known under what influence this maxim was produced; it dates itself. The economists believed that they had thus, with a stroke of the pen, resolved all questions concerning the *production* and *distribution* of wealth; they have consigned the realization of this broad concept to *personal interest*, not dreaming that each individual, no matter how profound his view, cannot, in the environment within which he lives, judge the whole of things, cannot see from the depths of the valley what can be discovered only from the highest summit. We are witnesses to the disasters that have already resulted from this *opportunist principle (principe de circonstance)* and if we were to cite the striking examples, they would crowd together to testify to the impotence of a theory that was supposed to fertilize industrial growth. If there are a few monopolies today, a few enterprises based on exclusive privilege, most of them owe their existence entirely to legislative dispensation. The fact is that liberty is widespread, and the maxim of the economists is generally the rule in France and England.

Well, then, what is the scene that we have before our eyes? Each separate industrialist, without a guide, without any compass but his *personal* observation, which is always incomplete no matter how extensive his connections in the world, seeks to instruct himself in the needs of consumption. Rumor has it that a certain branch of production has good possibilities: all efforts, all available funds, are steered in that direction, everyone plunging in blindly. Nobody even takes time out to ask himself what the proper measure of the situation might be, what the necessary limits are. The economists, meanwhile, applaud at the sight of this congested road, since a huge number of opponents indicates to them that the principle of *competition* is going to be widely applied. Alas! What is the result of this battle to the death? A few lucky ones are victorious—but it is a victory paid for by the complete ruin of innumerable victims.

The inevitable consequence of this manner of production that is so excessive in certain directions, of these incoherent efforts, is that the equilibrium between production and consumption is disturbed at every moment. Countless catastrophes result from this situation—these commercial crises that arise and terrify speculators, and put a stop to the execution of the worthiest projects. Then we are confronted with the spectacle of honest and hard-working men going down to ruin, a sight that undermines the morality of the onlookers, for it leads one to the conclusion that one evidently needs, in order to succeed, something more than honesty and industriousness. People then become subtle, adroit, deceitful, and they even glory in being so. Once they have taken this step, they are lost.

Let us now add that this fundamental principle, *laissez faire, laissez passer,* presupposes a personal interest that is always in harmony with the general interest, a supposition that innumerable facts tend to refute. To choose one example from a thousand, is it not evident that, if society in general conceives its interest to be in the construction of steam engines, the worker who makes his living by toiling with his hands cannot join his voice to that of society? The answer to this objection is well known. Printing, for example, is cited, and it is pointed out that printing today occupies more men than the task of copying ever did, as a result of society's having pursued the consequences of the invention of printing; and so it is said, *everything balances out in the end.* An admirable conclusion! And until this balancing-process has run its course, what do we do with the thousands of men who are starving? Will our calculations console them? Will they endure their misery with patience because the statistical tables assure them that they will have bread in a few years?

This is not to criticize mechanical progress, which should take every step that its genius inspires it to take; but, with some foresight, society could see to it that the conquests of *industry* are not like those of *war.* Funeral dirges ought not to be mixed in among the songs of joy.

The third aspect of industry that we want to examine is the relationship between the laborers and the owners of the instruments of labor, or capital. But this question is related to that of the constitution of property itself. . . . We will merely remark at this point that the lands, workshops, capital investments, etc., can be employed to the greatest possible advantage of production only on this one condition, that they be placed in the hands of those most able to make use of them, of those, in other words, who have a *capacity for industry.* Now, today, *capacity* by itself constitutes feeble grounds for claiming credit; in order to acquire something, you must already be in possession of something. The *accident of birth* blindly distributes the *instruments of labor*, whatever they may be, and if the inheritor, the idle property-owner, entrusts them into the hands of a capable worker, it goes without saying that the raw product, the major part of the earnings, goes to the incompetent or lazy proprietor.

What can we conclude from all the above, if not that the results we now so admire would be greatly surpassed, but without the woes to which we are daily witness, if the exploitation of the goods of the world were regularized, and if, therefore, a general conception were to preside over this exploitation? It is unity and wholeness, then, that we still lack.

Fourier's Phalanstery

The announcement does, I acknowledge, sound very improbable, of a method for combining three hundred families unequal in fortune, and rewarding each person,—man, woman, child—according to the three properties, *capital, labor, talent.* More than one reader will credit himself with humor when he remarks: "Let the author try to associate but three families, to reconcile three households in the same dwelling to social union, to arrangements of purchases and expenses, to perfect harmony in passions, character, and authority; when he shall have succeeded in reconciling three mistresses of associated households, we shall believe that he can succeed with thirty and with three hundred."

I have already replied to an argument which it is well to reproduce (for repetition will frequently be necessary here); I have observed *that as economy can spring only from large combinations, God had to create a social theory applicable to large masses and not to three or four families.*

An objection seemingly more reasonable, and which needs to be refuted more than once, is that of social discords. How conciliate the passions, the conflicting interests, the incompatible characters, —in short, the innumerable disparities which engender so much discord?

It may easily have been surmised that I shall make use of a lever

SOURCE: F. M. C. Fourier, *Selections from the Works of Fourier*, trans. Julia Franklin (Swan Sonnenschein, London, 1901), passim pp. 136–141, 142–144, 163–165.

entirely unknown, and whose properties cannot be judged until I shall have explained them. The passional contrasted Series draws its nourishment solely from those disparities which bewilder civilized policy; it acts like the husbandman who from a mass of filth draws the germs of abundance; the refuse, the dirt, and impure matter which would serve only to defile and infect our dwellings, are for him the sources of wealth.

If social experiments have miscarried, it is because some fatality has impelled all speculators to work with bodies of poor people whom they subjected to a *monastic-industrial* discipline, chief obstacle to the working of the series. Here, as in everything else, it is ever SIMPLISM (*simplisme*) which misleads the civilized, obstinately sticking to experiments with combinations of the poor; they cannot elevate themselves to the conception of a trial with combinations of the rich. They are veritable Lemming rats (migrating rats of Lapland), preferring drowning in a pond to deviating from the route which they have decided upon.

It is necessary for a company of 1,500 to 1,600 persons to have a stretch of land comprising a good square league, say a surface of six million square *toises* (do not let us forget that a third of that would suffice for the simple mode).

The land should be provided with a fine stream of water; it should be intersected by hills, and adapted to varied cultivation; it should be contiguous to forest, and not far removed from a large city, but sufficiently so to escape intruders.

The experimental Phalanx standing alone, and without the support of neighboring phalanxes, will, in consequence of this isolation, have so many gaps in attraction, and so many passional calms to dread in its workings, that it will be necessary to provide it with the aid of a good location fitted for a variety of functions. A flat country such as Antwerp, Leipsic, Orleans, would be totally unsuitable, and would cause many Series to fail, owing to the uniformity of the land surface. It will, therefore, be necessary to select a diversified region, like the surroundings of Lausanne, or, at the very least, a fine valley provided with a stream of water and a forest, like the valley of Brussels or of Halle. A fine location near Paris would be the stretch of country lying between Poissy and Confleurs, Poissy and Meulan.

A company will be collected consisting of from 1,500 to 1,600 persons of graduated degrees of fortune, age, character, of theoretical and practical knowledge; care will be taken to secure the greatest amount of variety possible, for the greater the number of variations either in the passions or the faculties of the members, the easier will it be to make them harmonize in a short space of time.

In this district devoted to experiment, there ought to be combined every species of practicable cultivation, including that in conservatories and hot-houses; in addition, there ought to be at least three accessory factories, to be used in winter and on rainy days; furthermore, various practical branches of science and the arts, independent of the schools.

Above all, it will be necessary to fix the valuation of the capital invested in shares; lands, materials, flocks, implements, etc. This point ought, it seems, to be among the first to receive attention; I think it best to dismiss it here. I shall limit myself to remarking that all these investments in transferable shares and stock-coupons will be represented.

A great difficulty to be overcome in the experimental Phalanx will be the formation of the ties of high mechanism or collective bonds of the Series, before the close of the first season. It will be necessary to accomplish the passional union of the mass of the members; to lead them to collective and individual devotion to the maintenance of the Phalanx, and, especially, to perfect harmony regarding the division of the profits, according to the three factors, *Capital, Labor, Talent.*

The difficulty will be greater in northern than in southern countries, owing to the difference between devoting eight months and five months to agricultural labor.

An experimental Phalanx, being obliged to start out with agricultural labor, will not be in full operation until the month of May (in a climate of 50 degrees, say in the region around London or Paris); and, since it will be necessary to form the bonds of general union, the harmonious ties of the Series, before the suspension of field labor, before the month of October, there will be barely five months of full practice in a region of 50 degrees: the work will have to be accomplished in that short space.

The trial would, therefore, be much more conveniently made in a temperate region, like Florence, Naples, Valencia, Lisbon, where they would have eight to nine months of full cultivation and a far better opportunity to consolidate the bonds of union, since there would be but two or three months of passional calm remaining to tide over until the advent of the second spring, a time when the Phalanx, resuming agricultural labor, would form its ties and cabals anew with much greater zeal, imbuing them with a degree of intensity far above that of the first year; it would thenceforth be in a state of complete consolidation, and strong enough to weather the passional calm of the second winter.

We shall see in the chapter on hiatuses of attraction, that the first Phalanx will, in consequence of its social isolation and other impediments inherent to the experimental canton, have twelve special obstacles to overcome, obstacles which the Phalanxes subsequently founded would not have to contend with. That is why it is so important that the experimental canton should have the assistance coming from field-work prolonged eight or nine months, like that in Naples and Lisbon.

Let us proceed with the details of composition.

At least seven-eighths of the members ought to be cultivators and manufacturers; the remainder will consist of capitalists, scholars, and artists.

The Phalanx would be badly graded and difficult to balance, if among its capitalists there were several having 100,000 francs, several 50,000 francs, without intermediate fortunes. In such a case it would be necessary to seek to procure intermediate fortunes of 60,000, 70,000, 80,000, 90,000 francs. The Phalanx best graduated in every respect raises social harmony and profits to the highest degree.

One is tempted to believe that our sybarites would not wish to be associated with Grosjean and Margot: they are so even now (as I believe I have already pointed out). Is not the rich man obliged to discuss his affairs with twenty peasants who occupy his farms, and who are all agreed in taking illegal advantage of him? He is, therefore, *the peasant's associate*, obliged to make inquiries about the good and bad farmers, their character, morals, solvency, and industry; *he does associate in a very direct and a very tiresome way* with Grosjean and Margot. In Harmony, he will be their indirect associate, being relieved of accounts regarding the management, which will be regulated by the regents, proctors, and special officers, without its being necessary for the capitalist to intervene or to run any risk of fraud. He will, therefore, be freed from the disagreeable features of his present association with the peasantry; he will form a new one, where he will not furnish them anything, and where they will only be his obliging and devoted friends, in accordance with the details given regarding the management of the Series and of reunions. If he takes the lead at festivals, it is because he has agreed to accept the rank of captain. If he gives them a feast, it is because he takes pleasure in acknowledging their continual kind attentions.

Thus the argument urged about the repugnance to association between Margot and Grosjean, *already associated in fact*, is only, like all the others, a quibble devoid of sense.

The edifice occupied by a Phalanx does not in any way resemble our constructions, whether of the city or country; and none of our buildings could be used to establish a large Harmony of 1,600 persons,—not even a great palace like Versailles, nor a great monastery like the Escurial. If, for the purposes of experiment, only an inconsiderable Harmony of 200 or 300 members, or a *hongrée* of 400 members is organized, a monastery or a palace (Meudon) could be used for it.

The lodgings, plantations, and stables of a Society conducted on the plan of Series of groups, must differ vastly from our villages and country towns, which are intended for families having no social connection, and which act in a perverse manner; in place of that class of little houses which rival each other in filth and ungainliness in our little towns, a Phalanx constructs an edifice for itself which is as regular as the ground permits: here is a sketch of distribution for a location favorable to development.

The central part of the Palace or Phalanstery ought to be appropriated to peaceful uses, and contain the dining halls, halls for finance, libraries, study, etc. In this central portion are located the place of worship, the *tour d' ordre*, the telegraph, the post-office boxes, the chimes for ceremonials, the observatory, the winter court adorned with resinous plants, and situated in the rear of the parade-court.

One of the wings ought to combine all the noisy workshops, such as the carpenter-shop, the forge, all hammer-work; it ought to contain also all the industrial gatherings of children, who are generally very noisy in industry and even in music. This combination will obviate a great annoyance of our civilized cities, where we find some man working with a hammer in every street, some dealer in iron or tyro on the clarinet, who shatter the tympanum of fifty families in the vicinity.

The other wing ought to contain the caravansery with its ballrooms and its halls appropriated to intercourse with outsiders, so that these may not encumber the central portion of the palace and embarrass the domestic relations of the Phalanx. . . .

In the civilized mechanism we find everywhere composite unhappiness instead of composite charm. Let us judge of it by the case of labor. It is, says the Scripture very justly, a punishment of man: Adam and his issue are condemned to earn their bread by the sweat of their brow. That, already, is an affliction; but this labor, this ungrateful labor upon which depends the earnings of our miserable bread, we cannot even get it! A laborer lacks the labor upon which his maintenance depends,—he asks in vain for a tribulation! He suffers a second, that of obtaining work at times whose fruit is his master's and not his, or of being employed in duties to which he is entirely unaccustomed. . . . The civilized laborer suffers a third affliction through the maladies with which he is generally stricken by the excess of labor demanded by his master. . . . He suffers a fifth affliction, that of being despised and treated as a beggar because he lacks those necessaries which he consents to purchase by the anguish of repugnant labor. He suffers, finally, a sixth affliction, in that he will obtain neither advancement nor sufficient wages, and that to the vexation of present suffering is added the perspective of future suffering, and of being sent to the gallows should he demand that labor which he may lack to-morrow.

Labor, nevertheless, forms the delight of various creatures, such as beavers, bees, wasps, ants, which are entirely at liberty to prefer inertia: but God has provided them with a social mechanism which attracts to industry, and causes happiness to be found in industry. Why should he not have accorded us the same favor as these animals? What a difference between their industrial condition and ours! A Russian, an Algerian, work from fear of the lash or the bastinado; an Englishman, a Frenchman, from fear of the famine which stalks close to his poor household; the Greeks and the Romans, whose freedom has been vaunted to us, worked as slaves, and from fear of punishment, like the negroes in the colonies to-day.

Associative labor, in order to exert a strong attraction upon people, will have to differ in every particular from the repulsive conditions which render it so odious in the existing state of things. It is necessary, in order that it become attractive, that associative labor fulfil the following seven conditions:

1. That every laborer be a partner, remunerated by dividends and not wages.

2. That every one, man, woman, or child, be remunerated in proportion to the three faculties, *capital, labor*, and *talent*.

3. That the industrial sessions be varied about eight times a day, it being impossible to sustain enthusiasm longer than an hour and a half or two hours in the exercise of agricultural or manufacturing labor.

4. That they be carried on by bands of friends, united spontaneously, interested and stimulated by very active rivalries.

5. That the workshops and husbandry offer the laborer the allurements of elegance and cleanliness.

6. That the division of labor be carried to the last degree, so that each sex and age may devote itself to duties that are suited to it.

7. That in this distribution, each one, man, woman, or child, be in full enjoyment of the right to labor or the right to engage in such branch of labor as they may please to select, provided they give proof of integrity and ability.

Finally, that, in this new order, people possess a guarantee of well-being, of a minimum sufficient for the present and the future, and that this guarantee free them from all uneasiness concerning themselves and their families.

We find all these properties combined in the associative mechanism. . . .

Proudhon on Property

If I were asked to answer the following question: *What is slavery?* and I should answer in one word, *It is murder*, my meaning would be understood at once. No extended argument would be required to show that the power to take from a man his thought, his will, his personality, is a power of life and death; and that to enslave a man is to kill him. Why, then, to this other question: *What is property?* may I not likewise answer, *It is theft*, without the certainty of being misunderstood; the second proposition being no other than a transformation of the first?

I undertake to discuss the vital principle of our government and our institutions, property: I am in my right. I may be mistaken in the conclusion which shall result from my investigations: I am in

SOURCE: P.-J. Proudhon, *What Is Property? An Inquiry into the Principle of Right and Government*, trans. B. R. Tucker (Reeves, London), pp. 37–40 and 60–63.

my right. I think best to place the last thought of my book first: still am I in my right.

Such an author teaches that property is a civil right born of occupation and sanctioned by law; another maintains that it is a natural right, originating in labor,—and both of these doctrines, totally opposed as they may seem, are encouraged and applauded. I contend that neither labor, nor occupation, nor law, can create property; that it is an effect without a cause: am I censurable?

But murmurs arise!

Property is theft! That is the war-cry of '93! That is the signal of revolutions!

Reader, calm yourself: I am no agent of discord, no firebrand of sedition. I anticipate history by a few days; I disclose a truth whose development we may try in vain to arrest; I write the preamble of our future constitution. This proposition which seems to you blasphemous—*property is theft*—would, if our prejudices allowed us to consider it, be recognized as the lightning-rod to shield us from the coming thunderbolt; but too many interests stand in the way! . . . Alas! philosophy will not change the course of events: destiny will fulfil itself regardless of prophecy. Besides, must not justice be done and our education be finished?

Property is theft! . . . What a revolution in human ideas! *Proprietor* and *thief* have been at all times expressions as contradictory as the beings whom they designate as hostile! All languages have perpetuated this opposition. On what authority, then, do you venture to attack universal consent, and give the lie to the human race? Who are you, that you should question the judgment of the nations and the ages?

Of what consequence to you, reader, is my obscure individuality? I live, like you, in a century in which reason submits only to fact and to evidence. My name, like yours, is TRUTHSEEKER. My mission is written in these words of the law: *Speak without hatred and without fear; tell that which thou knowest!* The work of our race is to build the temple of science, and this science includes man and Nature. Now truth reveals itself to all; to-day to Newton and Pascal, to-morrow to the herdsman in the valley and the journeyman in the shop. Each one contributes his stone to the edifice; and, his task accomplished, disappears. Eternity precedes us, eternity follows us; between the two infinites, of what account is one poor mortal that the century should inquire about him?

Disregard then, reader, my title and my character, and attend only to my arguments. It is in accordance with universal consent that I undertake to correct universal error; from the *opinion* of the human race I appeal to its *faith*. Have the courage to follow me; and, if your will is untrammelled, if your conscience is free, if your mind can unite two propositions and deduce a third therefrom, my ideas will inevitably become yours. In beginning by giving you my last word, it was my purpose to warn you, not to defy you; for I am certain that, if you read me, you will be compelled to assent. The things of which I am to speak are so simple and clear that you will be astonished at not having perceived them before, and you will say: "I have neglected to think." Others offer you the spectacle of genius wresting Nature's secrets from her, and unfolding before you her sublime messages; you will find here only a series of experiments upon *justice* and *right*, a sort of verification of the weights and measures of your conscience. The operations shall be conducted under your very eyes, and you shall weigh the result.

Nevertheless, I build no system. I ask an end to privilege, the abolition of slavery, equality of rights, and the reign of law. Justice, nothing else: that is the alpha and omega of my argument: to others I leave the business of governing the world.

One day I asked myself: Why is there so much sorrow and misery in society? Must man always be wretched? And not satisfied with the explanations given by the reformers—these attributing the general distress to governmental cowardice and incapacity, those to conspiracies and *émeutes*, still others to ignorance and general corruption—and weary of the interminable quarrels of the tribune and the press, I sought to fathom the matter myself. I have consulted the masters of science; I have read a hundred volumes of philosophy, law, political economy, and history; would to God that I had lived in a century in which so much reading had been useless! I have made every effort to obtain exact information, comparing doctrines, replying to objections, continually constructing equations and reductions from arguments, and weighing thousands of syllogisms in the scales of the most rigorous logic. In this laborious work, I have collected many interesting facts which I shall share with my friends and the public as soon as I have leisure. But I must say that I recognised at once that we had never understood the meaning of these words, so common and yet so sacred: *Justice, equality, liberty;* that concerning each of these principles our ideas have been utterly obscure; and, in fact, that this ignorance was the sole cause, both of the poverty that devours us, and of all the calamities that have ever afflicted the human race. . . .

Is political and civil inequality just?

Some say yes; others no. To the first I would reply that, when the people abolished all privileges of birth and caste, they did it, in all probability, because it was for their advantage; why then do they favor the privileges of fortune more than those of rank and race? Because, say they, political inequality is a result of property; and without property society is impossible: thus the question just raised becomes a question of property. To the second I content myself with this remark: If you wish to enjoy political equality, abolish property; otherwise, why do you complain?

Is property just?

Everybody answers without hesitation, "Yes, property is just." I say everybody, for up to the present time no one who thoroughly understood the meaning of his words has answered no. For it is no easy thing to reply understandingly to such a question; only time and experience can furnish an answer. Now, this answer is given; it is for us to understand it. I undertake to prove it.

We are to proceed with the demonstration in the following order:—

I. We dispute not at all, we refute nobody, we deny nothing; we accept as sound all the arguments alleged in favor of property, and confine ourselves to a search for its principle, in order that we may then ascertain whether this principle is faithfully expressed by property. In fact, property being defensible on no ground save that of justice, the idea, or at least the intention, of justice must of necessity underlie all the arguments that have been made in defense of property; and, as on the other hand the right of property is only exercised over those things which can be appreciated by the senses, justice, secretly objectifying itself, so to speak, must take the shape of an algebraic formula. By this method of investigation, we soon see that every argument which has been invented in behalf of property, *whatever it may be*, always and of necessity leads to equality; that is, to the negation of property.

The first part covers two chapters: one treating of occupation, the foundation of our right; the other, of labor and talent, considered as causes of property and social inequality.

The first of these chapters will prove that the right of occupation *obstructs* property; the second that the right of labor *destroys* it.

II. Property, then, being of necessity conceived as existing only in connexion with equality, it remains to find out why, in spite of this necessity of logic, equality does not exist. This new investigation also covers two chapters: in the first, considering the fact of property in itself, we inquire whether this fact is real, whether it exists, whether it is possible; for it would imply a contradiction, were these two opposite forms of society, equality and inequality, both possible. Then we discover, singularly enough, that property may indeed manifest itself accidentally; but that, as an institution and principle, it is mathematically impossible. So that the axiom of the school—*ab actu ad posse valet consecutio:* from the actual to the possible the inference is good—is given the lie as far as property is concerned.

Finally, in the last chapter, calling psychology to our aid, and probing man's nature to the bottom, we shall disclose the principle of *justice*—its formula and character; we shall state with precision the organic law of society; we shall explain the origin of property, the causes of its establishment, its long life, and its approaching death; we shall definitively establish its identity with theft. And, after having shown that these three prejudices—the *sovereignty of man, the inequality of conditions, and property*—are one and the same; that they may be taken for each other, and are reciprocally convertible—we shall have no trouble in inferring therefrom, by the principle of contradiction, the basis of government and right. There our investigations will end, reserving the right to continue them in future works.

The importance of the subject which engages our attention is recognized by all minds.

"Property," says M. Hennequin, "is the creative and conservative principle of civil society. Property is one of those basic institutions, new theories concerning which cannot be presented too soon; for it must not be forgotten, and the publicist and statesman must know, that on the answer to the question whether property is the principle or the result of the social order, whether it is to be considered as a cause, or an effect, depends all morality, and, consequently, all the authority of human institutions."

These words are a challenge to all men of hope and faith; but, although the cause of equality is a noble one, no one has yet picked up the gauntlet thrown down by the advocates of property; no one has been courageous enough to enter upon the struggle. The spurious learning of haughty jurisprudence, and the absurd aphorisms of a political economy controlled by property have puzzled the most generous minds; it is a sort of password among the influential friends of liberty and the interests of the people that *equality is a chimera!* So many false theories and meaningless analogies influence minds otherwise keen, which are unconsciously controlled by popular prejudice. Equality advances every day—*fit æqualitas.* Soldiers of liberty, shall we desert our flag in the hour of triumph?

A defender of equality, I shall speak without bitterness and without anger, with the independence becoming a philosopher, with the courage and firmness of a free man. May I, in this momentous struggle, carry into all hearts the light with which I am filled; and show, by the success of my argument, that equality failed to conquer by the sword only that it might conquer by the pen!

C. KARL MARX AND FRIEDRICH ENGELS: AUTHORITARIAN SOCIALISM

Karl Marx (1818–1883) and Friedrich Engels (1820–1895) were born in western Germany. The former belonged to a Jewish family freed from ghetto life by French revolutionary armies, and later converted to Protestantism. In the freer environment created by the French, the fathers of both prospered. The sons attended Prussian schools and universities, then probably the best in Europe. Intellectual curiosity in the case of Marx, business activity on his father's behalf in the case of Engels, took them both abroad in their twenties—to France and to Belgium, which was then the freest and fastest developing Continental nation. Their writings appeared in a publication Marx edited early in 1844. In Brussels they became friends and initiated a literary cooperation that became a permanent feature of their lives. As a philosophy student Marx, who wrote his doctoral dissertation on the materialist philosopher of ancient Greece Democritus, was attracted by the Left Hegelian school of which Feuerbach was a major spokesman. Engels was widely read in the literature of British economists. Both were interested in history. Both became acquainted with socialist ideas in France. The emotion caused by a deep concern for the poor in the wake of industrialization (a concern shared by many who did not become socialists) was the catalyst that arranged in a neat ideological formula what the two friends had learned from a variety of sources. Back in Prussia, Marx edited a newspaper during the revolutionary upheaval of 1848 to 1849. He was one of well over a million Germans who left Germany, partly or wholly for political reasons, when the revolution ended with the failure first of the liberals and then of the democrats. In 1849 he settled in London, the major rendezvous of Continental exiles. He resided there until his death, despising the country that sheltered him and provided him with the freedom of expression necessary for the formulation and diffusion of new ideas. In London he received visits from Engels, who was successfully pursuing a business career and who helped him financially.

The *Communist Manifesto,* printed shortly before the February, 1848, Revolution in France, made the names of Engels and Marx known in the socialist circles of the time. The circles were small; at the presidential elections of 1848 in France, where most socialists were to be found, the candidate of socialists and Jacobins received one vote in twenty. The circles were also deeply divided, the Proudhonian school of thought being the major one. Engels always maintained modestly that the ideas expressed in the Manifesto were Marx's. In 1867 appeared the first volume of *Capital,* Marx's major work, based largely on the analysis of recent economic developments in Great Britain seen through the lenses of historical dialectical materialism. From the manuscripts left by Marx, Engels edited the second and third volumes after his friend's death. Two articles Engels published in 1869 summarize Marx's *Capital.* The dialectical process was clearly explained by Engels in *Socialism: Utopian and Scientific,* published in 1880. The books, pamphlets, and articles produced by the two friends, during four decades by Marx, over five by Engels, composed a large literary output, so abundant that it is bound to contain some statements at variance with others. Consequently, the search for the "real" Marx and Engels is likely to be unending.

The complex web of concepts they elaborated is woven around the major themes of materialism, dialectics, the economic class as mankind's unit, the class struggle, the labor theory of value, and a number of derived ideas, several of which became household words for Marxist and many non-Marxist socialists: surplus value, inevitability of socialism, phases of the historical scheme, distinction between socialism ("to each according to the work done") and communism ("to each according to his needs"), dictatorship of the proletariat. It was reported that toward the end of their lives Marx and Engels worried about the Marxists' misinterpretations of their ideas. It is possible that they were veering toward a democratic position. Leaving these speculations aside, a few points concerning approach, emotions, and omissions help one to see clearly the relationship between the ideas of Marx and Engels and the later Marxist ideology:

Marx and Engels were certain that they knew the truth. The modest measure of doubt indicative of minds that have reached the level of critical thinking was absent. This absence makes unscientific the socialism the two thinkers defined as scientific. From the dogmatism implicit in certainty came contempt, evident in their writings, for all holding different views; came, too, intolerance of opposition and dissent.

Together with capitalism—the by-product of the emancipation brought about by the partial success of European liberalism—Marx and Engels rejected the twin institutional pillars of liberalism: intellectual and political liberty. Owen saw in socialism the fulfillment of the two liberties through the elimination of capitalism. In the socialism of Marx and Engels, which negated the two liberties, were implicit conformity and absolutism, intellectual and political coercion.

Much of the ideological system of Marx and Engels is the rationalization, through selective historical evidence and dialectical simplification, of an aspiration toward the well-ordered and disciplined society, peaceful because uniform.

Marx and Engels devoted their energies to the attack against capitalism, not to the clarification of socialism. They derided, as utopian, thinkers who acted responsibly in trying to figure out the institutions of the system that would replace capitalism. Consequently, Marxists can have divergent views on what socialism should be. Comforted by the unproven conviction that socialism means harmony, liberty, and everything else their generation thought desirable, Marx and Engels ignored problems fundamental to all social systems, which instead were central in democratic thinking: the coexistence of groups holding differing views and pursuing different aims, the proper use of power, the control of violence. Having read Marx and Engels, most of their disciples concluded that violence is good, that the end justifies the means, that socialists should aim at total power; and they acted accordingly.

Manifesto of the Communist Party

PREFACE TO THE ENGLISH EDITION OF 1888

THE MANIFESTO was published as the platform of the Communist League, a workingmen's association, first exclusively German, later on international, and, under the political conditions of the Continent before 1848, unavoidably a secret society. At a Congress of the League, held in London in November, 1847, Marx and Engels were commissioned to prepare for publication a complete theoretical and practical party program. The manuscript, drawn up in German in January, 1848, was sent to the printer in London a few weeks before the French Revolution of February 24. A French

SOURCE: K. Marx and F. Engels, *Communist Manifesto* (F. Engels, ed., authorized translation, London 1888), complete text, except Part III.

translation was brought out in Paris shortly before the insurrection of June, 1848. The first English translation, by Miss Helen Macfarlane, appeared in George Julian Harney's *Red Republican*, London, 1850. A Danish and a Polish edition had also been published.

. . . when it was written, we could not have called it a *Socialist* Manifesto. By socialists, in 1847, were understood, on the one hand, the adherents of the various utopian systems: Owenites in England, Fourierists in France, both of them already reduced to the position of mere sects, and gradually dying out; on the other hand, the most multifarious social quacks, who, by all manners of tinkering, professed to redress, without any danger to capital and profit, all sorts of social grievances, in both cases men outside the working-class movement and looking rather to the "educated" classes for support. Whatever portion of the working class had become convinced of the insufficiency of mere political revolutions and had proclaimed the necessity of a total social change, that portion then called itself communist. It was a crude, rough-hewn, purely instinctive sort of communism; still, it touched the cardinal point and was powerful enough among the working class to produce the utopian communism, in France, of Cabet and, in Germany, of Weitling. Thus socialism was, in 1847, a middle-class movement, communism a working-class movement. Socialism was, on the Continent at least, "respectable"; communism was the very opposite. And as our notion, from the very beginning, was that "the emancipation of the working class must be the act of the working class itself," there could be no doubt as to which of the two names we must take. Moreover, we have, ever since, been far from repudiating it.

The Manifesto being our joint production, I consider myself bound to state that the fundamental proposition, which forms its nucleus, belongs to Marx. That proposition is that in every historical epoch the prevailing mode of economic production and exchange and the social organization necessarily following from it form the basis upon which is built up, and from which alone can be explained, the political and intellectual history of that epoch; that consequently the whole history of mankind (since the dissolution of primitive tribal society, holding land in common ownership) has been a history of class struggles, contests between exploiting and

exploited, ruling and oppressed classes; that the history of these
class struggles forms a series of evolutions in which, nowadays, a
stage has been reached where the exploited and oppressed class—
the proletariat—cannot attain its emancipation from the sway of
the exploiting and ruling class—the bourgeoisie—without, at the
same time, and once and for all, emancipating society at large from
all exploitation, oppression, class distinctions, and class struggles.

Friedrich Engels

A specter is haunting Europe—the specter of communism. All
the powers of old Europe have entered into a holy alliance to
exorcise this specter: Pope and Czar, Metternich and Guizot,
French radicals and German police spies.

Where is the party in opposition that has not been decried as
communistic by its opponents in power? Where the opposition
that has not hurled back the branding reproach of communism
against the more advanced opposition parties, as well as against its
reactionary adversaries?

Two things result from this fact:

I. Communism is already acknowledged by all European powers
to be itself a power.

II. It is high time that communists should openly, in the face of
the whole world, publish their views, their aims, their tendencies,
and meet this nursery tale of the specter of communism with a
Manifesto of the party itself.

To this end, communists of various nationalities have assembled
in London and sketched the following Manifesto, to be published
in the English, French, German, Italian, Flemish, and Danish
languages.

I. BOURGEOIS AND PROLETARIANS[1]

The history of all hitherto existing society[2] is the history of class
struggles.

[1] By "bourgeoisie" is meant the class of modern capitalists, owners of the
means of social production and employers of wage labor. By proletariat, the
class of modern wage laborers who, having no means of production of their
own, are reduced to selling their labor power in order to live. [All notes are
Engels', from the English edition of 1888.]

[2] That is, all *written* history. In 1847 the pre-history of society, the social
organisation existing previous to recorded history, was all but unknown.
Since then Haxthausen discovered common ownership of land in Russia,

Free man and slave, patrician and plebeian, lord and serf, guild master[3] and journeyman, in a word, oppressor and oppressed, stood in constant opposition to one another, carried on an uninterrupted, now hidden, now open fight, a fight that each time ended either in a revolutionary reconstitution of society at large or in the common ruin of the contending classes.

In the earlier epochs of history we find almost everywhere a complicated arrangement of society into various orders, a manifold gradation of social rank. In ancient Rome we have patricians, knights, plebeians, slaves; in the Middle Ages, feudal lords, vassals, guild masters, journeymen, apprentices, serfs; in almost all of these classes, again, subordinate gradations.

The modern bourgeois society that has sprouted from the ruins of feudal society has not done away with class antagonisms. It has but established new classes, new conditions of oppression, new forms of struggle in place of the old ones.

Our epoch, the epoch of the bourgeoisie, possesses, however, this distinctive feature: it has simplified the class antagonisms. Society as a whole is more and more splitting up into two great hostile camps, into two great classes directly facing each other: bourgeoisie and proletariat.

From the serfs of the Middle Ages sprang the chartered burghers of the earliest towns. From these burgesses the first elements of the bourgeoisie were developed.

The discovery of America, the rounding of the Cape opened up fresh ground for the rising bourgeoisie. The East Indian and Chinese markets, the colonization of America, trade with the colonies, the increase in the means of exchange and in commodities generally, gave to commerce, to navigation, to industry an impulse

---

Maurer proved it to be the social foundation from which all Teutonic races started in history, and by and by village communities were found to be, or to have been, the primitive form of society everywhere from India to Ireland. The inner organization of this primitive communistic society was laid bare, in its typical form, by Morgan's crowning discovery of the true nature of the *gens* and its relation to the *tribe*. With the dissolution of these primeval communities society begins to be differentiated into separate and finally antagonistic classes. I have attempted to retrace this process of dissolution in *Der Ursprung der Familie, des Privateigentums und des Staats* [*The Origin of the Family, Private Property and the State*], second edition, Stuttgart, 1886.

[3] Guild master, that is, a full member of a guild, a master within, not a head of a guild.

never before known, and thereby, to the revolutionary element in the tottering feudal society, a rapid development.

The feudal system of industry, under which industrial production was monopolized by closed guilds, now no longer sufficed for the growing wants of the new markets. The manufacturing system took its place. The guild masters were pushed on one side by the manufacturing middle class; division of labor between the different corporate guilds vanished in the face of division of labor in each single workshop.

Meantime the markets kept ever growing, the demand ever rising. Even manufacture no longer sufficed. Thereupon steam and machinery revolutionized industrial production. The place of manufacture was taken by the giant, modern industry, the place of the industrial middle class by industrial millionaires, the leaders of whole industrial armies, the modern bourgeois.

Modern industry has established the world market, for which the discovery of America paved the way This market has given an immense development to commerce, to navigation, to communication by land. This development has, in its turn, reacted on the extension of industry; and in proportion as industry, commerce, navigation, railways extended, in the same proportion the bourgeoisie developed, increased its capital, and pushed into the background every class handed down from the Middle Ages.

We see, therefore, how the modern bourgeoisie is itself the product of a long course of development, of a series of revolutions in the modes of production and of exchange.

Each step in the development of the bourgeoisie was accompanied by a corresponding political advance of that class. An oppressed class under the sway of the feudal nobility, an armed and self-governing association in the medieval commune;[4] here independent urban republic (as in Italy and Germany), there taxable "third estate" of the monarchy (as in France), afterwards, in the period of manufacture proper, serving either the semi-feudal or the absolute monarchy as a counterpoise against the nobility, and, in fact, cornerstone of the great monarchies in general, the bour-

[4] "Commune" was the name taken, in France, by the nascent towns even before they had conquered from their feudal lords and masters local self-government and political rights as the "third estate." Generally speaking, for the economic development of the bourgeoisie, England is here taken as the typical country; for its political development, France.

geoisie has at last, since the establishment of modern industry and of the world market, conquered for itself, in the modern representative state, exclusive political sway. The executive of the modern state is but a committee for managing the common affairs of the whole bourgeoisie.

The bourgeoisie, historically, has played a most revolutionary part.

The bourgeoisie, wherever it has got the upper hand, has put an end to all feudal, patriarchal, idyllic relations. It has pitilessly torn asunder the motley feudal ties that bound man to his "natural superiors," and has left remaining no other nexus between man and man than naked self-interest, than callous "cash payment." It has drowned the most heavenly ecstasies of religious fervor, of chivalrous enthusiasm, of Philistine sentimentalism in the icy water of egotistical calculation. It has resolved personal worth into exchange value and, in place of the numberless indefeasible chartered freedoms, has set up that single, unconscionable freedom—free trade. In one word, for exploitation, veiled by religious and political illusions, it has substituted naked, shameless, direct, brutal exploitation.

The bourgeoisie has stripped of its halo every occupation hitherto honored and looked up to with reverent awe. It has converted the physician, the lawyer, the priest, the poet, the man of science into its paid wage laborers.

The bourgeoisie has torn away from the family its sentimental veil, and has reduced the family relation to a mere money relation.

The bourgeoisie has disclosed how it came to pass that the brutal display of vigor in the Middle Ages, which reactionists so much admire, found its fitting complement in the most slothful indolence. It has been the first to show what man's activity can bring about. It has accomplished wonders far surpassing Egyptian pyramids, Roman aqueducts, and Gothic cathedrals; it has conducted expeditions that put in the shade all former exoduses of nations and crusades.

The bourgeoisie cannot exist without constantly revolutionizing the instruments of production, and thereby the relations of production, and with them the whole relations of society. Conservation of the old modes of production in unaltered form was, on the contrary, the first condition of existence for all earlier industrial classes. Constant revolutionizing of production, uninterrupted disturbance of all social conditions, everlasting uncertainty and agitation distinguish the bourgeois epoch from all earlier ones. All fixed, fast-frozen relations, with their train of ancient and venerable prejudices and opinions, are swept away, all new-formed ones become antiquated before they can ossify. All that is solid melts into air, all that is holy is profaned, and man is at last compelled to face with sober senses his real conditions of life and his relations with his kind.

The need of a constantly expanding market for its products chases the bourgeoisie over the whole surface of the globe. It must nestle everywhere, settle everywhere, establish connections everywhere.

The bourgeoisie has through its exploitation of the world market given a cosmopolitan character to production and consumption in every country. To the great chagrin of reactionists, it has drawn from under the feet of industry the national ground on which it stood. All old-established national industries have been destroyed or are daily being destroyed. They are dislodged by new industries, whose introduction becomes a life and death question for all civilized nations, by industries that no longer work up indigenous raw material, but raw material drawn from the remotest zones; industries whose products are consumed not only at home, but in every quarter of the globe. In place of the old wants, satisfied by the productions of the country, we find new wants, requiring for their satisfaction the products of distant lands and climes. In place of the old local and national seclusion and self-sufficiency we have intercourse in every direction, universal interdependence of nations. And as in material, so also in intellectual production. The intellectual creations of individual nations become common property. National one-sidedness and narrow-mindedness become more and more impossible, and from the numerous national and local literatures there arises a world literature.

The bourgeoisie, by the rapid improvement of all instruments of production, by the immensely facilitated means of communication, draws all, even the most barbarian, nations into civilization. The cheap prices of its commodities are the heavy artillery with which it batters down all Chinese walls, with which it forces the barbarians' intensely obstinate hatred of foreigners to capitulate. It compels all nations, on pain of extinction, to adopt the bourgeois mode of production; it compels them to introduce what it calls civilization into their midst, i.e., to become bourgeois themselves. In one word, it creates a world after its own image.

The bourgeoisie has subjected the country to the rule of the towns. It has created enormous cities, has greatly increased the urban population as compared with the rural, and has thus rescued a considerable part of the population from the idiocy of rural life. Just as it has made the country dependent on the towns, so it has made barbarian and semi-barbarian countries dependent on the civilized ones, nations of peasants on nations of bourgeois, the East on the West.

The bourgeoisie keeps more and more doing away with the scattered state of the population, of the means of production, and of property. It has agglomerated population, centralized means of production, and has concentrated property in a few hands. The necessary consequence of this was political centralization. Independent, or but loosely connected provinces, with separate interests, laws, governments and systems of taxation, became lumped together into one nation, with one government, one code of laws, one national class interest, one frontier, and one customs tariff.

The bourgeoisie, during its rule of scarce one hundred years, has created more massive and more colossal productive forces than have all preceding generations together. Subjection of nature's forces to man, machinery, application of chemistry to industry and agriculture, steam navigation, railways, electric telegraphs, clearing of whole continents for cultivation, canalization of rivers, whole populations conjured out of the ground—what earlier century had even a presentiment that such productive forces slumbered in the lap of social labor?

We see then: the means of production and of exchange, on whose foundation the bourgeoisie built itself up, were generated in feudal society. At a certain stage in the development of these means of production and of exchange, the conditions under which feudal society produced and exchanged, the feudal organization of agriculture and manufacturing industry, in one word, the feudal relations of property, became no longer compatible with the already developed productive forces; they became so many fetters. They had to be burst asunder; they were burst asunder.

Into their place stepped free competition, accompanied by a social and political constitution adapted to it, and by the economic and political sway of the bourgeois class.

A similar movement is going on before our own eyes. Modern bourgeois society with its relations of production, of exchange, and of property, a society that has conjured up such gigantic means of production and of exchange, is like the sorcerer who is no longer able to control the powers of the nether world whom he called up by his spells. For many a decade past, the history of industry and commerce is but the history of the revolt of modern productive forces against modern conditions of production, against the property relations that are the conditions for the existence of the bourgeoisie and of its rule. It is enough to mention the commercial crises that by their periodic return put on its trial, each time more threateningly, the existence of the entire bourgeois society. In these crises a great part not only of the existing products but also of the previously created productive forces are periodically destroyed. In these crises there breaks out an epidemic that in all earlier epochs would have seemed an absurdity—the epidemic of overproduction. Society suddenly finds itself put back into a state of momentary barbarism; it appears as if a famine, a universal war of devastation had cut off the supply of every means of subsistence; industry and commerce seem to be destroyed; and why? Because there is too much civilization, too much means of subsistence, too much industry, too much commerce. The productive forces at the disposal of society no longer tend to further the development of the conditions of bourgeois property; on the contrary, they have become too powerful for these conditions, by which they are fettered, and as soon as they overcome these fetters they bring disorder into the whole of bourgeois society, endanger the existence of bourgeois property. The conditions of bourgeois society are too narrow to comprise the wealth created by them. And how does the bourgeoisie get over these crises? On the one hand, by enforced destruction of a mass of productive forces; on the other, by the conquest of new markets, and by the more thorough exploitation of the old ones. That is to say, by paving the way for more extensive and more destructive crises, and by diminishing the means whereby crises are prevented.

The weapons with which the bourgeoisie felled feudalism to the ground are now turned against the bourgeoisie itself.

But not only has the bourgeoisie forged the weapons that bring death to itself; it has also called into existence the men who are to wield those weapons—the modern working class—the proletarians.

In proportion as the bourgeoisie, i.e., capital, is developed, in the same proportion is the proletariat, the modern working class, developed—a class of laborers, who live only so long as they find work, and who find work only so long as their labor increases capital. These laborers, who must sell themselves piecemeal, are a commodity, like every other article of commerce, and are consequently exposed to all the vicissitudes of competition, to all the fluctuations of the market.

Owing to the extensive use of machinery and to division of labor, the work of the proletarians has lost all individual character and, consequently, all charm for the workman. He becomes an appendage of the machine, and it is only the simplest, most monotonous, and most easily acquired knack that is required of him. Hence the cost of production of a workman is restricted, almost entirely, to the means of subsistence that he requires for his maintenance and for the propagation of his race. But the price of a commodity, and therefore also of labor, is equal to its cost of production. In proportion, therefore, as the repulsiveness of the work increases, the wage decreases. Nay, more, in proportion as the use of machinery and division of labor increases, in the same proportion the burden of toil also increases, whether by prolongation of the working hours, by increase of the work exacted in a given time, or by increased speed of the machinery, etc.

Modern industry has converted the little workshop of the patriarchal master into the great factory of the industrial capitalist. Masses of laborers, crowded into the factory, are organized like soldiers. As privates of the industrial army they are placed under the command of a perfect hierarchy of officers and sergeants. Not only are they slaves of the bourgeois class, and of the bourgeois state; they are daily and hourly enslaved by the machine, by the overlooker, and, above all, by the individual bourgeois manufacturer himself. The more openly this despotism proclaims gain to be its end and aim, the more petty, the more hateful, and the more embittering it is.

The less the skill and exertion of strength implied in manual labor, in other words, the more modern industry becomes developed, the more is the labor of men superseded by that of women. Differences of age and sex have no longer any distinctive social validity for the working class. All are instruments of labor, more or less expensive to use, according to their age and sex.

No sooner is the exploitation of the laborer by the manufacturer over, to the extent that he receives his wages in cash, than he is set upon by the other portions of the bourgeoisie, the landlord, the shopkeeper, the pawnbroker, etc.

The lower strata of the middle class—the small tradespeople, shopkeepers, and retired tradesmen generally, the handicraftsmen and peasants—all these sink gradually into the proletariat, partly because their diminutive capital does not suffice for the scale on which modern industry is carried on, and is swamped in the competition with the large capitalists, partly because their specialized skill is rendered worthless by new methods of production. Thus the proletariat is recruited from all classes of the population.

The proletariat goes through various stages of development. With its birth begins its struggle with the bourgeoisie. At first the contest is carried on by individual laborers, then by the workpeople of a factory, then by the operatives of one trade, in one locality, against the individual bourgeois who directly exploits them. They direct their attacks not against the bourgeois conditions of production, but against the instruments of production themselves; they destroy imported wares that compete with their labor, they smash to pieces machinery, they set factories ablaze, they seek to restore by force the vanished status of the workman of the Middle Ages.

At this stage the laborers still form an incoherent mass scattered over the whole country and broken up by their mutual competition. If anywhere they unite to form more compact bodies, this is not yet the consequence of their own active union, but of the union of the bourgeoisie, which class, in order to attain its own political ends, is compelled to set the whole proletariat in motion, and is moreover yet, for a time, able to do so. At this stage, therefore, the proletarians do not fight their enemies, but the enemies of their enemies, the remnants of absolute monarchy, the landowners, the non-industrial bourgeois, the petty bourgeoisie. Thus the whole historical movement is concentrated in the hands of the bourgeoisie; every victory so obtained is a victory for the bourgeoisie.

But with the development of industry the proletariat not only increases in number; it becomes concentrated in greater masses, its strength grows, and it feels that strength more. The various interests and conditions of life within the ranks of the proletariat are more and more equalized, in proportion as the machinery obliterates all distinctions of labor and nearly everywhere reduces wages to the same low level. The growing competition among the bourgeois and the resulting commercial crises make the wages of the workers ever more fluctuating. The unceasing improvement of machinery, ever more rapidly developing, makes their livelihood more and more precarious; the collisions between individual workmen and individual bourgeois take more and more the character of collisions between two classes. Thereupon the workers begin to form combinations (trade unions) against the bourgeois; they club together in order to keep up the rate of wages; they found permanent associations in order to make provision beforehand for these occasional revolts. Here and there the contest breaks out into riots.

Now and then the workers are victorious, but only for a time. The real fruit of their battles lies not in the immediate result, but in the ever expanding union of the workers. This union is helped on by the improved means of communication that are created by modern industry and that place the workers of different localities in contact with one another. It was just this contact that was needed to centralize the numerous local struggles, all of the same character, into one national struggle between classes. But every class struggle is a political struggle. And that union, to attain which the burghers of the Middle Ages, with their miserable highways, required centuries, the modern proletarians, thanks to railways, achieve in a few years.

This organization of the proletarians into a class, and consequently into a political party, is continually being upset again by the competition between the workers themselves. But it ever rises up again, stronger, firmer, mightier. It compels legislative recognition of particular interests of the workers by taking advantage of the divisions among the bourgeoisie itself. Thus the ten-hour bill in England was carried.

Altogether collisions between the classes of the old society further, in many ways, the course of development of the proletariat. The bourgeoisie finds itself involved in a constant battle. At first with the aristocracy; later on, with those portions of the bourgeoisie itself whose interests have become antagonistic to the progress of industry; at all times, with the bourgeoisie of foreign countries. In all these battles it sees itself compelled to appeal to the proletariat, to ask for its help, and thus to drag it into the political arena. The bourgeoisie itself, therefore, supplies the proletariat with its own elements of political and general education; in other words, it furnishes the proletariat with weapons for fighting the bourgeoisie.

Further, as we have already seen, entire sections of the ruling classes are, by the advance of industry, precipitated into the proletariat, or are at least threatened in their conditions of existence. These also supply the proletariat with fresh elements of enlightenment and progress.

Finally, in times when the class struggle nears the decisive hour, the process of dissolution going on within the ruling class, in fact within the whole range of old society, assumes such a violent, glaring character that a small section of the ruling class cuts itself adrift and joins the revolutionary class, the class that holds the future in its hands. Just as, therefore, at an earlier period, a section of the nobility went over to the bourgeoisie, so now a portion of the bourgeoisie goes over to the proletariat, and in particular a portion of the bourgeois ideologists, who have raised themselves to the level of comprehending theoretically the historical movement as a whole.

Of all the classes that stand face to face with the bourgeoisie today, the proletariat alone is a really revolutionary class. The other classes decay and finally disappear in the face of modern industry; the proletariat is its special and essential product.

The lower-middle class, the small manufacturer, the shopkeeper, the artisan, the peasant, all these fight against the bourgeoisie, to save from extinction their existence as fractions of the middle class. They are therefore not revolutionary, but conservative. Nay, more, they are reactionary, for they try to roll back the wheel of history. If by chance they are revolutionary they are so only in view of their impending transfer into the proletariat; they thus defend not their present but their future interests, they desert their own standpoint to place themselves at that of the proletariat.

The "dangerous class," the social scum, that passively rotting mass thrown off by the lowest layers of old society, may, here and there, be swept into the movement by a proletarian revolution; its conditions of life, however, prepare it far more for the part of a bribed tool of reactionary intrigue.

In the conditions of the proletariat those of old society at large are already virtually swamped. The proletarian is without property; his relation to his wife and children has no longer anything in common with the bourgeois family relations; modern industrial labor, modern subjection to capital, the same in England as in France, in America as in Germany, has stripped him of every trace of national character. Law, morality, religion are to him so many bourgeois prejudices, behind which lurk in ambush just as many bourgeois interests.

All the preceding classes that got the upper hand sought to fortify their already acquired status by subjecting society at large to their conditions of appropriation. The proletarians cannot become masters of the productive forces of society, except by abolishing their own previous mode of appropriation, and thereby also every other previous mode of appropriation. They have nothing of their own to secure and to fortify; their mission is to destroy all previous securities for, and insurances of, individual property.

All previous historical movements were movements of minorities, or in the interest of minorities. The proletarian movement is the self-conscious, independent movement of the immense majority, in the interests of the immense majority. The proletariat, the lowest stratum of our present society, cannot stir, cannot raise itself up, without the whole superincumbent strata of official society being sprung into the air.

Though not in substance, yet in form, the struggle of the proletariat with the bourgeoisie is at first a national struggle. The proletariat of each country must, of course, first of all settle matters with its own bourgeoisie.

In depicting the most general phases of the development of the proletariat, we traced the more or less veiled civil war, raging within existing society, up to the point where that war breaks out into open revolution, and where the violent overthrow of the bourgeoisie lays the foundation for the sway of the proletariat.

Hitherto every form of society has been based, as we have already seen, on the antagonism of oppressing and oppressed classes. But in order to oppress a class certain conditions must be assured to it under which it can, at least, continue its slavish existence. The serf, in the period of serfdom, raised himself to membership in the commune, just as the petty bourgeois, under the yoke of feudal absolutism, managed to develop into a bourgeois. The modern laborer, on the contrary, instead of rising with the progress of industry, sinks deeper and deeper below the conditions of existence of his own class. He becomes a pauper, and pauperism develops more rapidly than population and wealth. And here it becomes evident that the bourgeoisie is unfit any longer to be the ruling class in society, and to impose its conditions of existence upon society as an overriding law. It is unfit to rule because it is incompetent to assure an existence to its slave within his slavery, because it cannot help letting him sink into such a state that it has to feed him instead of being fed by him. Society can no longer live under this bourgeoisie: in other words, its existence is no longer compatible with society.

The essential condition for the existence, and for the sway of the bourgeois class, is the formation and augmentation of capital; the condition for capital is wage labor. Wage labor rests exclusively on competition between the laborers. The advance of industry, whose involuntary promoter is the bourgeoisie, replaces the isolation of the laborers, due to competition, by their revolutionary combination, due to association. The development of modern industry, therefore, cuts from under its feet the very foundation on which the bourgeoisie produces and appropriates products. What the bourgeoisie, therefore, produces, above all, is its own gravediggers. Its fall and the victory of the proletariat are equally inevitable.

II. PROLETARIANS AND COMMUNISTS

In what relation do the communists stand to the proletarians as a whole?

The communists do not form a separate party opposed to other working-class parties.

They have no interests separate and apart from those of the proletariat as a whole.

They do not set up any sectarian principles of their own, by which to shape and mold the proletarian movement.

The communists are distinguished from the other working-class parties by this only: 1. In the national struggles of the proletarians of the different countries they point out and bring to the front the common interests of the entire proletariat, independent of all nationality. 2. In the various stages of development which the struggle of the working class against the bourgeoisie has to pass through, they always and everywhere represent the interests of the movement as a whole.

The communists, therefore, are on the one hand, practically, the most advanced and resolute section of the working-class parties of every country, that section which pushes forward all others; on the other hand, theoretically, they have over the great mass of the proletariat the advantage of clearly understanding the line of march, the conditions, and the ultimate general results of the proletarian movement.

The immediate aim of the communists is the same as that of all the other proletarian parties: formation of the proletariat into a class, overthrow of the bourgeois supremacy, conquest of political power by the proletariat.

The theoretical conclusions of the communists are in no way based on ideas or principles that have been invented, or discovered, by this or that would-be universal reformer.

They merely express, in general terms, actual relations springing from an existing class struggle, from a historical movement going on under our very eyes. The abolition of existing property relations is not at all a distinctive feature of communism.

All property relations in the past have continually been subject to historical change consequent upon the change in historical conditions.

The French Revolution, for example, abolished feudal property in favor of bourgeois property.

The distinguishing feature of communism is not the abolition of property generally, but the abolition of bourgeois property. But modern bourgeois private property is the final and most complete expression of the system of producing and appropriating products that is based on class antagonisms, on the exploitation of the many by the few.

In this sense the theory of the communists may be summed up in the single sentence: Abolition of private property.

We communists have been reproached with the desire of abolishing the right of personally acquiring property as the fruit of a man's own labor, which property is alleged to be the groundwork of all personal freedom, activity, and independence.

Hard-won, self-acquired, self-earned property! Do you mean the property of the petty artisan and of the small peasant, a form of property that preceded the bourgeois form? There is no need to abolish that; the development of industry has to a great extent already destroyed it, and is still destroying it daily.

Or do you mean modern bourgeois private property?

But does wage labor create any property for the laborer? Not a bit. It creates capital, i.e., that kind of property which exploits wage labor, and which cannot increase except upon condition of begetting a new supply of wage labor for fresh exploitation. Property, in its present form, is based on the antagonism of capital and wage labor. Let us examine both sides of this antagonism.

To be a capitalist is to have not only a purely personal but a social *status* in production. Capital is a collective product, and only by the united action of many members, nay, in the last resort only by the united action of all members of society, can it be set in motion.

Capital is, therefore, not a personal, it is a social power.

When, therefore, capital is converted into common property, into the property of all members of society, personal property is not thereby transformed into social property. It is only the social character of the property that is changed. It loses its class character.

Let us now take wage labor.

The average price of wage labor is the minimum wage, i.e., that quantum of the means of subsistence which is absolutely requisite to keep the laborer in bare existence as a laborer. What, therefore, the wage laborer appropriates by means of his labor merely suffices to prolong and reproduce a bare existence. We by no means intend to abolish this personal appropriation of the products of labor, an appropriation that is made for the maintenance and reproduction of human life, and that leaves no surplus wherewith to command the labor of others. All that we want to do away with is the miserable character of this appropriation, under which the laborer lives merely to increase capital, and is allowed to live only in so far as the interest of the ruling class requires it.

In bourgeois society living labor is but a means to increase accumulated labor. In communist society accumulated labor is but a means to widen, to enrich, to promote the existence of the laborer.

In bourgeois society, therefore, the past dominates the present; in communist society the present dominates the past. In bourgeois society capital is independent and has individuality, while the living person is dependent and has no individuality.

And the abolition of this state of things is called by the bourgeois abolition of individuality and freedom! And rightly so. The abolition of bourgeois individuality, bourgeois independence, and bourgeois freedom is undoubtedly aimed at.

By freedom is meant, under the present bourgeois conditions of production, free trade, free selling and buying. But if selling and buying disappear, free selling and buying disappear also. This talk about free selling and buying, and all the other "brave words" of our bourgeoisie about freedom in general, have a meaning, if any, only in contrast with restricted selling and buying, with the fettered traders of the Middle Ages, but have no meaning when opposed to the communistic abolition of buying and selling, of the bourgeois conditions of production, and of the bourgeoisie itself.

You are horrified at our intending to do away with private property. But in your existing society private property is already done away with for nine-tenths of the population; its existence for the few is solely due to its non-existence in the hands of those nine tenths. You reproach us, therefore, with intending to do away with a form of property the necessary condition for whose existence is the non-existence of any property for the immense majority of society.

In one word, you reproach us with intending to do away with your property. Precisely so; that is just what we intend.

From the moment when labor can no longer be converted into capital, money, or rent, into a social power capable of being monopolized, i.e., from the moment when individual property can no longer be transformed into bourgeois property, into capital, from that moment, you say, individuality vanishes.

You must, therefore, confess that by "individual" you mean no other person than the bourgeois, than the middle-class owner of property. This person must, indeed, be swept out of the way and made impossible.

Communism deprives no man of the power to appropriate the products of society; all that it does is to deprive him of the power to subjugate the labor of others by means of such appropriation.

It has been objected that upon the abolition of private property all work will cease and universal laziness will overtake us.

According to this, bourgeois society ought long ago have gone to the dogs through sheer idleness, for those of its members who work acquire nothing and those who acquire anything do not work. The whole of this objection is but another expression of the tautology that there can no longer be any wage labor when there is no longer any capital.

All objections urged against the communistic mode of producing and appropriating material products have, in the same way, been urged against the communistic modes of producing and appropriating intellectual products. Just as, to the bourgeois, the disappearance of class property is the disappearance of production itself, so the disappearance of class culture is to him identical with the disappearance of all culture.

That culture, the loss of which he laments, is, for the enormous majority, a mere training to act as a machine.

But don't wrangle with us so long as you apply, to our intended abolition of bourgeois property, the standard of your bourgeois notions of freedom, culture, law, etc. Your very ideas are but the outgrowth of the conditions of your bourgeois production and bourgeois property, just as your jurisprudence is but the will of your class made into a law for all, a will whose essential character and direction are determined by the economic conditions of existence of your class.

The selfish misconception that induces you to transform into eternal laws of nature and of reason the social forms springing from your present mode of production and form of property—historical relations that rise and disappear in the progress of production—this misconception you share with every ruling class that has preceded you. What you see clearly in the case of ancient property, what you admit in the case of feudal property you are of course forbidden to admit in the case of your own bourgeois form of property.

Abolition of the family! Even the most radical flare up at this infamous proposal of the communists.

On what foundation is the present family, the bourgeois family, based? On capital, on private gain. In its completely developed form this family exists only among the bourgeoisie. But this state of things finds its complement in the practical absence of the family among the proletarians, and in public prostitution.

The bourgeois family will vanish as a matter of course when its complement vanishes, and both will vanish with the vanishing of capital.

Do you charge us with wanting to stop the exploitation of children by their parents? To this crime we plead guilty.

But, you will say, we destroy the most hallowed of relations when we replace home education by social.

And your education! Is not that also social, and determined by the social conditions under which you educate, by the intervention, direct or indirect, of society, by means of schools, etc.? The communists have not invented the intervention of society in education; they do but seek to alter the character of that intervention, and to rescue education from the influence of the ruling class.

The bourgeois claptrap about the family and education, about the hallowed co-relation of parent and child, becomes all the more disgusting, the more, by the action of modern industry, all family ties among the proletarians are torn asunder and their children transformed into simple articles of commerce and instruments of labor.

"But you communists would introduce community of women," screams the whole bourgeoisie in chorus.

The bourgeois sees in his wife a mere instrument of production. He hears that the instruments of production are to be exploited in common and, naturally, can come to no other conclusion than that the lot of being common to all will likewise fall to the women.

He has not even a suspicion that the real point aimed at is to do away with the status of women as mere instruments of production.

For the rest, nothing is more ridiculous than the virtuous indignation of our bourgeois at the community of women which, they pretend, is to be openly and officially established by the communists. The communists have no need to introduce community of women; it has existed almost from time immemorial.

Our bourgeois, not content with having the wives and daughters of their proletarians at their disposal, not to speak of common prostitutes, take the greatest pleasure in seducing each other's wives.

Bourgeois marriage is in reality a system of wives in common and thus, at the most, what the communists might possibly be reproached with is that they desire to introduce, in substitution for a hypocritically concealed, an openly legalized community of women. For the rest, it is self-evident that the abolition of the present system of production must bring with it the abolition of the community of women springing from the system, i.e., of prostitution, both public and private.

The communists are further reproached with desiring to abolish countries and nationality.

The workingmen have no country. We cannot take from them what they have not got. Since the proletariat must first of all acquire political supremacy, must rise to be the leading class of the nation, must constitute itself *the* nation, it is, so far, itself national, though not in the bourgeois sense of the word.

National differences and antagonisms between peoples are daily more and more vanishing, owing to the development of the bourgeoisie, to freedom of commerce, to the world market, to uniformity in the mode of production and in the conditions of life corresponding thereto.

The supremacy of the proletariat will cause them to vanish still faster. United action, of the leading civilized countries at least, is one of the first conditions for the emancipation of the proletariat.

In proportion as the exploitation of one individual by another is put to an end, the exploitation of one nation by another will also be put to an end. In proportion as the antagonism between classes within the nation vanishes, the hostility of one nation to another will come to an end.

The charges against communism made from a religious, a philosophical, and, generally, from an ideological standpoint are not deserving of serious examination.

Does it require deep intuition to comprehend that man's ideas, views, and conception, in one word, man's consciousness, change with every change in the conditions of his material existence, in his social relations, and in his social life?

What else does the history of ideas prove than that intellectual production changes its character in proportion as material production is changed? The ruling ideas of each age have ever been the ideas of its ruling class.

When people speak of ideas that revolutionize society they do but express the fact that within the old society the elements of a new one have been created, and that the dissolution of the old ideas keep even pace with the dissolution of the old conditions of existence.

When the ancient world was in its last throes, the ancient religions were overcome by Christianity. When Christian ideas succumbed in the eighteenth century to rationalist ideas, feudal society fought its death battle with the then revolutionary bourgeoisie. The ideas of religious liberty and freedom of conscience merely gave expression to the sway of free competition within the domain of knowledge.

"Undoubtedly," it will be said, "religious, moral, philosophical, and juridical ideas have been modified in the course of historical development. But religion, morality, philosophy, political science, and law constantly survived this change.

"There are, besides, eternal truths, such as freedom, justice, etc., that are common to all states of society. But communism abolishes eternal truths, it abolishes all religion, and all morality, instead of constituting them on a new basis; it therefore acts in contradiction to all past historical experience." What does this accusation reduce itself to? The history of all past society has consisted in the development of class antagonisms, antagonisms that assumed different forms at different epochs.

But whatever form they may have taken, one fact is common to all past ages, viz., the exploitation of one part of society by the other. No wonder then that the social consciousness of past ages, despite all the multiplicity and variety it displays, moves within certain common forms, or general ideas, which cannot completely vanish except with the total disappearance of class antagonisms.

The communist revolution is the most radical rupture with traditional property relations; no wonder that its development involves the most radical rupture with traditional ideas.

But let us have done with the bourgeois objections to communism.

We have seen above that the first step in the revolution by the working class is to raise the proletariat to the position of ruling class, to win the battle of democracy.

The proletariat will use its political supremacy to wrest, by degrees, all capital from the bourgeoisie, to centralize all instruments of production in the hands of the state, i.e., of the proletariat organized as the ruling class, and to increase the total of productive forces as rapidly as possible.

Of course, in the beginning this cannot be effected except by means of despotic inroads on the rights of property and on the conditions of bourgeois production; by means of measures, therefore, which appear economically insufficient and untenable, but which, in the course of the movement, outstrip themselves, necessitate further inroads upon the old social order, and are unavoidable as a means of entirely revolutionizing the mode of production.

These measures will of course be different in different countries.

Nevertheless, in the most advanced countries the following will be pretty generally applicable:

1. Abolition of property in land and application of all rents of land to public purposes.

2. A heavy progressive or graduated income tax.

3. Abolition of all right of inheritance.

4. Confiscation of the property of all emigrants and rebels.

5. Centralization of credit in the hands of the state, by means of a national bank with state capital and an exclusive monopoly.

6. Centralization of the means of communication and transport in the hands of the state.

7. Extension of factories and instruments of production owned by the state; the bringing into cultivation of wastelands, and the improvement of the soil generally in accordance with a common plan.

8. Equal liability of all to labor. Establishment of industrial armies, especially for agriculture.

9. Combination of agriculture with manufacturing industries; gradual abolition of the distinction between town and country, by a more equable distribution of the population over the country.

10. Free education for all children in public schools. Abolition of children's factory labor in its present form. Combination of education with industrial production, etc.

When, in the course of development, class distinctions have disappeared and all production has been concentrated in the hands of a vast association of the whole nation, the public power will lose its political character. Political power, properly so called, is merely the organized power of one class for oppressing another. If the proletariat during its contest with the bourgeoisie is compelled, by the force of circumstances, to organize itself as a class, if, by means of a revolution, it makes itself the ruling class and, as such, sweeps away by force the old conditions of production, then it will, along with these conditions, have swept away the conditions for the existence of class antagonisms and of classes generally and will thereby have abolished its own supremacy as a class.

In place of the old bourgeois society, with its classes and class antagonisms, we shall have an association in which the free development of each is the condition for the free development of all.

[Under the headings of Reactionary (Feudal, Petty-Bourgeois, and German, or "True") Socialism, of Conservative, or bourgeois, Socialism, and of Critical Utopian Socialism and Communism, in Section III Marx and Engels attack the then existing socialist schools of thought that did not agree with their own.]

IV. POSITION OF THE COMMUNISTS IN RELATION TO
THE VARIOUS EXISTING OPPOSITION PARTIES

Section II has made clear the relations of the communists to the existing working-class parties, such as the Chartists in England and the agrarian reformers in America.

The communists fight for the attainment of the immediate aims, for the enforcement of the momentary interests of the working class, but in the movement of the present they also represent and take care of the future of that movement. In France the communists ally themselves with the social democrats,[5] against the conservative and radical bourgeoisie, reserving, however, the right to take up a critical position in regard to phrases and illusions traditionally handed down from the Great Revolution.

In Switzerland they support the radicals, without losing sight of the fact that this party consists of antagonistic elements, partly of democratic socialists, in the French sense, partly of radical bourgeois.

In Poland they support the party that insists on an agrarian revolution as the prime condition for national emancipation, that party which fomented the insurrection of Cracow in 1846.

In Germany they fight with the bourgeoisie whenever it acts in a revolutionary way, against the absolute monarchy, the feudal squirearchy, and the petty bourgeoisie.

But they never cease, for a single instant, to instill into the working class the clearest possible recognition of the hostile antagonism between bourgeoisie and proletariat, in order that the German workers may straightway use, as so many weapons against the

[5] The party then represented in Parliament by Ledru-Rollin, in literature by Louis Blanc, in the daily press by the *Reforme*. The name of social democracy signified, with these its inventors, a section of the democratic or republican party more or less tinged with socialism.

bourgeoisie, the social and political conditions that the bourgeoisie must necessarily introduce along with its supremacy, and in order that, after the fall of the reactionary classes in Germany, the fight against the bourgeoisie itself may immediately begin.

The communists turn their attention chiefly to Germany, because that country is on the eve of a bourgeois revolution that is bound to be carried out under more advanced conditions of European civilization, and with a much more developed proletariat, than that of England was in the seventeenth and of France in the eighteenth century, and because the bourgeois revolution in Germany will be but the prelude to an immediately following proletarian revolution.

In short, the communists everywhere support every revolutionary movement against the existing social and political order of things.

In all these movements they bring to the front, as the leading question in each, the property question, no matter what its degree of development at the time.

Finally, they labor everywhere for the union and agreement of the democratic parties of all countries.

The communists disdain to conceal their views and aims. They openly declare that their ends can be attained only by the forcible overthrow of all existing social conditions. Let the ruling classes tremble at a communistic revolution. The proletarians have nothing to lose but their chains. They have a world to win.

WORKINGMEN OF ALL COUNTRIES, UNITE!

Capital *Explained by Engels*

As long as there have been capitalists and workers on earth, no book has appeared which is of as much importance for the workers as the one before us. The relation between capital and labor, the hinge on which our entire present system of society turns, is here treated scientifically for the first time, and with a thoroughness and acuity possible only for a German. Valuable as the writings of an Owen, Saint-Simon, Fourier, are and will remain—it was reserved for a German to climb to the height from which the whole field of modern social relations can be seen clearly and in full view just as

SOURCE: Friedrich Engels, *Engels on* Capital (International Publishers, New York, 1937), pp. 3–11.

the lower mountain scenery is seen by an observer standing at the topmost peak.

Political economy up to now has taught us that labor is the source of all wealth and the measure of all values, so that two objects whose production has cost the same labor time also possess the same value and must also be exchanged for each other, since on the average only equal values are exchangeable for one another. At the same time, however, it teaches that there exists a kind of stored-up labor, which it calls capital; that this capital, owing to the auxiliary sources contained in it, raises the productivity of living labor a hundred and a thousandfold, and in return claims a certain compensation which is termed profit or gain. As we all know, this occurs in reality in such a way that the profits of stored-up, dead labor become ever more massive, the capital of the capitalists becomes ever more colossal, while the wages of living labor become constantly less, and the mass of workers living solely on wages becomes ever more numerous and poverty-stricken. How is this contradiction to be solved? How can there remain a profit for the capitalists, if the worker gets back in another form the full value of the labor he adds to his product? And this should be the case, nevertheless, since only equal values are exchanged. On the other hand, how can equal values be exchanged, how can the worker receive the full value of his product, if, as is admitted by many economists, this product is divided between him and the capitalists? Economics up to now has been helpless in the face of this contradiction, and writes or stutters embarrassed phrases which say nothing. Even the previous socialist critics of economics have not been able to do more than to emphasize the contradiction; no one has solved it, until now at last Marx has traced the process by which this profit arises right to its birthplace and has thereby made everything clear.

In tracing the development of capital, Marx starts out from the simple, notoriously obvious fact that the capitalists turn their capital to account by exchange: they buy commodities for their money and afterwards sell them for more money than they cost. For example a capitalist buys cotton for 1,000 talers and resells it for 1,100, thus "earning" 100 talers. This excess of 100 talers over the original capital, Marx calls *surplus value*. What is the origin of this surplus value? According to the economists' assumption, only equal values are exchanged, and in the sphere of abstract theory this is correct. Hence, the purchase of cotton and its subsequent sale can just as little yield surplus value as the exchange of a silver taler for thirty silver groschen and the reexchange of the small coins for a silver taler, a process by which one becomes neither richer nor poorer. But surplus value can just as little arise from sellers selling commodities above their value, or purchasers buying them below their value, because each one is in turn buyer and seller and this would, therefore, again balance. Just as little can it arise from buyers and sellers reciprocally over-reaching each other, for this would create no new or surplus value, but would only divide the existing capital differently between the capitalists. In spite of the fact that the capitalist buys the commodities at their value and sells them at their value, he gets more value out than he put in. How does this happen?

The capitalist finds on the market, under present social conditions, *one commodity* which has the peculiar property that *its use is a source of new value, is a creation of new value.* This commodity is *labor-power.*

What is the value of labor-power? The value of every commodity is measured by the labor required for its production. Labor-power exists in the form of the living worker who requires a definite amount of means of subsistence for his existence, as well as for the maintenance of his family, which ensures the continuance of labor-power even after his death. Hence the labor time necessary for producing these means of subsistence represents the value of labor-power. The capitalist pays him weekly and purchases for that the use of one week's labor of the worker. So far Messrs. the economists will be pretty well in agreement with us as to the value of labor-power.

The capitalist now sets his worker to work. In a certain period of time the worker will have delivered as much labor as was represented by his weekly wages. Supposing that the weekly wage of a worker represents three labor days, then, if the worker begins on Monday, he has by Wednesday evening *replaced for the capitalist the full value of the wage paid.* But does he then stop working? Not at all. The capitalist has bought his *week's* labor and the worker must also go on working during the last three days of the week. This *surplus labor* of the worker, over and above the time necessary to replace his wages, is the *source of surplus value,* of profit, of the continually growing accumulation of capital.

Do not say it is an arbitrary assumption that the worker reproduces in three days the wages he has received and works the remaining three days for the capitalist. Whether he takes exactly three days to replace his wages, or two or four, is, to be sure, quite immaterial here and varies according to circumstances; the main point is that the capitalist, besides the labor he pays for, also extracts labor that he *does not pay for*, and this is no arbitrary assumption, for the day the capitalist only extracts from the worker as much labor in the long run as he paid him in wages, on that day he would shut down his workshops, since indeed his whole profit would come to naught.

Here we have the solution of all those contradictions. The origin of surplus value (of which the capitalist's profit forms an important part) is now quite clear and natural. The value of the labor-power is paid for, but this value is far less than that which the capitalist can extract from the labor-power, and it is precisely the difference, the *unpaid labor*, that constitutes the share of the capitalist, or more accurately, of the capitalist class. For even the profit that the cotton dealer made on his cotton in the above example must consist of unpaid labor, if cotton prices have not risen. The trader must have sold to a cotton manufacturer, who is able to extract a profit for himself from his product besides the 100 talers, and therefore, divides with him the unpaid labor he has pocketed. In general, it is this unpaid labor which maintains all the non-working members of society. The state and municipal taxes, as far as they affect the capitalist class, are paid from it, as is the rent of the landowners, etc. On it rests the whole existing social system.

It would, however, be absurd to assume that unpaid labor arose only under present conditions where production is carried on by capitalists on one hand and wage workers on the other. On the contrary, the oppressed class at all times has had to perform unpaid labor. During the whole long period when slavery was the prevailing form of the organization of labor, the slaves had to perform much more labor than was returned to them in the form of means of subsistence. The same was the case under the rule of serfdom and right up to the abolition of peasant *corvée* labor; here in fact the difference stands out palpably between the time during which the peasant works for his own maintenance and the surplus labor for the feudal lord, precisely because the latter is carried out separately from the former. The form has now been changed, but the substance remains and as long as "a part of society possesses the monopoly of the means of production, the laborer, free or not free, must add to the working time necessary for his own maintenance an extra working time in order to produce the means of subsistence for the owners of the means of production."

In the previous article we saw that every worker employed by the capitalist performs two kinds of labor: during one part of his working time he replaces the wages advanced to him by the capitalist, and this part of his labor Marx terms the *necessary labor*. But afterwards he has to go on working and during that time he produces *surplus value* for the capitalist, a significant portion of which constitutes profit. That part of the labor is called surplus labor.

Let us assume that the worker works three days of the week to replace his wages and three days to produce surplus value for the capitalist. Putting it otherwise, it means that, with a twelve-hour working day, he works six hours daily for his wages and six hours for the production of surplus value. One can only get six days out of the week, at most seven, even by including Sunday, but one can extract six, eight, ten, twelve, fifteen or even more hours of labor out of every working day. The worker sells the capitalist a working day for his day's wages. But, *what is a working day?* Eight hours or eighteen?

It is to the capitalist's interest to make the working day as long as possible. The longer it is, the more surplus value he obtains. The worker correctly feels that every hour of labor which he performs over and above the replacement of the wage is unjustly extorted from him; he experiences in his own person what it means to work excessive hours. The capitalist fights for his profit, the worker for his health, for a few hours of daily rest, to be able to occupy himself as a human being as well, in other ways besides working, sleeping and eating. It may be remarked in passing that it does not depend at all upon the good will of the individual capitalists whether they desire to embark on this struggle or not, since competition compels even the most philanthropic among them to join with his colleagues and to make a working time as long as theirs the rule.

The struggle for the fixing of the working day has lasted from the first historical appearance of free workers on the scene up to the present day. In various trades, different traditional working days prevail; but in reality they are seldom adhered to. Only where the law fixes the working day and supervises its observance can one really say that there exists a normal working day. And up to now this is the case almost solely in the factory districts of England. Here the ten-hour working day (ten-and-a-half hours on five days, seven-and-a-half on Saturday) has been fixed for all women and for youths of thirteen to eighteen, and since the men cannot work without them, they also come under the ten-hour working day. This law has been won by English factory workers through years of endurance, through the most persistent, stubborn struggle with the factory owners, through freedom of the press, the right of association and assembly, as well as through adroit utilization of the divisions within the ruling class itself. It has become the palladium of the English workers; it has gradually become extended to all branches of large-scale industry and last year to almost *all trades*, at least to all those employing women and children. The present work contains most exhaustive material on the history of this legislative regulation of the working day in England. The next "North German Reichstag" will also have factory regulations to discuss and therefore the regulation of factory labor. We expect that none of the deputies elected by German workers will proceed to discuss this bill without previously making themselves thoroughly conversant with *Marx's* book. *There is much to be achieved there.* The divisions within the ruling classes are more favorable to the workers than they ever were in England, because *universal suffrage compels the ruling classes to court the favor of the workers*. Under these circumstances, four or five representatives of the proletariat are *a power*, if they know how to use their position, if above all they know what is at issue, which the bourgeois do not know. And for this purpose, Marx's book gives them all the material in ready form.

We will pass over a number of other very fine investigations of more theoretical interest and will halt only at the final chapter which deals with the accumulation of capital. Here it is first shown that the capitalist mode of production, *i.e.*, that effected by capitalists on one hand and by wage workers on the other, not only continually reproduces the capital of the capitalist, but also continually reproduces the poverty of the workers at the same time. Thereby it is ensured that there always exist anew, on the one hand, capitalists who are the owners of all means of subsistence, raw materials and instruments of labor, and, on the other, the great mass of workers who are compelled to sell their labor-power to these capitalists for an amount of the means of subsistence which at best just suffices to maintain them in a condition capable of working and to bring up a new generation of able-bodied proletarians. But capital does not merely reproduce itself; it is continually increased and multiplied—hence its power over the propertyless class of workers. And just as it itself is reproduced on an ever-greater scale, so the modern capitalist mode of production reproduces the class of propertyless workers also on an ever-greater scale and in ever-greater numbers. ". . . accumulation [of capital] reproduces the capital relation on a progressive scale, more capitalists or larger capitalists at this pole, more wage workers at that. . . . *Accumulation of capital is, therefore, increase of the proletariat.*"

Since, however, owing to the progress of machinery, owing to improved agriculture, etc., fewer and fewer workers are necessary in order to produce the same quantity of products, since this perfecting, *i.e.*, this making the workers superfluous, grows more rapidly than the growing capital itself, what becomes of this ever-increasing number of workers? They form an industrial reserve army, which is paid *below* the value of its labor and is irregularly employed, or comes under the care of public Poor Law institutions during times of bad or moderate business, but which is indispensable to the capitalist class at times when business is especially lively, as is palpably evident in England—but which *under all circumstances* serves to break the power of resistance of the regularly employed workers and to keep their wages down. "The greater the social wealth . . . the greater is the [relative surplus population or] industrial reserve army. . . . But the greater this reserve army in proportion to the active labor army, the greater is the mass of a consolidated [permanent] surplus population [or strata of workers] whose misery is in inverse ratio to its torment of labor. Finally, the more extensive the Lazarus-layers of the working class, and the industrial reserve army, the greater is official pauperism. *This is the absolute general law of capitalist accumulation.*"

These, strictly scientifically proved—and the official economists take great care not to make even an attempt at refutation—are some of the chief laws of the modern, capitalist social system. But with this is everything said? By no means. Just as sharply as Marx stresses the bad sides of capitalist production, does he also clearly prove that this social form was necessary to develop the productive forces of society to a level which will make possible an equal development, worthy of human beings, for *all* members of society. All earlier forms of society were too poor for this. Capitalist production for the first time creates the wealth and the productive forces necessary for this but at the same time it also creates in the mass of oppressed workers the social class which is more and more compelled to claim the utilization of this wealth and these productive forces for the whole of society—instead of as today for a monopolist class.

The Dialectical Process in History

The materialist conception of history starts from the proposition that the production of the means to support human life and, next to production, the exchange of things produced, is the basis of all social structure; that in every society that has appeared in history, the manner in which wealth is distributed and society divided into classes or orders is dependent upon what is produced, how it is produced, and how the products are exchanged. From this point of view the final causes of all social changes and political revolutions are to be sought, not in men's brains, not in man's better insight into eternal truth and justice, but in changes in the modes of production and exchange. They are to be sought, not in the *philosophy*, but in the *economics* of each particular epoch. The growing perception that existing social institutions are unreasonable and unjust, that reason has become unreason, and right wrong, is only proof that in the modes of production and exchange changes have silently taken place, with which the social order, adapted to earlier economic conditions, is no longer in keeping. From this it also follows that the means of getting rid of the incongruities that have been brought to light must also be present, in a more or less developed condition, within the changed modes of production themselves. These means are not to be invented by deduction from fundamental principles, but are to be discovered in the stubborn facts of the existing system of production.

Active social forces work exactly like natural forces; blindly, forcibly, destructively, so long as we do not understand and

SOURCE: Friedrich Engels, *Socialism, Utopian and Scientific* (Swan Sonnenschein, London, 1892), passim Part III.

reckon with them. But when once we understand them, when once we grasp their action, their direction, their effects, it depends only upon ourselves to subject them more and more to our own will, and by means of them to reach our own ends. And this holds quite especially of the mighty productive forces of today. As long as we obstinately refuse to understand the nature of the character of these social means of action—and this understanding goes against the grain of the capitalist mode of production and its defenders—so long these forces are at work in spite of us, in opposition to us, so long they master us, as we have shown above in detail.

But when once their nature is understood, they can, in the hands of the producers working together, be transformed from master demons into willing servants. The difference is as that between the destructive force of electricity in the lightning of the storm, and electricity under command in the telegraph and the voltaic arc; the difference between a conflagration, and fire working in the service of man. With this recognition at last of the real nature of the productive forces of today, the social anarchy of production gives place to a social regulation of production upon a definite plan, according to the needs of the community and each individual. Then the capitalist mode of appropriation, in which the product enslaves first the producer and then the appropriator, is replaced by the mode of appropriation of the products that is based upon the nature of the modern means of production; upon the one hand, direct social appropriation, as means to the maintenance and extension of production—on the other, direct individual appropriation, as means of subsistence and of enjoyment.

Whilst the capitalist mode of production more and more completely transforms the great majority of the population into proletarians, it creates the power which, under penalty of its own destruction, is forced to accomplish this revolution. Whilst it forces on more and more the transformation of the vast means of production, already socialized, into state property, it shows itself the way to accomplishing this revolution. *The proletariat seizes political power and turns the means of production into state property.*

But, in doing this, it abolishes itself as proletariat, abolishes all class distinctions and class antagonisms, abolishes also the state as state. Society thus far, based upon class antagonisms, had need of the state. That is, of an organization of the particular class which was *pro tempore* the exploiting class, an organization for the purpose of preventing any interference from without with the existing conditions of production, and therefore, especially, for the purpose of forcibly keeping the exploited classes in the condition of oppression corresponding with the given mode of production (slavery, serfdom, wage labor). The state was the official representative of society as a whole; the gathering of it together into a visible embodiment. But it was this only in so far as it was the state of that class which itself represented, for the time being, society as a whole; in ancient times, the state of slave-owning citizens; in the Middle Ages, the feudal lords; in our own time, the bourgeoisie. When at last it becomes the real representative of the whole of society, it renders itself unnecessary. As soon as there is no longer any social class to be held in subjection; as soon as class rule and the individual struggle for existence based upon our present anarchy in production, with the collisions and excesses arising from these, are removed, nothing more remains to be repressed, and a special repressive force, a state, is no longer necessary. The first act by virtue of which the state really constitutes itself the representative of the whole of society—the taking possession of the means of production in the name of society—this is, at the same time, its last independent act as a state. State interference in social relations becomes, in one domain after another, superfluous, and then dies out of itself; the government of persons is replaced by the administration of things, and by the conduct of processes of production. The state is not "abolished." *It dies out.* This gives the measure of the value of the phrase "a free state," both as to its justifiable use at times by agitators, and as to its ultimate scientific insufficiency; and also of the demands of the so-called anarchists for the abolition of the state out of hand.

Since the historical appearance of the capitalist mode of production, the appropriation by society of all the means of production has often been dreamed of, more or less vaguely, by individuals, as well as by sects, as the ideal of the future. But it could become possible, could become a historical necessity, only when the actual conditions for its realization were there. Like every other social advance, it becomes practicable, not by men understanding that the existence of classes is in contradiction to justice, equality, etc., not by the mere willingness to abolish these classes, but by virtue of certain new economic conditions. The separation of society into an exploiting and an exploited class, a ruling and an oppressed class, was the necessary consequence of the deficient and restricted development of production in former times. So long as the total social labor only yields a produce which but slightly exceeds that barely necessary for the existence of all; so long, therefore, as labor engages all or almost all the time of the great majority of the members of society—so long, of necessity, this society is divided into classes. Side by side with the great majority, exclusively bond slaves to labor, arises a class freed from directly productive labor, which looks after the general affairs of society, the direction of labor, state business, law, science, art, etc. It is, therefore, the law of division of labor that lies at the basis of the division into classes. But this does not prevent this division into classes from being carried out by means of violence and robbery, trickery and fraud. It does not prevent the ruling class, once having the upper hand, from consolidating its power at the expense of the working class, from turning their social leadership into an intensified exploitation of the masses.

But if, upon this showing, division into classes has a certain historical justification, it has this only for a given period, only under given social conditions. It was based upon the insufficiency of production. It will be swept away by the complete development of modern productive forces. And, in fact, the abolition of classes in society presupposes a degree of historical evolution, at which the existence, not simply of this or that particular ruling class, but of any ruling class at all, and, therefore, the existence of class distinction itself has become an obsolete anachronism. It presupposes, therefore, the development of production carried out to a degree at which appropriation of the means of production and of the products, and, with this, of political domination, of the monopoly of culture, and of intellectual leadership by a particular class of society, has become not only superfluous, but economically, politically, intellectually a hindrance to development.

This point is now reached. Their political and intellectual bankruptcy is scarcely any longer a secret to the bourgeoisie themselves. Their economic bankruptcy recurs regularly every ten years. In every crisis, society is suffocated beneath the weight of its own productive forces and products, which it cannot use, and stands helpless, face to face with the absurd contradiction that the producers have nothing to consume, because consumers are wanting.

The expansive force of the means of production bursts the bonds that the capitalist mode of production had imposed upon them. Their deliverance from these bonds is the one precondition for an unbroken, constantly accelerated development of the productive forces, and therewith for a practically unlimited increase of production itself. Nor is this all. The socialized appropriation of the means of production does away not only with the present artificial restrictions upon production, but also with the positive waste and devastation of productive forces and products that are at the present time the inevitable concomitants of production, and that reach their height in the crises. Further, it sets free for the community at large a mass of means of production and of products, by doing away with the senseless extravagance of the ruling classes of today, and their political representatives. The possibility of securing for every member of society, by means of socialized production, an existence not only fully sufficient materially, and becoming day by day more full, but an existence guaranteeing to all the free development and exercise of their physical and mental faculties—this possibility is now for the first time here, but *it is here*.

With the seizing of the means of production by society, production of commodities is done away with, and simultaneously, the mastery of the product over the producer. Anarchy in social production is replaced by systematic definite organization. The struggle for individual existence disappears. Then for the first time, man, in a certain sense, is finally marked off from the rest of the animal kingdom, and emerges from mere animal conditions of existence into really human ones. The whole sphere of the conditions of life which environ man, and which have hitherto ruled man, now comes under the domination and control of man, who for the first time becomes the real, conscious lord of nature, because he has now become master of his own social organization. The laws of his own social action, hitherto standing face to face with man as laws of nature foreign to and dominating him, will then be used with full understanding, and so mastered by him. Man's own social organization, hitherto confronting him as a necessity imposed by nature and history, now becomes the result of his own free action. The extraneous objective forces that have hitherto governed history pass under the control of man himself. Only from that time will man himself, more and more consciously, make his own history—only from that time will the social causes set in movement by him have, in the main and in a constantly growing measure, the results intended by him. It is the ascent of man from the kingdom of necessity to the kingdom of freedom.

Let us briefly sum up our sketch of historical evolution.

I. *Medieval Society*—Individual production on a small scale. Means of production adapted for individual use; hence primitive, ungainly, petty, dwarfed in action. Production for immediate consumption, either of the producer himself or of his feudal lords. Only where an excess of production over this consumption occurs is such excess offered for sale, enters into exchange. Production of commodities therefore, is only in its infancy. But already it contains within itself, in embryo, *anarchy in the production of society at large*.

II. *Capitalist Revolution*—Transformation of industry, at first by means of simple co-operation and manufacture. Concentration of the means of production, hitherto scattered, into great workshops. As a consequence, their transformation from individual to social means of production—a transformation which does not, on the whole, affect the form of exchange. The old forms of appropriation remain in force. The capitalist appears. In his capacity as owner of the means of production, he also appropriates the products and turns them into commodities. Production has become a *social* act. Exchange and appropriation continue to be *individual* acts, the acts of individuals. *The social product is appropriated by the individual capitalist.* Fundamental contradiction, whence arises all the contradiction in which our present day society moves, and which modern industry brings to light.

A. Severance of the producer from the means of production. Condemnation of the worker to wage labor for life. *Antagonism between the proletariat and the bourgeoisie.*

B. Growing predominance and increasing effectiveness of the laws governing the production of commodities. Unbridled competition. *Contradiction between socialized organization in the individual factory and social anarchy in production as a whole.*

C. On the one hand, perfecting of machinery, made by competition compulsory for each individual manufacturer, and complemented by a constantly growing displacement of laborers. *Industrial reserve army*. On the other hand, unlimited extension of production, also compulsory under competition, for every manufacturer. On both sides, unheard of development of productive forces, excess of supply over demand, overproduction, glutting of the markets, crises every ten years, the vicious circle: excess here, of means of production and products—excess there, of laborers, without employment and without means of existence. But these two levers of production and of social well-being are unable to work together because the capitalist form of production prevents the productive forces from working and the products from circulating, unless they are first turned into capital—which their very superabundance prevents. The contradiction has grown into an absurdity. *The mode of production rises in rebellion against the form of exchange.* The bourgeoisie are convicted of incapacity further to manage their own social productive forces.

D. Partial recognition of the social character of the productive forces forced upon the capitalists themselves. Taking over of the great institutions for production and communication, first by joint-stock companies, later on by trusts, then by the state. The bourgeoisie demonstrated to be a superfluous class. All its social functions are now performed by salaried employees.

III. *Proletarian Revolution*—Solution of the contradictions. The proletariat seizes the public power, and by means of this transforms the socialized means of production, slipping from the hands of the bourgeoisie, into public property. By this act, the proletariat frees the means of production from the character of capital they have thus far borne, and gives their socialized character complete freedom to work itself out. Socialized production upon a predetermined plan becomes henceforth possible. The development of production makes the existence of different classes of society thenceforth an anachronism. In proportion as anarchy in social production vanishes, the political authority of the state dies out. Man, at last the master of his own form of social organization, becomes at the same time the lord over nature, his own master—free.

To accomplish this act of universal emancipation is the historical mission of the modern proletariat. To thoroughly comprehend the historical conditions and thus the very nature of this act, to impart to the now oppressed proletarian class a full knowledge of the conditions and of the meaning of the momentous act it is called upon to accomplish, this is the task of the theoretical expression of the proletarian movement, scientific socialism.

D.   THE ANARCHIST COMPONENT OF SOCIALISM

In varying measure, the anarchist component has been present in most socialist schools of thought. European Continental socialism, from which most of today's world socialism derives, was linked to the French Revolution ideologically and emotionally. Continental socialists agreed that capitalism was the main enemy of the 1789 revolutionary trinity: liberty, equality, and fraternity. Capitalism had to be destroyed. What about the state, the instrument through which, socialists maintained, the capitalists—the bourgeoisie—dominated society? Early socialists who lived in societies in which the role of the state was minimal (Great Britain, France after 1830, the United States) had ignored the state. A few decades later there was general awareness among socialists that the state could not be ignored. Marxists maintained that socialists must seize the state and use it to destroy capitalism; this objective achieved, the state would disappear, would "wither away." "Nonsense," said other socialists, "the state is always oppression, there can be no socialism with the state. This must be eliminated immediately." This was Proudhon's position. This was also the anti-Marxist anarchist socialism of Mikhail Bakunin (1814–1876), scion of an upper-class Russian family. He was educated in a military academy, and commissioned in the Czarist army. Endowed with a powerful, inquisitive mind, widely read, vaguely acquainted with progressive ideas, Bakunin resigned his commission. He left Russia in 1840. For several years he traveled extensively in western Europe, studying in German universities, meeting Russian expatriates like Herzen, getting to know revolutionaries of all hues and nationalities. Proudhon had the greatest influence on his ideas. Arrested in Germany in 1849, Bakunin spent eight years in Prussian, Austrian, and Russian prisons, after which Alexander II changed his imprisonment into banishment to Siberia. Bakunin escaped in 1861, reaching London via Japan. All his life he was an indefatigable activist. He wrote, attracted disciples, and organized secret societies and conspiracies. As head of the International Alliance for Social Democracy, he joined the International in 1868. Marx had him expelled in 1872.

Anarchism was for a long time a thorn in the side of statist socialism. Anarchist socialists were not allowed to join the Second International, established in 1889. Bakunin's disciples could be found in many countries, but only in Italy and Spain were they able to launch politically meaningful movements. Bakunin was the main inspirer of the anarchism (or syndicalism or anarchosyndicalism) that played an important role in Spain until the victory of the nationalists in the civil war of 1936 to 1939. British Guild Socialism and the American I.W.W. (Industrial Workers of the World, organized in 1905) also had ideological links with Bakuninism.

Bakunin was a lively but disorderly writer. The excerpts in this selection are taken from the writings edited by G. P. Maximoff in *The Political Philosophy of Bakunin: Scientific Anarchism.*

The Frenchman Georges Sorel (1847–1922) considered himself a Marxist but was closer to Proudhon and Bakunin. An engineer and a civil servant, he wrote copiously after his retirement, formulating the concept of the general strike as the key to revolutionary transformation: once workers are sufficiently organized, their strike will be enough to paralyze the economy and the state; stateless collectivism will then replace capitalism. Sorel achieved popularity among socialists with his book *Reflections on Violence*, published in 1908. The book impressed Lenin: Sorel as the theoretical advocate of violence found in Lenin and his friends his best pupils. Benito Mussolini (1883–1945), before 1914 leader of the revolutionary wing of the Italian socialist movement and founder of Italian fascism in 1919, considered himself a disciple of Sorel.

On Socialism without the State

NOT ONLY are we averse to the idea of persuading our Slave brothers to join the ranks of the Social-Democratic party of German workers, headed by the duumvirate invested with dictatorial power—Marx and Engels—followed by Bebel, Liebknecht, and a few Jewish litterateurs. On the contrary, we shall use all efforts to turn the Slavic proletariat away from a suicidal union with that party, which, by its tendency, aims, and means, is not a folk party, but a purely bourgeois party, and is in addition a German party, that is, anti-Slavic.

. . . Idealists of all sorts, metaphysicians, positivists, those who uphold the priority of science over life, the doctrinaire revolutionists—all of them champion, with equal zeal although differing in their argumentation, the idea of the State and State power, seeing in them, quite logically from their point of view, the only salvation of society. *Quite logically*, I say, having taken as their basis the tenet—a fallacious tenet in our opinion—that thought is prior to life, and abstract theory is prior to social practice, and that therefore sociological science must become the starting point for social upheavals and social reconstruction—they necessarily arrived at the conclusion that since thought, theory, and science are, for the present at least, the property of only a very few people, those

SOURCE: Mikhail A. Bakunin, *The Political Philosophy of Bakunin: Scientific Anarchism* (G. P. Maximoff, ed., The Free Press of Glencoe, New York), passim pp. 283–301.

few should direct social life, and not only foment and stimulate but rule all movements of the people; and that on the morrow of the Revolution the new social organization should be set up not by the free integration of workers' associations, villages, communes, and regions from below upward, conforming to the needs and instincts of the people, but solely by the dictatorial power of this learned political and economic enslavement of the masses of people.

. . . It is upon this fiction of people's representation and upon the actual fact of the masses of people being ruled by a small handful of privileged individuals elected, or for that matter not even elected, by throngs herded together on election day and ever ignorant of why and whom they elect; it is upon this fictitious and abstract expression of the fancied general will and thought of the people, of which the living and real people have not the slightest conception—that the theory of the State and that of revolutionary dictatorship are based in equal measure.

Between revolutionary dictatorship and the State principle the difference is only in the external situation. In substance both are one and the same: the ruling of the majority by the minority in the name of the alleged stupidity of the first and the alleged superior intelligence of the second. Therefore both are equally reactionary, both having as their result the invariable consolidation of the political and economic privileges of the ruling minority and the political and economic enslavement of the masses of people.

The Workers' Social-Democratic Party and the General Association of German Workers founded by Lassalle are both Socialist organizations in the sense that they want a socialist reform in the relations between capital and labor. The Lassalleans, as well as the party of Eisenach, are unanimous on that point—that in order to obtain this reform, *it is necessary first to reform the State,* and that if this cannot be achieved in a peaceful manner, by means of extensive propaganda and a peaceful, legal labor movement, then force should be resorted to in order to bring about State reform— in other words, the change is to be effected through a political revolution.

According to the almost unanimous view of the German Socialists, *a political revolution should precede a social revolution,* which in my opinion is a great and fatal error, because every political revolution taking place prior to and consequently without a social revolution must necessarily be a bourgeois revolution, and a bourgeois revolution can only be instrumental in bringing about bourgeois Socialism—that is, it is bound to end in a new, more hypocritical and more skillful, but no less oppressive, exploitation of the proletariat by the bourgeoisie.

This unfortunate idea of a political revolution which, so the German Socialists say, is to precede the Social Revolution, opens wide the door of the Workers' Social-Democratic Party to all the exclusively political radical democrats of Germany who have very little Socialism in them. Thus it has happened that on several occasions the Workers' Social-Democratic Party was prevailed upon by its leaders—not by its own collective instinct, which is socialistic to a much greater degree than the ideas of its leaders—to fraternize with the bourgeois democrats of the People's Party (*Volkspartei*), an exclusively political party which is not only foreign but downright hostile to any serious Socialism.

Effect of the Great Principles Proclaimed by the French Revolution. From the time when the Revolution brought down to the masses its Gospel—not the mystic but the rational, not the heavenly but the earthly, not the divine but the human Gospel, the Gospel of the Rights of Man—ever since it proclaimed that all men are equal, that all men are entitled to liberty and equality, the masses of all European countries, of all the civilized world, awakening gradually from the sleep which had kept them in bondage ever since Christianity drugged them with its opium, began to ask themselves whether they too, had the right to equality, freedom, and humanity.

As soon as this question was posed, the people, guided by their admirable sound sense as well as by their instincts, realized that the first condition of their real emancipation, or of their *humanization*, was above all a radical change in their economic situation. The question of daily bread is to them justly the first question, for as it was noted by Aristotle, man, in order to think, in order to feel himself free, in order to become man, must be freed from the material cares of daily life. For that matter, the bourgeois, who are so vociferous in their outcries against the materialism of the people and who preach to the latter the abstinences of idealism, know it very well, for they themselves preach it only by word and not by example.

The second question arising before the people—that of leisure after work—is the indispensable condition of humanity. But bread and leisure can never be obtained apart from a radical transformation of existing society, and that explains why the Revolution, impelled by the implications of its own principles, gave birth to Socialism.

Socialism is Justice. . . . Socialism is *justice*. When we speak of justice, we understand thereby not the justice contained in the Codes and in Roman jurisprudence—which were based to a great extent upon facts of violence achieved by force, violence consecrated by time and by the benedictions of some church or other (Christian or pagan), and as such accepted as absolute principles, from which all law is to be deduced by a process of logical reasoning—no, we speak of that justice which is based solely upon human conscience, the justice to be found in the consciousness of every man—even in that of children—and which can be expressed in a single word: *equity*.

This universal justice which, owing to conquests by force and religious influences, has never yet prevailed in the political or juridical or economic worlds, would become the basis of the new world. Without it there can be neither liberty, nor republic, nor prosperity, nor peace. It then must govern our resolutions in order that we work effectively toward the establishment of peace. And this justice urges us to take upon ourselves the defense of the interests of the terribly maltreated people and demand their economic and social emancipation along with political freedom.

The Basic Principle of Socialism. We do not propose here, gentlemen, this or any other socialist system. What we demand now is the proclaiming anew of the great principle of the French Revolution: that *every human being should have the material and moral means to develop all his humanity*, a principle which, in our opinion, is to be translated into the following problem:

To organize society in such a manner that every individual, man or woman, should find, upon entering life, approximately equal means for the development of his or her diverse faculties and their utilization in his or her work. And to organize such a society that, rendering impossible the exploitation of anyone's labor, will enable every individual to enjoy the social wealth, which in reality is produced only by collective labor, but to enjoy it only in so far as he contributes directly toward the creation of that wealth.

State Socialism Rejected. The carrying out of this task will of course take centuries of development. But history has already brought it forth and henceforth we cannot ignore it without condemning ourselves to utter impotence. We hasten to add here that we vigorously reject any attempt at social organization which would not admit the fullest liberty of individuals and organizations, or which would require the setting up of any regimenting power whatever. In the name of freedom, which we recognize as the only foundation and the only creative principle of any organization, economic or political, we shall protest against anything even remotely resembling State Communism, or State Socialism.

Abolition of the Inheritance Law. The only thing which, in our opinion, the State can and should do, is first to modify little by little the inheritance law so as to arrive as soon as possible at its complete abolition. That law being purely a creation of the State, and one of the essential conditions of the very existence of the authoritarian and divine State, it can and should be abolished by freedom in the State. In other words, the State should dissolve itself into a society freely organized in accordance with the principles of justice. Inheritance right, in our opinion, should be abolished, for so long as it exists there will be hereditary economic inequality, not the natural inequality of individuals, but the artificial man-made inequality of classes—and the latter will always beget hereditary inequality in the development and shaping of minds, continuing to be the source and consecration of all political and social inequalities.

The task of justice is to establish equality for everyone, inasmuch as that equality will depend upon the economic and political organization of society—an equality with which everyone is going to begin his life, so that everyone, guided by his own nature, will be the product of his own efforts. In our opinion, the property of the deceased should accrue to a social fund for the instruction and education of children of both sexes, including their maintenance from birth until they come of age. As Slavs and as Russians, we shall add that with us the fundamental social idea, based upon the general and traditional instinct of our populations, is that land, the property of all the people, should be owned only by those who cultivate it with their own hands.

We are convinced, gentlemen, that this principle is just, that it is the essential and inevitable condition of all serious social reform, and that consequently Western Europe in turn will not fail to recognize and accept this principle, notwithstanding the difficulties of its realization in some countries, as in France, for instance, where the majority of peasants own the land which they cultivate, but where most of those very peasants will soon end up owning next to nothing, owing to the parceling out of land coming as the inevitable result of the political and economic system now prevailing in France. We shall, however, refrain from offering any proposals on the land question. . . . We shall confine ourselves now to proposing the following declaration:

The Declaration of Socialism. "Convinced that the serious realization of liberty, justice, and peace will be impossible so long as the vast majority of the population remains dispossessed of elementary needs, so long as it is deprived of education and is condemned to political and social insignificance and slavery—in fact if not by law—by poverty as well as by the necessity of working without rest or leisure, producing all the wealth upon which the world now prides itself, and receiving in return only such a small part thereof that it hardly suffices to assure its livelihood for the next day;

"Convinced that for all that mass of population, terribly maltreated for centuries, the problem of bread is the problem of mental emancipation, of freedom and humanity;

"Convinced that freedom without Socialism is privilege and injustice, and that Socialism without freedom is slavery and brutality;

"The League [for Peace and Freedom] loudly proclaims the necessity of a radical social and economic reconstruction, having for its aim the emancipation of people's labor from the yoke of capital and property owners, a reconstruction based upon strict justice—neither juridical nor theological nor metaphysical justice, but simply human justice—upon positive science and upon the widest freedom."

Organization of Productive Forces in Place of Political Power. It is necessary to abolish completely, both in principle and in fact, all that which is called political power; for, so long as political power exists, there will be ruler and ruled, masters and slaves, exploiters and exploited. Once abolished, political power should be replaced by an organization of productive forces and economic service.

Notwithstanding the enormous development of modern states—

a development which in its ultimate phase is quite logically reducing the State to an absurdity—it is becoming evident that the days of the State and the State principle are numbered. Already we can see approaching the full emancipation of the toiling masses and their free social organization, free from governmental intervention, formed by economic associations of the people and brushing aside all the old State frontiers and national distinctions, and having as its basis only productive labor, humanized labor, having one common interest in spite of its diversity.

The Ideal of the People. This ideal of course appears to the people as signifying first of all the end of want, the end of poverty, and the full satisfaction of all material needs by means of collective labor, equal and obligatory for all, and then, as the end of domination and the free organization of the people's lives in accordance with their needs—not from the top down, as we have it in the State, but from the bottom up, an organization formed by the people themselves, apart from all governments and parliaments, a free union of associations of agricultural and factory workers, of communes, regions, and nations, and finally, in the more remote future, the universal human brotherhood, triumphing above the ruins of all States.

The Program of a Free Society. Outside of the Mazzinian system, which is the system of the republic in the form of a State, there is no other system but that of the republic as a commune, the republic as a federation, a Socialist and a genuine people's republic —the system of Anarchism. It is the politics of the Social Revolution, which aims at the abolition of the State, and the economic, altogether free organization of the people, an organization from below upward, by means of a federation.

. . . There will be no possibility of the existence of a political government, for this government will be transformed into a simple administration of common affairs.

Our program can be summed up in a few words:

Peace, emancipation, and the happiness of the oppressed.

War upon all oppressors and all despoilers.

Full restitution to workers: all the capital, the factories, and all the instruments of work and raw materials to go to the associations, and the land to those who cultivate it with their own hands.

Liberty, justice, and fraternity in regard to all human beings born upon the earth.

Equality for all.

To all, with no distinction whatever, all the means of development, education and upbringing, and the equal possibility of living while working.

Organizing of a society by means of a free federation from below upward, of workers' associations, industrial as well as agricultural, scientific as well as literary associations—first into a commune, then a federation of communes into regions, of regions into nations, and of nations into an international fraternal association.

Correct Tactics During a Revolution. In a social revolution, which in everything is diametrically opposed to a political revolution, the actions of individuals hardly count at all, whereas the spontaneous action of the masses is everything. All that individuals can do is to clarify, propagate, and work out ideas corresponding to the popular instinct, and, what is more, to contribute their incessant efforts to revolutionary organization of the natural power of the masses—but nothing else beyond that; the rest can and should be done by the people themselves. Any other method would lead to political dictatorship, to the re-emergence of the State, of privileges, of inequalities, of all the oppressions of the State—that is, it would lead in a roundabout but logical way toward re-establishment of political, social, and economic slavery of the masses of people.

Varlin and all his friends, like all sincere Socialists, and in general like all workers born and brought up among the people, shared to a high degree this perfectly legitimate bias against the initiative coming from isolated individuals, against the domination exercised by superior individuals, and being above all consistent, they extended the same prejudice and distrust to their own persons.

Revolution by Decrees Is Doomed to Failure. Contrary to the ideas of the authoritarian Communists, altogether fallacious in my opinion, that the Social Revolution can be decreed and organized by means of a dictatorship or a Constituent Assembly—our friends, the Parisian Socialists, held the opinion that that revolution can be waged and brought to its full development only through the spontaneous and continued mass action of groups and associations of the people.

Our Parisian friends were a thousand times right. For, indeed, there is no mind, much as it may be endowed with the quality of a genius,—or if we speak of a collective dictatorship consisting of several hundred supremely endowed individuals—there is no combination of intellects so vast as to be able to embrace all the infinite multiplicity and diversity of the real interests, aspirations, wills, and needs constituting in their totality the collective will of the people; there is no intellect that can devise a social organization capable of satisfying each and all.

Such an organization would ever be a Procrustean bed into which violence, more or less sanctioned by the State, would force the unfortunate society. But it is this old system of organization based upon force that the Social Revolution should put an end to by giving full liberty to the masses, groups, communes, associations, and even individuals, and by destroying once and for all the historic cause of all violence—the very existence of the State, the fall of which will entail the destruction of all the iniquities of juridical right and all the falsehood of various cults, that right and those cults having ever been simply the complaisant consecration, ideal as well as real, of all violence represented, guaranteed, and authorized by the State.

It is evident that only when the State has ceased to exist humanity will obtain its freedom, and the true interests of society, of all groups, of all local organizations, and likewise of all the individuals forming such organization, will find their real satisfaction.

Free Organization to Follow Abolition of the State. Abolition of the State and the Church should be the first and indispensable condition of the real enfranchisement of society. It will be only after this that society can and should begin its own reorganization; that, however, should take place not from the top down, not according to an ideal plan mapped by a few sages or savants, and not by means of decrees issued by some dictatorial power or even by a National Assembly elected by universal suffrage. Such a system, as I have already said, inevitably would lead to the formation of a governmental aristocracy, that is, a class of persons which has nothing in common with the masses of people; and, to be sure, this class would again turn to exploiting and enthralling the masses under the pretext of common welfare or of the salvation of the State.

Freedom Must Go Hand-in-Hand with Equality. I am a convinced partisan of *economic and social equality*, for I know that outside of this equality, freedom, justice, human dignity, morality, and the well-being of individuals as well as the prosperity of nations are all nothing but so many falsehoods. But being at the same time a partisan of freedom—the first condition of humanity—I believe that equality should be established in the world by a spontaneous organization of labor and collective property, by the free organization of producers' associations into communes, and the free federation of communes—but nowise by means of the supreme and tutelary action of the State.

The Difference Between Authoritarian and Libertarian Revolutionists. It is this point which mainly divides the Socialists or revolutionary collectivists from the authoritarian Communists, the partisans of the absolute initiative of the State. The goal of both is the same: both parties want the creation of a new social order based exclusively upon collective labor, under economic conditions that are equal for all—that is, under conditions of collective ownership of the tools of production.

Only the Communists imagine that they can attain it through development and organization of the political power of the working classes, and chiefly of the city proletariat, aided by bourgeois radicalism—whereas the revolutionary Socialists, the enemies of all ambiguous alliances, believe, on the contrary, that this common goal can be attained not through the political but through the social (and therefore anti-political) organization and power of the working masses of the cities and villages, including all those who, though belonging by birth to the higher classes, have broken with their past of their own free will, and have openly joined the proletariat and accepted its program.

The Methods of the Communists and the Anarchists. Hence the two different methods. The Communists believe that it is necessary to organize the forces of the workers in order to take possession of the political might of the State. The revolutionary Socialists organize with the view of destroying, or if you prefer a more refined expression, of liquidating the State. The Communists are the partisans of the principle and practice of authority, while revolutionary Socialists place their faith only in freedom. Both are equally the partisans of science, which is to destroy superstition and take the place of faith; but the first want to impose science upon the people, while the revolutionary collectivists try to diffuse science and knowledge among the people, so that the various groups of human society, when convinced by propaganda, may organize and spontaneously combine into federations, in accordance with their natural tendencies and their real interests, but never according to a plan traced in advance and *imposed upon the ignorant masses* by a few "superior" minds.

Revolutionary Socialists believe that there is much more of practical reason and intelligence in the instinctive aspirations and real needs of the masses of people than in the profound minds of all these learned doctors and self-appointed tutors of humanity, who, having before them the sorry examples of so many abortive attempts to make humanity happy, still intend to keep on working in the same direction. But revolutionary Socialists believe, on the contrary, that humanity has permitted itself to be ruled for a long time, much too long, and that the source of its misfortunes lies not in this or any other form of government but in the principle and the very existence of the government, whatever its nature may be.

It is this difference of opinion, which already has become historic, that now exists between the scientific Communism, developed by the German school and partly accepted by American and English Socialists, and Proudhonism, extensively developed and pushed to its ultimate conclusions, and by now accepted by the proletariat of the Latin countries. Revolutionary Socialism has made its first brilliant and practical appearance in the Paris Commune.

On the Pan-German banner is written: *Retention and strengthening of the State at any cost.* On our banner, the social-revolutionary banner, on the contrary, are inscribed, in fiery and bloody letters: the destruction of all States, the annihilation of bourgeois civilization, free and spontaneous organization from below upward, by means of free associations, the organization of the unbridled rabble of toilers, of all emancipated humanity, and the creation of a new universally human world.

Before creating, or rather aiding the people to create, this new organization, it is necessary to achieve a victory. It is necessary to overthrow that which is, in order to be able to establish that which should be. . . .

Sorel's Introduction to Reflections on Violence

. . . For a long time I had been struck by the fact that the *normal development* of strikes is accompanied by an important series of acts of violence; but certain learned sociologists seek to disguise a

SOURCE: G. Sorel, *Reflections on Violence*, trans. T. E. Hulme and J. Roth (Collier Books, New York, 1961), passim pp. 57–178.

phenomenon that every one who cares to use his eyes must have noticed. Revolutionary syndicalism keeps alive in the minds of the masses the desire to strike, and only prospers when important strikes, accompanied by violence, take place. Socialism tends to appear more and more as a theory of revolutionary syndicalism— or rather as a philosophy of modern history, in as far as it is under the influence of this syndicalism. It follows from these incontestable data, that if we desire to discuss Socialism with any benefit, we must first of all investigate the functions of violence in actual social conditions.

I do not believe that this question has yet been approached with the care it admits of; I hope that these reflections will lead a few thinkers to examine the problems of proletarian violence more closely. I cannot too strongly recommend this investigation to the *new school* which, inspired by the principles of Marx rather than by the formulas taught by the official proprietors of Marxism, is about to give to Socialist doctrines a sense of reality and a gravity which it certainly has lacked for several years. Since the *new school* calls itself Marxist, syndicalist, revolutionary, it should have nothing so much at heart as the investigation of the exact historical significance of the spontaneous movements which are being produced in the working classes, movements which may possibly ensure that the future direction of social development will conform to Marx's ideas.

It seems to me that the problem of violence has been very badly formulated by many Socialists; as a proof of this, I instance an article published in the *Socialiste* on October 21, 1905, by Rappoport. The author, who has written a book on the philosophy of history, ought, it seems to me, to have discussed the question by examining the remoter consequences of these events; but, on the contrary, he considered them under their most immediate, most paltry, and, consequently, least historical aspect. According to him, syndicalism tends necessarily to opportunism, and as this law does not seem to be verified in France, he adds: "If in some Latin countries it assumes revolutionary attitudes, that is mere appearance. It shouts louder, but that is always for the purpose of demanding reforms inside the framework of existing society. It is a meliorism by blows, but it is always meliorism."

Thus there would be two kinds of meliorism: the one patronised by the *Musée Social*, the Direction du Travail, and Jaurès, which would work with the aid of maxims, half-lies and supplication to eternal justice; the other proceeds by blows—that latter being the only one that is within the scope of uneducated people who have not yet been enlightened by a knowledge of advanced social economics. These worthy people, democrats devoted to the cause of the Rights of man and the Duties of the informer, sociologist members of the Bloc, think that violence will disappear when popular education becomes more advanced; they recommend, then, a great increase in the numbers of courses and lectures; they hope to overturn revolutionary syndicalism by the breath of the professors. It is very strange that a revolutionary like Rappoport should agree with these worthy progressives and their acolytes in their estimate of the meaning of syndicalism; this can only be explained by admitting that even for the best-informed Socialists the problems of violence still remain very obscure.

To examine the effects of violence it is necessary to start from its distant consequences and not from its immediate results. We should not ask whether it is more or less directly advantageous for contemporary workmen than adroit diplomacy would be, but we should inquire what will result from the introduction of violence into the relations of the proletariat with society. We are not comparing two kinds of reformism, but we are endeavouring to find out what contemporary violence is in relation to the future social revolution.

Many will reproach me for not having given any information which might be useful for tactical purposes; no formulas, no recipes. . . .

Marx also was accused by the great lords of positivism of having, in *Capital*, treated economics metaphysically; they were astonished "that he had confined himself to a mere critical analysis of actual facts, instead of formulating receipts." This reproach does not seem to have moved him very much; moreover, in his preface to his book, he had warned the reader that he would not determine the social position of any particular country, and that he would confine himself to an investigation of the laws of capitalist production, "the tendencies working with iron necessity towards inevitable results."

One does not need a great knowledge of history to perceive that the mystery of historical development is only intelligible to men who are far removed from superficial disturbances; the chroniclers and the actors of the drama do not see at all, what, later on, will be regarded as fundamental; so that one might formulate this apparently paradoxical rule, "It is necessary to be outside in order to see the inside. . . ."

Sorel on the Proletarian Strike

. . . [Previously] I compared the general strike to the Napoleonic battle which definitely crushes an adversary; this comparison will help us to understand the part played by the general strike in the world of ideas.

Military writers of to-day, when discussing the new methods of war necessitated by the employment of troops infinitely more numerous than those of Napoleon, equipped with arms much more deadly than those of his time, do not for all that imagine that wars will be decided in any other way than that of the Napoleonic battle. The new tactics proposed must fit into the drama Napoleon had conceived; the detailed development of the combat will doubtless be quite different from what it used to be, but the end must always be the catastrophic defeat of the enemy. The methods of military instruction are intended to prepare the soldier for this great and terrible action, in which everybody must be ready to take part at the first signal. From the highest to the lowest, the members of a really solid army have always in mind this catastrophic issue of international conflicts.

The revolutionary Syndicates argue about Socialist action exactly in the same manner as military writers argue about war; they restrict the whole of Socialism to the general strike; they look upon every combination as one that should culminate in the catastrophe; they see in each strike a reduced facsimile, an essay, a preparation for the great final upheaval.

The *new school*, which calls itself Marxist, Syndicalist, and revolutionary, declared in favour of the idea of the general strike as soon as it became clearly conscious of the true sense of its own doctrine, of the consequences of its activity, and of its own originality. It was thus led to leave the old official, Utopian, and political tabernacles, which hold the general strike in horror, and to launch itself into the true current of the proletarian revolutionary movement; for a long time past the proletariat had made adherence to the principle of the general strike the *test* by means of which the

Socialism of the workers was distinguished from that of the amateur revolutionaries.

. . . revolutionary Syndicalism takes its stand, and endeavours . . . to leave nothing in a state of indecision; its ideas are honestly expressed, without trickery and without mental reservations; no attempt is made to dilute doctrines by a stream of confused commentaries. Syndicalism endeavours to employ methods of expression which throw a full light on things, which put them exactly in the place assigned to them by their nature, and which bring out the whole value of the forces in play. Oppositions, instead of being glozed over, must be thrown into sharp relief if we desire to obtain a clear idea of the Syndicalist movement; the groups which are struggling one against the other must be shown as separate and as compact as possible; in short, the movements of the revolted masses must be represented in such a way that the soul of the revolutionaries may receive a deep and lasting impression.

These results could not be produced in any very certain manner by the use of ordinary language; use must be made of a body of images which, *by intuition alone*, and before any considered analyses are made, is capable of evoking as an undivided whole the mass of sentiments which corresponds to the different manifestations of the war undertaken by Socialism against modern society. The Syndicalists solve this problem perfectly, by concentrating the whole of Socialism in the drama of the general strike; there is thus no longer any place for the reconciliation of contraries in the equivocations of the professors; everything is clearly mapped out, so that only one interpretation of Socialism is possible. This method has all the advantages which "integral" knowledge has over analysis, according to the doctrine of Bergson; and perhaps it would not be possible to cite another example which would so perfectly demonstrate the value of the famous professor's doctrines.

The possibility of the actual realization of the general strike has been much discussed; it has been stated that the Socialist war could not be decided in one single battle. To the people who think themselves cautious, practical, and scientific the difficulty of setting great masses of the proletariat in motion at the same moment seems prodigious; they have analysed the difficulties of detail which such an enormous struggle would present. It is the opinion of the Socialist-sociologists, as also of the politicians, that the general strike is a popular dream, characteristic of the beginnings of a working-class movement; we have had quoted against us the authority of Sidney Webb, who has decreed that the general strike is an illusion of youth, of which the English workers—whom the monopolists of sociology have so often presented to us as the depositaries of the true conception of the working-class movement —soon rid themselves.

That the general strike is not popular in contemporary England, is a poor argument to bring against the historical significance of the idea, for the English are distinguished by an extraordinary lack of understanding of the class war; their ideas have remained very much dominated by medieval influences: the guild, privileged, or at least protected by laws, still seems to them the ideal of working-class organisation; it is for England that the term *working-class aristocracy*, as a name for the trades unionists, was invented, and, as a matter of fact, trades unionism does pursue the acquisition of legal privileges. We might therefore say that the aversion felt by England for the general strike should be looked upon as strong presumptive evidence in favour of the latter by all those who look upon the class war as the essence of Socialism.

Moreover, Sidney Webb enjoys a reputation for competence which is very much exaggerated; all that can be put to his credit is that he has waded through uninteresting blue-books, and has had the patience to compose an extremely indigestible compilation on the history of trades unionism; he has a mind of the narrowest description, which could only impress people unaccustomed to reflection. Those who introduced his fame into France knew nothing at all about Socialism; and if he is really in the first rank of contemporary authors of economic history, as his translator affirms, it is because the intellectual level of these historians is rather low; moreover, many examples show us that it is possible to be a most illustrious professional historian and yet possess a mind something less than mediocre.

Neither do I attach any importance to the objections made to the general strike based on considerations of a practical order. The attempt to construct hypotheses about the nature of the struggles of the future and the means of suppressing capitalism, on the model furnished by history, is a return to the old methods of the Utopists. There is no process by which the future can be predicted scientifically, nor even one which enables us to discuss whether one hypothesis about it is better than another; it has been proved by too many memorable examples that the greatest men have committed prodigious errors in thus desiring to make predictions about even the least distant future.

And yet without leaving the present, without reasoning about this future, which seems for ever condemned to escape our reason, we should be unable to act at all. Experience shows that the *framing of a future, in some indeterminate time*, may, when it is done in a certain way, be very effective, and have very few inconveniences; this happens when the anticipations of the future take the form of those myths, which enclose with them all the strongest inclinations of a people, of a party or of a class, inclinations which recur to the mind with the insistence of instincts in all the circumstances of life; and which give an aspect of complete reality to the hopes of immediate action by which, more easily than by any other method, men can reform their desires, passions, and mental activity. We know, moreover, that these social myths in no way prevent a man profiting by the observations which he makes in the course of his life, and form no obstacle to the pursuit of his normal occupations.

. . . the general strike is . . . the *myth* in which Socialism is wholly comprised, *i.e.* a body of images capable of evoking instinctively all the sentiments which correspond to the different manifestations of the war undertaken by Socialism against modern society. Strikes have engendered in the proletariat the noblest, deepest, and most moving sentiments that they possess; the general strike groups them all in a co-ordinated picture, and, by bringing them together, gives to each one of them its maximum of intensity; appealing to their painful memories of particular conflicts, it colours with an intense life all the details of the composition presented to consciousness. We thus obtain that intuition of Socialism which language cannot give us with perfect clearness—and we obtain it as a whole, perceived instantaneously.

I have already called attention to the terrible nature of the revolution as conceived by Marx and the Syndicalists, and I have said that it is very important that its character of absolute and irrevocable transformation should be preserved, because it is that which gives Socialism its high educational value. The comfort-loving followers of our politicians could not view with any approval the profoundly serious work which is being carried on by the proletariat; the former desire to reassure the middle class, and promise not to allow the people to give themselves up entirely to their anarchical instincts. They explain to the middle class that they do not by any means dream of suppressing the great State machine, but wise Socialists desire two things: (1) to take possession of this machine so that they may improve its works, and make them run to further their friends' interests as much as possible, and (2) to assure the stability of the Government, which will be very advantageous for all business men. Tocqueville had observed that, since the beginning of the nineteeth century, the administrative institutions of France having changed very little, revolutions had no longer produced any very great upheavals. Socialist financiers have not read Tocqueville, but they understand instinctively that the preservation of a highly centralised, very authoritative and very democratic State puts immense resources at their disposal, and protects them from proletarian revolution. The transformations which their friends, the Parliamentary Socialists, may carry out will always be of a very limited scope, and it will always be possible, thanks to the State, to correct any imprudences they may commit.

The general strike of the Syndicalists drives away from Socialism all financiers in quest of adventures; the political strike rather pleases these gentlemen, because it would be carried out in circumstances favourable to the power of politicians, and consequently to the operations of their financial allies.

Marx supposes, exactly as the Syndicalists do, that the revolution will be absolute and irrevocable, because it will place the forces of production in the hands of *free men*, *i.e.* of men who will be capable of running the workshop created by capitalism without any need of masters. This conception would not at all suit the financiers and the politicians whom they support, for both are only fit to exercise the noble profession of masters. Therefore, the authors of all enquiries into *moderate Socialism* are forced to acknowledge that the latter implies the division of society into two groups: the first of these is a select body, organised as a political party, which has adopted the mission of thinking for the thoughtless masses, and which imagines that, because it allows the latter to enjoy the results of its superior enlightenment, it has done something admirable. The second is the whole body of the producers. The select body of politicians has no other profession than that of using its wits, and they find that it is strictly in accordance with the principles of immanent justice (of which they are sole owners) that the proletariat should work to feed them and furnish them with the means for an existence that only distantly resembles an ascetic's.

The study of the political strike leads us to a better understanding of a distinction we must always have in mind when we reflect on contemporary social questions. Sometimes the terms *force* and *violence* are used in speaking of acts of authority, sometimes in speaking of acts of revolt. It is obvious that the two cases give rise to very different consequences. I think it would be better to adopt a terminology which would give rise to no ambiguity, and that the term *violence* should be employed only for acts of revolt; we should say, therefore, that the object of force is to impose a certain social order in which the minority governs, while violence tends to the destruction of that order. The middle class have used force since the beginning of modern times, while the proletariat now reacts against the middle class and against the State by violence.

For a long time I was convinced that it is very important that the theory of social forces should be thoroughly investigated—in a large measure, the forces may be compared to those acting on matter; but I was not able to perceive the capital distinction in question here until I had come to consider the problem of the general strike. Moreover, I do not think that Marx had ever examined any other form of social constraints except force. In my *Saggi di critica del marxismo* I endeavoured, a few years ago, to sum up the arguments of Marx with respect to the adaptation of man to the conditions of capitalism, and I presented these arguments in the following manner, on pages 38–40:—

"(1) There is a social system which is to a certain extent mechanical, in which man seems subject to true *natural laws:* classical economists place at the beginning of things that automatism which is in reality the last product of the capitalistic régime. 'But the advance of capitalist production,' says Marx, 'develops a more and more numerous class of workers who, by education, tradition, and habit, look upon the conditions of that mode of production as self-evident laws of nature.' The intervention of an intelligent will in this mechanism would appear as an exception.

"(2) There is a régime of emulation and of keen competition

which impels men to set aside traditional obstacles, to seek constantly for what is new, and to imagine conditions of existence which seem to them to be better. According to Marx, it is in this revolutionary task that the middle class excelled.

"(3) There is a régime of violence, which plays an important part in history, and which assumes several distinct forms:

"(a) On the lowest level, we find a scattered kind of violence, which resembles the struggle for life, which acts through economic conditions, and which carries out a slow but sure expropriation; violence of this character works especially with the aid of fiscal arrangements.

"(b) Next comes the concentrated and organised force of the State, which acts directly on labour, 'to regulate wages,' i.e. force them within the limits suitable to surplus value making, to lengthen the working day, and to maintain the labourer himself in the normal degree of dependence; this is an essential element of the so-called primitive accumulation.

"(c) We have, finally, violence properly so called, which occupies so great a place in the history of primitive accumulation, and which constitutes the principal subject of history."

A few supplementary observations may be useful here.

We must first of all observe that these different phases are placed in a logical sequence, starting from states which most resemble an organism, and in which no independent will appears, and ending in states in which individual minds bring forward their considered plans; but the historical order is quite the contrary of this order.

At the origin of capitalist accumulation we find some very distinct historical facts, which appear each in its proper time, with its own characteristics, and under conditions so clearly marked that they are described in the chronicles. We find, for instance, the expropriation of the peasants and the suppression of the old legislation which had constituted "serfdom and the industrial hierarchy." Marx adds: "The history of this expropriation is not a matter of conjecture; it is inscribed in the annals of humanity in indelible letters of blood and fire."

Farther on Marx shows how the dawn of modern times was marked by the conquest of America, the enslavement of negroes and the colonial wars: "The different methods of primitive accumulation which the capitalist era brought about are divided in a more or less chronological order first of all [between] Portugal,

Spain, France and England, until the latter combined the lot, during the last thirty years of the seventeenth century, into a systematic whole, embracing simultaneously the colonial system, public credit, modern finance and the protectionist system. Some of these methods are backed by the employment of brute force; but all, without exception, exploit the power of the State, the concentrated and organised force of society, in order to precipitate violently the passage from the feudal economic order to the capitalist economic order, and to shorten the phases of the transition." It is on this occasion that he compared force to a midwife, and says that it multiplies the social movement.

Thus we see that economic forces are closely bound up with political power, and capitalism finally perfects itself to the point of being able to dispense with any direct appeal to the public force, except in very exceptional cases. "In the ordinary run of things, the worker can be left to the action of the *natural laws of production*, *i.e.* to his dependence on capital, a dependence springing from guaranteed, and perpetuated by the very mechanism of production."

When we reach the last historical stage, the action of independent wills disappears, and the whole of society resembles an organised body, working automatically; observers can then establish an economic science which appears to them as exact as the sciences of physical nature. The error of many economists consisted in their ignorance of the fact that this system, which seemed natural or primitive to them, is the result of a series of transformations which might not have taken place, and always remains a very unstable structure, for it could be destroyed by force, as it had been created by the intervention of force; moreover, contemporary economic literature is full of complaints respecting the intervention of the State, which has thereby upset *natural laws*.

Nowadays economists are little disposed to believe that these *natural laws* are in reality laws of Nature; they are well aware that the capitalist system was reached but slowly, but they consider that it was reached by a progress which should enchant the minds of all enlightened men. This progress, in fact, is demonstrated by three remarkable facts: it has become possible to set up a science of economics; laws can be stated in the simplest, surest, and most elegant formulas, since the law of contract dominates every country of advanced capitalism, the caprices of the rulers of the

State are no longer so apparent, and thus the path towards liberty is open. Any return to the past seems to them a crime against science, law, and human dignity.

Socialism looks upon this evolution as being a history of middle-class force, and it only sees differences of degree where the economists imagine that they are discovering differences of kind. Whether force manifests itself under the aspect of historical acts of coercion, or of fiscal oppression, or of conquest, or labour legislation, or whether it is wholly bound up with the economic system, it is always a middle-class force labouring with more or less skill to bring about the capitalist order of society.

The *new school* . . . cannot accept the idea that the historical mission of the proletariat is to imitate the middle class; it cannot conceive that a revolution as vast as that which would abolish capitalism could be attempted for a trifling and doubtful result, for a change of masters, for the satisfaction of theorists, politicians, and speculators—all worshippers and exploiters of the State. It does not wish to restrict itself to the formulas of Marx; although he gave no other theory than that of middle-class force, that, in his eyes, is no reason why it should confine itself to a scrupulous imitation of middle-class force.

In the course of his revolutionary career, Marx was not always happily inspired, and too often he followed inspirations which belong to the past; he even allowed from time to time a quantity of old rubbish which he found in the Utopists to creep into his writings. The *new school* does not in the least feel itself bound to admire the illusions, the faults, and the errors of the man who did so much to work out revolutionary ideas; it endeavours to separate what disfigures the work of Marx from what will immortalise his name; its attitude is thus the reverse of that of official Socialists, who admire especially in Marx that which is not Marxian. We shall therefore attach no importance whatever to the numerous extracts which may be quoted against us to prove that Marx often understood history as the politicians do.

We know now the reason for his attitude: he did not know the distinction, which appears to us nowadays so obvious, between middle-class force and proletarian violence, because he did not move in circles which had acquired a satisfactory notion of the general strike. We now possess sufficient material to enable us to understand the Syndicalist strike as thoroughly as we do the political strike; we know what differentiates the proletarian movement from the older middle-class movement; we find in the attitude of the revolutionaries towards the State a means of elucidating ideas which were still very confused in Marx's mind.

IV

Marxism

The ten points mentioned on pp. 19–20 of the Introduction summarize the main concepts of the ideology accepted by most of those who during the last hundred years or so have described themselves as Marxists. It must be added that Marxism as a movement (today, the world's most influential ideological and political movement), has been characterized essentially by the total acceptance of a set of ideas. In other words, integralism, which implicitly rejects the legitimacy of any other idea, has been a major feature of Marxism. Marxist integralism at the ideological level necessarily led to political authoritarianism at the level of political activities. Several practical consequences derive from integralism.

The border between Marxism and non-Marxism is represented not so much by the rejection of any major point of the ideology as by the abandonment of integralism. In the opinion of most Marxists, a Marxist ceases to be such when he accepts the legitimacy of a non-Marxist position, when he falls under the influence of liberalism, the Marxists' main ideological enemy; when, therefore, pluralism, criticism, and tolerance replace monism, dogmatism, and intolerance, and the principle of the equality of divergent ideological positions replaces the hierarchical inequality implicit in any integralism. Another consequence of integralism is that a Marxist school of thought rejects other Marxist schools of thought as vehemently as it rejects non-Marxist positions. This explains the hatred between Trotskyites and Stalinists a few decades ago, between Maoists and Soviet Marxists in the 1960's. None of the ten points mentioned in the Introduction concerns socialist organization and socialist policies. On the topic of the organization of a socialist party or, more important, of a socialist society, and on the topics of policies of parties and governments, equally convinced Marxists could hold different views. Differences being incompatible with integralism, Marxist parties in free societies underwent a continuous process of splits and mergers; and Marxist factions in a Marxist-controlled state were destroyed by the dominant faction. There is no more room for Maoist Marxism in the Soviet Union than there is for Lockeian empiricism, Hegelian idealism, or Comtian positivism (and their political manifestations).

Because Bukharin's and Preobrazhensky's *ABC of Communism* reflects Lenin's ideas, excerpts from this book are presented in Selection A.

According to Lenin, Bukharin, a much younger man, was the best interpreter of Marxism. Then come a few excerpts from Lenin's writings. It was Lenin who resurrected the term communism and introduced the distinction between socialism and communism conventionally accepted by all Marxists and many non-Marxists today. Three major versions of Marxism-Leninism are represented by excerpts from the works of Trotsky, Stalin, and Mao Tse-tung. No excerpts from the works describing the position of the "revisionist" Marxist-Leninist Tito have been included in this section. The reasons for this are explained in the introductions to Section VI and Selection A of the same section on Yugoslav nationalcommunism.

A. N. Bukharin and E. Preobrazhensky

In the twenties, *The ABC of Communism*, the book from which this selection's excerpts are taken, was a must for all Marxists and a test for all students in Soviet Russia (from 1922 on, the Soviet Union). Because the authors fell into disgrace when Stalin ruled the Soviet Union with an iron hand and led the world communist movement with firm determination, the book was shelved. It remains, however, the clearest and simplest exposé of what Lenin meant by Marxism. It was written in 1919 in order to explain the program approved at the Eighth Congress of the Communist Party of Soviet Russia. The program superseded the previous one of 1903, approved when the faction led by Lenin acquired the majority at the party congress. One-third of the book was devoted to a theoretical explanation of Marxist basic tenets as interpreted by Lenin. The rest was a comment on the party's new program. The excerpts are from Chapter 3 of Part I.

Of the two authors, by far the better known was Nikolai I. Bukharin (1888–1938), Lenin's disciple, thought by his teacher to be the foremost Marxist-Leninist ideologue. When Lenin became incapacitated in 1923, Bukharin was one of the top Communist leaders in a position to express views of their own. He had prestige but no organized following. During the succession struggle of 1924 to 1927 he vacillated between rather meaningless leftist, rightist, and centrist positions. He ended however by supporting Stalin. After his triumph, Stalin deprived Bukharin, always a potential rival, of any possibility of influencing the party leadership. Arrested during the purges of 1936 to 1938, Bukharin was executed in 1938. The other author, Evgeny A. Preobrazhensky (1886–1937), sided with Trotsky during the succession crisis. He was harassed by Stalin, and executed in 1937.

Communism and the Dictatorship of the Proletariat

Characteristics of the Communist System. Production under Communism. . . . The capitalist system . . . is now perishing under

source: N. Bukharin, and E. Preobrazhensky, *The ABC of Communism* (The University of Michigan Press, Ann Arbor, Michigan, 1966), passim pp. 69–84.

our very eyes. It is perishing because it is affected by two fundamental contradictions: on the one hand, anarchy of production,
leading to competition, crises, and wars; on the other hand, the
class character of society, owing to which one part of society
inevitably finds itself in mortal enmity with the other part (class
war). Capitalist society is like a badly constructed machine, in
which one part is continually interfering with the movements of
another. That is why it was inevitable that this machine would
break down sooner or later.

It is evident that the new society must be much more solidly
constructed than capitalism. As soon as the fundamental contradictions of capitalism have destroyed the capitalist system, upon the
ruins of that system there must arise a new society which will be
free from the contradictions of the old. That is to say, the communist method of production must present the following characteristics: In the first place it must be an *organised* society; it must
be free from anarchy of production, from competition between
individual entrepreneurs, from wars and crises. In the second place
it must be a *classless* society, not a society in which the two halves
are at eternal enmity one with the other; it must not be a society in
which one class exploits the other. Now a society in which there
are no classes, and in which production is organised, can only be *a
society of comrades, a communist society based upon labour.*

Let us examine this society more closely.

The basis of communist society must be the social ownership of
the means of production and exchange. Machinery, locomotives,
steamships, factory buildings, warehouses, grain elevators, mines,
telegraphs and telephones, the land, sheep, horses, and cattle, must
all be at the disposal of society. All these means of production must
be under the control of society as a whole, and not as at present
under the control of individual capitalists or capitalist combines.
What do we mean by "society as a whole"? We mean that
ownership and control is not the privilege of a class but of all the
persons who make up society. In these circumstances society will
be transformed into a huge working organization for cooperative
production. There will then be neither disintegration of production nor anarchy of production. In such a social order, production
will be organised. No longer will one enterprise compete with
another; the factories, workshops, mines, and other productive
institutions will all be subdivisions, as it were, of one vast people's
workshop, which will embrace the entire national economy of

production. It is obvious that so comprehensive an organisation presupposes a general plan of production. If all the factories and workshops together with the whole of agricultural production are combined to form an immense cooperative enterprise, it is obvious that everything must be precisely calculated. We must know in advance how much labour to assign to the various branches of industry; what products are required and how much of each it is necessary to produce; how and where machines must be provided. These and similar details must be thought out beforehand, with approximate accuracy at least; and the work must be guided in conformity with our calculations. This is how the organisation of communist production will be effected. Without a general plan, without a general directive system, and without careful calculation and book-keeping, there can be no organisation. But in the communist social order, there is such a plan.

Mere organisation does not, however, suffice. The essence of the matter lies in this, that the organisation shall be a cooperative organisation of *all* the members of society. The communist system, in addition to affecting organisation, is further distinguished by the fact that *it puts an end to exploitation*, that *it abolishes the division of society into classes*. We might conceive the organisation of production as being effected in the following manner: a small group of capitalists, a capitalist combine, controls everything; production has been organised, so that capitalist no longer competes with capitalist; conjointly they extract surplus value from the workers, who have been practically reduced to slavery. Here we have organisation, but we also have the exploitation of one class by another. Here there is a joint ownership of the means of production, but it is joint ownership by one class, an exploiting class. This is something very different from communism, although it is characterised by the organisation of production. Such an organisation of society would have removed only one of the fundamental contradictions, the anarchy of production. But it would have strengthened the other fundamental contradiction of capitalism, the division of society into two warring halves; the class war would be intensified. Such a society would be organised along one line only; on another line, that of class structure, it would still be rent asunder. Communist society does not merely organise production; in addition, it frees people from oppression by others. It is organised throughout.

The cooperative character of communist production is likewise displayed in every detail of organisation. Under communism, for example, there will not be permanent managers of factories, nor will there be persons who do one and the same kind of work throughout their lives. Under capitalism, if a man is a bootmaker, he spends his whole life in making boots (the cobbler sticks to his last); if he is a pastrycook, he spends all his life baking cakes; if he is the manager of a factory, he spends his days in issuing orders and in administrative work; if he is a mere labourer, his whole life is spent in obeying orders. Nothing of this sort happens in communist society. Under communism people receive a many-sided culture, and find themselves at home in various branches of production: to-day I work in an administrative capacity, I reckon up how many felt boots or how many French rolls must be produced during the following month; tomorrow I shall be working in a soap factory, next month perhaps in a steam laundry, and the month after in an electric power station. This will be possible when all the members of society have been suitably educated.

Distribution in the Communist System. The communist method of production presupposes in addition that production is not for the market, but for use. Under communism, it is no longer the individual manufacturer or the individual peasant who produces; the work of production is effected by the gigantic cooperative as a whole. In consequence of this change, we no longer have *commodities*, but only *products*. These products are not exchanged one for another; they are neither bought nor sold. They are simply stored in the communal warehouses, and are subsequently delivered to those who need them. In such conditions, money will no longer be required. "How can that be?" some of you will ask. "In that case one person will get too much and another too little. What sense is there in such a method of distribution?" The answer is as follows. At first, doubtless, and perhaps for twenty or thirty years, it will be necessary to have various regulations. Maybe certain products will only be supplied to those persons who have a special entry in their work-book or on their work-card. Subsequently, when communist society has been consolidated and fully developed, no such regulations will be needed. There will be an ample quantity of all products, our present wounds will long since have been healed, and everyone will be able to get just as much as he needs.

168   MARXISM

"But will not people find it to their interest to take more than they need?" Certainly not. To-day, for example, no one thinks it worth while when he wants one seat in a tram, to take three tickets and keep two places empty. It will be just the same in the case of all products. A person will take from the communal storehouse precisely as much as he needs, no more. No one will have any interest in taking more than he wants in order to sell the surplus to others, since all these others can satisfy their needs whenever they please. Money will then have no value. Our meaning is that at the outset, in the first days of communist society, products will probably be distributed in accordance with the amount of work done by the applicant; at a later stage, however, they will simply be supplied according to the needs of the comrades.

It has often been contended that in the future society everyone will have the right to the full product of his labour. "What you have made by your labour, that you will receive." This is false. It would never be possible to realise it fully. Why not? For this reason, that if everyone were to receive the full product of his labour, there would never be any possibility of developing, expanding, and improving production. Part of the work done must always be devoted to the development and improvement of production. If we had to consume and to use up everything we have produced, then we could never produce machines, for these cannot be eaten or worn. But it is obvious that the bettering of life will go hand in hand with the extension and improvement of machinery. It is plain that more and more machines must continually be produced. Now this implies that part of the labour which has been incorporated in the machines will not be returned to the person who has done the work. It implies that no one can ever receive the full product of his labour. But nothing of the kind is necessary. With the aid of good machinery, production will be so arranged that all needs will be satisfied.

To sum up, at the outset products will be distributed *in proportion to the work done* (which does not mean that the worker will receive "the full product of his labour"); subsequently, products will be distributed *according to need,* for there will be an abundance of everything.

Administration in the Communist System. In a communist society there will be no classes. But if there will be no classes, this implies that *in communist society there will likewise be no State.* . . . The State is a class organisation of the rulers. The State is always directed by one class against the other. A bourgeois State is directed against the proletariat, whereas a proletarian State is directed against the bourgeoisie. In the communist social order there are neither landlords, nor capitalists, nor wage workers; there are simply people—comrades. If there are no classes, then there is no class war, and there are no class organisations. Consequently the State has ceased to exist. Since there is no class war, the State has become superfluous. There is no one to be held in restraint, and there is no one to impose restraint.

But how, they will ask us, can this vast organisation be set in motion without any administration? Who is going to work out the plans for social production? Who will distribute labour power? Who is going to keep account of social income and expenditure? In a word, who is going to supervise the whole affair?

It is not difficult to answer these questions. The main direction will be entrusted to various kinds of book-keeping offices or statistical bureaux. There, from day to day, account will be kept of production and all its needs; there also it will be decided whither workers must be sent, whence they must be taken, and how much work there is to be done. And inasmuch as, from childhood onwards, all will have been accustomed to social labour, and since all will understand that this work is necessary and that life goes easier when everything is done according to a prearranged plan and when the social order is like a well-oiled machine, all will work in accordance with the indications of these statistical bureaux. There will be no need for special ministers of State, for police and prisons, for laws and decrees—nothing of the sort. Just as in an orchestra all the performers watch the conductor's baton and act accordingly, so here all will consult the statistical reports and will direct their work accordingly.

The State, therefore, has ceased to exist. There are no groups and there is no class standing above all other classes. Moreover, in these statistical bureaux one person will work today, another tomorrow. The bureaucracy, the permanent officialdom, will disappear. The State will die out.

Manifestly this will only happen in the fully developed and strongly established communist system, after the complete and definitive victory of the proletariat; nor will it follow immediately upon that victory. For a long time yet, the working class will have to fight against all its enemies, and in especial against the relics of the past, such as sloth, slackness, criminality, pride. All these will have to be stamped out. Two or three generations of persons will have to grow up under the new conditions before the need will pass for laws and punishments and for the use of repressive measures by the workers' State. Not until then will all the vestiges of the capitalist past disappear. Though in the intervening period the existence of the workers' State is indispensable, subsequently, in the fully developed communist system, when the vestiges of capitalism are extinct, the proletarian State authority will also pass away. The proletariat itself will become mingled with all the other strata of the population, for everyone will by degrees come to participate in the common labour. Within a few decades there will be quite a new world, with new people and new customs.

The Development of Productive Forces in the Communist System. (The Advantages of Communism.) As soon as victory has been achieved and as soon as all our wounds have been healed, the communist system will rapidly develop the forces of production. This more rapid development of the forces of production will be due to the following causes.

In the first place, there will have ensued the liberation of the vast quantity of human energy which is now absorbed in the class struggle. Just think how great is the waste of nervous energy, strength, and labour—upon the political struggle, upon strikes, revolts and their suppression, trials in the law-courts, police activities, the State authority, upon the daily effort of the two hostile classes. The class war now swallows up vast quantities of energy and material means. In the new system this energy will be liberated; people will no longer struggle one with another. The liberated energy will be devoted to the work of production.

Secondly, the energy and the material means which now are destroyed or wasted in competition, crises, and wars, will all be saved. If we consider how much is squandered upon wars alone, we shall realise that this amounts to an enormous quantity. How much, again, is lost to society through the struggle of sellers one with another, of buyers one with another, and of sellers with buyers. How much futile destruction results from commercial crises. How much needless outlay results from the disorganisation and confusion that prevail in production. All these energies, which now run to waste, will be saved in communist society.

Thirdly, the organisation of industry on a purposive plan will not merely save us from needless waste, in so far as large-scale production is always more economical. In addition, it will be possible to improve production from the technical side, for work will be conducted in very large factories and with the aid of perfected machinery. Under capitalism, there are definite limits to the introduction of new machinery. The capitalist only introduces new machinery when he cannot procure a sufficiency of cheap labour. If he can hire an abundance of cheap labour, the capitalist will never install new machinery, since he can secure ample profit without this trouble. The capitalist finds machinery requisite only when it reduces his expenses for highly paid labour. Under capitalism, however, labour is usually cheap. The bad conditions that prevail among the working class become a hindrance to the improvement of manufacturing technique. This causal sequence is peculiarly obvious in agriculture. Here labour power has always been cheap, and for that reason, the introduction of machinery in agricultural work has been extremely slow. In communist society, our concern will not be for profit but for the workers. There every technical advance will be immediately adopted. The chains which capitalism imposed will no longer exist. Technical advances will continue to take place under communism, for all will now enjoy a good education, and those who under capitalism perished from want—mentally gifted workers for instance—will be able to turn their capacities to full account.

In communist society parasitism will likewise disappear. There will be no place for the parasites who do nothing and who live at others' cost. That which in capitalist society is squandered by the capitalists in gluttony, drunkenness, and riotous living, will in communist society be devoted to the needs of production. The capitalists, their lackeys, and their hangers-on (priests, prostitutes, and the rest), will disappear, and all the members of society will be occupied in productive labour.

The communist method of production will signify an enormous development of productive forces. As a result, no worker in communist society will have to do as much work as of old. The working day will grow continually shorter, and people will be to an increasing extent freed from the chains imposed on them by nature. As soon as man is enabled to spend less time upon feeding and clothing himself, he will be able to devote more time to the work of mental development. Human culture will climb to heights never attained before. It will no longer be a class culture, but will become a genuinely human culture. Concurrently with the disappearance of man's tyranny over man, the tyranny of nature over man will likewise vanish. Men and women will for the first time be able to lead a life worthy of thinking beings instead of a life worthy of brute beasts.

The opponents of communism have always described it as a process of sharing things out equally. They declared that the communists wanted to confiscate everything and to divide everything up; to parcel out the land, to divide up the other means of production, and to share out also all the articles of consumption. Nothing could be more absurd than this notion. Above all, such a general division is impossible. We could share out land, horses and cattle, money, but could not share out railways, machinery, steamboats, and various other things of the sort. So much for that. Furthermore, such a division, as far as practicable, would not merely do no good to anyone, but would be a backward step for mankind. It would create a vast number of petty proprietors. . . . Out of petty proprietorship and the competition among petty proprietors there issues large-scale proprietorship. Thus even if it were possible to realise such an equal division, the same old cycle would be reproduced.

Proletarian communism (or proletarian socialism) is a huge cooperative commonwealth. It is a sequence of the whole development of capitalist society and of the condition of the proletariat in that society. It must be carefully distinguished from the four following things:

1. *Lumpenproletarian socialism* (*anarchism*). The anarchists reproach the communists on the ground that communism (so they contend) will maintain the State authority in the future society. As we have seen, the assertion is false. The essential difference consists in this, that the anarchists are far more concerned with dividing up than with the organisation of production; and that they conceive the organisation of production as taking the form, not of a huge cooperative commonwealth, but of a great number of "free," small, self-governing communes. It need hardly be said that such a social system would fail to liberate mankind from nature's yoke, for in it the forces of production would not be developed even to the degree to which they have been developed under capitalism. Anarchism would not increase production, but would disintegrate

it. It is natural that, in practice, the anarchists should advocate the dividing up of articles of consumption and should oppose the organisation of large-scale production. They do not, for the most part, represent the interests and aspirations of the working class; they represent those of what is termed the lumpenproletariat, the loafer-proletariat; they represent the interests of those who live in bad conditions under capitalism, but who are quite incapable of independent creative work.

2. *Petty-bourgeois socialism.* This finds its main supporters, not in the proletariat, but in the decaying class of independent artisans, among the lower middle-class townsfolk, and in part among the intelligentsia (professional classes). It protests against large-scale capital, but it does so in the name of the "freedom" of petty enterprise. For the most part the petty-bourgeois socialists advocate bourgeois democracy and oppose the social revolution; they hope to attain their ideals "peacefully"—through the development of cooperatives, a unified organisation of home workers, and so on. In Russia, most of the urban cooperatives formed by the social revolutionists exhibit this complexion. Under capitalism, cooperative enterprises are apt to degenerate into ordinary capitalistic organisations, and the cooperators can in this case hardly be distinguished from bourgeois.

3. *Agrarian peasant socialism.* This assumes various forms, and at times closely resembles peasant anarchism. Its most distinctive characteristic is the way in which it habitually fails to look upon socialism as a system of large-scale production, and the way in which it inclines towards dividing up and towards equalisation. Its main distinction from anarchism is that it demands the creation of a strong central authority which shall protect it, on the one hand from the landlords and on the other from the proletariat. In this form of socialism we have the "socialisation of the land" advocated by the social revolutionists, who desire to establish small-scale production in perpetuity, who dread the proletariat, and who oppose the formation of a great and united cooperative commonwealth. In addition, among certain strata of the peasantry, we find yet other varieties of socialism more or less akin to anarchism. Here the State authority is repudiated, but the advocates of these trends are distinguished by their pacifist views (various communistically inclined sectaries, such as the Dukhobors, etc.). The agrarian types of socialism will not be eradicated until after the lapse of a good

many years. They will disappear as soon as the masses of the peasantry come to realise the advantages of large-scale production. . . .

4. *Slaveholding and large-scale capitalistic socialism (so-called).* In this form we cannot discern so much as a trace of socialism. In the three varieties previously mentioned, we find at least some tincture of socialism, and we find in them a protest against oppression; but in the fourth variety, the one we are now considering, the "socialism" is a mere word, fraudulently employed by those who want a new shuffle of the cards. This variety was introduced by bourgeois intellectuals and was taken over from them by the socialist advocates of class collaboration (and in part by Kautsky & Co.). Of such a character, for example, was the communism of Plato, the philosopher of ancient Greece. The essential characteristic of his system was that the slaveholders' organisation would in "comradely" fashion and "jointly" exploit the mass of slaves—who were to have no legal rights. As far as the slave-owners were concerned there would be perfect equality and all things would be held in common. The case of the slaves was to be very different; they were to become mere cattle. Obviously this has nothing whatever to do with socialism. A similar sort of "socialism" has been advocated by certain bourgeois professors under the name of "State socialism." The only difference from Plato's variety is that contemporary proletarians have taken the place of slaves, while the capitalist magnates sit in the seats of the mighty in place of the slave-owners. Here, likewise, there is no trace of socialism. We have State capitalism, based upon forced labour. . . .

Petty-bourgeois, agrarian, and lumpenproletarian socialism have one characteristic common to them all. Such varieties of non-proletarian socialism are outside the general course of evolution. The course of social evolution leads to the expansion of production. But in these non-proletarian varieties the whole trend is towards small-scale production. Inevitably, therefore, socialism of this kind is nothing more than a utopian dream. There is no likelihood of its actual realisation.

The Dictatorship of the Proletariat. For the realisation of the communist system the proletariat must have all authority and all power in its hands. The proletariat cannot overthrow the old world unless it has power in its hands, unless for a time it becomes the ruling class. Manifestly the bourgeoisie will not abandon its position without a fight. For the bourgeoisie, communism signifies the loss of its former power, the loss of its "freedom" to extort blood and sweat from the workers; the loss of its right to rent, interest, and profit. Consequently the communist revolution of the proletariat, the communist transformation of society, is fiercely resisted by the exploiters. It follows that the principal task of the workers' government is to crush this opposition ruthlessly. Precisely because the opposition will inevitably be so embittered, it is necessary that the workers' authority, the proletarian rule, shall take the form of a dictatorship. Now "dictatorship" signifies very strict methods of government and a resolute crushing of enemies. It is obvious that in such a state of affairs there can be no talk of "freedom" for everyone. The dictatorship of the proletariat is incompatible with freedom for the bourgeoisie. This is the very reason why the dictatorship of the proletariat is needed: to deprive the bourgeoisie of freedom; to bind it hand and foot; to make it impossible for it to carry on a struggle against the revolutionary proletariat. The more vigorous the resistance of the bourgeoisie, the more desperate the mobilisation of its forces, the more threatening its attitude, the sterner and harsher must be the proletarian dictatorship. In extreme cases the workers' government must not hesitate to use the method of the terror. Only when the suppression of the exploiters is complete, when they have ceased to resist, when it is no longer in their power to injure the working class, will the proletarian dictatorship grow progressively milder. Meanwhile the bourgeoisie, little by little, will fuse with the proletariat; the workers' State will gradually die out; society as a whole will be transformed into a communist society in which there will be no classes.

Under the dictatorship of the proletariat (a temporary institution) the means of production will from the nature of the case belong, not to society as a whole, but only to the proletariat, to its State organisation. For the time being, the working class, that is the majority of the population, monopolises the means of production. Consequently there does not yet exist communist production in all its completeness. There still exists the division of society into classes; there is still a governing class (the proletariat); all the means of production are monopolised by this new governing class; there is still a State authority (the proletarian authority) which crushes its enemies. But as the resistance of the sometime capitalists, landlords, bankers, generals, and bishops, is crushed, in like measure the system of proletarian dictatorship will without any revolution undergo transformation into communism.

The dictatorship of the proletariat is not only an instrument for the crushing of enemies; it is likewise a lever for effecting economic transformation. Private ownership of the means of production must be replaced by social ownership; the bourgeoisie must be deprived of the means of production and exchange, must be "expropriated." Who will and can do this? Obviously no isolated individual could do it, even if he should be of proletarian origin. If it were done by an isolated individual or even by isolated groups of individuals, at the best it would be nothing more than a dividing up, and at the worst it would be a mere act of robbery. We understand, therefore, why the expropriation of the bourgeoisie must be effected by the *organised* power of the proletariat. Now this organised power takes the form of the dictatorial workers' state.

Objections to the dictatorship of the proletariat arise from various quarters. First of all come the *anarchists*. They say that they are in revolt against all authority and against every kind of State, whereas the communist bolsheviks are the sustainers of the Soviet Government. Every kind of government, they continue, involves the abuse of power and the limitation of freedom. For this reason it is necessary to overthrow the bolsheviks, the Soviet Government, the dictatorship of the proletariat. No dictatorship is necessary, no State is necessary. Such are the arguments of the anarchists. Only in appearance is their criticism revolutionary. In actual fact the anarchists do not stand more to the left, but more to the right than the bolsheviks. Why, indeed, do we need the dictatorship? We need it for the *organised* destruction of the bourgeois regime; we need it that we may crush the enemies of the proletariat *by force*. Quite openly we say, by force. The dictatorship is the axe in the hands of the proletariat. Anyone who is opposed to the dictatorship of the proletariat is one who is afraid of decisive action, is afraid of hurting the bourgeoisie, is no revolutionist. When we have completely vanquished the bourgeoisie, the need for the dictatorship of the proletariat will no longer exist. But as long as the life-and-death struggle continues it is absolutely incumbent upon the working class to crush its enemies utterly. AN EPOCH OF PROLETARIAN DICTATORSHIP MUST INEVITABLY INTERVENE BETWEEN A CAPITALIST AND A COMMUNIST SOCIETY.

Next, as objectors to the dictatorship, come the *social democrats*, and in especial the mensheviks. These worthies have completely forgotten what they wrote about the matter in former days. In our old program, drawn up by ourselves and the mensheviks together, it is expressly stated: "An essential condition of the social revolution is the dictatorship of the proletariat, that is to say the conquest of political power by the proletariat, which will enable the workers to crush all resistance on the part of the exploiters." The mensheviks signed this statement. But when the time came for action, they raised a clamour against the crushing of the freedom of the bourgeoisie, against the suppression of bourgeois newspapers, against the bolshevist "reign of terror," and so on. Even Plekhanoff, at one time, thoroughly approved of the most ruthless measures against the bourgeoisie, saying that we could deprive the bourgeois of their electoral rights, and so on. Nowadays the mensheviks have forgotten all this; they have taken refuge in the camp of the bourgeoisie.

Finally, a number of *moral* considerations are brought into the argument against us. We are told that we form our judgments like the savage Hottentots. The Hottentot says: "When I steal my neighbour's wife, it is good; when he steals my wife, it is bad." the bolsheviks, it is contended, resemble these savages, for they say: "When the bourgeoisie uses force to crush the proletariat, it is bad; but when the proletariat uses force to crush the bourgeoisie, it is good." Those who argue thus, do not know what they are talking about. In the case of the Hottentots we are concerned with two equal individuals who are stealing one another's wives for identical reasons. But the proletariat and the bourgeoisie are not on equal terms. Proletarians comprise an enormous class, bourgeois form a comparatively small group. The proletariat is fighting for the liberation of all mankind; but the bourgeoisie is fighting for the maintenance of oppression, wars, exploitation. The proletariat is fighting for communism, the bourgeoisie for the preservation of capitalism. If capitalism and communism were one and the same thing, then the bourgeoisie and the proletariat could be compared to the two Hottentots. The proletariat is fighting solely on behalf of the new social order. Whatever helps in the struggle is good; whatever hinders, is bad.

The Conquest of political Power. The proletariat makes its dictatorship actual through the conquest of the State power. But what do we mean by the conquest of power? Many persons imagine that it is quite an easy matter to wrest power from the bourgeoisie, as easy as to transfer a ball from one pocket to another. First, power is in the hands of the bourgeoisie; then the proletariat will drive the bourgeoisie from power and will take the reins into its own hands. According to this view, the problem is not the creation of a new power, but the seizure of a power that already exists.

Such a notion is utterly false, and a very little reflection will show us where the error lies.

The State power is an organisation. The bourgeois State power is a bourgeois organisation, and in that organisation people are assigned their roles in a distinctive manner. At the head of the army are generals, members of the wealthy class; at the head of the administration are ministers, members of the wealthy class; and so on. When the proletariat is fighting for power, against whom and what is it fighting? In the first place, against this bourgeois organisation. Now when it is fighting this organisation, its task is to deliver blows that will destroy the organisation. But since the main strength of the government resides in the army, if we wish to gain the victory over the bourgeoisie, the first essential is to disorganise and destroy the bourgeois army. The German communists could not overthrow the regime of Scheidemann and Noske unless they could destroy the army of White Guards. If the opposing army remain intact, the victory of the revolution will be impossible; if the revolution be victorious, the army of the bourgeoisie will disintegrate and crumble. This, for example, is why the victory over tsarism signified no more than a partial destruction of the tsarist State and a partial decomposition of the army; but the victory of the November revolution denoted the final overthrow of the State organisation of the Provisional Government and the total dissolution of the Kerenskyite army.

Thus the revolution destroys the old power and creates a new one, a different power from that which existed before. Of course

the new power takes over some of the constituent parts of the old,
but it uses them in a different way.

It follows that the conquest of State power is not the conquest
of the pre-existent organisation, but the creation of a new organisation, an organisation brought into being by the class which has
been victorious in the struggle.

The practical importance of this question is enormous. The
German bolsheviks, for example, have been reproached (as the
Russian bolsheviks were formerly reproached) on the ground that
they have led to disintegration in the army and have promoted
indiscipline, have encouraged disobedience to officers. This used to
be considered, and by many is still considered, a terrible charge.
But there is nothing terrible about it. We must promote disintegration in an army which is ranged against the workers and is at the
orders of the bourgeoisie, even though the latter consists of our
fellow-countrymen. Failing this, the revolution will succumb. Consequently, there is nothing to be afraid of in working for the
disintegration of such a bourgeois army; a revolutionist who destroys the State apparatus of the bourgeoisie may consider that he
is doing excellent service. Where bourgeois discipline remains
intact, the bourgeoisie is invincible. Those who wish to overthrow
the bourgeoisie must not shrink from hurting it.

B. Lenin, Architect of the Socialist State

Vladimir Ilyich Ulyanov (1870–1924), universally known as Lenin, has
left a deep mark on the twentieth century. He was a convinced
Marxist at the age of twenty. As a first-rank ideologue he clarified and
redefined, as mentioned on pp. 24–25 of the Introduction, a few basic
Marxist tenets. He also filled gaps in the Marxist ideological system,
particularly concerning the organization of a socialist party and a
socialist society; today most Marxists are Marxist-Leninists. He was
the strategist who led his faction of the Russian socialist movement (in
March, 1917, the smallest of the three major factions) to the conquest
of power in November, 1917. He was the statesman who reorganized a
Russia disrupted by six and a half years of wars and civil wars, creating
the totalitarian one-party state, the most successful political formula of
the twentieth century. He was the charismatic leader who inspired
intellectuals and nonintellectuals in all continents, and made of a small
Russian political sect a powerful world-wide movement. Other leaders
have come and gone; Lenin lives on.

Lenin was well-born. His father had achieved distinction as a civil servant. A tragedy may have been the turning point in Lenin's life: he was still in his teens when a beloved older brother, Alexander, was executed as a political conspirator. In high school and at the university Lenin read avidly. He had a vast store of knowledge in science, philosophy, history, economics. Politics was his major passion—not of course the politicians' politics, but the politics of a man with a mission. His mission was his duty, and he never doubted what his duty was. At the university he became acquainted with the writings of Plekhanov (1857–1918) and, through Plekhanov, of Marx and Engels. Marxism made sense to him. Unlike his brother Alexander and Plekhanov, he was never attracted by Narodnism, the well-meaning and vague ideology of the Russian Populists. Arrested, he was banished to Siberia. There he met his future wife, a woman nearly as remarkable as her husband. He was released, and went into exile in 1895. As a member of the Social Democratic Party, he cooperated with Plekhanov and a few others to start a new periodical in 1901, *Iskra* (or *Spark*). At the party congress of 1903, held abroad in Brussels and London with the participation of a few dozen delegates, Lenin presented the ideas on the organization of revolutionary activists that he had already put forth in one of his most important works, *What Is to Be Done?*, printed in 1902. At the congress, he unequivocally opposed the faction that stood for internal democracy, advocating instead rigidly centralized authority in the hands of the party leaders, discipline and obedience for the rank and file. The absence of some delegates gave Lenin's faction the majority in the congress. A few years later, that faction, the Bolsheviks, organized itself as a separate party. There had been no more than a couple of dozen Bolsheviks in 1903; by 1949, the Bolsheviks (Communists since 1918) ruled thirteen states including the two giants, the Soviet Union and China.

Before 1914, Lenin had been one of several leaders of the revolutionary wing of European Marxist socialism. During World War I he passionately advocated the transforming of the war into civil wars. He was writing his major work *The State and Revolution* when revolution broke out in Russia, in March, 1917. In April, German authorities helped him to reach Russia's capital, Petrograd (now Leningrad). Under his leadership, the Bolsheviks achieved control of the Petrograd Soviet. Through the Red Guard organized by his loyal collaborator Trotsky, he overthrew the provisional government in November. His first measures consolidated his dictatorship: establishment of a powerful secret police, censorship of the press, ejection of the freely elected Constituent Assembly in which Bolsheviks had held only one-quarter of the seats. In the summer of 1918 opposition to Bolshevik rule became civil war. Terror eliminated the opposition in the areas controlled by the Bolsheviks, Trotsky's Red Army defeated opponents on the battlefield. The failure of the wartime collectivist experiments led

Lenin to grant private enterprise a limited respite with the New Economic Policy of 1921. Incapacitated in 1923, Lenin died early in 1924.

Clear ideas gave direction to Lenin's action. Personality traits made his action effective: single-mindedness, forcefulness, total devotion to the cause he believed in, strong will, a capacity for combining rigidity of aims with tactical flexibility. Ever since, Leninists have tried to mold themselves on their leader. The two excerpts here are taken from the works mentioned above.

The Professional Revolutionary

. . . THE ORGANIZATION of a revolutionary Social-Democratic Party must inevitably *differ* from the organizations of the workers designed for the latter['s] struggle. A worker's organization must in the first place be a trade organization; secondly, it must be as wide as possible; and thirdly, it must be as public as conditions will allow. . . . On the other hand, the organizations of revolutionaries must consist first and foremost of people whose profession is that of a revolutionary (that is why I speak of organizations of *revolutionaries*, meaning revolutionary Social-Democrats). In view of this coming feature of the members of such an organization, *all distinctions as between workers and intellectuals*, and certainly distinctions of trade and profession, must be obliterated. Such an organization must of necessity be not too extensive and as secret as possible. . . .

A small, compact core, consisting of reliable, experienced and hardened workers, with responsible agents in the principal districts and connected by all the rules of strict secrecy with the organizations of revolutionaries, can, with the wide support of the masses and without an elaborate organization, perform *all* the functions of a trade union organization, and perform them, moreover, in the manner Social-Democrats desire. Only in this way can we secure the *consolidation* and development of a *Social-Democratic* trade union movement, in spite of the gendarmes.

It may be objected that an organization which is so loose that it is not even definitely formed, and which even has no enrolled and

SOURCE: N. (or V. I.) Lenin, *What Is to Be Done?* (*Selected Works*, International Publishers, New York), Vol. II, passim pp. 126–156.

registered members, cannot be called an organization at all. That may very well be. I am not out for names. But this "organization without members" can do everything that is required, and will, from the very outset, guarantee the closest contact between our future trade unions and socialism. Only an incorrigible utopian would want a *wide* organization of workers, with elections, reports, universal suffrage, etc., under the autocracy.

The moral to be drawn from this is a simple one. If we begin with the solid foundation of a strong organization of revolutionaries, we can guarantee the stability of the movement as a whole and carry out the aims of both Social-Democracy and of trade unionism. If, however, we begin with a wide workers' organization, supposed to be most "accessible" to the masses, when as a matter of fact it will be most accessible to the gendarmes and will make the revolutionaries most accessible to the police, we shall achieve the aims neither of Social-Democracy nor of trade unionism.

I assert: 1) that no movement can be durable without a stable organization of leaders to maintain continuity; 2) that the more widely the masses are spontaneously drawn into the struggle and form the basis of the movement and participate in it, the more necessary is it to have such an organization, and the more stable must it be (for it is much easier for demagogues to side-track the more backward sections of the masses); 3) that the organization must consist chiefly of persons engaged in revolutionary activities as a profession; 4) that in a country with an autocratic government, the more we *restrict* the membership of this organization to persons who are engaged in revolutionary activities as a profession and who have been professionally trained in the art of combating the political police, the more difficult will it be to catch the organization, and 5) the *wider* will be the circle of men and women of the working class or of other classes of society able to join the movement and perform active work in it.

I invite our Economists, terrorists and "Economists-terrorists" to confute these propositions. At the moment, I shall deal only with the last two points. The question as to whether it is easier to catch "a dozen wise men" or "a hundred fools" reduces itself to the question . . . whether it is possible to have a mass *organization* when the maintenance of strict secrecy is essential. We can never give a mass organization that degree of secrecy which is essential for the persistent and continuous struggle against the government. But to concentrate all secret functions in the hands of as small a number of professional revolutionaries as possible does not mean that the latter will "do the thinking for all" and that the crowd will not take an active part in the *movement*. On the contrary, the crowd will advance from its ranks increasing numbers of professional revolutionaries, for it will know that it is not enough for a few students and workingmen, waging economic war, to gather together and form a "committee," but that it takes years to train professional revolutionaries; the crowd will "think" not of primitive ways but of training professional revolutionaries. The centralization of the secret functions of the *organization* does not mean the centralization of all the functions of the *movement*. The active participation of the broad masses in the dissemination of illegal literature will not diminish because a dozen professional revolutionaries centralize the secret part of the work; on the contrary, it will *increase tenfold*. Only in this way will the reading of illegal literature, the contribution to illegal literature and to some extent even the distribution of illegal literature *almost cease to be secret work*, for the police will soon come to realize the folly and futility of setting the whole judicial and administrative machine into motion to intercept every copy of a publication that is being broadcast in thousands. This applies not only to the press, but to every function of the movement, even to demonstrations. The active and widespread participation of the masses will not suffer; on the contrary, it will benefit by the fact that a "dozen" experienced revolutionaries, no less professionally trained than the police, will centralize all the secret side of the work—prepare leaflets, work out approximate plans and appoint bodies of leaders for each urban district, for each factory district and for each educational institution, etc. . . . . The centralization of the more secret functions in an organization of revolutionaries will not diminish, but rather increase the extent and the quality of the activity of a large number of other organizations intended for wide membership and which, therefore, can be as loose and as public as possible, for example, trade unions, workers' circles for self-education and the reading of illegal literature, and socialist and also democratic circles for *all other sections of the population*, etc., etc. We must have *as large a number as possible* of such organizations having the widest possible variety of functions, but it is absurd and dangerous to *confuse these with organizations of revolutionaries,* to erase the line of demarcation between them, to dim still more the masses' already incredibly hazy appreciation of the fact that in order to "serve" the mass movement we must have people who will devote themselves exclusively to Social-Democratic activities, and that such people must *train* themselves patiently and steadfastly to be professional revolutionaries.

Aye, this appreciation has become incredibly dim. The most grievous sin we have committed in regard to organization is that *by our primitiveness we have lowered the prestige of revolutionaries in Russia.* A man who is weak and vacillating on theoretical questions, who has a narrow outlook, who makes excuses for his own slackness on the ground that the masses are awakening spontaneously, who resembles a trade union secretary more than a people's tribune, who is unable to conceive of a broad and bold plan, who is incapable of inspiring even his opponents with respect for himself, and who is inexperienced and clumsy in his own professional art—the art of combating the political police—such a man is not a revolutionary but a wretched amateur!

In order to be fully prepared for his task, the working class revolutionary must also become a professional revolutionary. Hence B——————v is wrong when he says that as the worker is engaged for eleven and a half hours a day in the factory, therefore, the brunt of all the other revolutionary functions (apart from agitation) "*must necessarily* fall mainly upon the shoulders of an extremely small intellectual force." It need not "necessarily" be so. It is so because we are backward, because we do not recognize our duty to assist every capable worker to become a *professional* agitator, organizer, propagandist, literature distributor, etc., etc. In this respect, we waste our strength in a positively shameful manner; we lack the ability to husband that which should be tended and reared with special care. Look at the Germans: they have a hundred times more forces than we have. But they understand perfectly well that the "average" does not too frequently promote really capable agitators, etc., from its ranks. Hence they immediately try to place every capable workingman in such conditions as will enable him to develop and apply his abilities to the utmost: he is made a professional agitator, he is encouraged to widen the field of his activity, to spread it from one factory to the whole of his trade, from one locality to the whole country. He acquires experience and dexterity in his profession, his outlook becomes wider, his knowledge increases, he observes the prominent political leaders from other localities and other parties, he strives to rise to their level and combine within himself the knowledge of working class environment and freshness of socialist convictions with professional skill, without which the proletariat *cannot* carry on a stubborn struggle with the excellently trained enemy. Only in this way can men of the stamp of Bebel and Auer be promoted from the ranks of the working class. But what takes place very largely automatically in a politically free country must in Russia be done deliberately and systematically by our organizations. A workingman agitator who is at all talented and "promising" *must not be left* to work eleven hours a day in a factory. We must arrange that he be maintained by the Party, that he may in due time go underground, that he change the place of his activity, otherwise he will not enlarge his experience, he will not widen his outlook, and will not be able to stay in the fight against the gendarmes for at least a few years. As the spontaneous rise of the working class masses becomes wider and deeper, they not only promote from their ranks an increasing number of talented agitators, but also of talented organizers, propagandists and "practical workers" in the best sense of the term (of whom there are so few among our intelligentsia who, in the majority of cases, are somewhat careless and sluggish in their habits, so characteristic of Russians). When we have detachments of specially trained working class revolutionaries who have gone through long years of preparation (and, of course, revolutionaries "of all arms"), no political police in the world will be able to contend against them, for these detachments of men absolutely devoted and loyal to the revolution will themselves enjoy the absolute confidence and devotion of the broad masses of the workers. The *sin* we commit is that we do not sufficiently "stimulate" the workers to take this path, "common" to them and to the "intellectuals," of professional revolutionary training, and that we too frequently drag them back by our silly speeches about what "can be understood" by the masses of the workers, by the "average workers," etc.

In this, as in other cases, the narrowness of our field of organizational work is without a doubt directly due (although the over-

whelming majority of the Economists and the novices in practical
work do not appreciate it) to the fact that we restrict our theories
and our political tasks to a narrow field. Subservience to spontaneity seems to inspire a fear of taking even one step away from
what "can be understood" by the masses, a fear of rising too high
above mere subservience to the immediate requirements of the
masses. Have no fear, gentlemen! Remember that we stand so low
on the plane of organization that the very idea that we could rise
too high is absurd!

There are many people among us who are so sensitive to the
"voice of life" that they fear it more than anything in the world
and accuse those who adhere to the views here expounded of
"Narodovolism," of failing to understand "democracy," etc. . . .

These accusations are called forth by a twofold misunderstand-
ing. First, the history of the revolutionary movement is so little
known among us that the very idea of a militant centralized
organization which declares a determined war upon tsarism is
described as Narodovolist. But the magnificent organization that
the revolutionaries had in the seventies, and which should serve us
all as a model, was not formed by the Narodovolists but by the
adherents of *Zemlya i Volya*, who split up into Chernoperedelists
and Narodovolists. Consequently, to regard a militant revolutionary organization as something specifically Narodovolist is absurd
both historically and logically, because no revolutionary tendency,
if it seriously thinks of fighting, can dispense with such an organization. But the mistake the Narodovolists committed was not that
they strove to recruit to their organization *all* the discontented, and
to hurl this organization into the decisive battle against the autocracy; on the contrary, that was their great historical merit. Their
mistake was that they relied on a theory which in substance was
not a revolutionary theory at all, and they either did not know
how, or circumstances did not permit them, to link up their
movement inseparably with the class struggle that went on within
developing capitalist society. And only a gross failure to understand Marxism (or an "understanding" of it in the spirit of Struve-
ism) could prompt the opinion that the rise of a mass, spontaneous
labor movement *relieves* us of the duty of creating as good an
organization of revolutionaries as *Zemlya i Volya* had in its time,

and even an incomparably better one. On the contrary, this movement *imposes* this duty upon us, because the spontaneous struggle of the proletariat will not become a genuine "class struggle" until it is led by a strong organization of revolutionaries.

Secondly, many . . . misunderstood the polemics that Social-Democrats have always waged against the "conspirative" view of the political struggle. We have always protested, and will, of course, continue to protest against *restricting* the political struggle to conspiracies. But this does not, of course, mean that we deny the need for a strong revolutionary organization. And in the pamphlet [The tasks of Russian Social-Democrats] . . . after the polemics against reducing the political struggle to a conspiracy, a description is given (as a Social-Democratic ideal) of an organization so strong as to be able to "resort to rebellion" and to "every other form of attack," in order to "deliver a smashing blow against absolutism." According to its *form* a strong revolutionary organization of that kind in an autocratic country may also be described as a "conspirative" organization, because the French word *"conspiration"* means in Russian "conspiracy," and we must have the utmost conspiracy for an organization of that kind. Secrecy is such a necessary condition for such an organization that all the other conditions (number and selection of members, functions, etc.) must all be subordinated to it. It would be extremely naive indeed, therefore, to fear the accusation that we Social-Democrats desire to create a conspirative organization. Such an accusation would be as flattering to every opponent of Economism as the accusation of being followers of Narodovolism would be.

Against us it will be argued: such a powerful and strictly secret organization, which concentrates in its hands all the threads of secret activities, an organization which of necessity must be a centralized organization, may too easily throw itself into a premature attack, may thoughtlessly intensify the movement before political discontent, the ferment and anger of the working class, etc., are sufficiently ripe for it. To this we reply: speaking abstractly, it cannot be denied, of course, that a militant organization *may* thoughtlessly commence a battle, which *may* end in defeat, which might have been avoided under other circumstances. But we cannot confine ourselves to abstract reasoning on such a question, because every battle bears within itself the abstract possibility of defeat, and there is no other way of *reducing this possibility* than by organized preparation for battle. If, however, we base our argument on the concrete conditions prevailing in Russia at the present time, we must come to the positive conclusion that a strong revolutionary organization is absolutely necessary precisely for the purpose of giving firmness to the movement, and of *safeguarding* it against the possibility of its making premature attacks. It is precisely at the present time, when no such organization exists yet, and when the revolutionary movement is rapidly and spontaneously growing, that we *already observe* two opposite extremes (which, as is to be expected, "meet"), *i.e.*, absolutely unsound Economism and the preaching of moderation, and equally unsound "excitative terror," which strives artificially to "call forth symptoms of its end in a movement which is developing and becoming strong, but which is as yet nearer to its beginning than to its end." . . . And the example of *Rabocheye Dyelo* shows that *there are already* Social-Democrats who give way to both these extremes. This is not surprising because, apart from other reasons, the "economic struggle against the employers and the government" *can never* satisfy revolutionaries, and because opposite extremes will always arise here and there. Only a centralized, militant organization that consistently carries out a Social-Democratic policy, that satisfies, so to speak, all revolutionary instincts and strivings, can safeguard the movement against making thoughtless attacks and prepare it for attacks that hold out the promise of success.

It will be further argued against us that the views on organization here expounded contradict the "principles of democracy." Now while the first-mentioned accusation was of purely Russian origin, this one is of *purely foreign* origin. And only an organization abroad (the League of Russian Social-Democrats) would be capable of giving its editorial board instructions like the following:

> *Principles of Organization.* In order to secure the successful development and unification of Social-Democracy, broad democratic principles of Party organization must be emphasized, developed and fought for; and this is particularly necessary in view of the anti-democratic tendencies that have become revealed in the ranks of our Party. (*Two Congresses.*)

. . . We shall examine more closely the "principle" that the Economists advance. Everyone will probably agree that "broad democratic principles" presuppose the two following conditions:

first, full publicity, and second, election to all functions. It would be absurd to speak about democracy without publicity, that is, a publicity that extends beyond the circle of the membership of the organization. We call the German Socialist Party a democratic organization because all it does is done publicly; even its Party congresses are held in public. But no one would call an organization that is hidden from every one but its members by a veil of secrecy, a democratic organization. What is the use of advancing "*broad* democratic principles" when the fundamental condition for these principles *cannot be fulfilled* by a secret organization? "Broad principles" turns out to be a resonant but hollow phrase. More than that, this phrase proves that the urgent tasks in regard to organization are totally misunderstood. Everyone knows how great is the lack of secrecy among the "broad" masses of revolutionaries. We have heard the bitter complaints of B———v on this score, and his absolutely just demand for a "strict selection of members." (*Rabocheye Dyelo*, No. 6.) And people who boast about their "sensitiveness to life" come forward in a situation like this, and *urge*, not strict secrecy and a strict (and therefore more restricted) selection of members but "*broad* democratic principles"! This is what we call being absolutely wide of the mark.

Nor is the situation with regard to the second attribute of democracy, namely, the principle of election, any better. In politically free countries, this condition is taken for granted. "Membership of the Party is open to those who accept the principles of the Party program, and render all the support they can to the Party"— says point 1 of the rules of the German Social-Democratic Party. And as the political arena is as open to the public view as is the stage in a theatre, this acceptance or non-acceptance, support or opposition, is known to all from the press and public meetings. Everyone knows that a certain political worker commenced in a certain way, passed through a certain evolution, behaved in difficult periods in a certain way and possesses certain qualities and, consequently, knowing all the facts of the case, *every* Party member can decide for himself whether or not to elect this person for a certain Party office. The general control (in the literal sense of the term) that the Party exercises over every act this person commits in the political field brings into existence an automatically operating mechanism which brings about what in biology is called "survival of the fittest." "Natural selection" of full publicity, the principle of election and general control provide the guarantee that, in the last analysis, every political worker will be "in his proper place," will do the work for which he is best fitted by his strength and abilities, will feel the effects of his mistakes on himself, and prove before all the world his ability to recognize mistakes and to avoid them.

Try to put this picture in the frame of our autocracy! Is it possible in Russia for all those "who accept the principles of the Party program and render all the support they can to the Party" to control every action of the revolutionary working in secret? Is it possible for all the revolutionaries to elect one of their number to any particular office, when, in the very interests of the work, he *must* conceal his identity from nine out of ten of these "all"? Ponder a little over the real meaning of the high-sounding phrases that *Rabocheye Dyelo* gives utterance to, and you will realize that "broad democracy" in Party organization, amidst the gloom of autocracy and the domination of gendarme selection, is nothing more than a *useless and harmful toy*. It is a useless toy because, as a matter of fact, no revolutionary organization has ever practiced *broad* democracy, nor could it, however much it desired to do so. It is a harmful toy because any attempt to practice the "broad democratic principles" will simply facilitate the work of the police in making big raids, it will perpetuate the prevailing primitiveness, divert the thoughts of the practical workers from the serious and imperative task of training themselves to become professional revolutionaries to that of drawing up detailed "paper" rules for election systems. Only abroad, where very often people who have no opportunity of doing real live work gather together, can the "game of democracy" be played here and there, especially in small groups.

. . . The only serious organizational principle the active workers of our movement can accept is strict secrecy, strict selection of members and the training of professional revolutionaries. If we possessed these qualities, something even more than "democracy" would be guaranteed to us, namely, complete, comradely, mutual confidence among revolutionaries. And this is absolutely essential for us because in Russia it is useless thinking that democratic control can serve as a substitute for it. It would be a great mistake to believe that because it is impossible to establish real "democratic" control, the members of the revolutionary organization will remain altogether uncontrolled. They have not the time to think about the toy forms of democracy (democracy within a close and compact body of comrades in which complete, mutual confidence prevails), but they have a lively sense of their *responsibility*, because they know from experience that an organization of real revolutionaries will stop at nothing to rid itself of an undesirable member.

On Transition to the Higher Form of Communism

Marx continues:

> Between capitalist and communist society lies the period of the revolutionary transformation of the one into the other. There corresponds to this also a political transition period in which the state can be nothing but *the revolutionary dictatorship of the proletariat.*

Marx bases this conclusion on an analysis of the role played by the proletariat in modern capitalist society, on the data concerning the development of this society, and on the irreconcilability of the antagonistic interests of the proletariat and the bourgeoisie.

Earlier the question was put in this way: in order to achieve its emancipation, the proletariat must overthrow the bourgeoisie, conquer political power and establish its own revolutionary dictatorship.

Now the question is put somewhat differently: the transition from capitalist society—which is developing towards communism —to a communist society is impossible without a "political transition period," and the state in this period can only be the revolutionary dictatorship of the proletariat.

What, then, is the relation of this dictatorship to democracy?

. . . *The Communist Manifesto* simply places the two ideas side by side: "to raise the proletariat to the position of the ruling class" and "to win the battle of democracy." On the basis of all that has been said above, it is possible to determine more precisely how democracy changes in the transition from capitalism to communism.

In capitalist society, under the conditions most favorable to its development, we have more or less complete democracy in the democratic republic. But this democracy is always restricted by the narrow framework of capitalist exploitation, and consequently

SOURCE: N. (or V. I.) Lenin, *The State and Revolution* (in H. M. Christman, ed., *Essential Works of Lenin,* Bantam Books, New York, 1966), pp. 335–340 and 346–349.

always remains, in reality, a democracy for the minority, only for the possessing classes, only for the rich. Freedom in capitalist society always remains about the same as it was in the ancient Greek republics: freedom for the slave-owners. Owing to the conditions of capitalist exploitation the modern wage-slaves are also so crushed by want and poverty that "they cannot be bothered with democracy," "they cannot be bothered with politics"; in the ordinary peaceful course of events the majority of the population is debarred from participating in social and political life.

The correctness of this statement is perhaps most clearly proved by Germany, precisely because in that country constitutional legality lasted and remained stable for a remarkably long time—for nearly half a century (1871–1914)—and because during this period Social-Democracy was able to achieve far more in Germany than in other countries in the way of "utilizing legality," and was able to organize a larger proportion of the working class into a political party than anywhere else in the world.

What is this largest proportion of politically conscious and active wage-slaves that has so far been observed in capitalist society? One million members of the Social-Democratic Party—out of fifteen million wage-workers! Three million organized in trade unions—out of fifteen million!

Democracy for an insignificant minority, democracy for the rich—that is the democracy of capitalist society. If we look more closely into the mechanism of capitalist democracy, everywhere, in the "petty"—so-called petty—details of the suffrage (residential qualification, exclusion of women, etc.), and in the technique of the representative institutions, in the actual obstacles to the right of assembly (public buildings are not for "beggars"!), in the purely capitalist organization of the daily press, etc. etc.—on all sides we see restriction after restriction upon democracy. These restrictions, exceptions, exclusions, obstacles for the poor, seem slight, especially in the eyes of one who has never known want himself and has never been in close contact with the oppressed classes in their mass life (and nine-tenths, if not ninety-nine hundredths, of the bourgeois publicists and politicians are of this category); but in their sum total these restrictions exclude and squeeze out the poor from politics, from taking an active part in democracy.

Marx grasped this *essence* of capitalist democracy splendidly, when, in analyzing the experience of the Commune, he said that the oppressed were allowed, once every few years, to decide which particular representatives of the oppressing class should misrepresent them in parliament!

But from this capitalist democracy—inevitably narrow, tacitly repelling the poor, and therefore hypocritical and false to the core—development does not proceed simply, smoothly and directly to "greater and greater democracy," as the liberal professors and petty-bourgeois opportunists would have us believe. No, development—towards communism—proceeds through the dictatorship of the proletariat; it cannot do otherwise, for the *resistance* of the capitalist exploiters cannot be *broken* by anyone else or in any other way.

But the dictatorship of the proletariat, *i.e.*, the organization of the vanguard of the oppressed as the ruling class for the purpose of crushing the oppressors, cannot result merely in an expansion of democracy. *Simultaneously* with an immense expansion of democracy which *for the first time* becomes democracy for the poor, democracy for the people, and not democracy for the rich, the dictatorship of the proletariat imposes a series of restrictions on the freedom of the oppressors, the exploiters, the capitalists. We must crush them in order to free humanity from wage-slavery; their resistance must be broken by force; it is clear that where there is suppression there is also violence, there is no freedom, no democracy.

Engels expressed this splendidly in his letter to Bebel when he said, as the reader will remember, that

> so long as the proletariat still *uses* the state it does not use it in the interests of freedom but in order to hold down its adversaries, and as soon as it becomes possible to speak of freedom the state as such ceases to exist.

Democracy for the vast majority of the people, and suppression by force, *i.e.*, exclusion from democracy, of the exploiters and oppressors of the people—this is the change democracy undergoes during the transition from capitalism to communism.

Only in communist society, when the resistance of the capitalists has been completely broken, when the capitalists have disappeared, when there are no classes (*i.e.* when there is no difference between the members of society as regards their relation to the social means of production), *only then* does "the state . . . cease to exist," and it *"becomes possible to speak of freedom."* Only then will really complete democracy, democracy without any exceptions, be possible and be realized. And only then will democracy itself begin to *wither away* owing to the simple fact that, freed from capitalist slavery, from the untold horrors, savagery, absurdities and infamies of capitalist exploitation, people will gradually *become accustomed* to observing the elementary rules of social life that have been known for centuries and repeated for thousands of years in all copy-book maxims; they will become accustomed to observing them without force, without compulsion, without subordination, without the *special apparatus* for compulsion which is called the state.

The expression "the state *withers away*" is very well chosen, for it indicates both the gradual and the spontaneous nature of the process. Only habit can, and undoubtedly will, have such an effect; for we see around us millions of times how readily people become accustomed to observing the necessary rules of social life if there is no exploitation, if there is nothing that causes indignation, that calls forth protest and revolt and has to be *suppressed*.

Thus, in capitalist society we have a democracy that is curtailed, wretched, false; a democracy only for the rich, for the minority. The dictatorship of the proletariat, the period of transition to communism, will, for the first time, create democracy for the people, for the majority, in addition to the necessary suppression of the minority—the exploiters. Communism alone is capable of giving really complete democracy, and the more complete it is the more quickly will it become unnecessary and wither away of itself.

In other words: under capitalism we have a state in the proper sense of the word, that is, a special machine for the suppression of one class by another, and of the majority by the minority at that. Naturally, the successful discharge of such a task as the systematic suppression of the exploited majority by the exploiting minority calls for the greatest ferocity and savagery in the work of suppression, it calls for seas of blood through which mankind has to wade in slavery, serfdom and wage-labor.

Furthermore, during the *transition* from capitalism to communism, suppression is *still* necessary; but it is the suppression of the exploiting minority by the exploited majority. A special apparatus, a special machine for suppression, the "state," is *still* necessary, but this is now a transitory state; it is no longer a state in the proper sense; for the suppression of the minority of exploiters by the majority of the wage-slaves *of yesterday* is comparatively so easy, simple and natural a task that it will entail far less bloodshed than the suppression of the risings of slaves, serfs or wage-laborers, and it will cost mankind far less. This is compatible with the diffusion of democracy among such an overwhelming majority of the population that the need for a *special machine* of suppression will begin to disappear. The exploiters are, naturally, unable to suppress the people without a very complex machine for performing this task; but *the people* can suppress the exploiters with a very simple "machine," almost without a "machine," without a special apparatus, by the simple *organization of the armed masses* (such as the Soviets of Workers' and Soldiers' Deputies, we may remark, running ahead a little).

Finally, only communism makes the state absolutely unnecessary, for there is *no one* to be suppressed—"no one" in the sense of a *class*, in the sense of a systematic struggle against a definite section of the population. We are not utopians, and we do not in the least deny the possibility and inevitability of excesses on the part of *individual persons*, or the need to suppress *such* excesses. But, in the first place, no special machine, no special apparatus of repression is needed for this: this will be done by the armed people itself, as simply and as readily as any crowd of civilized people, even in modern society, parts two people who are fighting, or interferes to prevent a woman from being assaulted. And, secondly, we know that the fundamental social cause of excesses, which consist in violating the rules of social life, is the exploitation of the masses, their want and their poverty. With the removal of this chief cause, excesses will inevitably begin to *"wither away."* We do not know how quickly and in what order, but we know that they will wither away. With their withering away, the state will also *wither away*.

. . . the scientific difference between socialism and communism is clear. What is generally called socialism was termed by Marx the "first" or lower phase of communist society. In so far as the means of production become *common* property, the word "communism" is also applicable here, providing we do not forget that it is *not* complete communism. The great significance of Marx's explanation lies in that here, too, he consistently applies materialist dialectics, the theory of development, and regards communism as something which develops *out* of capitalism. Instead of scholastically invented, "concocted" definitions and fruitless disputes about words (what is socialism? what is communism?), Marx gives an analysis of what may be called stages in the economic ripeness of communism.

In its first phase, or first stage, communism *cannot* as yet be economically ripe and entirely free from all the traditions and all traces of capitalism. Hence the interesting phenomenon that communism in its first phase retains "the narrow horizon of *bourgeois right.*" Of course, bourgeois right in regard to distribution of articles of *consumption* inevitably presupposes the existence of the *bourgeois state*, for right is nothing without an apparatus capable of *enforcing* the observance of the standards of right.

Consequently, for a certain time not only bourgeois right, but even the bourgeois state remains under communism, without the bourgeoisie!

This may sound like a paradox or simply a dialectical puzzle which Marxism is often accused of inventing by people who would not take the slightest trouble to study its extraordinarily profound content.

As a matter of fact, however, the remnants of the old surviving in the new confront us in life at every step, in nature as well as in society. Marx did not smuggle a scrap of "bourgeois" right into communism of his own accord; he indicated what is economically and politically inevitable in the society which is emerging *from the womb* of capitalism.

Democracy is of great importance for the working class in its struggle for freedom against the capitalists. But democracy is by no means a boundary that must not be overstepped; it is only one of the stages in the process of development from feudalism to capitalism, and from capitalism to communism.

Democracy means equality. The great significance of the proletariat's struggle for equality and the significance of equality as a slogan will be clear if we correctly interpret it as meaning the abolition of *classes*. But democracy means only *formal* equality. As soon as equality is obtained for all members of society *in relation to* the ownership of the means of production, that is, equality of labor and equality of wages, humanity will inevitably be confronted with the question of going beyond formal equality to real equality, *i.e.*, to applying the rule, "from each according to his ability, to each according to his needs." By what stages, by what practical measures humanity will proceed to this higher aim—we do not and cannot know. But it is important to realize how infinitely mendacious is the ordinary bourgeois conception of socialism as something lifeless, petrified, fixed once for all, whereas in reality *only* under socialism will a rapid, genuine, really mass movement, embracing first the *majority* and then the whole of the population, commence in all spheres of social and individual life.

Democracy is a form of state, one of its varieties. Consequently, like every state, it, on the one hand, represents the organized, systematic application of force against persons; but, on the other hand, it signifies the formal recognition of the equality of all citizens, the equal right of all to determine the structure and administration of the state. This, in turn, is connected with the fact that, at a certain stage in the development of democracy, it first rallies the proletariat as a revolutionary class against capitalism, and gives it the opportunity to crush, to smash to atoms, to wipe off the face of the earth the bourgeois, even the republican bourgeois, state machine, the standing army, the police and bureaucracy; to substitute for all this a *more* democratic, but still a state machine in the shape of the armed masses of workers who become transformed into a universal people's militia.

Here "quantity is transformed into quality": *such* a degree of democracy is connected with overstepping the boundaries of bourgeois society, with the beginning of its socialist reconstruction. If, indeed, *all* take part in the administration of the state, capitalism cannot retain its hold. The development of capitalism, in turn, itself creates the *prerequisites* that *enable* indeed "all" to take part in the administration of the state. Some of these prerequisites are: universal literacy, already achieved in most of the advanced capitalist countries, then the "training and disciplining" of millions of workers by the huge, complex and socialized apparatus of the post-office, the railways, the big factories, large-scale commerce, banking, etc. etc.

With such *economic* prerequisites it is quite possible, immediately, overnight, after the overthrow of the capitalists and bureaucrats, to supersede them in the *control* of production and distribution, in the work of *keeping account* of labor and its products by the armed workers, by the whole of the armed population. (The question of control and accounting must not be confused with the question of the scientifically educated staff of engineers, agronomists and so on. These gentlemen are working today and obey the capitalists; they will work even better tomorrow and obey the armed workers.)

Accounting and control—these are the *principal* things that are necessary for the "setting up" and correct functioning of the *first phase* of communist society. *All* citizens are transformed into the salaried employees of the state, which consists of the armed workers. *All* citizens become employees and workers of a *single* national state "syndicate." All that is required is that they should work equally—do their proper share of work—and get paid equally. The accounting and control necessary for this have been so utterly *simplified* by capitalism that they have become the extraordinarily simple operations of checking, recording and issuing receipts, which anyone who can read and write and who knows the first four rules of arithmetic can perform.

When the *majority* of the people themselves begin everywhere to keep such accounts and maintain such control over the capitalists (now converted into employees) and over the intellectual gentry, who preserve their capitalist habits, this control will really become universal, general, national; and there will be no way of getting away from it, there will be "nowhere to go."

The whole of society will have become a single office and a single factory with equality of work and equality of pay.

But this "factory" discipline, which the proletariat will extend to the whole of society after the defeat of the capitalists and the overthrow of the exploiters, is by no means our ideal, or our ultimate goal. It is but a necessary *step* for the purpose of thoroughly purging society of all the hideousness and foulness of capitalist exploitation, *and for the purpose of advancing further*.

From the moment all members of society, or even only the overwhelming majority, have learned to administer the state *themselves*, have taken this business into their own hands, have "set up" control over the insignificant minority of capitalists, over the gentry, who wish to preserve their capitalist habits, and over the workers who have been completely demoralized by capitalism—from this moment the need for government begins to disappear. The more complete democracy becomes, the nearer the moment approaches when it becomes unnecessary. The more democratic the "state" of the armed workers—which is "no longer a state in the proper sense of the word"—becomes, the more rapidly does *the state* begin to wither away.

For when *all* have learned the art of administration, and will indeed independently administer social production, will independently keep accounts, control the idlers, the gentlefolk, the swindlers and similar "guardians of capitalist traditions," the escape from this national accounting and control will inevitably become so increasingly difficult, such a rare exception, and will probably be accompanied by such swift and severe punishment (for the armed workers are practical men and not sentimental intellectuals, and they will scarcely allow anyone to trifle with them), that very soon the *necessity* of observing the simple, fundamental rules of human intercourse will become a *habit*.

C. Leon Trotsky, Thinker and Doer

In the crucial three-year period when the Bolsheviks (Communists) seized power in Russia, annihilated the internal unarmed opposition through terror, and defeated their armed enemies in an epic struggle on the battlefield, Leon Trotsky (1879–1940) was second only to Lenin in leading the Bolsheviks to their triumph. Trotsky, born Lev D. Bronstein, belonged to a family in which education more than occupation gave middle-class status. He was dynamic in action as well as an intellectual of great stature. From his teens, he was acquainted with Populism, and soon, like Plekhanov, transferred his allegiance to Marxism. Imprisoned and later banished to Siberia, he escaped in 1902 and joined Lenin in London. In the dispute at the 1903 Congress of the Social Democratic Party, he sided at first with Lenin's opponents, the Mensheviks, forming his own separate group later. When revolution broke out in 1905 at St. Petersburg, he went there and helped to organize the first workers' council or soviet, inspired by the myth of the 1871 Paris Commune. He was arrested and escaped again, spending ten years in Austria, France, Switzerland, and the United States. The March, 1917, Revolution enabled him to return to Russia, where he became Lenin's most trusted right-hand man. Largely from his personal followers he organized the Red Guard, which carried out the November, 1917, *coup d'état*. With the cooperation of former Czarist officers, he organized soldiers, workers, and peasants in a Red Army that defeated the opposition made up mainly of two distinct groups—a weak coalition of democrats, democratic socialists and anti-Bolshevik Social Revolutionaries, and military units loyal to the Czarist régime. It was expected that Trotsky would be Lenin's successor, but Stalin, helped by most other major communist leaders, outmaneuvered him. Expelled from the Soviet Communist Party in 1927 and from the

Soviet Union in 1929, he went eventually to Mexico City, where he was assassinated in 1940 by a Stalinist agent.

Trotsky's name is linked with the advocacy of relentless revolutionary activities toward the total victory of communism, with the use of extreme violence to achieve this goal, and with his attack against Stalin, whose despotism was founded on an efficient, rigid, and hierarchical party bureaucracy. No more than Lenin, Stalin, or Mao, could Trotsky conceive equality of rights between those holding his views and those holding different views. Nothing indicates that if he had won in the succession struggle of 1924 to 1927 he would have been less ruthless than Stalin. However, being less patient than Stalin, he would have jeopardized communist success in the Soviet Union by promoting more intense revolutionary activities everywhere. The excerpts here are from *Permanent Revolution* (1930), *The Defence of Terrorism* (1921), and *The New Course* (1924).

Permanent Revolution

THE PERMANENT revolution, in the sense which Marx attached to this concept, means a revolution which makes no compromise with any single form of class rule, which does not stop at the democratic stage, which goes over to socialist measures and to war against reaction from without; that is, a revolution whose every successive stage is rooted in the preceding one and which can end only in complete liquidation of class society.

To dispel the chaos that has been created around the theory of the permanent revolution, it is necessary to distinguish three lines of thought that are united in this theory.

First, it embraces the problem of the transition from the democratic revolution to the socialist. This is in essence the historical origin of the theory.

The concept of the permanent revolution was advanced by the great Communists of the middle of the nineteenth century, Marx and his co-thinkers, in opposition to the democratic ideology which, as we know, claims that with the establishment of a "rational" or democratic state all questions can be solved peacefully by reformist or evolutionary measures. Marx regarded the bourgeois revolution of 1848 as the direct prelude to the proletarian revolution. Marx "erred." Yet his error has a factual and not a methodological character. The Revolution of 1848 did not turn into the socialist revolution. But that is just why it also did not

SOURCE: L. D. Trotsky, *The Permanent Revolution*, trans. M. Schachtman (Pioneer Publications: New York, 1931) pp. 6–10.

achieve democracy. As to the German Revolution of 1918, it was no democratic completion of the bourgeois revolution; it was a proletarian revolution decapitated by the Social Democrats; more correctly, it was a bourgeois counterrevolution, which was compelled to preserve pseudodemocratic forms after its victory over the proletariat.

Vulgar "Marxism" has worked out a pattern of historical development according to which every bourgeois society sooner or later secures a democratic régime, after which the proletariat, under conditions of democracy, is gradually organized and educated for socialism. The actual transition to socialism has been variously conceived: the avowed reformists picture this transition as the reformist filling of democracy with a socialist content (Jaurès); the formal revolutionists acknowledge the inevitability of applying revolutionary violence in the transition to socialism (Guesde). But both the former and the latter considered democracy and socialism, for all peoples and countries, as two stages in the development of society which are not only entirely distinct but also separated by great distances of time from each other. This view was predominant also among those Russian Marxists who, in the period of 1905, belonged to the Left Wing of the Second International. [George] Plekhanov, the brilliant progenitor of Russian Marxism, considered the idea of the dictatorship of the proletariat a delusion in contemporary Russia. The same standpoint was defended not only by the Mensheviks but also by the overwhelming majority of the leading Bolsheviks, in particular by those present party leaders, without exception, who in their day were resolute revolutionary democrats but for whom the problems of the socialist revolution, not only in 1905 but also on the eve of 1917, still signified the vague music of a distant future.

The theory of the permanent revolution, which originated in 1905, declared war upon those ideas and moods. It pointed out that the democratic tasks of the backward bourgeois nations led directly, in our epoch, to the dictatorship of the proletariat and that the dictatorship of the proletariat puts socialist tasks on the order of the day. Therein lay the central idea of the theory. While the traditional view was that the road to the dictatorship of the proletariat led through a long period of democracy, the theory of the permanent revolution established the fact that for backward bourgeois countries the road to democracy passed through the dictatorship of the proletariat. Thus democracy is not a régime that remains self-sufficient for decades, but is only a direct prelude to the socialist revolution. Each is bound to the other by an unbroken chain. Thus there is established between the democratic revolution and the socialist reconstruction of society a permanent state of revolutionary development.

The second aspect of the theory has to do with the socialist revolution as such. For an indefinitely long time and in constant internal struggle, all social relations undergo transformation. Society keeps on changing its skin. Each stage of transformation stems directly from the preceding. This process necessarily retains a political character, that is, it develops through collisions between various groups in the society, which is in transformation. Outbreaks of civil war and foreign wars alternate with periods of "peaceful" reform. Revolutions in economy, technique, science, the family, morals, and everyday life develop in complex reciprocal action and do not allow society to achieve equilibrium. Therein lies the permanent character of the socialist revolution as such.

The international character of the socialist revolution, which constitutes the third aspect of the theory of the permanent revolution, flows from the present state of the economy and the social structure of humanity. Internationalism is no abstract principle but a theoretical and political reflection of the character of world economy, of the world development of productive forces, and of the world scale of the class struggle. The socialist revolution begins on national foundations—but cannot be completed on these foundations alone. The maintenance of the proletarian revolution within a national framework can only be a provisional state of affairs, even though, as the experience of the Soviet Union shows, one of long duration. In an isolated proletarian dictatorship, the internal and external contradictions grow inevitably along with the successes achieved. If it remains isolated, the proletarian state must finally fall victim to these contradictions. The way out for it lies only in the victory of the proletariat of the advanced countries. Viewed from this standpoint, a national revolution is not a self-contained whole; it is only a link in the international chain. The international revolution constitutes a permanent process, despite temporary declines and ebbs.

The struggle of the epigones is directed, even if not always with the same clarity, against all three aspects of the theory of the permanent revolution. And how could it be otherwise, when it is a question of three inseparably connected parts of a whole? The epigones mechanically separate *democracy* and the *socialist* dictatorship. They separate the *national* socialist revolution from the *international*. They consider that, in essence, the conquest of power within national limits is not the initial act but the final act of the revolution; after that follows the period of reforms that lead to the national socialist society. In 1905, they did not even grant the idea that the proletariat could conquer power in Russia earlier than in Western Europe. In 1917, they preached the self-sufficing democratic revolution in Russia and spurned the dictatorship of the proletariat. In 1925–27, they steered a course toward national revolution in China under the leadership of the national bourgeoisie. Subsequently, they raised the slogan for China of the democratic dictatorship of the workers and peasants in opposition to the slogan of the dictatorship of the proletariat. They proclaimed the possibility of the construction of an isolated and self-sufficient socialist society in the Soviet Union. The world revolution became for them, instead of an indispensable condition for victory, only a favorable circumstance. This profound breach with Marxism was reached by the epigones [i.e., the Stalinists, whom Trotsky considers the epigones of Lenin] in the process of permanent struggle against the theory of the permanent revolution. . . .

Terrorism

The problem of revolution, as of war, consists in breaking the will of the foe, forcing him to capitulate and to accept the conditions of the conqueror. The will, of course, is a fact of the psychical world, but in contradistinction to a meeting, a dispute, or a congress, the revolution carries out its object by means of the employment of material resources—though to a less degree than war. The bourgeoisie itself conquered power by means of revolts, and consolidated it by the civil war. In the peaceful period, it retains power by means of a system of repression. As long as class society, founded on the most deep-rooted antagonisms, continues to exist, repressions remain a necessary means of breaking the will of the opposing side.

Even if, in one country or another, the dictatorship of the

SOURCE: L. D. Trotsky, *The Defence of Terrorism* (The Labour Publishing Co., London, 1920), pp. 51–58.

proletariat grew up within the external framework of democracy, this would by no means avert the civil war. The question as to who is to rule the country, *i.e.*, of the life or death of the bourgeoisie, will be decided on either side, not by references to the paragraphs of the constitution, but by the employment of all forms of violence. However deeply Kautsky goes into the question of the food of the anthropopithecus (see page 122 et seq. of his book) and other immediate and remote conditions which determine the cause of human cruelty, he will find in history no other way of breaking the class will of the enemy except the systematic and energetic use of violence.

The degree of ferocity of the struggle depends on a series of internal and international circumstances. The more ferocious and dangerous is the resistance of the class enemy who has been overthrown, the more inevitably does the system of repression take the form of a system of terror.

But here Kautsky unexpectedly takes up a new position in his struggle with Soviet terrorism. He simply waves aside all reference to the ferocity of the counter-revolutionary opposition of the Russian bourgeoisie.

"Such ferocity," he says, "could not be noticed in November, 1917, in Petrograd and Moscow, and still less more recently in Budapest." . . . With such a happy formulation of the question, revolutionary terrorism merely proves to be a product of the bloodthirstiness of the Bolsheviks, who simultaneously abandoned the traditions of the vegetarian anthropopithecus and the moral lessons of Kautsky.

The first conquest of power by the Soviets at the beginning of November, 1917 (new style), was actually accomplished with insignificant sacrifices. The Russian bourgeoisie found itself to such a degree estranged from the masses of the people, so internally helpless, so compromised by the course and the result of the war, so demoralised by the régime of Kerensky, that it scarcely dared show any resistance. In Petrograd the power of Kerensky was overthrown almost without a fight. In Moscow its resistance was dragged out, mainly owing to the indecisive character of our own actions. In the majority of the provincial towns, power was transferred to the Soviet on the mere receipt of a telegram from Petrograd or Moscow. If the matter had ended there, there would have been no word of the Red Terror. But in November, 1917, there was already evidence of the beginning of the resistance of the propertied classes. True, there was required the intervention of the imperialist governments of the West in order to give the Russian counter-revolution faith in itself, and to add ever-increasing power to its resistance. This can be shown from facts, both important and insignificant, day by day during the whole epoch of the Soviet revolution.

Kerensky's "Staff" felt no support forthcoming from the mass of the soldiery, and was inclined to recognise the Soviet Government, which had begun negotiations for an armistice with the Germans. But there followed the protest of the military missions of the Entente, followed by open threats. The Staff was frightened; incited by "Allied" officers, it entered the path of opposition. This led to armed conflict and to the murder of the chief of the field staff, General Dukhonin, by a group of revolutionary sailors.

In Petrograd, the official agents of the Entente, especially the French Military Mission, hand in hand with the S.R.s and the Mensheviks, openly organised the opposition, mobilising, arming, inciting against us the cadets, and the bourgeois generally, from the second day of the Soviet revolution. The rising of the junkers on November 10 brought about a hundred times more victims than the revolution of November 7. The campaign of the adventurers Kerensky and Krasnov against Petrograd, organised at the same time by the Entente, naturally introduced into the struggle the first elements of savagery. Nevertheless, General Krasnov was set free on his word of honour. The Yaroslav rising (in the summer of 1918) which involved so many victims, was organised by Savinkov on the instructions of the French Embassy, and with its resources. Archangel was captured according to the plans of British naval agents, with the help of British warships and aeroplanes. The beginning of the empire of Kolchak, the nominee of the American Stock Exchange, was brought about by the foreign Czecho-Slovak Corps maintained by the resources of the French Government. Kaledin and Krasnov (liberated by us), the first leaders of the counter-revolution on the Don, could enjoy partial success only thanks to the open military and financial aid of Germany. In the Ukraine the Soviet power was overthrown in the beginning of 1918 by German militarism. The Volunteer Army of Denikin was created with the financial and technical help of Great Britain and France. Only in the hope of British intervention and of British military support was Yudenich's army created. The politicians, the diplomats, and the journalists of the Entente have for two years on end been debating with complete frankness the question of whether the financing of the civil war in Russia is a sufficiently profitable enterprise. In such circumstances, one needs truly a brazen forehead to seek the reason for the sanguinary character of the civil war in Russia in the malevolence of the Bolsheviks, and not in the international situation.

The Russian proletariat was the first to enter the path of the social revolution, and the Russian bourgeoisie, politically helpless, was emboldened to struggle against its political and economic expropriation only because it saw its elder sister in all countries still in power, and still maintaining economic, political, and, to a certain extent, military supremacy.

If our November revolution had taken place a few months, or even a few weeks, after the establishment of the rule of the proletariat in Germany, France, and England, there can be no doubt that our revolution would have been the most "peaceful," the most "bloodless" of all possible revolutions on this sinful earth. But this historical sequence—the most "natural" at the first glance, and, in any case, the most beneficial for the Russian working class—found itself infringed—not through our fault, but through the will of events. Instead of being the last, the Russian proletariat proved to be the first. It was just this circumstance, after the first period of confusion, that imparted desperation to the character of the resistance of the classes which had ruled in Russia previously, and forced the Russian proletariat, in a moment of the greatest peril, foreign attacks, and internal plots and insurrections, to have recourse to severe measures of State terror. No one will now say that those measures proved futile. But, perhaps, we are expected to consider them "intolerable"?

The working class, which seized power in battle, had as its object and its duty to establish that power unshakeably, to guarantee its own supremacy beyond question, to destroy its enemies' hankering for a new revolution, and thereby to make sure of carrying out Socialist reforms. Otherwise there would be no point in seizing power.

The revolution "logically" does not demand terrorism, just as "logically" it does not demand an armed insurrection. What a profound commonplace! But the revolution does require of the revolutionary class that it should attain its end by all methods at its disposal—if necessary, by an armed rising; if required, by terrorism. A revolutionary class which has conquered power with arms in its hands is bound to, and will, suppress, rifle in hand, all attempts to tear the power out of its hands. Where it has against it a hostile army, it will oppose to it its own army. Where it is confronted with armed conspiracy, attempt at murder, or rising, it will hurl at the heads of its enemies an unsparing penalty. Perhaps Kautsky has invented other methods? Or does he reduce the whole question to the *degree* of repression, and recommend in all circumstances imprisonment instead of execution?

The question of the form of repression, or of its degree, of course, is not one of "principle." It is a question of expediency. In a revolutionary period, the party which has been thrown from power, which does not reconcile itself with the stability of the ruling class, and which proves this by its desperate struggle against the latter, cannot be terrorised by the threat of imprisonment, as it does not believe in its duration. It is just this simple but decisive fact that explains the widespread recourse to shooting in a civil war.

Or, perhaps, Kautsky wishes to say that execution is not expedient, that "classes cannot be cowed." This is untrue. Terror is helpless—and then only "in the long run"—if it is employed by reaction against a historically rising class. But terror can be very efficient against a reactionary class which does not want to leave the scene of operations. *Intimidation* is a powerful weapon of policy, both internationally and internally. War, like revolution, is founded upon intimidation. A victorious war, generally speaking, destroys only an insignificant part of the conquered army, intimidating the remainder and breaking their will. The revolution works in the same way: it kills individuals, and intimidates thousands. In this sense, the Red Terror is not distinguishable from the armed insurrection, the direct continuation of which it represents. The State terror of a revolutionary class can be condemned "morally" only by a man who, as a principle, rejects (in words) every form of violence whatsoever—consequently, every war and every rising. For this one has to be merely and simply a hypocritical Quaker.

"But, in that case, in what do your tactics differ from the tactics of Tsarism?" we are asked, by the high priests of Liberalism and Kautskianism.

You do not understand this, holy men? We shall explain to you. The terror of Tsarism was directed against the proletariat. The gendarmerie of Tsarism throttled the workers who were fighting for the Socialist order. Our Extraordinary Commissions shoot landlords, capitalists, and generals who are striving to restore the capitalist order. Do you grasp this . . . distinction? Yes? For us Communists it is quite sufficient.

"Freedom of the Press"

One point particularly worries Kautsky, the author of a great many books and articles—the freedom of the Press. Is it permissible to suppress newspapers?

During war all institutions and organs of the State and of public opinion become, directly or indirectly, weapons of warfare. This is particularly true of the Press. No government carrying on a serious war will allow publications to exist on its territory which, openly or indirectly, support the enemy. Still more so in a civil war. The nature of the latter is such that each of the struggling sides has in the rear of its armies considerable circles of the population on the side of the enemy. In war, where both success and failure are repaid by death, hostile agents who penetrate into the rear are subject to execution. This is inhumane, but no one ever considered war a school of humanity—still less civil war. Can it be seriously demanded that, during a civil war with the White Guards of Denikin, the publications of parties supporting Denikin should come out unhindered in Moscow and Petrograd? To propose this in the name of the "freedom" of the Press is just the same as, in the name of open dealing, to demand the publication of military secrets. "A besieged city," wrote a Communard, Arthur Arnould of Paris, "cannot permit within its midst that hopes for its fall should openly be expressed, that the fighters defending it should be incited to treason, that the movements of its troops should be communicated to the enemy. Such was the position of Paris under the Commune." Such is the position of the Soviet Republic during the two years of its existence.

Let us, however, listen to what Kautsky has to say in this connection.

"The justification of this system (*i.e.*, repressions in connection with the Press) is reduced to the naive idea that an absolute truth (!) exists, and that only the Communists possess it (!) "Similarly," continues Kautsky, "it reduces itself to another point of view, that all writers are by nature liars (!) and that only Communists are fanatics for truth (!). In reality, liars and fanatics for what they consider truth are to be found in all camps." And so on, and so on, and so on.

In this way, in Kautsky's eyes, the revolution, in its most acute phase, when it is a question of the life and death of classes, continues as hitherto to be a literary discussion with the object of establishing . . . the truth. What profundity! . . . Our "truth," of course, is not absolute. But as in its name we are, at the present moment, shedding our blood, we have neither cause nor possibility to carry on a literary discussion as to the relativity of truth with those who "criticise" us with the help of all forms of arms. Similarly, our problem is not to punish liars and to encourage just men amongst journalists of all shades of opinion, but to throttle the class lie of the bourgeoisie and to achieve the class truth of the proletariat, irrespective of the fact that in both camps there are fanatics and liars.

"The Soviet Government," Kautsky thunders, "has destroyed the sole remedy that might militate against corruption: the freedom of the Press. Control by means of unlimited freedom of the Press alone could have restrained those bandits and adventurers who will inevitably cling like leeches to every unlimited, uncontrolled power." . . . And so on.

The Press as a trusty weapon of the struggle with corruption! This liberal recipe sounds particularly pitiful when one remembers the two countries with the greatest "freedom" of the Press—North America and France—which, at the same time, are countries of the most highly developed stage of capitalist corruption.

Feeding on the old scandal of the political ante-rooms of the Russian revolution, Kautsky imagines that without Cadet and Menshevik freedom the Soviet apparatus is honeycombed with "bandits" and "adventurers." Such was the voice of the Mensheviks a year or eighteen months ago. Now even they will not dare to repeat this. With the help of Soviet control and party selection, the Soviet Government, in the intense atmosphere of the struggle, has dealt with the bandits and adventurers who appeared on the surface at the moment of the revolution incomparably better than any government whatsoever, at any time whatsoever.

We are fighting. We are fighting a life-and-death struggle. The Press is a weapon not of an abstract society, but of two irreconcilable, armed and contending sides. We are destroying the Press of the counter-revolution, just as we destroyed its fortified positions, its stores, its communications, and its intelligence system. Are we depriving ourselves of Cadet and Menshevik criticisms of the corruption of the working class? In return we are victoriously destroying the very foundations of capitalist corruption.

Bureaucratism

In the debates and articles of recent times, it has been underlined that "pure," "complete," "ideal" democracy is not realizable and that in general for us it is not an end in itself. That is incontestable. But it can be stated with just as much reason that pure, absolute centralism is unrealizable and incompatible with the nature of a mass party, and that it can no more be an end in itself than can the party apparatus. Democracy and centralism are two aspects of party organization. The question is to harmonize them in the most correct manner, that is, the manner best corresponding to the situation. During the last period there was no such equilibrium. The center of gravity was wrongly placed in the apparatus. The initiative of the party was reduced to the minimum. Thence, the habits and the procedures of leadership, fundamentally contradicting the spirit of revolutionary proletarian organization. The excessive centralization of the apparatus at the expense of initiative engendered a feeling of *uneasiness*, an uneasiness which, at the extremities of the party, assumed an exceedingly morbid form and was translated, among other things, in the appearance of illegal groupings directed by elements indubitably hostile to Communism. At the same time, the whole of the party disapproved more and more of bureaucratic methods in coping with questions. The idea, or at the very least the feeling, that bureaucratism threatened to get the party into a blind alley, had become pretty general. Voices were raised to point out the danger. The [Politburo's] resolution on the new course is the first official expression of the change that

SOURCE: L. D. Trotsky, *The New Course*, trans. and ed. M. Schachtman (New International Publishing Co., New York, 1944), passim pp. 45–60, pp. 90–92.

has taken place in the party. It will be realized to the degree that the party, that is, its four hundred thousand members, will want to realize it and will succeed in doing so.

In a number of articles, efforts are being made to demonstrate that in order to give life to the party, it is necessary to begin by raising the level of its members, after which everything else, that is, workers' democracy, will come of its own accord. It is incontestable that we must raise the ideological level of our party in order to enable it to accomplish the gigantic tasks devolving upon it. But precisely because of this, such a purely *pedagogical*, professorial way of putting the question is insufficient and, hence, erroneous. To persist in it is to produce unfailingly an aggravation of the crisis.

The party cannot raise its level except by accomplishing its essential tasks, by the collective leadership that displays the initiative of the working class and the proletarian state. The question must be approached not from the *pedagogical* but from the *political* point of view. The application of workers' democracy cannot be made dependent upon the degree of "preparation" of the party members for this democracy. A party is a party. We can make stringent demands upon those who want to enter and stay in it; but once they are members, they ought to participate most actively, by that fact, in all the work of the party.

Bureaucratism kills initiative and thus prevents the elevation of the general level of the party. That is its cardinal defect. As the apparatus is made up inevitably of the most experienced and most meritorious comrades, it is upon the political training of the young Communist generations that bureaucratism has its most grievous repercussions. Also, it is the youth, the most reliable barometer of the party, that reacts most vigorously against party bureaucratism.

Nevertheless, it should not be thought that our system of solving questions—settled almost exclusively by the party functionaries—has no influence on the older generation, which incarnates the political experience and the revolutionary traditions of the party. There too the danger is very great. It is not necessary to speak of the immense, not only national but also international, authority of the group of our party veterans; that is universally recognized. But it would be a crude mistake to regard it as *absolute. It is only by a constant active collaboration with the new generation, within the framework of democracy, that the old guard can preserve itself as*

a revolutionary factor. Otherwise, it may ossify and become un-
wittingly the most consummate expression of bureaucratism.

It is unworthy of a Marxist to consider that bureaucratism is
only the aggregate of the bad habits of office holders. Bureaucratism is a social phenomenon in that it is a definite system of
administration of men and things. Its profound causes lie in the
heterogeneity of society, the difference between the daily and the
fundamental interests of various groups of the population. Bureaucratism is complicated by the fact of the lack of culture of the
broad masses. With us, the essential source of bureaucratism resides
in the necessity of creating and sustaining a state apparatus that
unites the interests of the proletariat and those of the peasantry in a
perfect economic harmony, from which we are still far removed.
The necessity of maintaining a permanent army is likewise another
important source of bureaucratism.

It is quite plain that precisely the negative social phenomena we
have just enumerated and which now nurture bureaucratism could
place the revolution in peril should they continue to develop. We
have mentioned above this hypothesis: the growing discord between state and peasant economy, the growth of the kulaks in the
country, their alliance with private commercial-industrial capital,
these would be—given the low cultural level of the toiling masses
of the countryside and in part of the towns—the causes of the
eventual counter-revolutionary dangers.

In other words, bureaucratism in the state and party apparatus is
the expression of the most vexatious tendencies inherent in our
situation, of the defects and deviations in our work which, under
certain social conditions, might sap the basis of the revolution.
And, in this case as in many others, quantity will at a certain stage
be transformed into quality.

The struggle against the bureaucratism of the state apparatus is
an exceptionally important but prolonged task, one that runs more
or less parallel to our other fundamental tasks: economic reconstruction and the elevation of the cultural level of the masses.

The most important historical instrument for the accomplishment of all these tasks is the party. Naturally, not even the party
can tear itself away from the social and cultural conditions of the
country. But as the voluntary organization of the vanguard, of
the best, the most active and the most conscious elements of the

working class, it is able to preserve itself much better than can the state apparatus from the tendencies of bureaucratism. For that, it must see the danger clearly and combat it without let-up.

Thence the immense importance of the education of the party youth, based upon personal initiative, in order to serve the state apparatus in a new manner and to transform it completely. . . .

The more ingrown the party apparatus, the more imbued it is with the feeling of its own intrinsic importance, the slower it reacts to needs emanating from the ranks and the more inclined it is to set formal tradition against new needs and tasks. And if there is one thing likely to strike a mortal blow to the spiritual life of the party and to the doctrinal training of the youth, it is certainly the transformation of Leninism from a method demanding for its application initiative, critical thinking and ideological courage into a canon which demands nothing more than interpreters appointed for good and aye.

Leninism cannot be conceived of without theoretical breadth, without a critical analysis of the material bases of the political process. The weapon of Marxian investigation must be constantly sharpened and applied. It is precisely in this that tradition consists, and not in the substitution of a formal reference or of an accidental quotation. Least of all can Leninism be reconciled with ideological superficiality and theoretical slovenliness.

Lenin cannot be chopped up into quotations suited for every possible case, because for Lenin the formula never stands higher than the reality; it is always the tool that makes it possible to grasp the reality and to dominate it. It would not be hard to find in Lenin dozens and hundreds of passages which, formally speaking, seem to be contradictory. But what must be seen is not the formal relationship of one passage to another, but the real relationship of each of them to the concrete reality in which the formula was introduced as a lever. The Leninist truth is always concrete!

As a system of revolutionary action, Leninism presupposes a revolutionary sense sharpened by reflection and experience which, in the social realm, is equivalent to the muscular sensation in physical labor. But revolutionary sense cannot be confused with demagogical flair. The latter may yield ephemeral successes, some-times even sensational ones. But it is a political instinct of an inferior type. It always leans toward the line of least resistance. Leninism, on the other hand, seeks to pose and resolve the fundamental revolutionary problems, to overcome the principal obstacles; its demagogical counterpart consists in evading the problems, in creating an illusory appeasement, in lulling critical thought to sleep.

Leninism is, first of all, the highest qualitative and quantitative appreciation of reality, from the standpoint of revolutionary action. Precisely because of this it is irreconcilable with the flight from reality behind the screen of hollow agitationalism, with the passive loss of time, with the haughty justification of yesterday's mistakes on the pretext of saving the tradition of the party.

Leninism is genuine freedom from formalistic prejudices, from moralizing doctrinalism, from all forms of intellectual conservatism attempting to bind the will to revolutionary action. But to believe that Leninism signifies that "anything goes," would be an irremediable mistake. Leninism includes the morality, not formal but genuinely revolutionary, of mass action and the mass party. Nothing is so alien to it as functionary-arrogance and bureaucratic cynicism. A mass party has its own morality, which is the bond of fighters in and for action. Demagogy is irreconcilable with the spirit of a revolutionary party because it is deceitful: by presenting one or another simplified solution of the difficulties of the hour, it inevitably undermines the next future, weakens the party's self-confidence.

Swept by the wind and gripped by a serious danger, demagogy easily dissolves into panic. It is hard to juxtapose, even on paper, panic and Leninism.

Leninism is warlike from head to foot. War is impossible without cunning, without subterfuge, without deception of the enemy. Victorious war cunning is a constituent element of Leninist politics. But at the same time, Leninism is supreme revolutionary honesty toward the party and the working class. It admits of no fiction, no bubble-blowing, no pseudo-grandeur!

Leninism is orthodox, obdurate, irreducible, but it does not contain so much as a hint of formalism, canon, nor bureaucratism. In the struggle, it takes the bull by the horns. To make out of the traditions of Leninism a supratheoretical guarantee of the infallibility of all the words and thought of the interpreters of these traditions, is to scoff at genuine revolutionary tradition and transform it into official bureaucratism. It is ridiculous and pathetic to try to hypnotize a great revolutionary party by the repetition of the same formulæ, according to which the right line should be sought not in the essence of each question, not in the methods of posing and solving this question, but in information . . . of a biographical character.

Since I am obliged to speak of myself for a moment, I will say that I do not consider the road by which I came to Leninism as less safe and reliable than the others. I came to Lenin fighting, but I came fully and all the way. My actions in the service of the party are the only guarantee of this: I can give no other supplementary guarantees. And if the question is to be posed in the field of biographical investigation, then at least it ought to be done properly.

It would then be necessary to reply to thorny questions: Were all those who were faithful to the master in the small matters also faithful to him in the great? Did all those who showed such docility in the presence of the master thereby offer guarantees that they would continue his work in his absence? Does the whole of Leninism lie in docility? I have no intention whatever of analyzing these questions by taking as examples individual comrades with whom, so far as I am concerned, I intend to continue working hand in hand.

Whatever the difficulties and the differences of opinion may be in the future, they can be victoriously overcome only by the collective work of the party's mind, checking up each time by itself and thereby maintaining the continuity of development.

This character of the revolutionary tradition is bound up with the peculiar character of revolutionary discipline. Where tradition is conservative, discipline is passive and is violated at the first moment of crisis. Where, as in our party, tradition consists in the highest revolutionary activity, discipline attains its maximum point, for its decisive importance is constantly checked in action. Thence, the indestructible alliance of revolutionary initiative, of critical, bold elaboration of questions, with iron discipline in action. And it is only by this superior activity that the youth can receive from the old this tradition of discipline and carry it on.

We cherish the traditions of Bolshevism as much as anybody. But let no one dare identify bureaucratism with Bolshevism, tradition with officious routine.

Certain comrades have adopted very singular methods of political criticism: they assert that I am mistaken today in this or that question because I was wrong in this or that question a dozen years ago. This method considerably simplifies the task.

The question of today in itself needs to be studied in its full contents. But a question raised several years ago has long since been exhausted, judged by history and, to refer to it again does not require great intellectual effort; all that is needed is memory and good faith.

But I cannot say that in this last respect all goes well with my critics. And I am going to prove it by an example from one of the most important questions.

One of the favorite arguments of certain circles during recent times consists of pointing out—mainly by indirection—that I "underestimate" the rôle of the peasantry. But one would seek in vain among my adversaries for an analysis of this question, for facts, quotations, in a word, for any proof.

Ordinarily, their argumentation boils down to allusions to the theory of the "permanent revolution," and to two or three bits of corridor gossip. And between the theory of the "permanent revolution" and the corridor gossip there is nothing, a void.

As to the theory of the "permanent revolution," I see no reason to renounce what I wrote on this subject in 1904, 1905, 1906, and later. To this day, I persist in considering that the thoughts I developed at that time are much closer, taken as a whole, to the genuine essence of Leninism than much of what a number of Bolsheviks wrote in those days.

The expression *"permanent revolution"* is an expression of Marx which he applied to the revolution of 1848. In Marxian, naturally not in revisionist but in revolutionary Marxian literature, this term has always had citizenship rights. Franz Mehring employed it for the revolution of 1905–1907. The permanent revolution, in an exact translation, is the continuous revolution, the uninterrupted revolution. What is the political idea embraced in this expression?

It is, for us communists, that the revolution does not come to an end after this or that political conquest, after obtaining this or that social reform, but that it continues to develop further and its only boundary is the socialist society. Thus, once begun, the revolution (insofar as we participate in it and particularly when we lead it) is in no case interrupted by us at any formal stage whatever. On the contrary, we continually and constantly advance it in conformity, of course, with the situation, so long as the revolution has not exhausted all the possibilities and all the resources of the movement. This applies to the conquests of the revolution inside of a country as well as to its extension over the international arena.

For Russia, this theory signified: what we need is not the bourgeois republic as a political crowning, nor even the democratic dictatorship of the proletariat and peasantry, but a workers' government supporting itself upon the peasantry and opening up the era of the international socialist revolution.

D. JOSEPH STALIN, MOLDER OF THE USSR

In the course of his pre-1917 clandestine activities for the Russian Social Democratic Party, Joseph V. Djugashvili (1879–1953) took the appropriate name of Stalin. By nationality a Georgian from the Caucasus, Stalin came from a family of artisans, between the middle and lower classes. Lenin appreciated his ability as a conspirator, his courage, his self-control, his devotion to socialism. Stalin was the least known of the top Bolshevik leaders when appointed Commissar of Nationalities. But as a result of Stalin's genius for organization and his capacity for patient effort even in the most difficult situations, Lenin chose him to be the secretary general of the Soviet Communist Party. (It seems that Lenin had begun to regret his choice when, happily for Stalin, he became incapacitated.) As secretary general, Stalin built his own solid machine within the party. This gave him success against brilliant opponents in the struggle for power that followed Lenin's death. From the end of 1927 until 1953, Stalin guided the Soviet Union and the communist movement with a firm hand and an exceptionally clear mind. From a communist point of view he was right, when to Trotsky's "permanent revolution" he opposed "socialism in one country," an all-out effort to develop the Soviet Union before the country entered the international arena again, as it had done unsuccessfully from 1918 to 1923.

Stalin dealt ruthlessly with his opponents. Millions died in the course of the land collectivization of the early 1930's, of the so-called purges of 1936 to 1938 and the lesser ones after World War II, of the forcible annexation to the Soviet Union of vast territories in 1939 and 1940 and again in 1945. Millions died in forced-labor camps, which provided the cheap labor needed for fast industrialization. Stalin's writings testify to his gifts as an intellectual. He devised a formula for running a collectivist economy, and put it into practice with success. He played for the Soviet Union in World War II the role Churchill played for Great Britain. He expanded the Soviet Union—economically, politically, and militarily the number two power in world affairs after 1945—into a Soviet empire supported by a vast and disciplined world-wide fifth column. Many communists were as afraid of Stalin as anti-communists

were, and took a partial revenge with the denunciation of his crimes in
1956. In spite of the anti-Stalinist reaction, however, and in spite, too,
of several errors, Stalin left an imprint on Marxism-Leninism that
cannot be erased. The following excerpt is from Stalin's *The Foundations of Leninism*, which appeared originally as a series of articles in
1924.

Stalin on Marxism-Leninism

FROM THIS theme [theory] I take three topics:
  (a) the significance of theory for the proletarian movement;
  (b) criticism of the "theory" of spontaneity;
  (c) the theory of the proletarian revolution.

1. *The significance of theory.* Some think that Leninism is the
precedence of practice over theory in the sense that its main point
is the translation of Marxist theses into deeds, their "execution"; as
for theory, it is alleged that Leninism is rather unconcerned about
it. We know that Plekhanov time and again chaffed Lenin about
his "unconcern" for theory, and particularly for philosophy. We
also know that theory is not held in great favor by many present-
day Leninist practical workers, particularly in view of the immense
amount of practical work imposed upon them by the situation. I
must declare that this more than odd opinion about Lenin and
Leninism is quite wrong and bears no relation whatever to the truth
and that the attempt of practical workers to brush theory aside
runs counter to the whole spirit of Leninism and is fraught with
serious dangers to the work.

Theory is the experience of the working-class movement in all
countries taken in its general aspect. Of course, theory becomes
purposeless if it is not connected with revolutionary practice, just
as practice gropes in the dark if its path is not illumined by
revolutionary theory. But theory can become a tremendous force
in the working-class movement if it is built up in indissoluble connection with revolutionary practice; for theory, and theory alone,
can give the movement confidence, the power of orientation, and
an understanding of the inner relation of surrounding events; for it,
and it alone, can help practice to realize not only how and in which
direction classes are moving at the present time, but also how and
in which direction they will move in the near future. None other

SOURCE: J. V. Stalin, *Foundations of Leninism* (International Publishers,
New York, 1937), pp. 28–46.

than Lenin said and repeated scores of times the well-known thesis that:

Without a revolutionary theory there can be no revolutionary movement.

Lenin, better than anyone else, understood the great importance of theory, particularly for a party such as ours, in view of the role of vanguard fighter of the international proletariat which has fallen to its lot, and in view of the complicated internal and international situation in which it finds itself. Foreseeing this special role of our Party as far back as 1902, he thought it necessary even then to point out that:

The role of the vanguard fighter can be fulfilled only by a party that is guided by the most advanced theory.

It scarcely needs proof that now, when Lenin's prediction about the role of our Party has come true, this thesis of Lenin's acquires special force and special importance.

Perhaps the most striking expression of the great importance which Lenin attached to theory is the fact that none other than Lenin undertook the very serious task of generalizing, on the basis of materialist philosophy, the most important achievements of science from the time of Engels down to his own time, as well as subjecting to comprehensive criticism the antimaterialistic trends among Marxists. Engels said that "materialism must assume a new aspect with every new great discovery." It is well known that none other than Lenin accomplished this task for his own time in his remarkable work *Materialism and Empirio-Criticism.* It is well known that Plekhanov, who loved to chaff Lenin about his "unconcern" for philosophy, did not even dare to make a serious attempt to undertake such a task.

2. *Criticism of the "theory" of spontaneity, or the role of the vanguard in the movement.* The "theory" of spontaneity is a theory of opportunism, a theory of worshiping the spontaneity of the labor movement, a theory which actually repudiates the leading role of the vanguard of the working class, the party of the working class.

The theory of worshiping spontaneity is decidedly opposed to the revolutionary character of the working-class movement; it is opposed to the movement taking the line of struggle against the foundations of capitalism; it is in favor of the movement proceeding exclusively along the line of "realizable" demands, of demands "acceptable" to capitalism; it is wholly in favor of the "line of least resistance." The theory of spontaneity is the ideology of trade unionism.

The theory of worshiping spontaneity is decidedly opposed to giving the spontaneous movement a politically conscious, planned character. It is opposed to the Party marching at the head of the working class, to the Party raising the masses to the level of political consciousness, to the Party leading the movement. It is in favor of the politically conscious elements of the movement not hindering the movement from taking its own course; it is in favor of the Party only heeding the spontaneous movement and dragging at the tail of it. The theory of spontaneity is the theory of belittling the role of the conscious element in the movement, the ideology of "tailism" (*khvostism*); the logical basis of *all* opportunism.

In practice this theory, which appeared on the scene even before the first revolution in Russia, led its adherents, the so-called "Economists," to deny the need for an independent workers' party in Russia, to oppose the revolutionary struggle of the working class for the overthrow of tsarism, to preach a purely trade-unionist policy in the movement, and, in general, to surrender the labor movement to the hegemony of the liberal bourgeoisie.

The fight of the old *Iskra* and the brilliant criticism of the theory of "tailism" in Lenin's pamphlet *What Is to Be Done?* not only smashed so-called "Economism," but also created the theoretical foundations for a truly revolutionary movement of the Russian working class.

Without this fight it would have been quite useless even to think of creating an independent workers' party in Russia and of its playing a leading part in the revolution.

But the theory of worshiping spontaneity is not an exclusively Russian phenomenon. It is extremely widespread—in a somewhat different form, it is true—in all the parties of the Second International, without exception. I have in mind the so-called "productive forces" theory as debased by the leaders of the Second International, which justifies everything and conciliates everybody, which records facts and explains them after everyone has become sick and tired of them, and, having recorded them, rests content. Marx said that the materialist theory could not confine itself to explaining the world, that it must also change it. But Kautsky and

Co. are not concerned with this; they prefer to rest content with the first part of Marx's formula.

Here is one of the numerous examples of the application of this "theory." It is said that before the imperialist war the parties of the Second International theatened to declare "war against war" if the imperialists should start a war. It is said that on the very eve of the war these parties pigeonholed the "war against war" slogan and applied an opposite one, *viz.*, "war for the imperialist fatherland." It is said that as a result of this change of slogan millions of workers were sent to their death. But it would be a mistake to think that there were some people to blame for this, that someone was unfaithful to the working class or betrayed it. Not at all! Everything happened as it should have happened. Firstly, because the International, it seems, is "an instrument of peace," and not of war. Secondly, because, in view of the "level of the productive forces" which then prevailed, nothing else could be done. The "productive forces" are "to blame." That is the precise explanation vouchsafed to "us" by Mr. Kautsky's "theory of the productive forces." And whoever does not believe in that "theory" is not a Marxist. The role of the parties? Their importance for the movement? But what can a party do against so decisive a factor as the "level of the productive forces"? . . .

One could cite a host of similar examples of the falsification of Marxism.

It scarcely needs proof that this spurious "Marxism," designed to hide the nakedness of opportunism, is merely a European variety of the same theory of "tailism" which Lenin fought even before the first Russian revolution.

It scarcely needs proof that the demolition of this theoretical falsification is a preliminary condition for the creation of truly revolutionary parties in the West.

3. *The theory of the proletarian revolution.* Lenin's theory of the proletarian revolution proceeds from three fundamental theses.

First thesis: The domination of finance capital in the advanced capitalist countries; the issue of stocks and bonds as one of the principal operations of finance capital; the export of capital to the sources of raw materials, which is one of the foundations of imperialism; the omnipotence of a financial oligarchy, which is the result of the domination of finance capital—all this reveals the grossly parasitic character of monopolist capitalism, makes the yoke of the capitalist trusts and syndicates a hundred times more burdensome, intensifies the indignation of the working class against the foundations of capitalism, and leads the masses to proletarian revolution as their only salvation. (See Lenin, *Imperialism*.)

Hence the first conclusion: intensification of the revolutionary crisis within the capitalist countries and growth of explosive elements on the internal, proletarian front in the "metropolises."

Second thesis: The increase in the export of capital to the colonies and dependent countries; the expansion of "spheres of influence" and colonial possessions until they cover the whole globe; the transformation of capitalism into a *world system* of financial enslavement and colonial oppression of the vast majority of the population of the world by a handful of "advanced" countries—all this has, on the one hand, converted the separate national economies and national territories into links in a single chain called world economy, and, on the other hand, split the population of the globe into two camps: a handful of "advanced" capitalist countries which exploit and oppress vast colonies and dependencies, and the huge majority consisting of colonial and dependent countries which are compelled to wage a struggle for liberation from the imperialist yoke. (See *Imperialism*.)

Hence the second conclusion: intensification of the revolutionary crisis in the colonial countries and growth of the elements of revolt against imperialism on the external, colonial front.

Third thesis: The monopolistic possession of "spheres of influence" and colonies; the uneven development of the capitalist countries, leading to a frenzied struggle for the redivision of the world between the countries which have already seized territories and those claiming their "share"; imperialist wars as the only means of restoring the disturbed "equilibrium"—all this leads to the intensification of the struggle on the third front, the intercapitalist front, which weakens imperialism and facilitates the union of the first two fronts against imperialism, the front of the revolutionary proletariat and the front of colonial emancipation. (See *Imperialism*.)

Hence the third conclusion: that under imperialism wars cannot be averted, and that a coalition between the proletarian revolution in Europe and the colonial revolution in the East in a united world front of revolution against the world front of imperialism is inevitable.

Lenin combines all these conclusions into one general conclusion that *"imperialism is the eve of the socialist revolution."* . . .

The very approach to the question of the proletarian revolution, of the character of the revolution, its scope and its depth, of the pattern of the revolution in general, changes accordingly.

Formerly, the analysis of the prerequisites for the proletarian revolution was usually approached from the point of view of the economic state of individual countries. Now, this approach is no longer adequate. Now the matter must be approached from the point of view of the economic state of all or the majority of countries, from the point of view of the state of the world economy; for individual countries and individual national economies have ceased to be self-sufficient units and have become links in a single chain called world economy; for the old "cultured" capitalism has evolved into imperialism, and imperialism is a world system of financial enslavement and colonial oppression of the vast majority of the population of the world by a handful of "advanced" countries.

Formerly it was the accepted thing to speak of the existence or absence of objective conditions for the proletarian revolution in individual countries, or, to be more precise, in one or another developed country. Now this point of view is no longer adequate. Now we must speak of the existence of objective conditions for revolution in the entire system of the world imperialist economy as an integral whole. Moreover, the existence within this system of some countries that are not sufficiently developed industrially cannot serve as an insuperable obstacle to the revolution, *if* the system as a whole or, more correctly, *since* the system as a whole is already ripe for revolution.

Formerly it was the accepted thing to speak of the proletarian revolution in one or another developed country as of a separate and self-sufficient entity opposing a separate national front of capital as its antipode. Now, this point of view is no longer adequate. Now we must speak of the world proletarian revolution; for the separate national fronts of capital have become links in a single chain called the world front of imperialism, which must be opposed by a common front of the revolutionary movement in all countries.

Formerly the proletarian revolution was regarded exclusively as the result of the internal development of a given country. Now, this point of view is no longer adequate. Now the proletarian revolution must be regarded primarily as the result of the development of the contradictions within the world system of imperialism, as the result of the breaking of the chain of the world imperialist front in one country or another.

Where will the revolution begin? Where, in what country, can the front of capital be pierced first?

Where industry is more developed, where the proletariat constitutes the majority, where there is more culture, where there is more democracy—that was the reply usually given formerly.

No, objects the Leninist theory of revolution, *not necessarily where industry is more developed,* and so forth. The front of capital will be pierced where the chain of imperialism is weakest, for the proletarian revolution is the result of the breaking of the chain of the world imperialist front at its weakest link; and it may turn out that the country which has started the revolution, which has made a breach in the front of capital, is less developed in a capitalist sense than other, more developed, countries, which have, however, remained within the framework of capitalism.

In 1917 the chain of the imperialist world front proved to be weaker in Russia than in the other countries. It was there that the chain broke and provided an outlet for the proletarian revolution. Why? Because in Russia a great popular revolution was unfolding, and at its head marched the revolutionary proletariat, which had such an important ally as the vast mass of the peasantry, oppressed and exploited by the landlords. Because the revolution there was opposed by such a hideous representative of imperialism as tsarism, which lacked all moral prestige and was deservedly hated by the whole population. The chain proved to be weaker in Russia, although Russia was less developed in a capitalist sense than, say, France or Germany, Britain or America.

Where will the chain break in the near future? Again, where it is weakest. It is not precluded that the chain may break, say, in India. Why? Because that country has a young, militant, revolutionary proletariat, which has such an ally as the national liberation movement—an undoubtedly powerful and undoubtedly important ally. Because there the revolution is confronted by such a well-known foe as foreign imperialism, which has no moral credit and is deservedly hated by all the oppressed and exploited masses of India.

It is also quite possible that the chain will break in Germany.

Why? Because the factors which are operating, say, in India are beginning to operate in Germany as well; but, of course, the enormous difference in the level of development between India and Germany cannot but stamp its imprint on the progress and outcome of a revolution in Germany.

That is why Lenin said that:

> The West-European capitalist countries will consummate their development towards socialism . . . not by the even "maturing" of socialism in them, but by the exploitation of some countries by others, by the exploitation of the first of the countries to be vanquished in the imperialist war combined with the exploitation of the whole of the East. On the other hand, precisely as a result of the first imperialist war, the East has definitely come into revolutionary movement, has been definitely drawn into the general maelstrom of the world revolutionary movement. . . .

Briefly: the chain of the imperialist front must, as a rule, break where the links are weaker and, at all events, not necessarily where capitalism is more developed, where there is such and such a percentage of proletarians and such and such a percentage of peasants, and so on.

That is why in deciding the question of proletarian revolution statistical estimates of the percentage of the proletarian population in a given country lose the exceptional importance so eagerly attached to them by the doctrinaires of the Second International, who have not understood imperialism and who fear revolution like the plague.

To proceed. The heroes of the Second International asserted (and continue to assert) that between the bourgeois-democratic revolution and the proletarian revolution there is a chasm, or at any rate a Chinese Wall, separating one from the other by a more or less protracted interval of time, during which the bourgeoisie having come into power, develops capitalism, while the proletariat accumulates strength and prepares for the "decisive struggle" against capitalism. This interval is usually calculated to extend over many decades, if not longer. It scarcely needs proof that this Chinese Wall "theory" is totally devoid of scientific meaning under the conditions of imperialism, that it is and can only be a means of concealing and camouflaging the counterrevolutionary aspirations of the bourgeoisie. It scarcely needs proof that under the conditions of imperialism, fraught as it is with collisions and wars, under the conditions of the "eve of the socialist revolution," when "flourishing" capitalism becomes "moribund" capitalism (Lenin) and the revolutionary movement is growing in all countries of the world; when imperialism is allying itself with all reactionary forces without exception, down to and including tsarism and serfdom, thus making imperative the coalition of all revolutionary forces, from the proletarian movement of the West to the national liberation movement of the East; when the overthrow of the survivals of the regime of feudal serfdom becomes impossible without a revolutionary struggle against imperialism—it scarcely needs proof that the bourgeois-democratic revolution, in a more or less developed country, must under such circumstances verge upon the proletarian revolution, that the former must pass into the latter. The history of the revolution in Russia has provided palpable proof that this thesis is correct and incontrovertible. It was not without reason that Lenin, as far back as 1905, on the eve of the first Russian revolution, in his pamphlet *Two Tactics* depicted the bourgeois-democratic revolution and the socialist revolution as two links in the same chain, as a single and integral picture of the sweep of the Russian revolution:

> *The proletariat must carry to completion the democratic revolution, by allying to itself the mass of the peasantry in order to crush by force the resistance of the autocracy and to paralyze the instability of the bourgeoisie. The proletariat must accomplish the socialist revolution, by allying to itself the mass of the semiproletarian elements of the population in order to crush by force the resistance of the bourgeoisie and to paralyze the instability of the peasantry and the petty bourgeoisie.* Such are the tasks of the proletariat, which the new *Iskra*-ists present so narrowly in all their arguments and resolutions about the sweep of the revolution. . . .

There is no need to mention other, later works of Lenin's, in which the idea of the bourgeois revolution passing into the proletarian revolution stands out in greater relief than in *Two Tactics* as one of the cornerstones of the Leninist theory of revolution.

Some comrades believe, it seems, that Lenin arrived at this idea only in 1916, that up to that time he had thought that the revolution in Russia would remain within the bourgeois framework, that power, consequently, would pass from the hands of the organ of the dictatorship of the proletariat and peasantry into the hands of the bourgeoisie and not of the proletariat. It is said that this assertion has even penetrated into our communist press. I must say that this assertion is absolutely wrong, that it is totally at variance with the facts.

I might refer to Lenin's well-known speech at the Third Congress of the Party (1905), in which he defined the dictatorship of the proletariat and peasantry, *i.e.*, the victory of the democratic revolution, not as the "organization of 'order' " but as the "organization of war."

Further, I might refer to Lenin's well-known article "On a Provisional Government" (1905), where, outlining the prospects of the unfolding Russian revolution, he assigns to the Party the task of "ensuring that the Russian revolution is not a movement of a few months, but a movement of many years, that it leads, not merely to slight concessions on the part of the powers that be, but to the complete overthrow of those powers." Enlarging further on these prospects and linking them with the revolution in Europe, he goes on here to say:

> And if we succeed in doing that, . . . then the revolutionary conflagration will spread all over Europe. The European worker, languishing under bourgeois reaction, will rise in his turn and will show us "how it is done." Then the revolutionary wave in Europe will sweep back again into Russia and will convert an epoch of a few revolutionary years into an epoch of several revolutionary decades. . . .

I might further refer to a well-known article by Lenin published in November 1915, in which he writes:

> The proletariat is fighting, and will fight valiantly, for the conquest of power, for a republic, for the confiscation of the land . . . for the participation of the "*non*proletarian masses of the people" in the liberation of *bourgeois* Russia from *military-feudal* "imperialism" (= tsarism). And the proletariat will *immediately* take advantage of this liberation of bourgeois Russia from tsarism, from the agrarian power of the landlords, not to aid the rich peasants in their struggle against the rural worker, but to bring about the socialist revolution in alliance with the proletarians of Europe.

Finally, I might refer to the well-known passage in Lenin's pamphlet *The Proletarian Revolution and the Renegade Kautsky*, where, referring to the above-quoted passage in *Two Tactics* on the sweep of the Russian revolution, he arrives at the following conclusion:

> Things turned out just as we said they would. The course taken by the revolution confirmed the correctness of our reasoning. *First*, with the "whole" of the peasantry against the monarchy, against the landlords, against the medieval regime (and to that extent the revolution remains bourgeois, bourgeois-democratic). *Then*, with the poor peasants, with the semiproletarians, with all the exploited, *against capitalism*, including the rural rich, the kulaks, the profiteers, and to that extent the revolution becomes a *socialist* one. To attempt to raise an artificial Chinese Wall between the first and second, to separate them by anything else *than* the degree of preparedness of the proletariat and the degree of its unity with the poor peasants, means monstrously to distort Marxism, to vulgarize it, to replace it by liberalism.

That is sufficient, I think.

Very well, we may be told; but if that is the case, why did Lenin combat the idea of "permanent (uninterrupted) revolution"?

Because Lenin proposed that the revolutionary capacities of the peasantry be "exhausted" and that the fullest use be made of their revolutionary energy for the complete liquidation of tsarism and for the transition to the proletarian revolution, whereas the adherents of "permanent revolution" did not understand the important role of the peasantry in the Russian revolution, underestimated the strength of the revolutionary energy of the peasantry, underestimated the strength and ability of the Russian proletariat to lead the peasantry, and thereby hampered the work of emancipating the peasantry from the influence of the bourgeoisie, the work of rallying the peasantry around the proletariat.

Because Lenin proposed that the revolution be *crowned* with the transfer of power to the proletariat, whereas the adherents of "permanent" revolution wanted to *begin* at once with the establishment of the power of the proletariat, failing to realize that in so doing they were closing their eyes to such a "minor detail" as the survivals of serfdom and were leaving out of account so important a force as the Russian peasantry, failing to understand that such a policy could only retard the winning of the peasantry over to the side of the proletariat.

Consequently, Lenin fought the adherents of "permanent" revolution, not over the question of uninterruptedness, for Lenin himself maintained the point of view of uninterrupted revolution, but because they underestimated the role of the peasantry, which is an enormous reserve of the proletariat, because they failed to understand the idea of the hegemony of the proletariat.

The idea of "permanent" revolution should not be regarded as a new idea. It was first advanced by Marx at the end of the forties in his well-known *Address* to the *Communist League* (1850). It is from this document that our "permanentists" took the idea of uninterrupted revolution. It should be noted that in taking it from Marx our "permanentists" altered it somewhat, and in altering it "spoilt" it and made it unfit for practical use. The experienced hand of Lenin was needed to rectify this mistake, to take Marx's idea of uninterrupted revolution in its pure form and make it a cornerstone of his theory of revolution.

Here is what Marx says in his *Address* about uninterrupted (permanent) revolution, after enumerating a number of revolutionary-democratic demands which he calls upon the Communists to win:

> While the democratic petty bourgeoisie wish to bring the revolution to a conclusion as quickly as possible, and with the achievement of as many of the above demands as possible, it is our interest and our task to make the revolution permanent, until all the more or less propertied classes have been forced out of their position of dominance, until the proletariat has conquered state power, and the association of proletarians, not only in one country but in all the dominant countries of the world, has advanced so far that competition among the proletarians of these countries has ceased and that at least the decisive productive forces are concentrated in the hands of the proletarians.

In other words:

(a) Marx did not at all propose *to begin* the revolution in the Germany of the fifties with the immediate establishment of proletarian power—*contrary* to the plans of our Russian "permanentists."

(b) Marx proposed only that the revolution *be crowned* with the establishment of proletarian state power, by hurling, step by step, one section of the bourgeoisie after another from the heights of power, in order, after the attainment of power by the proletariat, to kindle the fire of revolution in every country. And everything that Lenin taught and carried out in the course of our revolution in pursuit of his theory of the proletarian revolution under the conditions of imperialism was *fully in line* with that proposition.

It follows, then, that our Russian "permanentists" have not only underestimated the role of the peasantry in the Russian revolution and the importance of the idea of the hegemony of the proletariat, but have altered (for the worse) Marx's idea of "permanent" revolution and made it unfit for practical use.

That is why Lenin ridiculed the theory of our "permanentists," calling it "original" and "fine," and accusing them of refusing to "think why, for ten whole years, life has passed by this fine theory." (Lenin's article was written in 1915, ten years after the appearance of the theory of the "permanentists" in Russia.)

That is why Lenin regarded this theory as a semi-Menshevik theory and said that it "borrows from the Bolsheviks their call for a resolute revolutionary struggle by the proletariat and the conquest of political power by the latter, and from the Mensheviks the 'repudiation' of the role of the peasantry."

This, then, is Lenin's idea of the bourgeois-democratic revolution passing into the proletarian revolution, of utilizing the bourgeois revolution for the "immediate" transition to the proletarian revolution.

To proceed. Formerly, the victory of the revolution in one country was considered impossible, on the assumption that it would require the combined action of the proletarians of all or at least of a majority of the advanced countries to achieve victory over the bourgeoisie. Now this point of view no longer fits the facts. Now we must proceed from the possibility of such a victory, for the uneven and spasmodic character of the development of the various capitalist countries under the conditions of imperialism, the development within imperialism of catastrophic contradictions leading to inevitable wars, the growth of the revolutionary movement in all countries of the world—all this leads, not only to the possibility, but also to the necessity of the victory of the proletariat in individual countries. The history of the revolution in Russia is direct proof of this. At the same time, however, it must be borne in mind that the overthrow of the bourgeoisie can be successfully accomplished only when certain absolutely necessary conditions exist, in the absence of which one could not even think of the proletariat taking power.

Here is what Lenin says about these conditions in his pamphlet *"Left-Wing" Communism:*

> The fundamental law of revolution, which has been confirmed by all revolutions and, particularly, by all three Russian revolutions in the twentieth century, is as follows: it is not enough for revolution that the exploited and oppressed masses should understand the impossibility of living in the old way and demand changes; it is essential for revolution that the exploiters should not be able to live and rule in the old way. Only when the "lower classes" *do not want* the old way, and when the "upper classes" *cannot carry on in the old way*—only then can revolution triumph. This truth may be expressed in other words: *revolution is impossible without a nation-wide crisis (affecting both the exploited and the exploiters).* It follows that for revolution it is essential, first, that a majority of the workers (or at least a majority of the class-conscious, thinking, politically active workers) should fully understand that revolution is necessary and be ready to sacrifice their lives for it; secondly, that the ruling classes should be ready to sacrifice their lives for it; finally, that the ruling classes should be passing through a governmental crisis, which draws even the most backward masses into politics . . . weakens the government and makes it possible for the revolutionaries to overthrow it rapidly.

But the overthrow of the power of the bourgeoisie and establishment of the power of the proletariat in one country does not yet mean that the complete victory of socialism has been ensured. After consolidating its power and leading the peasantry in its wake, the proletariat of the victorious country can and must build a socialist society. But does this mean that it will thereby achieve the complete and final victory of socialism, *i.e.*, does it mean that with the forces of only one country it can finally consolidate socialism and fully guarantee that country against intervention and, consequently, also against restoration? No, it does not. For this victory of the revolution in at least several countries is needed. Therefore, the development and support of revolution in other countries is an essential task of the victorious revolution. Therefore, the revolution which has been victorious in one country must regard itself not as a self-sufficient entity, but as an aid, as a means for hastening the victory of the proletariat in other countries.

Lenin expressed this thought succinctly when he said that the task of the victorious revolution is to do "the utmost possible in one country *for* the development, support and awakening of the revolution *in all countries.*"

These, in general, are the characteristic features of Lenin's theory of proletarian revolution.

E. MAO TSE-TUNG, MOLDER OF COMMUNIST CHINA

After the death of Stalin in 1953, Soviet leaders for a while maintained the ideological and political preeminence among communists that they had enjoyed since Lenin's time. This preeminence was gradually lost, however, and even before the end of the 1950's the Chinese Mao Tse-tung had become a commanding figure in the communist movement. At first he acted independently of Soviet leaders, later antagonistically to them. Mao, who was in control of his own armed forces, could not be dealt with in the manner that dissident communists had been dealt with within the Soviet Union, and then in most of eastern Europe, until their complete obliteration. In the second half of the 1960's more Marxist-Leninist revolutionaries—fascinated by Mao's success in mankind's largest nation, by his strong determination founded on clear ideas, by his absolute intransigence, by the simplicity of his concepts and the austerity of his ethics—followed the Maoist line than the Soviet one. Maoism became a household word. The "little red book" of *Chairman Mao's Quotations* became for hundreds of millions of young Chinese and for many millions outside China a sacred text, to be studied, memorized, commented upon, used as a guide to action, never questioned. Maoist China was playing a greater role than the Soviet Union had ever played in appealing to revolutionaries everywhere, and in stimulating revolutionary activities in scores of nations. Combining Stalinist ruthlessness with Trotskyite universalism, Maoism proved more dynamic than post-Stalin Soviet communism. In the dangerous game of international brinkmanship, Maoists were willing to go considerably further than Soviet leaders and their supporters.

Mao Tse-tung was born in 1893 of yeoman stock, a few social notches above the peasantry. He received a good traditional education. To this he added the knowledge of modern foreign ideologies, avidly reading all books by Western thinkers that came his way. The 1911 Revolution in China was followed by a chaotic situation that provided an ideal ground for the diffusion of new ideas and the development of new movements. In 1921, Mao was among those who founded the Chinese Communist Party, organized under Soviet auspices, and for several years linked to the nationalist Kuomintang. At the time of the break in 1926 and 1927 between the Kuomintang (by then led by Chiang Kai-shek) and the Communists, Mao led those who tried to establish a communist republic in central China. This meant war with the Kuomintang. It lasted until 1949. With some support from the

Soviet Union, Mao battled nationalist troops, warlords, and Japanese. For the Chinese Communists, poorly armed and often outnumbered, this was an epic struggle. It was to continue with the intervention in North Korea from 1950 to 1953, the aid to communists in southeast Asia, the attack against India in 1962. There had been quarrels among Chinese Communist leaders, in the 1930's particularly, but the rank and file never wavered in their devotion to the man who stood as solid as a rock, whose will was strengthened by the clarity of his ideas, and who led them to victory. With victory came reconstruction and with it the forcible obliteration of millenary traditions. As usual with Marxist-Leninists, there were massacres of opponents, elimination of members of former privileged classes, of ideological groups, of some rebellious ethnic communities. Having destroyed the opposition to the party, Mao turned, with the Great Proletarian Cultural Revolution, to the destruction of opposition within the party. Economically, Chinese progress under Maoism was remarkable, though inferior to that of neighboring countries like Japan and Taiwan. Leninism had been Marxist in action: Maoism was Marxist thought and Leninist action applied dynamically, intelligently, and effectively to mankind's potentially strongest nation. Even if the revolution devours Mao the individual, his stamp will remain.

The first two excerpts are from Selected Works of Mao Tse-tung (1961), the third from Quotations from Chairman Mao Tse-tung (1967).

On the People's Democratic Dictatorship

. . . WESTERN BOURGEOIS civilization, bourgeois democracy and the plan for a bourgeois republic have all gone bankrupt in the eyes of the Chinese people. Bourgeois democracy has given way to people's democracy under the leadership of the working class and the bourgeois republic to the people's republic. This has made it possible to achieve socialism and communism through the people's republic, to abolish classes and enter a world of Great Harmony. Kang Yu-wei wrote Ta Tung Shu, or the Book of Great Harmony, but he did not and could not find the way to achieve Great Harmony. There are bourgeois republics in foreign lands, but China cannot have a bourgeois republic because she is a country suffering under imperialist oppression. The only way is through a people's republic led by the working class.

All other ways have been tried and failed. Of the people who hankered after those ways, some have fallen, some have awakened

SOURCE: Mao Tse-tung, Selected Works of Mao Tse-tung (Foreign Language Press, Peking, 1965), Vol. II, pp. 31–33, and Vol. IV, pp. 414–420.

and some are changing their ideas. Events are developing so swiftly that many feel the abruptness of the change and the need to learn anew. This state of mind is understandable and we welcome this worthy desire to learn anew.

The vanguard of the Chinese proletariat learned Marxism-Leninism after the October Revolution and founded the Communist Party of China. It entered at once into political struggles and only now, after a tortuous course of twenty-eight years, has it won basic victory. From our twenty-eight years' experience we have drawn a conclusion similar to the one Sun Yat-sen drew in his testament from his "experience of forty years"; that is, we are deeply convinced that to win victory, "we must arouse the masses of the people and unite in a common struggle with those nations of the world which treat us as equals." Sun Yat-sen had a world outlook different from ours and started from a different class standpoint in studying and tackling problems; yet, in the 1920's he reached a conclusion basically the same as ours on the question of how to struggle against imperialism.

Twenty-four years have passed since Sun Yat-sen's death, and the Chinese revolution, led by the Communist Party of China, has made tremendous advances both in theory and practice and has radically changed the face of China. Up to now the principal and fundamental experience the Chinese people have gained is twofold:

1. Internally, arouse the masses of the people. That is, unite the working class, the peasantry, the urban petty bourgeoisie and the national bourgeoisie, form a domestic united front under the leadership of the working class, and advance from this to the establishment of a state which is a people's democratic dictatorship under the leadership of the working class and based on the alliance of workers and peasants.

2. Externally, unite in a common struggle with those nations of the world which treat us as equals and unite with the peoples of all countries. That is, ally ourselves with the Soviet Union, with the People's Democracies and with the proletariat and the broad masses of the people in all other countries, and form an international united front.

"You are leaning to one side." Exactly. The forty years' experience of Sun Yat-sen and the twenty-eight years' experience of the Communist Party have taught us to lean to one side, and we are firmly convinced that in order to win victory and consolidate it we must lean to one side. In the light of the experiences accumulated in these forty years and these twenty-eight years, all Chinese without exception must lean either to the side of imperialism or to the side of socialism. Sitting on the fence will not do, nor is there a third road. We oppose the Chiang Kai-shek reactionaries who lean to the side of imperialism, and we also oppose the illusions about a third road.

"You are too irritating." We are talking about how to deal with domestic and foreign reactionaries, the imperialists and their running dogs, not about how to deal with anyone else. With regard to such reactionaries, the question of irritating them or not does not arise. Irritated or not irritated, they will remain the same because they are reactionaries. Only if we draw a clear line between reactionaries and revolutionaries, expose the intrigues and plots of the reactionaries, arouse the vigilance and attention of the revolutionary ranks, heighten our will to fight and crush the enemy's arrogance can we isolate the reactionaries, vanquish them or supersede them. We must not show the slightest timidity before a wild beast. We must learn from Wu Sung on the Chingyang Ridge. As Wu Sung saw it, the tiger on Chingyang Ridge was a man-eater, whether irritated or not. Either kill the tiger or be eaten by him— one or the other.

"We want to do business." Quite right, business will be done. We are against no one except the domestic and foreign reactionaries who hinder us from doing business. Everybody should know that it is none other than the imperialists and their running dogs, the Chiang Kai-shek reactionaries, who hinder us from doing business and also from establishing diplomatic relations with foreign countries. When we have beaten the internal and external reactionaries by uniting all domestic and international forces, we shall be able to do business and establish diplomatic relations with all foreign countries on the basis of equality, mutual benefit and mutual respect for territorial integrity and sovereignty.

"Victory is possible even without international help." This is a mistaken idea. In the epoch in which imperialism exists, it is impossible for a genuine people's revolution to win victory in any country without various forms of help from the international revolutionary forces, and even if victory were won, it could not be consolidated. This was the case with the victory and consolidation of the great October Revolution, as Lenin and Stalin told us long ago. This was also the case with the overthrow of the three imperialist powers in World War II and the establishment of the People's Democracies. And this is also the case with the present and the future of People's China. Just imagine! If the Soviet Union had not existed, if there had been no victory in the anti-fascist Second World War, if Japanese imperialism had not been defeated, if the People's Democracies had not come into being, if the oppressed nations of the East were not rising in struggle and if there were no struggle of the masses of the people against their reactionary rulers in the United States, Britain, France, Germany, Italy, Japan and other capitalist countries—if not for all these in combination, the international reactionary forces bearing down upon us would certainly be many times greater than now. In such circumstances, could we have won victory? Obviously not. And even with victory, there could be no consolidation. The Chinese people have had more than enough experience of this kind. This experience was reflected long ago in Sun Yat-sen's death-bed statement on the necessity of uniting with the international revolutionary forces.

"We need help from the British and U. S. governments." This, too, is a naive idea in these times. Would the present rulers of Britain and the United States, who are imperialists, help a people's state? Why do these countries do business with us and, supposing they might be willing to lend us money on terms of mutual benefit in the future, why would they do so? Because their capitalists want to make money and their bankers want to earn interest to extricate themselves from their own crisis—it is not a matter of helping the Chinese people. The Communist Parties and progressive groups in these countries are urging their governments to establish trade and even diplomatic relations with us. This is good will, this is help, this cannot be mentioned in the same breath with the conduct of the bourgeoisie in the same countries. Throughout his life, Sun Yat-sen appealed countless times to the capitalist countries for help and got nothing but heartless rebuffs. Only once in his whole life did Sun Yat-sen receive foreign help, and that was Soviet help. Let readers refer to Dr. Sun Yat-sen's testament; his earnest advice was not to look for help from the imperialist countries but to "unite with those nations of the world which treat us as equals." Dr. Sun had experience; he had suffered, he had been deceived. We should remember his words and not allow ourselves to be deceived again. Internationally, we belong to the side of the anti-imperialist front headed by the Soviet Union, and so we can turn only to this side for genuine and friendly help, not to the side of the imperialist front.

"You are dictatorial." My dear sirs, you are right, that is just what we are. All the experience the Chinese people have accumulated through several decades teaches us to enforce the people's democratic dictatorship, that is, to deprive the reactionaries of the right to speak and let the people alone have that right.

Who are the people? At the present stage in China, they are the working class, the peasantry, the urban petty bourgeoisie and the national bourgeoisie. These classes, led by the working class and the Communist Party, unite to form their own state and elect their own government; they enforce their dictatorship over the running dogs of imperialism—the landlord class and bureaucrat-bourgeoisie, as well as the representatives of those classes, the Kuomintang reactionaries and their accomplices—suppress them, allow them only to behave themselves and not be unruly in word and deed. If they speak or act in an unruly way, they will be promptly stopped and punished. Democracy is practised within the ranks of the people, who enjoy the rights of freedom of speech, assembly, association and so on. The right to vote belongs only to the people, not to the reactionaries. The combination of these two aspects, democracy for the people and dictatorship over the reactionaries, is the people's democratic dictatorship.

Why must things be done this way? The reason is quite clear to everybody. If things were not done this way, the revolution would fail, the people would suffer, the country would be conquered.

"Don't you want to abolish state power?" Yes, we do, but not right now; we cannot do it yet. Why? Because imperialism still exists, because domestic reaction still exists, because classes still exist in our country. Our present task is to strengthen the people's state apparatus—mainly the people's army, the people's police and the people's courts—in order to consolidate national defence and protect the people's interests. Given this condition, China can develop steadily, under the leadership of the working class and the Communist Party, from an agricultural into an industrial country and from a new-democratic into a socialist and communist society, can abolish classes and realize the Great Harmony. The state apparatus, including the army, the police and the courts, is the instrument by which one class oppresses another. It is an instrument for the oppression of antagonistic classes; it is violence and not "benevo-lence." "You are not benevolent!" Quite so. We definitely do not apply a policy of benevolence to the reactionaries and towards the reactionary activities of the reactionary classes. Our policy of benevolence is applied only within the ranks of the people, not beyond them to the reactionaries or to the reactionary activities of reactionary classes.

The people's state protects the people. Only when the people have such a state can they educate and remould themselves on a country-wide scale by democratic methods and, with everyone taking part, shake off the influence of domestic and foreign reac-tionaries (which is still very strong, will survive for a long time and cannot be quickly destroyed), rid themselves of the bad habits and ideas acquired in the old society, not allow themselves to be led astray by the reactionaries, and continue to advance—to advance towards a socialist and communist society.

Here, the method we employ is democratic, the method of persuasion, not of compulsion. When anyone among the people breaks the law, he too should be punished, imprisoned or even sentenced to death; but this is a matter of a few individual cases, and it differs in principle from the dictatorship exercised over the reactionaries as a class.

As for the members of the reactionary classes and individual reactionaries, so long as they do not rebel, sabotage or create trouble after their political power has been overthrown, land and work will be given to them as well in order to allow them to live and remould themselves through labour into new people. If they are not willing to work, the people's state will compel them to work. Propaganda and educational work will be done among them too and will be done, moreover, with as much care and thorough-ness as among the captured army officers in the past. This, too, may be called a "policy of benevolence" if you like, but it is imposed by us on the members of the enemy classes and cannot be mentioned in the same breath with the work of self-education which we carry on within the ranks of the revolutionary people.

Such remoulding of members of the reactionary classes can be accomplished only by a state of the people's democratic dictator-ship under the leadership of the Communist Party. When it is well done, China's major exploiting classes, the landlord class and the bureaucrat-bourgeoisie (the monopoly capitalist class), will be eliminated for good. There remain the national bourgeoisie; at the present stage, we can already do a good deal of suitable educational work with many of them. When the time comes to realize socialism, that is, to nationalize private enterprise, we shall carry the work of educating and remoulding them a step further. The people have a powerful state apparatus in their hands—there is no need to fear rebellion by the national bourgeoisie.

The serious problem is the education of the peasantry. The peasant economy is scattered, and the socialization of agriculture, judging by the Soviet Union's experience, will require a long time and painstaking work. Without socialization of agriculture, there can be no complete, consolidated socialism. The steps to socialize agriculture must be co-ordinated with the development of a powerful industry having state enterprise as its backbone. The state of the people's democratic dictatorship must systematically solve the problems of industrialization. Since it is not proposed to discuss economic problems in detail in this article, I shall not go into them further.

In 1924 a famous manifesto was adopted at the Kuomintang's First National Congress, which Sun Yat-sen himself led and in which Communists participated. The manifesto stated:

> The so-called democratic system in modern states is usually monopolized by the bourgeoisie and has become simply an instrument for oppressing the common people. On the other hand, the Kuomintang's Principle of Democracy means a democratic system shared by all the common people and not privately owned by the few.

Apart from the question of who leads who, the Principle of Democracy stated above corresponds as a general political programme to what we call People's Democracy or New Democracy. A state system which is shared only by the common people and which the bourgeoisie is not allowed to own privately—add to this the leadership of the working class, and we have the state system of the people's democratic dictatorship.

Combat Liberalism

We stand for active ideological struggle because it is the weapon for ensuring unity within the Party and the revolutionary organizations in the interest of our fight. Every Communist and revolutionary should take up this weapon.

But liberalism rejects ideological struggle and stands for unprincipled peace, thus giving rise to a decadent, philistine attitude and bringing about political degeneration in certain units and individuals in the Party and the revolutionary organizations.

Liberalism manifests itself in various ways.

To let things slide for the sake of peace and friendship when a person has clearly gone wrong, and refrain from principled argument because he is an old acquaintance, a fellow townsman, a schoolmate, a close friend, a loved one, an old colleague or old subordinate. Or to touch on the matter lightly instead of going into it thoroughly, so as to keep on good terms. The result is that both the organization and the individual are harmed. This is one type of liberalism.

To indulge in irresponsible criticism in private instead of actively putting forward one's suggestions to the organization. To say nothing to people to their faces but to gossip behind their backs, or to say nothing at a meeting but to gossip afterwards. To show no regard at all for the principles of collective life but to follow one's own inclination. This is a second type.

To let things drift if they do not affect one personally; to say as little as possible while knowing perfectly well what is wrong, to be worldly wise and play safe and seek only to avoid blame. This is a third type.

Not to obey orders but to give pride of place to one's own opinions. To demand special consideration from the organization but to reject its discipline. This is a fourth type.

To indulge in personal attacks, pick quarrels, vent personal spite or seek revenge instead of entering into an argument and struggling against incorrect views for the sake of unity or progress or getting the work done properly. This is a fifth type.

To hear incorrect views without rebutting them and even to hear counter-revolutionary remarks without reporting them, but instead to take them calmly as if nothing had happened. This is a sixth type.

To be among the masses and fail to conduct propaganda and agitation or speak at meetings or conduct investigations and inquiries among them, and instead to be indifferent to them and show no concern for their well-being, forgetting that one is a Communist and behaving as if one were an ordinary non-Communist. This is a seventh type.

To see someone harming the interests of the masses and yet not feel indignant, or dissuade or stop him or reason with him, but to allow him to continue. This is an eighth type.

To work half-heartedly without a definite plan or direction; to work perfunctorily and muddle along—"So long as one remains a monk, one goes on tolling the bell." This is a ninth type.

To regard oneself as having rendered service to the revolution, to pride oneself on being a veteran, to disdain minor assignments while being quite unequal to major tasks, to be slipshod in work and slack in study. This is a tenth type.

To be aware of one's own mistakes and yet make no attempt to correct them, taking a liberal attitude towards oneself. This is an eleventh type.

We could name more. But these eleven are the principal types.

They are all manifestations of liberalism.

Liberalism is extremely harmful in a revolutionary collective. It is a corrosive which eats away unity, undermines cohesion, causes apathy and creates dissension. It robs the revolutionary ranks of compact organization and strict discipline, prevents policies from being carried through and alienates the Party organizations from the masses which the Party leads. It is an extremely bad tendency.

Liberalism stems from petty-bourgeois selfishness, it places personal interests first and the interests of the revolution second, and this gives rise to ideological, political and organizational liberalism.

People who are liberals look upon the principles of Marxism as abstract dogma. They approve of Marxism, but are not prepared to practise it or to practise it in full; they are not prepared to replace their liberalism by Marxism. These people have their Marxism, but they have their liberalism as well—they talk Marxism but practise liberalism; they apply Marxism to others but liberalism to themselves. They keep both kinds of goods in stock and find a use for each. This is how the minds of certain people work.

Liberalism is a manifestation of opportunism and conflicts fundamentally with Marxism. It is negative and objectively has the effect of helping the enemy; that is why the enemy welcomes its preservation in our midst. Such being its nature, there should be no place for it in the ranks of the revolution.

We must use Marxism, which is positive in spirit, to overcome liberalism, which is negative. A Communist should have largeness of mind and he should be staunch and active, looking upon the interests of the revolution as his very life and subordinating his personal interests to those of the revolution; always and everywhere he should adhere to principle and wage a tireless struggle against all incorrect ideas and actions, so as to consolidate the collective life of the Party and strengthen the ties between the Party and the masses; he should be more concerned about the Party and the masses than about any private person, and more concerned about others than about himself. Only thus can he be considered a Communist.

All loyal, honest, active and upright Communists must unite to oppose the liberal tendencies shown by certain people among us, and set them on the right path. This is one of the tasks on our ideological front.

Quotations on Methods of Thinking, Socialism and Communism

The history of mankind is one of continuous development from the realm of necessity to the realm of freedom. This process is never ending. In any society in which classes exist class struggle will never end. In classless society the struggle between the new and the old and between truth and falsehood will never end. In the fields of the struggle for production and scientific experiment, mankind makes constant progress and nature undergoes constant change; they never remain at the same level. Therefore, man has constantly to sum up experience and go on discovering, inventing, creating and advancing. Ideas of stagnation, pessimism, inertia and complacency are all wrong. They are wrong because they agree neither with the historical facts of social development over the past million years, nor with the historical facts of nature so far known to us (*i.e.*, nature as revealed in the history of celestial bodies, the earth, life, and other natural phenomena).

Natural science is one of man's weapons in his fight for freedom. For the purpose of attaining freedom in society, man must use social science to understand and change society and carry out social revolution. For the purpose of attaining freedom in the

SOURCE: Mao Tse-tung, *Quotations from Chairman Mao Tse-tung* (Bantam Books, New York, 1967), passim, sections III and XXII.

world of nature, man must use natural science to understand, conquer and change nature and thus attain freedom from nature.

The Marxist philosophy of dialectical materialism has two outstanding characteristics. One is its class nature: it openly avows that dialectical materialism is in the service of the proletariat. The other is its practicality: it emphasizes the dependence of theory on practice, emphasizes that theory is based on practice and in turn serves practice.

Marxist philosophy holds that the most important problem does not lie in understanding the laws of the objective world and thus being able to explain it, but in applying the knowledge of these laws actively to change the world.

Where do correct ideas come from? Do they drop from the skies? No. Are they innate in the mind? No. They come from social practice, and from it alone; they come from three kinds of social practice, the struggle for production, the class struggle and scientific experiment.

It is man's social being that determines his thinking. Once the correct ideas characteristic of the advanced class are grasped by the masses, these ideas turn into a material force which changes society and changes the world.

In their social practice, men engage in various kinds of struggle and gain rich experience, both from their successes and from their failures. Countless phenomena of the objective external world are reflected in a man's brain through his five sense organs—the organs of sight, hearing, smell, taste and touch. At first, knowledge is perceptual. The leap to conceptual knowledge, *i.e.* to ideas, occurs when sufficient perceptual knowledge is accumulated. This is one process in cognition. It is the first stage in the whole process of cognition, the stage leading from objective matter to subjective consciousness, from existence to ideas. Whether or not one's consciousness or ideas (including theories, policies, plans or measures) do correctly reflect the laws of the objective external world is not yet proved at this stage, in which it is not yet possible to ascertain whether they are correct or not. Then comes the second stage in the process of cognition, the stage leading from consciousness back to matter, from ideas back to existence, in which the knowledge gained in the first stage is applied in social practice to ascertain whether the theories, policies, plans or measures meet with the anticipated success. Generally speaking, those that succeed are correct and those that fail are incorrect, and this is especially true of man's struggle with nature. In social struggle, the forces representing the advanced class sometimes suffer defeat not because their ideas are incorrect but because, in the balance of forces engaged in struggle, they are not as powerful for the time being as the forces of reaction; they are therefore temporarily defeated, but they are bound to triumph sooner or later. Man's knowledge makes another leap through the test of practice. This leap is more important than the previous one. For it is this leap alone that can prove the correctness or incorrectness of the first leap in cognition, *i.e.* of the ideas, theories, policies, plans or measures formulated in the course of reflecting the objective external world. There is no other way of testing truth.

Often, correct knowledge can be arrived at only after many repetitions of the process leading from matter to consciousness and then back to matter, that is, leading from practice to knowledge and then back to practice. Such is the Marxist theory of knowledge, the dialectical materialist theory of knowledge.

Whoever wants to know a thing has no way of doing so except by coming into contact with it, that is, by living (practising) in its environment. . . . If you want knowledge, you must take part in the practice of changing reality. If you want to know the taste of a pear, you must change the pear by eating it yourself. . . . If you want to know the theory and methods of revolution, you must take part in revolution. All genuine knowledge originates in direct experience.

Knowledge begins with practice, and theoretical knowledge which is acquired through practice must then return to practice. The active function of knowledge manifests itself not only in the active leap from perceptual to rational knowledge, but—and this is more important—it must manifest itself in the leap from rational knowledge to revolutionary practice.

It is well known that when you do anything, unless you understand its actual circumstances, its nature and its relations to other things, you will not know the laws governing it, or know how to do it, or be able to do it well.

If a man wants to succeed in his work, that is, to achieve the anticipated results, he must bring his ideas into correspondence with the laws of the objective external world; if they do not correspond, he will fail in his practice. After he fails, he draws his lessons, corrects his ideas to make them correspond to the laws of the external world, and can thus turn failure into success; this is what is meant by "failure is the mother of success" and "a fall into the pit, a gain in your wit."

Communism is at once a complete system of proletarian ideology and a new social system. It is different from any other ideological and social system, and is the most complete, progressive, revolutionary and rational system in human history. The ideological and social system of feudalism has a place only in the museum of history. The ideological and social system of capitalism has also become a museum piece in one part of the world (in the Soviet Union), while in other countries it resembles "a dying person who is sinking fast, like the sun setting beyond the western hills," and will soon be relegated to the museum. The communist ideological and social system alone is full of youth and vitality, sweeping the world with the momentum of an avalanche and the force of a thunderbolt.

The socialist system will eventually replace the capitalist system; this is an objective law independent of man's will. However much the reactionaries try to hold back the wheel of history, sooner or later revolution will take place and will inevitably triumph.

We Communists never conceal our political views. Definitely and beyond all doubt, our future or maximum programme is to carry China forward to socialism and communism. Both the name of our Party and our Marxist world outlook unequivocally point to this supreme ideal of the future, a future of incomparable brightness and splendour.

Taken as a whole, the Chinese revolutionary movement led by the Communist Party embraces the two stages, *i.e.*, the democratic and the socialist revolutions, which are two essentially different revolutionary processes, and the second process can be carried through only after the first has been completed. The democratic revolution is the necessary preparation for the socialist revolution, and the socialist revolution is the inevitable sequel to the democratic revolution. The ultimate aim for which all communists strive is to bring about a socialist and communist society.

Socialist revolution aims at liberating the productive forces. The change-over from individual to socialist, collective ownership in agriculture and handicrafts and from capitalist to socialist ownership in private industry and commerce is bound to bring about a tremendous liberation of the productive forces. Thus the social conditions are being created for a tremendous expansion of industrial and agricultural production.

We are now carrying out a revolution not only in the social system, the change from private to public ownership, but also in technology, the change from handicraft to large-scale modern machine production, and the two revolutions are interconnected. In agriculture, with conditions as they are in our country cooperation must precede the use of big machinery (in capitalist countries agriculture develops in a capitalist way). Therefore we must on no account regard industry and agriculture, socialist industrialization and the socialist transformation of agriculture as two separate and isolated things, and on no account must we emphasize the one and play down the other.

The new social system has only just been established and requires time for its consolidation. It must not be assumed that the new system can be completely consolidated the moment it is established, for that is impossible. It has to be consolidated step by step. To achieve its ultimate consolidation, it is necessary not only to bring about the socialist industrialization of the country and persevere in the socialist revolution on the economic front, but to carry on constant and arduous socialist revolutionary struggles and socialist education on the political and ideological fronts. Moreover, various contributory international factors are required.

In China the struggle to consolidate the socialist system, the struggle to decide whether socialism or capitalism will prevail, will still take a long historical period. But we should all realize that the new system of socialism will unquestionably be consolidated. We can assuredly build a socialist state with modern industry, modern agriculture, and modern science and culture.

We must have faith, first, that the peasant masses are ready to advance step by step along the road of socialism under the leadership of the Party, and second, that the Party is capable of leading the peasants along this road. These two points are the essence of the matter, the main current.

The leading bodies in co-operatives must establish the dominant position of the poor peasants and the new lower middle peasants in these bodies, with the old lower middle peasants and the upper middle peasants—whether old or new—as the supplementary force. Only thus can unity between the poor and middle peasants be attained, the co-operatives be consolidated, production be expanded and the socialist transformation of the entire countryside be correctly accomplished in accordance with the Party's policy. Otherwise, unity between the middle and poor peasants cannot be attained, the co-operatives cannot be consolidated, production cannot be expanded, and the socialist transformation of the entire countryside cannot be achieved.

It is essential to unite with the middle peasants, and it is wrong not to do so. But on whom must the working class and the Communist Party rely in the countryside in order to unite with the middle peasants and realize the socialist transformation of the entire countryside? Surely on none other than the poor peasants. That was the case when the struggle against the landlords was being waged and the land reform was being carried out, and that is the case today when the struggle against the rich peasants and other capitalist elements is being waged to achieve the socialist transformation of agriculture. In both these revolutionary periods, the middle peasants wavered in the initial stages. It is only after they clearly see the general trend of events and the approaching triumph of the revolution that the middle peasants will come in on the side of the revolution. The poor peasants must work on the middle peasants and win them over, so that the revolution will broaden from day to day until final victory.

After the country-wide victory of the Chinese revolution and the solution of the land problem, two basic contradictions will still exist in China. The first is internal, that is, the contradiction between the working class and the bourgeoisie. The second is external, that is, the contradiction between China and the imperialist countries. Consequently, after the victory of the people's democratic revolution, the state power of the people's republic under the leadership of the working class must not be weakened but must be strengthened.

Our state is a people's democratic dictatorship led by the working class and based on the worker-peasant alliance. What is this dictatorship for? Its first function is to suppress the reactionary classes and elements and those exploiters in our country who resist the socialist revolution, to suppress those who try to wreck our socialist construction, or in other words, to resolve the internal contradictions between ourselves and the enemy. For instance, to arrest, try and sentence certain counterrevolutionaries, and to deprive landlords and bureaucrat-capitalists of their right to vote and their freedom of speech for a specified period of time—all this comes within the scope of our dictatorship. To maintain public order and safeguard the interests of the people, it is likewise necessary to exercise dictatorship over embezzlers, swindlers, arsonists, murderers, criminal gangs and other scoundrels who seriously disrupt public order. The second function of this dictatorship is to protect our country from subversion and possible aggression by external enemies. In that event, it is the task of this dictatorship to resolve the external contradiction between ourselves and the enemy. The aim of this dictatorship is to protect all our people so that they can devote themselves to peaceful labour and build China into a socialist country with a modern industry, agriculture, science and culture.

The people's democratic dictatorship needs the leadership of the working class. For it is only the working class that is most farsighted, most selfless and most thoroughly revolutionary. The entire history of revolution proves that without the leadership of the working class revolution fails and that with the leadership of the working class revolution triumphs.

The people's democratic dictatorship is based on the alliance of the working class, the peasantry and the urban petty bourgeoisie, and mainly on the alliance of the workers and the peasants, because these two classes comprise 80 to 90 per cent of China's population. These two classes are the main force in overthrowing imperialism and the Kuomintang reactionaries. The transition from New Democracy to socialism also depends upon their alliance.

Class struggle, the struggle for production and scientific experiment are the three great revolutionary movements for building a mighty socialist country. These movements are a sure guarantee that Communists will be free from bureaucracy and immune against revisionism and dogmatism, and will for ever remain invincible. They are a reliable guarantee that the proletariat will be able to unite with the broad working masses and realize a democratic dictatorship. If, in the absence of these movements, the landlords, rich peasants, counterrevolutionaries, bad elements and ogres of all kinds were allowed to crawl out, while our cadres were to shut their eyes to all this and in many cases fail even to differentiate between the enemy and ourselves but were to collaborate with the enemy and were corrupted, divided and demoralized by him, if our cadres were thus pulled out or the enemy were able to sneak in, and if many of our workers, peasants, and intellectuals were left defenceless against both the soft and the hard tactics of the enemy, then it would not take long, perhaps only several years or a decade, or several decades at most, before a counterrevolutionary restoration on a national scale inevitably occurred, the Marxist-Leninist party would undoubtedly become a revisionist party or a fascist party, and the whole of China would change its colour.

The people's democratic dictatorship uses two methods. Towards the enemy, it uses the methods of dictatorship, that is, for as long a period of time as is necessary it does not let them take part in political activities and compels them to obey the law of the People's Government and to engage in labour and, through labour, transform themselves into new men. Towards the people, on the contrary, it uses the method not of compulsion but of democracy, that is, it must necessarily let them take part in political activities and does not compel them to do this or that, but uses the methods of democracy in educating and persuading them.

Under the leadership of the Communist Party, the Chinese people are carrying out a vigorous rectification movement in order to bring about the rapid development of socialism in China on a firmer basis. It is a movement for carrying out a nation-wide debate which is both guided and free, a debate in the city and the country-side on such questions as the socialist road versus the capitalist road, the basic system of the state and its major policies, the working style of Party and government functionaries, and the question of the welfare of the people, a debate which is conducted by setting forth facts and reasoning things out, so as correctly to resolve those actual contradictions among the people which demand immediate solution. This is a socialist movement for the self-education and self-remoulding of the people.

V

Democratic Socialism

The socialist dilemma in relation to democracy and the present division between antagonistic democratic and authoritarian wings have their origin (as noted in the Introduction) in the dual soul of nineteenth-century socialism. In the socialist ideological scheme, collectivism will make for uniformity of views, thus ending tensions and creating a permanently peaceful society. Socialists maintained that only in capitalistic societies did liberty make for diversity, and political liberty for divisions within the national community. For a majority of socialists before 1917, to be a democrat meant making use of what was derisively called bourgeois liberty and taking advantage of a nonviolent method to seize power in the state. It did not mean permanently accepting ideological and political pluralism and the equality of different tendencies. It did not mean abandoning the aspiration toward uniformity, which was to result inevitably from the replacement of capitalism with collectivism. This was the position of Ferdinand Lassalle (1825–1863), accepted in the 1870's and later by many prominent Marxist thinkers, the most authoritative of whom for several decades was Karl Kautsky (1854–1938). Before 1917 few socialists faced the fact that, whatever the economic structure, political and intellectual liberty is likely to make for diversity; that the advocacy of these two basic concepts of liberalism cannot be dissociated from the search for institutions enabling diverse tendencies to coexist peacefully. However, whatever their understanding of democracy, there were already a few socialists for whom democracy, with its pluralism, equal rights of different groups, free representative institutions, and the alternating in power of different tendencies was more important than socialist uniformity. The coming into power of socialists in Russia in 1917, in Germany in 1918, and in other European countries soon after, obliged more and more socialists to choose between democracy as the dictatorship of the majority (or, as was the case in Russia, of self-appointed spokesmen for the majority), as advocated by Lenin's followers, and democracy as political liberty that necessitated the limiting of socialist goals. Democratic socialism developed in the measure in which not only authoritarianism was opposed, but also in the measure in which the pseudodemocratic Lassallean position was abandoned. The clarification begun before the end of the nineteenth century was completed after World War II.

In this section, the first selection contains excerpts from contributions of G. B. Shaw to essays written for the Fabian Society of Great Britain. The second has excerpts from the most important ideological work written by a democratic socialist, the German Eduard Bernstein. In the third is the text of the Frankfurt Declaration, approved in 1951 by delegates of democratic socialist parties when they met to reorganize the Socialist International, and also the Oslo Declaration of 1962. The fourth and fifth selections give excerpts from works by two prominent democratic socialists, the American Norman Thomas and the Englishman Anthony Crosland.

A. George Bernard Shaw on Fabian Socialism

George Bernard Shaw (1856–1950), known to two generations of his contemporaries as G.B.S., came of a family of Irish gentry. In literary circles he is known as a foremost playwright, but he thought of himself primarily as a socialist thinker and as an economist. Shaw was an eccentric, the kind of brilliant and irksome individual to whom only a tolerant nation like the British would give full freedom of expression—to everyone's advantage. An American, Henry George (1839–1897), the author of *Progress and Poverty*, converted Shaw to socialism in 1882. Two years later the young intellectual joined the distinguished group that had, a few months earlier, established the Fabian Society, with the aim of gradually preparing the British nation to abandon capitalism for collectivism. The gradualism advocated was reminiscent of the tactics employed against a powerful enemy by the Roman general Fabius Cunctator, hence the adjective Fabian. Influential members of the Society were Sidney Webb and his wife (the former Beatrice Potter), Graham Wallas, Annie Besant, Ramsay MacDonald (Prime Minister in 1924 and again from 1929 to 1935), William Morris, and Henry Hyndman. In 1887, Shaw edited the publication of a number of essays prepared by members of the Society. The platforms from which the Labour Party fought elections in 1924 and in 1929 were largely worked out by Fabian socialists. Shaw opposed British participation in World War I, admired the Italian fascist dictator Mussolini (before 1914 a revolutionary socialist), visited the Soviet Union in 1931, and, unaware of what was going on in the collectivization of the land, praised Soviet Marxist-Leninists for their adherence to Fabian principles. For Shaw, democracy was more a habit he could not give up than a conviction.

G. B. Shaw's Sixty Years of Fabianism

[1889] . . . The economic analysis . . . convicts Private Property of being unjust even from the beginning, and utterly

source: G. B. Shaw, ed., *Fabian Essays* (George Allen & Unwin, London, 1948), passim pp. xxix–xxxiv, 22–27, 228–230.

impossible as a final solution of even the individualist aspect of the problem of adjusting the share of the worker in the distribution of wealth to the labour incurred by him in its production. All attempts yet made to construct true societies upon it have failed: the nearest things to societies so achieved have been civilizations, which have rotted into centres of vice and luxury, and eventually been swept away by uncivilized races. That our own civilization is already in an advanced stage of rottenness may be taken as statistically proved. That further decay instead of improvement must ensue if the institution of private property be maintained, is economically certain. Fortunately, private property in its integrity is not now practicable. Although the safety valve of emigration has been furiously at work during this century, yet the pressure of population has forced us to begin the restitution to the people of the sums taken from them for the ground landlords, holders of tenant right, and capitalists, by the imposition of an income tax, and by compelling them to establish out of their revenues a national system of education, besides imposing restrictions—as yet only of the forcible-feeble sort—on their terrible power of abusing the wage contract. . . . experience has lately convinced all economists that no exercise in abstract economics, however closely deduced, is to be trusted unless it can be experimentally verified by tracing its expression in history. It is true that the process which I have presented as a direct development of private property between free exchangers had to work itself out in the Old World indirectly and tortuously through a struggle with political and religious institutions and survivals quite antagonistic to it. It is true that cultivation did not begin in Western Europe with the solitary emigrant pre-empting his private property, but with the tribal communes in which arose subsequently the assertion of the right of the individual to private judgment and private action against the tyranny of primitive society. It is true that cultivation has not proceeded by logical steps from good land to less good; from less good to bad; and from bad to worse: the exploration of new countries and new regions, and the discovery of new uses for old products, has often made the margin of cultivation more fruitful than the centre, and, for the moment (whilst the centre was shifting to the margin), turned the whole movement of rent and wages directly counter to the economic theory. Nor is it true that, taking the world as one country, cultivation has yet spread from the snowline to the water's edge. There is free land still for the

poorest East End match-box maker if she could get there, reclaim
the wilderness there, speak the language there, stand the climate
there, and be fed, clothed, and housed there whilst she cleared her
farm; learned how to cultivate it; and waited for the harvest.
Economists have been ingenious enough to prove that this alternative really secures her independence; but I shall not waste time in
dealing with that. Practically, if there is no free land in England,
the economic analysis holds good of England, in spite of Siberia,
Central Africa, and the Wild West. Again, it is not immediately
true that men are governed in production solely by a determination
to realize the maximum of exchange value. The impulse to production often takes specific direction in the first instance; and a man
will insist on producing pictures or plays although he might gain
more money by producing boots or bonnets. But, his specific
impulse once gratified, he will make as much money as he can. He
will sell his picture or play for a hundred pounds rather than for
fifty. In short, though there is no such person as the celebrated
"economic man," man being wilful rather than rational, yet when
the wilful man has had his way he will take what else he can get;
and so he always does appear, finally if not primarily, as the
economic man. On the whole, history, even in the Old World,
goes the way traced by the economist. In the New World the
correspondence is exact. The United States and the Colonies have
been peopled by fugitives from the full-blown individualism of
Western Europe, pre-empting private property precisely as assumed in this investigation of the conditions of cultivation. The
economic relations of these cultivators have not since put on any of
the old political disguises. Yet among them, in confirmation of the
validity of our analysis, we see all the evils of our old civilizations
growing up; and though with them the end is not yet, still it is
from them to us that the great recent revival of the cry for
nationalization of the land has come, articulated by a man who had
seen the whole tragedy of private property hurried through its acts
with unprecedented speed in the mushroom cities of America.

On Socialism the analysis of the economic action of Individualism bears as a discovery, in the private appropriation of land, of the
source of those unjust privileges against which Socialism is aimed.
It is practically a demonstration that public property in land is the
basic economic condition of Socialism. But this does not involve at
present a literal restoration of the land to the people. The land is at

present in the hands of the people: its proprietors are for the most part absentees. The modern form of private property is simply a legal claim to take a share of the produce of the national industry year by year without working for it. It refers to no special part or form of that produce; and in process of consumption its revenue cannot be distinguished from earnings, so that the majority of persons, accustomed to call the commodities which form the income of the proprietor his private property, and seeing no difference between them and the commodities which form the income of a worker, extend the term private property to the worker's subsistence also, and can only conceive an attack on private property as an attempt to empower everybody to rob everybody else all round. But the income of a private proprietor can be distinguished by the fact that he obtains it unconditionally and gratuitously by private right against the public weal, which is incompatible with the existence of consumers who do not produce. Socialism involves discontinuance of the payment of these incomes, and addition of the wealth so saved to incomes derived from labour. As we have seen, incomes derived from private property consist partly of economic rent; partly of pensions, also called rent, obtained by the subletting of tenant rights; and partly of a form of rent called interest, obtained by special adaptations of land to production by the application of capital: all these being finally paid out of the difference between the produce of the worker's labour and the price of that labour sold in the open market for wages, salary, fees, or profits. The whole, except economic rent, can be added directly to the incomes of the workers by simply discontinuing its exaction from them. Economic rent, arising as it does from variations of fertility or advantages of situations, must always be held as common or social wealth, and used, as the revenues raised by taxation are now used, for public purposes, among which Socialism would make national insurance and the provision of capital matters of the first importance.

The economic problem of Socialism is thus solved; and the political question of how the economic solution is to be practically applied does not come within the scope of this essay. But if we have got as far as an intellectual conviction that the source of our social misery is no eternal well-spring of confusion and evil, but only an artificial system susceptible of almost infinite modification and readjustment—nay, of practical demolition and substitution at

the will of Man, then a terrible weight will be lifted from the
minds of all except those who are, whether avowedly to themselves
or not, clinging to the present state of things from base motives.
We have had in this century a stern series of lessons on the folly of
believing anything for no better reason than that it is pleasant to
believe it. It was pleasant to look round with a consciousness of
possessing a thousand a year, and say, with Browning's David,
"All's love; and all's law." It was pleasant to believe that the chance
we were too lazy to take in this world would come back to us in
another. It was pleasant to believe that a benevolent hand was
guiding the steps of society; overruling all evil appearances for
good; and making poverty here the earnest of a great blessedness
and reward hereafter. It was pleasant to lose the sense of worldly
inequality in the contemplation of our equality before God. But
utilitarian questioning and scientific answering turned all this tran-
quil optimism into the blackest pessimism. Nature was shewn to us
as "red in tooth and claw": if the guiding hand were indeed
benevolent, then it could not be omnipotent; so that our trust in it
was broken: if it were omnipotent, it could not be benevolent; so
that our love of it turned to fear and hatred. We had never
admitted that the other world, which was to compensate for the
sorrows of this, was open to horses and apes (though we had not
on that account been any the more merciful to our horses); and
now came Science to shew us the corner of the pointed ear of the
horse on our own heads, and present the ape to us as our blood
relation. No proof came of the existence of that other world and
that benevolent power to which we had left the remedy of the
atrocious wrongs of the poor: proof after proof came that what we
called Nature knew and cared no more about our pains and
pleasures than we know or care about the tiny creatures we crush
underfoot as we walk through the fields. Instead of at once
perceiving that this meant no more than that Nature was unmoral
and indifferent, we relapsed into a gross form of devil worship, and
conceived Nature as a remorselessly malignant power. This was no
better than the old optimism, and infinitely gloomier. It kept our
eyes still shut to the truth that there is no cruelty and selfishness
outside Man himself; and that his own active benevolence can
combat and vanquish both. When the Socialist came forward as a
meliorist on these lines, the old school of political economists, who
could see no alternative to private property, put forward in proof

of the powerlessness of benevolent action to arrest the deadly automatic production of poverty by the increase of the population, the very analysis I have just presented. Their conclusions exactly fitted in with the new ideas. It was Nature at it again—the struggle for existence—the remorseless extirpation of the weak—the survival of the fittest—in short, natural selection at work. Socialism seemed too good to be true: it was passed by as merely the old optimism foolishly running its head against the stone wall of modern science. But Socialism now challenges individualism, scepticism, pessimism, worship of Nature personified as a devil, on their own ground of science. The science of the production and distribution of wealth is Political Economy. Socialism appeals to that science, and, turning on Individualism its own guns, routs it in incurable disaster. Henceforth the bitter cynic who still finds the world an eternal and unimprovable doghole, with the placid person of means who repeats the familiar misquotation, "the poor ye shall have always with you," lose their usurped place among the cultured, and pass over to the ranks of the ignorant, the shallow, and the superstitious. As for the rest of us, since we were taught to revere proprietary respectability in our unfortunate childhood, and since we found our childish hearts so hard and unregenerate that they secretly hated and rebelled against respectability in spite of that teaching, it is impossible to express the relief with which we discover that our hearts were all along right, and that the current respectability of today is nothing but a huge inversion of righteous and scientific social order weltering in dishonesty, uselessness, selfishness, wanton misery, and idiotic waste of magnificent opportunities for noble and happy living. It was terrible to feel this, and yet to fear that it could not be helped—that the poor must starve and make you ashamed of your dinner—that they must shiver and make you ashamed of your warm overcoat. It is to economic science—once the Dismal, now the Hopeful—that we are indebted for the discovery that though the evil is enormously worse than we knew, yet it is not eternal—not even very long lived, if we only bestir ourselves to make an end of it.

[1908] Since 1889 the Socialist movement has been completely transformed throughout Europe; and the result of the transformation may fairly be described as Fabian Socialism. In the eighteeneighties, when Socialism revived in England for the first time since the suppression of the Paris Commune in 1871, it was not at first realized that what had really been suppressed for good and all was the romantic revolutionary Liberalism and Radicalism of 1848, to which the Socialists had attached themselves as a matter of course, partly because they were themselves romantic and revolutionary, and partly because both Liberals and Socialists had a common object in Democracy.

Besides this common object the two had a common conception of method in revolution. They were both catastrophic. Liberalism had conquered autocracy and bureaucracy by that method in England and France, and then left industry to make what it could of the new political conditions by the unregulated action of competition between individuals. Briefly, the Liberal plan was to cut off the King's head, and leave the rest to Nature, which was supposed to gravitate towards economic harmonies when not restrained by tyrannical governments. The Socialists were very far ahead of the Liberals in their appreciation of the preponderant importance of industry, even going so far as to maintain, with Buckle and Marx, that all social institutions whatever are imposed by economic conditions, and that there is fundamentally only one tyranny: the tyranny of Capital. Yet even the Socialists had so far formed their political habits in the Liberal school that they were quite disposed to believe that if you cut off the head of King Capital, you might expect to see things come right more or less spontaneously.

It was in 1885 that the Fabian Society, amid the jeers of the catastrophists, turned its back on the barricades and made up its mind to turn heroic defeat into prosaic success. We set ourselves two definite tasks: first, to provide a parliamentary program for a Prime Minister converted to Socialism as Peel was converted to Free Trade; and second, to make it as easy and matter-of-course for the ordinary respectable Englishman to be a Socialist as to be a Liberal or a Conservative.

These tasks we have accomplished, to the great disgust of our more romantic comrades. Nobody now conceives Socialism as a destructive insurrection ending, if successful, in millennial absurdities. Membership of the Fabian Society, though it involves an express avowal of Socialism, excites no more comment than membership of the Society of Friends, or even of the Church of

England. Incidentally, Labour has been organized as a separate political interest in the House of Commons, with the result that in the very next Budget it was confessed for the first time that there are unearned as well as earned incomes in the country: an admission which, if not a surrender of the Capitalist citadel to Socialism, is at all events letting down the drawbridge; for Socialism, on its aggressive side, is, and always has been, an attack on idleness. The resolution to make an end of private property is gathering force every day: people are beginning to learn the difference between a man's property and his walking stick, which is strictly limited by the public condition that he shall not use it to break his neighbour's head or extort money with menaces, and those private rights of property which enable the idle to levy an enormous tribute, amounting at present to no less than £630,000,000 a year, on the earnings of the rest of the community. The old attempt to confuse the issue by asserting that the existence of the family, religion, marriage, etc., etc., are inextricably bound up with the toleration of senseless social theft no longer imposes on anyone: after a whole year of unexampled exploitation of this particular variety of obscene vituperation by the most widely read cheap newspapers in London, no Socialist is a penny the worse for it.

[1948] . . . nowadays the word Socialism means no more than the word Christianity. Even in the last century Sir William Harcourt said "We are all Socialists now," just as every military recruit who describes himself as having no religion is at once catalogued as Church of England. The Labour Party now in power professes Socialism: the Tory Opposition has just been urged to rename itself the Democratic Party. In such nonsense and confusion what constitutes a citizen a genuine Fabian? Is there any such person now?

Decidedly yes.

There are people who, having thoroughly learnt the economic law of rent, and its corollaries that "real" private property is theft and must be abolished root and branch, no longer imagine childishly that this means that highway robbery will be made legal and no man's watch and umbrella be safe.

They also understand the economic law of exchange value, over which Marx blundered, and a much less gifted capitalist professor (Stanley Jevons) was the British pathfinder. It is essentially a mathematical law of supply and demand, dealing with continually varying utilities, and entirely opposed to the proletarian notion that mere labour can create value as well as realize it. They understand, too, that the democracy claimed by the British Parliamentary system is a sham, deliberately invented by a clever peer to enable King William the Third of England (a Dutchman) to fight King Louis the Fourteenth of France for the maintenance of the Reformation and the extradition of the Stuart monarchy. Under it we have seen two world wars declared and one abdication of the British throne effected without consulting or informing the House of Commons, whilst (for example) the urgent need for a new bridge across the Severn has been under discussion for a hundred years, and the bridge is still unbuilt.

It is evident that if the Fabians are to keep their ancient intellectual leadership in the Socialist movement, they must not dream, as H. G. Wells did, of vast numbers and huge subscription lists. They must remain a minority of cultural snobs and genuinely scientific Socialist tacticians, few enough to be negligible in the electoral count of noses, and with no time to spend on the conversion and elementary Socialist education of illiterates and political novices. The recurrent cry for fraternization and unity in the movement must have no illusory charm for them, as it had for Keir Hardie. When he at last succeeded in bringing all the Socialist Societies into a fraternal conference, they wrangled until, having expelled each other one by one, they left him finally with nobody but himself and a few personal disciples to face a hopeless fraternal fiasco. We Fabians were a middle-class lot; and when a proletarian joined us he could not work mentally at the same speed and in the same way against the same cultural background as we. He was therefore an obstruction to our work, and finally abandoned us with his class mistrust of us intensified, crying "Do not trust these men." As our relations were quite friendly as long as we worked in separate compartments we learnt that cultural segregation is essential in research, and indiscriminate fraternization fatal.

Rudimentary unskilled Socialism has no place in the Fabian Society. Every Fabian should be acquainted with the domestic life of Tolstoy (an appalling example) and with the history of the early Socialist colonies founded on "the new moral worlds" of Owen and Fourier, also with the highly cultivated and scholarly moralized Capitalism of Comte's Positive Philosophy. Socialists who have all this to learn and no intention to learn it are useless obstructives in the Fabian Society. There are plenty of millennium mongering Societies and Parties and Leagues for them to join and be happy. The Fabians must be unsentimental scientific pioneers of the next practicable steps, not dreamers of the New Jerusalem and the Second Advent or the Love panacea with justice nowhere. All Socialists do not begin in the Fabian way, nor did the Fabians themselves. Even so able and sensible a man as William Morris, who may go down to posterity as Saint William of Kelmscott, began by declaring that he saw no hope for the people but in revolution, and did not reach his final Fabian position until he had tried to work with commonplace "comrades" fathoms beneath him in mental speed, scope, and capacity, and had found the combination utterly unworkable. Meanwhile the handful of "bourgeois" Fabians meeting in each others' drawing rooms, without a fixed subscription or a banking account, successfully explored the path of Socialism on constitutional lines; made it respectable; and lived to see the gigantic Russian experiment completely converted to Fabianism by sheer force of experience under Lenin and Stalin. But they are still, and must remain, missionaries among savages.

But they must not, like the cruder sectarian missionaries, shove all their doctrines, relevant or irrelevant, down the throats of their converts as the Truth.

B. EDUARD BERNSTEIN ON REVISIONISM

In 1896 the socialist newspaper *Die Neue Zeit* published articles indicative of a crisis in sectors of Marxist socialism, which had been for some time ideologically and politically the most important socialist school of thought. The articles had profound repercussions, which increased as time went on, so much so that today's democratic socialism is to a great extent the heir to Bernstein's revisionism (as it was called at the time). The author of the articles, the German Eduard Bernstein (1850–1932), then living in London, was a petty bourgeois (lower middle class), belonging, that is, to the social stratum most despised by Marxists. Highly educated and deeply committed, Bernstein had in 1872 joined the German Social Democratic Party, founded in 1869. Intellectually, he had been a follower of the positivist philosopher Eugen Dühring (1833–1921) but he became a convert to Marxist dialectical materialism after reading Engels's *Anti-Dühring*. Bernstein spent the ten years from 1878 to 1888 in Switzerland, editing the *Sozialdemokrat* after 1881. Thirteen years in London followed, in close contact with Engels, Kautsky, Fabian socialists, and labor leaders. Engels, who died in 1895, appointed him as his executor. No one knows how much of what Bernstein published in 1896 was contributed by Engels himself, how much was the result of reflection in the Swiss and British free environments, how much was owed to the Fabians in London. Under the title *Evolutionary Socialism*, the articles were published in German in 1899 and in English in 1909. The excerpts here are from the English edition.

Having praised Marx for his pioneer work, Bernstein went on to contradict his analyses and predictions. Bernstein himself admitted that socialism continued the liberal tradition, and that democracy as the organization of liberty was the road to socialism. That was the time when, particularly in France, socialists were debating and quarreling on the question of parliamentary cooperation with progressive democrats, specifically Radical parties or the radical wing of Liberal parties. By admitting a link between liberalism and socialism, Bernstein abandoned the Lassallean pseudodemocratism and, more openly and cogently than the Fabians, encouraged socialists to be democrats. So-called orthodox Marxists and all revolutionary socialists labelled him a revisionist; actually, in his position there was more than a revision of Marxism—there was a rejection of basic Marxist tenets. A majority of German, Austrian and other Social Democrats continued to call themselves Marxists, but after the Revolution of 1918 they acted as democratic socialists, advocating reforms within, not outside, a democratic frame and recognizing the equal rights of nonsocialists.

Preface [*To Evolutionary Socialism*]

. . . It has been maintained . . . that the practical deductions from my treatises would be the abandonment of the conquest of political power by the proletariat organised politically and economically. That is quite an arbitrary deduction, the accuracy of which I altogether deny.

I set myself against the notion that we have to expect shortly a collapse of the bourgeois economy, and that social democracy should be induced by the prospect of such an imminent, great, social catastrophe to adapt its tactics to that assumption. That I maintain most emphatically.

The adherents of this theory of a catastrophe, base it especially on the conclusions of the *Communist Manifesto*. This is a mistake in every respect.

SOURCE: Eduard Bernstein, *Evolutionary Socialism: A Criticism and Affirmation*, trans. Edith C. Harvey (Independent Labour Party, London, 1909), pp. ix–xvii, 139–156, 202–210.

The theory which the *Communist Manifesto* sets forth of the evolution of modern society was correct as far as it characterised the general tendencies of that evolution. But it was mistaken in several special deductions, above all in the estimate of the *time* the evolution would take. The last has been unreservedly acknowledged by Friedrich Engels, the joint author with Marx of the *Manifesto*, in his preface to the *Class War in France*. But it is evident that if social evolution takes a much greater period of time than was assumed, it must also take upon itself *forms* and lead to forms that were not foreseen and could not be foreseen then.

Social conditions have not developed to such an acute opposition of things and classes as is depicted in the *Manifesto*. It is not only useless, it is the greatest folly to attempt to conceal this from ourselves. The number of members of the possessing classes is to-day not smaller but larger. The enormous increase of social wealth is not accompanied by a decreasing number of large capitalists but by an increasing number of capitalists of all degrees. The middle classes change their character but they do not disappear from the social scale.

The concentration in productive industry is not being accomplished even today in all its departments with equal thoroughness and at an equal rate. In a great many branches of production it certainly justifies the forecasts of the socialist critic of society; but in other branches it lags even to-day behind them. The process of concentration in agriculture proceeds still more slowly. Trade statistics show an extraordinarily elaborated graduation of enterprises in regard to size. No rung of the ladder is disappearing from it. The significant changes in the inner structure of these enterprises and their interrelationship cannot do away with this fact.

In all advanced countries we see the privileges of the capitalist bourgeoisie yielding step by step to democratic organisations. Under the influence of this, and driven by the movement of the working classes which is daily becoming stronger, a social reaction has set in against the exploiting tendencies of capital, a counteraction which, although it still proceeds timidly and feebly, yet does exist, and is always drawing more departments of economic life under its influence. Factory legislation, the democratising of local government, and the extension of its area of work, the freeing of trade unions and systems of co-operative trading from legal restrictions, the consideration of standard conditions of labour in the work undertaken by public authorities—all these characterise this phase of the evolution.

But the more the political organisations of modern nations are democratised the more the needs and opportunities of great political catastrophes are diminished. He who holds firmly to the catastrophic theory of evolution must, with all his power, withstand and hinder the evolution described above, which, indeed, the logical defenders of that theory formerly did. But is the conquest of political power by the proletariat simply to be by a political catastrophe? Is it to be the appropriation and utilisation of the power of the State by the proletariat exclusively against the whole non-proletarian world?

He who replies in the affirmative must be reminded of two things. In 1872 Marx and Engels announced in the preface to the new edition of the *Communist Manifesto* that the Paris Commune had exhibited a proof that "the working classes cannot simply take possession of the ready-made State machine and set it in motion for their own aims." And in 1895 Friedrich Engels stated in detail in the preface to *War of the Classes* that the time of political surprises, of the "revolutions of small conscious minorities at the head of unconscious masses" was to-day at an end, that a collision on a large scale with the military would be the means of checking the steady growth of social democracy and of even throwing it back for a time—in short, that social democracy would flourish far better by lawful than by unlawful means and by violent revolution. And he points out in conformity with this opinion that the next task of the party should be "to work for an uninterrupted increase of its votes" or to carry on a slow *propaganda of parliamentary activity*.

Thus Engels, who, nevertheless, as his numerical examples show, still somewhat overestimated the rate of process of the evolution! Shall we be told that he abandoned the conquest of political power by the working classes, because he wished to avoid the steady growth of social democracy secured by lawful means being interrupted by a political revolution?

If not, and if one subscribes to his conclusions, one cannot reasonably take any offence if it is declared that for a long time yet the task of social democracy is, instead of speculating on a great economic crash, "to organise the working classes politically and develop them as a democracy and to fight for all reforms in the

State which are adapted to raise the working classes and transform the State in the direction of democracy."

That is what I have said in my impugned article and what I still maintain in its full import. As far as concerns the question propounded above it is equivalent to Engels' dictum, for democracy is, at any given time, as much government by the working classes as these are capable of practising according to their intellectual ripeness and the degree of social development they have attained. Engels, indeed, refers at the place just mentioned to the fact that the *Communist Manifesto* has "proclaimed the conquest of the democracy as one of the first and important tasks of the fighting proletariat."

In short, Engels is so thoroughly convinced that the tactics based on the presumption of a catastrophe have had their day, that he even considers a revision of them necessary in the Latin countries where tradition is much more favourable to them than in Germany. "If the conditions of war between nations have altered," he writes, "no less have those for the war between classes." Has this already been forgotten?

No one has questioned the necessity for the working classes to gain the control of government. The point at issue is between the theory of a social cataclysm and the question whether with the given social development in Germany and the present advanced state of its working classes in the towns and the country, a sudden catastrophe would be desirable in the interest of the social democracy. I have denied it and deny it again, because in my judgment a greater security for lasting success lies in a steady advance than in the possibilities offered by a catastrophic crash.

And as I am firmly convinced that important periods in the development of nations cannot be leapt over I lay the greatest value on the next tasks of social democracy, on the struggle for the political rights of the working man, on the political activity of working men in town and country for the interests of their class, as well as on the work of the industrial organisation of the workers.

In this sense I wrote the sentence that the movement means everything for me and that what is *usually* called "the final aim of socialism" is nothing; and in this sense I write it down again to-day. Even if the word "usually" had not shown that the proposition was only to be understood conditionally, it was obvious that it *could* not express indifference concerning the final carrying out of socialist principles, but only indifference—or, as it would be better expressed, carelessness—as to the form of the final arrangement of things. I have at no time had an excessive interest in the future, beyond general principles; I have not been able to read to the end any picture of the future. My thoughts and efforts are concerned with the duties of the present and the nearest future, and I only busy myself with the perspectives beyond so far as they give me a line of conduct for suitable action now.

The conquest of political power by the working classes, the expropriation of capitalists, are no ends in themselves but only means for the accomplishment of certain aims and endeavours. As such they are demands in the programme of social democracy and are not attacked by me. Nothing can be said beforehand as to the circumstances of their accomplishment; we can only fight for their realisation. But the conquest of political power necessitates the possession of political *rights;* and the most important problem of tactics which German social democracy has at the present time to solve, appears to me to be to devise the best ways for the extension of the political and economic rights of the German working classes.

. . . [This work] differs in several important points from the ideas to be found in the theory of Karl Marx and Engels—men whose writings have exercised the greatest influence on my socialist line of thought, and one of whom—Engels—honoured me with his personal friendship not only till his death but who showed beyond the grave, in his testamentary arrangements, a proof of his confidence in me.

This deviation in the manner of looking at things certainly is not of recent date; it is the product of an inner struggle of years and I hold in my hand a proof that this was no secret to Friedrich Engels, and moreover I must guard Engels from the suspicion that he was so narrow-minded as to exact from his friends an unconditional adherence to his views. Nevertheless, it will be understood from the foregoing why I have till now avoided as much as possible giving to my deviating points of view the form of a systematic and detailed criticism of the Marx-Engels doctrine. This could the more easily be avoided up till now because as regards the practical questions with which we were concerned Marx and Engels in the course of time considerably modified their views.

Democracy and Socialism

. . . The trade unions are the democratic element in industry.
Their tendency is to destroy the absolutism of capital, and to
procure for the worker a direct influence in the management of an
industry. It is only natural that great differences of opinion should
exist on the degree of influence to be desired. To a certain mode of
thought it may appear a breach of principle to claim less for the
union than an unconditional right of decision in the trade. The
knowledge that such a right under present circumstances is just as
Utopian as it would be contrary to the nature of a socialist
community, has led others to deny trade unions any lasting part in
economic life, and to recognise them only temporarily as the
lesser of various unavoidable evils. There are socialists in whose
eyes the union is only an object lesson to prove the uselessness of
any other than political revolutionary action. As a matter of fact,
the union to-day—and in the near future—has very important
social tasks to fulfil for the trades, which, however, do not demand,
nor are even consistent with, its omnipotence in any way.

The merit of having first grasped the fact that trade unions are
indispensable organs of the democracy, and not only passing coalitions, belongs to a group of English writers. This is not wonderful
if one considers that trade unions attained importance in England
earlier than anywhere else, and that England in the last third of the
nineteenth century passed through a change from an oligarchic to
an almost democratic state of government. The latest and most
thorough work on this subject, the book on the theory and the
practice of the British Trade Unions, by Sidney and Beatrice
Webb, has been rightly described by the authors as a treatment of
Industrial Democracy. Before them the late Thorold Rogers, in his
lectures on the *Economic Interpretation of History* . . . called
the trade union, Labour Partnership—which comes to the same
thing in principle, but at the same time points out the limits to
which the function of a trade union can extend in a democracy,
and beyond which it has no place in a democratic community.
Independently of whether the state, the community, or capitalists
are employers, the trade union as an organisation of all persons
occupied in certain trades can only further simultaneously the
interests of its members and the general good as long as it is content

to remain a partner. Beyond that it would run into danger of degenerating into a close corporation with all the worst qualities of a monopoly. It is the same as with the co-operative society. The trade union, as mistress of a whole branch of production, the ideal of various older socialists, would really be only a monopolist productive association, and as soon as it relied on its monopoly or worked upon it, it would be antagonistic to socialism and democracy, let its inner constitution be what it may. Why it is contrary to socialism needs no further explanation. Associations against the community are as little socialism as is the oligarchic government of the state. But why should such a trade union not be in keeping with the principles of a democracy?

This question necessitates another. What is the principle of democracy?

The answer to this appears very simple. At first one would think it settled by the definition "government by the people." But even a little consideration tells us that by that only quite a superficial, purely formal definition is given, whilst nearly all who use the word democracy to-day understand by it more than a mere form of government. We shall come much nearer to the definition if we express ourselves negatively, and define democracy as an absence of class government, as the indication of a social condition where a political privilege belongs to no one class as opposed to the whole community. By that the explanation is already given as to why a monopolist corporation is in principle anti-democratic. This negative definition has, besides, the advantage that it gives less room than the phrase "government by the people" to the idea of the oppression of the individual by the majority which is absolutely repugnant to the modern mind. To-day we find the oppression of the minority by the majority "undemocratic," although it was originally held to be quite consistent with government by the people. The idea of democracy includes, in the conception of the present day, a notion of justice—an equality of rights for all members of the community, and in that principle the rule of the majority, to which in every concrete case the rule of the people extends, finds its limits. The more it is adopted and governs the general consciousness, the more will democracy be equal in meaning to the highest possible degree of freedom for all.

Democracy is in principle the suppression of class government, though it is not yet the actual suppression of classes. They speak of the conservative character of the democracy, and to a certain degree rightly. Absolutism, or semi-absolutism, deceives its supporters as well as its opponents as to the extent of their power. Therefore in countries where it obtains, or where its traditions still exist, we have flitting plans, exaggerated language, zigzag politics, fear of revolution, hope in oppression. In a democracy the parties, and the classes standing behind them, soon learn to know the limits of their power, and to undertake each time only as much as they can reasonably hope to carry through under the existing circumstances. Even if they make their demands rather higher than they seriously mean in order to give way in the unavoidable compromise —and democracy is the high school of compromise—they must still be moderate. The right to vote in a democracy makes its members virtually partners in the community, and this virtual partnership must in the end lead to real partnership. With a working class undeveloped in numbers and culture the general right to vote may long appear as the right to choose "the butcher"; with the growing number and knowledge of the workers it is changed, however, into the implement by which to transform the representatives of the people from masters into real servants of the people.

Universal suffrage in Germany could serve Bismarck temporarily as a tool, but finally it compelled Bismarck to serve it as a tool. It could be of use for a time to the squires of the East Elbe district, but it has long been the terror of these same squires. In 1878 it could bring Bismarck into a position to forge the weapon of socialistic law, but through it this weapon became blunt and broken, until by the help of it Bismarck was thoroughly beaten. Had Bismarck in 1878, with his then majority, created a politically exceptional law, instead of a police one, a law which would have placed the worker outside the franchise, he would for a time have hit social democracy more sharply than with the former. It is true, he would then have hit other people also. Universal franchise is, from two sides, the alternative to a violent revolution. But universal suffrage is only a part of democracy, although a part which in time must draw the other parts after it as the magnet attracts to itself the scattered portions of iron. It certainly proceeds more slowly than many would wish, but in spite of that it is at work. And social democracy cannot further this work better than by taking its stand unreservedly on the theory of democracy—on the ground of universal suffrage with all the consequences resulting therefrom to its tactics.

In practice—that is, in its actions—it has in Germany always done so. But in their explanations its literary advocates have often acted otherwise, and still often do so to-day. Phrases which were composed in a time when the political privilege of property ruled all over Europe, and which under these circumstances were explanatory, and to a certain degree also justified, but which to-day are only a dead weight, are treated with such reverence as though the progress of the movement depended on them and not on the understanding of what can be done, and what should be done. Is there any sense, for example, in maintaining the phrase of the "dictatorship of the proletariat" at a time when in all possible places representatives of social democracy have placed themselves practically in the arena of Parliamentary work, have declared for the proportional representation of the people, and for direct legislation—all of which is inconsistent with a dictatorship.

The phrase is to-day so antiquated that it is only to be reconciled with reality by stripping the word dictatorship of its actual meaning and attaching to it some kind of weakened interpretation. The whole practical activity of social democracy is directed towards creating circumstances and conditions which shall render possible and secure a transition (free from convulsive outbursts) of the modern social order into a higher one. From the consciousness of being the pioneers of a higher civilisation, its adherents are ever creating fresh inspiration and zeal. In this rests also, finally, the moral justification of the socialist expropriation towards which they aspire. But the "dictatorship of the classes" belongs to a lower civilisation, and apart from the question of the expediency and practicability of the thing, it is only to be looked upon as a reversion, as political atavism. If the thought is aroused that the transition from a capitalist to a socialist society must necessarily be accomplished by means of the development of forms of an age which did not know at all, or only in quite an imperfect form, the present methods of the initiating and carrying of laws, and which was without the organs fit for the purpose, reaction will set in.

I say expressly transition from a capitalist to a socialist society, and not from a "civic society," as is so frequently the expression used to-day. . . .

What is the struggle against, or the abolition of, a civic society?

What does it mean specially in Germany, in whose greatest and leading state, Prussia, we are still constantly concerned with first getting rid of a great part of feudalism which stands in the path of civic development? No man thinks of destroying civic society as a civilised ordered system of society. On the contrary, social democracy does not wish to break up this society and make all its members proletarians together; it labours rather incessantly at raising the worker from the social position of a proletarian to that of a citizen, and thus to make citizenship universal. It does not want to set up a proletarian society instead of a civic society, but a socialist order of society instead of a capitalist one. It would be well if one, instead of availing himself of the former ambiguous expression, kept to the latter quite clear declaration. Then one would be quite free of a good portion of other contradictions which opponents, not quite without reason, assert do exist between the phraseology and the practice of social democracy. A few socialist newspapers find a pleasure to-day in forced anti-civic language, which at the most would be in place if we lived in a sectarian fashion as anchorites, but which is absurd in an age which declares it to be no offence to the socialist sentiment to order one's private life throughout in a "bourgeois fashion."

Finally, it is to be recommended that some moderation should be kept in the declaration of war against "liberalism." It is true that the great liberal movement of modern times arose for the advantage of the capitalist bourgeoisie first of all, and the parties which assumed the names of liberals were, or became in due course, simple guardians of capitalism. Naturally, only opposition can reign between these parties and social democracy. But with respect to liberalism as a great historical movement, socialism is its legitimate heir, not only in chronological sequence, but also in its spiritual qualities, as is shown moreover in every question of principle in which social democracy has had to take up an attitude.

Wherever an economic advance of the socialist programme had to be carried out in a manner, or under circumstances, that appeared seriously to imperil the development of freedom, social democracy has never shunned taking up a position against it. The security of civil freedom has always seemed to it to stand higher than the fulfilment of some economic progress.

The aim of all socialist measures, even of those which appear outwardly as coercive measures, is the development and the securing of a free personality. Their more exact examination always shows that the coercion included will raise the sum total of liberty in society, and will give more freedom over a more extended area than it takes away. The legal day of a maximum number of hours' work, for example, is actually a fixing of a minimum of freedom, a prohibition to sell freedom longer than for a certain number of hours daily, and, in principle, therefore, stands on the same ground as the prohibition agreed to by all liberals against selling oneself into personal slavery. It is thus no accident that the first country where a maximum hours' day was carried out was Switzerland, the most democratically progressive country in Europe, and democracy is only the political form of liberalism. Being in its origin a counter-movement to the oppression of nations under institutions imposed from without or having a justification only in tradition, liberalism first sought its realisation as the principle of the sovereignty of the age and of the people, both of which principles formed the everlasting discussion of the philosophers of the rights of the state in the seventeenth and eighteenth centuries, until Rousseau set them up in his *Contrat Social* as the fundamental conditions of the legitimacy of every constitution, and the French Revolution proclaimed them—in the Democratic Constitution of 1793 permeated with Rousseau's spirit—as inalienable rights of men.

The Constitution of 1793 was the logical expression of the liberal ideas of the epoch, and a cursory glance over its contents shows how little it was, or is, an obstacle to socialism. Babœuf, and the believers in absolute equality, saw in it an excellent starting point for the realisation of their communistic strivings, and accordingly wrote "The Restoration of the Constitution of 1793" at the head of their demands.

There is actually no really liberal thought which does not also belong to the elements of the ideas of socialism. Even the principle of economic personal responsibility which belongs apparently so entirely to the Manchester School cannot, in my judgment, be denied in theory by socialism nor be made inoperative under any conceivable circumstances. Without responsibility there is no freedom; we may think as we like theoretically about man's freedom of action, we must practically start from it as the foundation of the moral law, for only under this condition is social morality possible. And similarly, in our states which reckon with millions, a healthy social life is, in the age of traffic, impossible if the economic personal responsibility of all those capable of work is not assumed. The recognition of individual responsibility is the return of the individual to society for services rendered or offered him by society.

Perhaps I may be allowed to quote some passages from my article on *The Social-Political Meaning of Space and Numbers.*

"Changes in the economic personal responsibility of those capable of work can, then, as far as we can see, only be made relatively. Labour statistics can be developed very much more, the exchange or adjustment of labour be very much perfected, the change of work be made easier and a right of the workers developed which renders possible an infinitely greater security of existence and facility for the choice of a calling than are given to-day. The most advanced organs of economic self-help—the great trade unions—already point out in this respect the way which evolution will presumably take. . . . If already strong trade unions secure to those of their members fit to work a certain right of occupation, when they impress the employers that it is very inadvisable to dismiss a member of the union without very valid reasons recognised also by the union, if they in giving information to members seeking occupation supply their wants in order of application, there is in all this an indication of the development of a democratic right to work." Other beginnings of it are found to-day in the form of industrial courts, trades councils, and similar creations in which democratic self-government has taken shape, though still often imperfectly. On the other side, doubtless, the extension of the public services, particularly of the system of education and of reciprocal arrangements (insurances, etc.) helps very much towards divesting economic personal responsibility of its hardness. But a right to work, in the sense that the state guarantees to everyone occupation in his calling, is quite improbable in a visible time, and also not even desirable. What its pleaders want can only be attained with advantage to the community in the way described by the combination of various organs, and likewise the common duty to work can only be realised in this way without a deadening bureaucracy. In such great and complicated organisms as our modern civilised states and their industrial centres an absolute right to work would simply result in disorganisation; it is "only conceivable as a source of the most odious arbitrariness and everlasting quarrelling."

Liberalism had historically the task of breaking the chains which the fettered economy and the corresponding organisations of law of the middle ages had imposed on the further development of society. That it at first strictly maintained the form of bourgeois liberalism did not stop it from actually expressing a very much wider-reaching general principle of society whose completion will be socialism.

Socialism will create no new bondage of any kind whatever. The individual is to be free, not in the metaphysical sense, as the anarchists dreamed—*i.e.*, free from all duties towards the community—but free from every economic compulsion in his action and choice of a calling. Such freedom is only possible for all by means of organisation. In this sense one might call socialism "organising liberalism," for when one examines more closely the organisations that socialism wants and how it wants them, he will find that what distinguishes them above all from the feudalistic organisations, outwardly like them, is just their liberalism, their democratic constitution, their accessibility. Therefore the trade union, striving after an arrangement similar to a guild, is, in the eyes of the socialist, the product of self-defence against the tendency of capitalism to overstock the labour market; but, at the same time, just on account of its tendency towards a guild, and to the degree in which that obtains, is it an unsocialistic corporate body.

The work here indicated is no very simple problem; it rather conceals within itself a whole series of dangers. Political equality alone has never hitherto sufficed to secure the healthy development of communities whose centre of gravity was in the giant towns. It is, as France and the United States show, no unfailing remedy against the rank growth of all kinds of social parasitism and corruption. If solidity did not reach so far down in the constitution of the French nation, and if the country were not so well favoured geographically, France would have long since been ruined by the land plague of the official class which has gained a footing there. In any case this plague forms one of the causes why, in spite of the great keenness of the French mind, the industrial development of France remains more backward than that of neighbouring countries. If democracy is not to excel centralised absolutism in the breeding of bureaucracies, it must be built up on an elaborately organised self-government with a corresponding economic, personal responsibility of all the units of administration as well as of the adult citizens of the state. Nothing is more injurious to its healthy development than enforced uniformity and a too abundant amount of protectionism or subventionism.

To create the organisations described—or, so far as they are already begun, to develop them further—is the indispensable preliminary to what we call socialism of production. Without them the so-called social appropriation of the means of production would only result presumably in reckless devastation of productive forces, insane experimentalising and aimless violence, and the political sovereignty of the working class would, in fact, only be carried out in the form of a dictatorial, revolutionary, central power, supported by the terrorist dictatorship of revolutionary clubs. As such it hovered before the Blanquists, and as such it is still represented in the *Communist Manifesto* and in the publications for which its authors were responsible at that time. But "in presence of the practical experience of the February revolution and much more of those of the Paris Commune when the proletariat retained political power for two months," the revolutionary programme given in the *Manifesto* has "here and there become out of date." "The Commune notably offers a proof that the working class cannot simply take possession of the state machinery and set it in motion for their own ends."

So wrote Marx and Engels in 1872 in the preface to the new edition of the *Manifesto*.

Conclusion

. . . My proposition, "To me that which is generally called the ultimate aim of socialism is nothing, but the movement is everything," has often been conceived as a denial of every definite aim of the socialist movement, and Mr. George Plechanow has even discovered that I have quoted this "famous sentence" from the book *To Social Peace*, by Gerhard von Schulze-Gavernitz. . . .

When eight years ago I reviewed the . . . book in *Neue Zeit*, although my criticism was strongly influenced by assumptions which I now no longer hold, yet I put on one side as immaterial that opposition of ultimate aim and practical activity in reform, and admitted—without encountering a protest—that for England a further peaceful development, such as Schulze-Gavernitz places in prospect before her was not improbable. I expressed the conviction that with the continuance of free development, the English working classes would certainly increase their demands, but would desire nothing that could not be shown each time to be necessary and attainable beyond all doubt. That is at the bottom nothing else than what I say to-day. And if anyone wishes to bring up against me the advances in social democracy made since then in England, I answer that with this extension a development of the English social democracy has gone hand in hand from the Utopian, revolutionary sect, as Engels repeatedly represented it to be, to the party of political reform which we now know. No socialist capable of thinking, dreams to-day in England of an imminent victory for socialism by means of a violent revolution—none dreams of a quick conquest of Parliament by a revolutionary proletariat. But they rely more and more on work in the municipalities and other self-governing bodies. The early contempt for the trade union movement has been given up; a closer sympathy has been won for it and, here and there also, for the co-operative movement.

And the ultimate aim? Well, that just remains an ultimate aim. "The working classes have no fixed and perfect Utopias to introduce by means of a vote of the nation. They know that in order to work out their own emancipation—and with it that higher form of life which the present form of society irresistibly makes for by its own economic development—they, the working classes, have to pass through long struggles, a whole series of historical processes, by means of which men and circumstances will be completely transformed. They have no ideals to realise, they have only to set at liberty the elements of the new society which have already been developed in the womb of the collapsing bourgeois society." So writes Marx in *Civil War in France*. I was thinking of this utterance, not in every point, but in its fundamental thought in writing down the sentence about the ultimate aim. For after all what does it say but that the movement, the series of processes, is everything, whilst every aim fixed beforehand in its details is immaterial to it. I have declared already that I willingly abandon the form of the sentence about the ultimate aim as far as it admits the interpretation that every general aim of the working class movement formulated as a principle should be declared valueless. But the preconceived theories about the drift of the movement which go beyond such a generally expressed aim, which try to determine the direction of the movement and its character without an ever-vigilant eye upon facts and experience, must necessarily always pass into Utopianism, and at some time or other stand in the way, and hinder the real theoretical and practical progress of the movement.

Whoever knows even but a little of the history of German social democracy also knows that the party has become important by continued action in contravention of such theories and of infringing resolutions founded on them. What Engels says in the preface to the new edition of *Civil War* with regard to the Blanquists and Proudhonists in the Paris Commune of 1871, namely that they both had been obliged in practice to act against their own theory, has often been repeated in another form. A theory or declaration of principle which does not allow attention being paid at every stage of development to the actual interests of the working classes, will always be set aside just as all foreswearing of reforming detail work and of the support of neighboring middle class parties has again and again been forgotten; and again and again at the congresses of the party will the complaint be heard that here and there in the electoral contest the ultimate aim of socialism has not been put sufficiently in the foreground.

In the quotation from Schulze-Gavernitz which Plechanow flings at me, it runs that by giving up the dictum that the condition of the worker in modern society is hopeless, socialism would lose its revolutionary point and would be absorbed in carrying out legislative demands. From this contrast it is clearly inferred that Schulze-Gavernitz always used the concept "revolutionary" in the sense of a struggle having revolution by violence in view. Plechanow turns the thing round, and because I have not maintained the condition of the worker to be hopeless, because I acknowledge its capability of improvement and many other facts which bourgeois economists have upheld, he carts me over to the "opponents of scientific socialism."

Unfortunately for the scientific socialism of Plechanow, the Marxist propositions on the hopelessness of the position of the worker have been upset in a book which bears the title, *Capital: A Criticism of Political Economy*. There we read of the "physical and moral regeneration" of the textile workers in Lancashire through the Factory Law of 1847, which "struck the feeblest eye." A bourgeois republic was not even necessary to bring about a certain improvement in the situation of a large section of workers! In the same book we read that the society of to-day is no firm crystal, but an organism capable of change and constantly engaged in a process of change, that also in the treatment of economic questions on the part of the official representatives of this society an "improvement was unmistakable." Further that the author had devoted so large a space in his book to the results of the English Factory Laws in order to spur the Continent to imitate them and thus to work so that the process of transforming society may be accomplished in ever more humane forms. All of which signifies not hopelessness but capability of improvement in the condition of the worker. And, as since 1866, when this was written, the legislation depicted has not grown weaker but has been improved, made more general, and has been supplemented by laws and organisations working in the same direction, there can be no more doubt to-day than formerly of the hopefulness of the position of the worker. If to state such facts means following the "immortal Bastiat," then among the first ranks of these followers is—Karl Marx.

Now, it can be asserted against me that Marx certainly recognised those improvements, but that the chapter on the historical tendency of capitalist accumulation at the end of the first volume of *Capital* shows how little these details influenced his fundamental mode of viewing things. To which I answer that as far as that is correct it speaks against that chapter and not against me.

. . . To me the chapter illustrates a dualism which runs through the whole monumental work of Marx, and which also finds expression in a less pregnant fashion in other passages—a dualism which consists in this, that the work aims at being a scientific inquiry and also at proving a theory laid down long before its drafting; a formula lies at the basis of it in which the result to which the exposition should lead is fixed beforehand. The return to the *Communist Manifesto* points here to a real residue of Utopianism in the Marxist system. Marx had accepted the solution of the Utopians in essentials, but had recognised their means and proofs as inadequate. He therefore undertook a revision of them, and this with the zeal, the critical acuteness, and love of truth of a scientific genius. He suppressed no important fact, he also forebore belittling artificially the importance of these facts as long as the object of the inquiry had no immediate reference to the final aim of the formula to be proved. To that point his work is free of every tendency necessarily interfering with the scientific method.

For the general sympathy with the strivings for emancipation of the working classes does not in itself stand in the way of the scientific method. But, as Marx approaches a point when that final aim enters seriously into the question, he becomes uncertain and unreliable. Such contradictions then appear as were shown in the book under consideration, for instance, in the section of the movement of incomes in modern society. It thus appears that this great scientific spirit was, in the end, a slave to a doctrine. . . .

C. PRINCIPLES OF THE SOCIALIST INTERNATIONAL

The Socialist (Second) International, established in 1889 by parties belonging to different tendencies, had been disrupted by serious dissensions at the outbreak of World War I, particularly between those socialists in whom pacifist internationalism prevailed and those who rallied to the defense of their countries involved in the war. When reorganized after the war, it had as competitor the Marxist-Leninist Third International, founded in 1919, dissolved in 1943, partly replaced after World War II by the Cominform and later by meetings usually held in connection with congresses of the Soviet Communist Party. Competition made for ideological clarification, and only parties in which democratic socialists prevailed joined the revived Second International. The Vienna International (also called the Two and a Half International of parties trying to hold a middle ground between the Second and the Third) merged with the Second in 1923. A Fourth International of Trotskyite parties never acquired much political weight. The upheavals of World War II caused another disruption of the Second International, this time not because of internal dissensions but because many European, Latin-American, and Asian democratic socialist parties, driven underground by fascist and semi-fascist revolutions, were not able to function. It was re-established at the eighth postwar international socialist conference held in Frankfurt in West Germany in the summer of 1951. From fewer than thirty the membership rose to nearly fifty parties. To the Socialist International were linked international organizations of socialist women and socialist youth. Headquarters of the secretariat were in London. In 1953, Asian democratic socialist parties decided to form their own separate association, the Asian Socialist Conference, more in order to avoid the accusation of acting as agents of Western powers than to divorce themselves from European contacts. The democratic socialist parties of Burma, Ceylon, India, Indonesia, Israel, Japan, and the Philippines were among those who joined the Asian Socialist Conference. The Frankfurt Declaration of 1951 attacks capitalism, communism, and dictatorships of all kinds, and stresses freedom, democracy, planning, partial nationalization only of enterprises, economic and social rights, and internationalism. The same principles were reiterated in the Oslo Declaration of 1962. The Socialist International is an instrument of cooperation between democratic socialist parties, not a supreme authority. The sum total of successes and failures on the world scene, in the 1960's, has been some loss of ground for democratic socialism. This is regrettable, because, in many countries of all continents, democratic socialists are still the most trustworthy supporters of free institutions, the most convinced advocates of flexibility in internal and international economic policies, and the most determined opponents of authoritarian and totalitarian socialism.

The 1951 Frankfurt Declaration

PREAMBLE

1. FROM THE nineteenth century onwards, capitalism has developed immense productive forces. It has done so at the cost of excluding the great majority of citizens from influence over production. It put the rights of ownership before the rights of man. It created a new class of wage-earners without property or social rights. It sharpened the struggle between the classes.

    Although the world contains resources which could be made to provide a decent life for everyone, capitalism has been incapable of satisfying the elementary needs of the world's population. It proved unable to function without devastating crises and mass unemployment. It produced social insecurity and glaring contrasts between rich and poor. It resorted to imperialist expansion and colonial exploitation, thus making conflicts between nations and races more bitter. In some countries powerful capitalist groups helped the barbarism of the past to raise its head again in the form of Fascism and Nazism.

2. Socialism was born in Europe as a movement of protest against the diseases inherent in capitalist society. Because the wage-earners suffered most from capitalism, Socialism first developed as a movement of the wage-earners. Since then more and more citizens—professional and clerical workers, farmers and fishermen, craftsmen and retailers, artists and scientists—are coming to understand that Socialism holds the key to their future. Socialism appeals to all men who believe that the exploitation of man by man must be abolished.

SOURCE: *Aims and Tasks of Democratic Socialism* (Socialist International, London, 1951), pp. 1–8.

3. Socialism aims to liberate the peoples from dependence on a minority which owns or controls the means of production. It aims to put economic power in the hands of the people as a whole, and to create a community in which free men work together as equals.

4. Socialism has become a major force in world affairs. It has passed from propaganda into practice. In some countries the foundations of a Socialist society have already been laid. Here the evils of capitalism are disappearing and the community has developed new vigour. The principles of Socialism are proving their worth in action.

5. In many countries uncontrolled capitalism is giving place to an economy in which state intervention and collective ownership limit the scope of private capitalists. More people are coming to recognise the need for planning. Social security, free trade unionism and industrial democracy are winning ground. This development is largely a result of long years of struggle by Socialists and trade unionists. Wherever Socialism is strong, important steps have been taken towards the creation of a new social order.

6. In recent years the peoples in the underdeveloped areas of the world have been finding Socialism a valuable aid in the struggle for national freedom and higher standards of life. Here different forms of democratic Socialism are evolving under the pressure of different circumstances. The main enemies of Socialism in these areas are parasitical exploitation by indigenous financial oligarchies and colonial exploitation by foreign capitalists. The Socialists fight for political and economic democracy, they seek to raise the standard of living for the masses through land reform and industrialization, the extension of public ownership and the development of producers' and consumers' co-operatives.

7. Meanwhile, as Socialism advances throughout the world, new forces have arisen to threaten the movement towards freedom and social justice. Since the Bolshevik Revolution in Russia, Communism has split the International Labour Movement and has set back the realisation of Socialism in many countries for decades.

8. Communism falsely claims a share in the Socialist tradition.

In fact it has distorted that tradition beyond recognition. It has built up a rigid theology which is incompatible with the critical spirit of Marxism.

9. Where Socialists aim to achieve freedom and justice by removing the exploitation which divides men under capitalism, Communists seek to sharpen those class divisions only in order to establish the dictatorship of a single party.

10. International Communism is the instrument of a new imperialism. Wherever it has achieved power it has destroyed freedom or the chance of gaining freedom. It is based on a militarist bureaucracy and a terrorist police. By producing glaring contrasts of wealth and privilege it has created a new class society. Forced labour plays an important part in its economic organisation.

11. Socialism is an international movement which does not demand a rigid uniformity of approach. Whether Socialists build their faith on Marxist or other methods of analysing society, whether they are inspired by religious or humanitarian principles, they all strive for the same goal—a system of social justice, better living, freedom and world peace.

12. The progress of science and technical skill has given man increased power either to improve his lot or to destroy himself. For this reason production cannot be left to the play of economic liberalism but must be planned systematically for human needs. Such planning must respect the rights of the individual personality. Socialism stands for freedom and planning in both national and international affairs.

13. The achievement of Socialism is not inevitable. It demands a personal contribution from all its followers. Unlike the totalitarian way it does not impose on the people a passive role. On the contrary, it cannot succeed without a thorough-going and active participation by the people. It is democracy in its highest form.

I. POLITICAL DEMOCRACY

1. Socialists strive to build a new society in freedom and by democratic means.

2. Without freedom there can be no Socialism. Socialism can be achieved only through democracy. Democracy can be fully realised only through Socialism.

3. Democracy is government of the people, by the people, for the people. It must secure:
   (a) The right of every human being to a private life, protected from arbitrary invasion by the state.
   (b) Political liberties like freedom of thought, expression, education, organisation and religion.
   (c) The representation of the people through free elections, under universal, equal and secret franchise.
   (d) Government by the majority and respect for the rights of the minority.
   (e) The equality before the law of all citizens, whatever their birth, sex, language, creed and colour.
   (f) Right to cultural autonomy for groups with their own language.
   (g) An independent judiciary system; every man must have the right to a public trial before an impartial tribunal by due process of law.

4. Socialists have always fought for the rights of man. The Universal Declaration of the Rights of Man which has been adopted by the General Assembly of the United Nations must be made effective in every country.

5. Democracy requires the right of more than one party to exist and the right of opposition. But democracy has the right and duty to protect itself against those who exploit its opportunities only in order to destroy it. The defense of political democracy is a vital interest of the people. Its preservation is a condition of realising economic and social democracy.

6. Policies based on the protection of capitalist interests cannot develop the strength and unity needed to defend democracy from totalitarian attack. Democracy can only be defended with the active help of the workers, whose fate depends on its survival.

7. Socialists express their solidarity with all peoples suffering under dictatorship, whether Fascist or Communist, in their efforts to win freedom.

8. Every dictatorship, wherever it may be, is a danger to the freedom of all nations and thereby to the peace of the world. Wherever there is unrestrained exploitation of forced labour, whether under private profit or under political dictatorship,

there is a danger to the living and moral standards of all the peoples.

II. ECONOMIC DEMOCRACY

1. Socialism seeks to replace capitalism by a system in which the public interest takes precedence over the interest of private profit. The immediate economic aims of Socialist policy are full employment, higher production, a rising standard of life, social security and a fair distribution of incomes and property.

2. In order to achieve these ends production must be planned in the interest of the people as a whole.

   Such planning is incompatible with the concentration of economic power in the hands of a few. It requires effective democratic control of the economy.

   Democratic Socialism therefore stands in sharp contradiction both to capitalist planning and to every form of totalitarian planning; these exclude public control of production and a fair distribution of its results.

3. Socialist planning can be achieved by various means. The structure of the country concerned must decide the extent of public ownership and the forms of planning to apply.

4. Public ownership can take the form of the nationalisation of existing private concerns or the creation of new public concerns, municipal or regional enterprises, consumers' or producers' co-operatives.

   These various forms of public ownership should be regarded not as ends in themselves but as means of controlling basic industries and services on which the economic life and welfare of the community depend, of rationalising inefficient industries or of preventing private monopolies and cartels from exploiting the public.

5. Socialist planning does not presuppose public ownership of all the means of production. It is compatible with the existence of private ownership in important fields, for instance in agriculture, handicraft, retail trade and small and middle-size industries. The state must prevent private owners from abusing their powers. It can and should assist them to contribute towards increased production and well-being within the framework of a planned economy.

6. Trade unions and organizations of producers and consumers are necessary elements in a democratic society; they should never be allowed to degenerate into the tools of a central bureaucracy or into a rigid corporative system. Such economic organizations should participate in shaping general economic policy without usurping the constitutional prerogatives of parliament.

7. Socialist planning does not mean that all economic decisions are placed in the hands of the government or central authorities. Economic power should be decentralized wherever this is compatible with the aims of planning.

8. All citizens should prevent the development of bureaucracy in public and private industry by taking part in the process of production through their organizations or by individual initiative. The workers must be associated democratically with the direction of their industry.

9. Democratic Socialism aims at extending individual freedom on the basis of economic and social security and an increasing prosperity.

III. SOCIAL DEMOCRACY AND CULTURAL PROGRESS

1. While the guiding principle of capitalism is private profit the guiding principle of Socialism is the satisfaction of human needs.

2. Basic human needs must make the first claim on the distribution of the fruits of production; this need not deprive the individual of the incentive to work according to his capacity. Socialists accept as self-evident the individual's right to be rewarded according to his efforts.

   But they believe that there are other incentives, like pride in doing work well, solidarity and team spirit which can be strengthened when men work for the common interest.

3. Socialism stands not only for basic political rights but also for economic and social rights. Among these rights are:

   the right to work;
   the right to medical and maternity benefits;
   the right to leisure;
   the right to economic security for citizens unable to work because of old age, incapacity or unemployment;

the right of children to welfare and of the youth to education
in accordance with their abilities;

the right to adequate housing.

4. Socialists strive to abolish all legal, economic and political
discriminations between the sexes, between social groups,
between town and countryside, between regional and between
racial groups.

5. Socialism means far more than a new economic and social
system. Economic and social progress have moral value to the
extent that they serve to liberate and develop the human
personality.

6. Socialists oppose capitalism not only because it is economically
wasteful and because it keeps the masses from their material
rights, but above all because it revolts their sense of justice.
They oppose totalitarianism in every form because it outrages
human dignity.

7. Socialism fights to liberate men from the fears and anxieties
from which all forms of political and economic insecurity are
inseparable. This liberation will open the way to the spiritual
development of men conscious of their responsibilities and to
the cultural evolution of complete personalities. Socialism is
a powerful factor in promoting this cultural development.

8. Socialism seeks to give men all the means to raise their cultural
standard and foster the creative aspiration of the human spirit.
The treasures of art and science must be made available to all
men.

IV. INTERNATIONAL DEMOCRACY

1. The Socialist movement has been an international movement
from the beginning.

2. Democratic Socialism is international because it aims at liberating all men from every form of economic, spiritual and
political bondage.

3. Democratic Socialism is international because it recognises
that no nation can solve all its economic and social problems
in isolation.

4. Absolute national sovereignty must be transcended.

5. The new world society for which Socialists strive can develop
fruitfully in peace only if it is based on voluntary cooperation
between nations. Democracy must, therefore, be established on

an international scale under an international rule of law which guarantees national freedom and the rights of man.

6. Democratic Socialism regards the establishment of the United Nations as an important step towards an international community; it demands the strict implementation of the principles of its Charter.

7. Democratic Socialism rejects every form of imperialism. It fights the oppression or exploitation of any people.

8. A negative anti-imperialism is not enough. Vast areas of the world suffer from extreme poverty, illiteracy and disease. Poverty in one part of the world is a threat to prosperity in other parts. Poverty is an obstacle to the development of democracy. Democracy, prosperity and peace require a redistribution of the world's wealth and an increase in the productivity of the underdeveloped areas. All people have an interest in raising the material and cultural standards in those areas. Democratic Socialism must inspire the economic, social and cultural development of these areas unless they are to fall victim to new forms of oppression.

9. Democratic Socialists recognise the maintenance of world peace as the supreme task in our time. Peace can be secured only by a system of collective security. This will create the conditions for international disarmament.

10. The struggle for the preservation of peace is inseparably bound up with the struggle for freedom. It is the threat to the independence of free peoples which is directly responsible for the danger of war in our time.

Socialists work for a world of peace and freedom, for a world in which the exploitation and enslavement of men by men and peoples by peoples is unknown, for a world in which the development of the individual personality is the basis for the fruitful development of mankind. They appeal to the solidarity of all working men in the struggle for this great aim.

From the 1962 Oslo Declaration

The most dynamic impulse towards social change has come in countries where democratic Socialist parties have been able to exert

SOURCE: *The World Today . . . The Socialist Perspective* (Socialist International, London, 1962), passim pp. 6–11.

effective influence. History has not confirmed the doctrine of the increasing misery of the proletariat. The worst excesses of capitalism have been corrected through the constant activity of the Socialist parties, the trade unions and the co-operative societies. New forms of ownership and control of production have emerged. Mass unemployment has been eliminated, social security extended, working hours have been reduced and educational and vocational opportunities widened.

Even where democratic Socialists have been in opposition, their opponents have often been obliged by public opinion to adopt essentially Socialist solutions for the problems of full employment and social welfare. Likewise, in the United States of America, pressures of trade unions and other progressive social forces have made their influence felt.

Democratic Socialism has achieved much, but greater tasks still lie ahead. There is no single method to remedy the evils of present-day society. To achieve a fair distribution of wealth, we require an extension of public ownership and control and other legislation to curb private monopolies, to effect a radical reform of the tax system and to protect consumers.

State action, authorised by democratic decisions, is essential to provide for a rapid rate of economic expansion, a sufficiently high level of investment and the swift application of modern scientific techniques. This involves economic and social planning as a central government responsibility.

In democracy, a framework must be created within which the workers can effectively influence decisions and conditions in industry and the economy generally.

The democracies must improve and extend the techniques which will enable them to direct their economic resources so as to serve the long-term interests of the people and to facilitate a more substantial contribution to world economic development. They have yet to establish sufficiently close co-operation with one another to assist the steady development of international trade, unimpeded by high tariff barriers and undisturbed by exchange and currency crises. Economic planning outgrows the borders of national States. The establishment of regional economic organizations is a recognition of this fact.

The free development of the human personality can be ensured only by a reform of the existing social and economic structure. For those still living in poverty, improvement of conditions must be realised by a system of fair wages and of effective social security and family allowances and individual care and help. A basic requirement is the provision of a general system of education with a truly democratic character and ensuring genuine equality of opportunity for all. Education in citizenship, vital to democracy, should be promoted both by the State, and by voluntary organisations, such as political parties, trade unions, co-operatives and educational associations.

The emergent nations, with their hundreds of millions of people, have a heavy burden of poverty to overcome. Their difficult task is an exciting one because independence has released great reservoirs of vitality. There should be available to the new States the whole stock of science, technology and political experience that has been accumulated by the developed countries.

These new states have the opportunity of escaping the evils of Capitalism and Communism alike. The capitalist methods of ruthless exploitation of the workers, involving the uprooting of the peasants and driving them into urban slums, are not only obnoxious, but also unnecessary. The Communist method is equally obsolete, consisting as it does of abstracting surplus value through terror and undertaking break-neck industrialisation by the sacrifice of the needs of the people and more particularly at the cost of agricultural development.

The future belongs no more to Communism than to Capitalism. Communism and Capitalism point back to an age where human beings were treated as raw materials and not as the source and objective of all efforts. The Socialist International greets with satisfaction the fact that so many of the new States, striving to plan their economic future, are inspired by the ideas of democracy and Socialism.

There is the danger that the people of new States will be lured by the false perspectives of authoritarianism. Recent experience in Europe, in Asia, in Africa, in Latin America shows how barren this repudiation of democracy can be.

Substantial economic expansion in the Soviet Union has led to improved living standards but, above all, to greater military potential. In China, industrialisation is advancing. The fact that the formidable power of a State containing 600 million people is subject to totalitarian rule and severe discipline, cannot be ignored. It presents a threat to other Asian countries. Industrialisation and modernisation at the tempo at which they are realised in the Communist sphere are maintained only at the cost either of preventing the essential freedoms from developing or destroying them where they are already in existence.

Communism is not merely a social, political and economic system, but a set of doctrines which its advocates claim to be infallible and which they strive to extend all over the world.

Rivalries in the Communist sphere between different centres of Communist power and currents of opinion concerning Communism, make it manifest that Communist pretensions to totalitarian control over the individual, the nation and the development of society, are incompatible with the nature of man, the role of the nation and the evolution of human society.

For Communists, the end justifies the means, and there is a permanent contradiction between what they say and do.

Although the Communist countries claim to be peace-loving, the way in which they have used their military power has aggravated tension in the world. Although they encourage the non-aligned countries when they can exploit the attitude of the latter in their own favour, they condemn them when they cannot.

Although the Communist countries use the strongest anti-colonial language, they have enslaved scores of millions of people.

Misusing the word Socialism, their one-party dictatorships represent in fact tyranny, denying those freedoms of speech, religion, criticism, voluntary organisation and contacts with the outside world which are the essence of a democratic society.

D. NORMAN THOMAS, AMERICAN DEMOCRATIC SOCIALIST

In the Introduction are listed (page 32) some of the widespread features of the American way of life that cut the ground from under ideological and political socialism in the United States. Some features are akin to socialist ones: a deeply felt sense of community, high

level of voluntary cooperation, concern for others, feeling of solidarity. Other features are alien or even antagonistic to socialism, but
make for the kind of life that most Americans appreciate: efficient free
enterprise system, cultural pluralism, high degree of permissiveness,
social and physical mobility, open road to multiplicity of experiences
in all fields. Akin or alien to socialism, these and other features made
socialism unnecessary. But even without much political success, socialism has had a long career in the United States and has numbered
distinguished adherents. It had native roots in the communalism and
solidarity of progressive sectors of Protestantism. It was enriched,
stimulated, and modified by European influences. In a period of about
four generations, down to the end of the nineteenth century, nearly a
hundred communities experimented with socialist principles. There
were religious socialists, beginning with the Shakers of the 1770's—
long before the word socialism was used. There were the communities
established by European reformers or by their disciples among native
Americans and immigrant Europeans. After 1849 there were possibly
more German socialists in the United States (among them Wilhelm
Weitling) then in Germany. Brisbane introduced Fourier's socialism to
the United States, and Henry George exported his American socialism
to countries beyond the Atlantic. Political action reflected ideas: the
1828 Workers' Party was a forerunner of socialist organizations established in the 1870's from which—through clarifications, agreements,
and dissensions, through secessions and mergers—came the existing
half-dozen or so democratic and authoritarian socialist parties of the
United States.

Norman Thomas (from whose book *A Socialist's Faith*, published in
1951, the excerpts in this selection are taken) is the embodiment in the
United States of native Christian socialism, of world-wide socialist
ideologies, of socialist political action. He was born in 1884, was
graduated from Princeton University, and became an active Presby-
terian minister. At first a liberal deeply concerned with the unfulfilled
promises of the American system, he was attracted to socialism as a
young man. He joined the American Socialist Party, created in 1901
through the merger of a section of the Socialist Labor Party led by
Morris Hillquit with a more recent socialdemocratic organization led
by Eugene V. Debs. Norman Thomas was the founder and from 1918
to 1921 editor of *World of To-morrow*, and later, from 1922 to 1937,
the executive director of the League for Industrial Democracy. On
Debs's death in 1926, Thomas succeeded him as leader of the American
Socialist Party, whose Presidential candidate he became six times
between 1928 and 1948. Under Debs and Thomas the party had greater
political influence than its electoral strength appeared to warrant.
This was owing to the personal prestige the two leaders enjoyed
nationally, to the fact that many labor leaders and prominent intellectuals were members or actively supported the party, also to the fact
that many American liberals agreed with the party's immediate goals.

The democratic socialism of Norman Thomas and his collaborators enriched American liberalism.

Socialist Planning

THE FIRST insistence, then, of democratic socialism must be that free enterprise is not enough. Freedom, yes, and enterprise are essential. But "free enterprise" as a euphemism for a capitalist economy under the supremacy of private profit is not working and cannot work to solve the problems of peace and plenty or to establish true liberty in the modern world. It is very dangerous to permit a philosophy of the adequacy of capitalist free enterprise to go unchallenged while in practice every group flouts it. The right sort of loyalty is essential to the right sort of economic and political plan. It is not a mere by-product of any inevitable movement in history or any change of the tools of production. It must be consciously taught with intelligent reference to the power of modern technology and the growth of interdependence among men and nations. If we are incapable of this cooperative loyalty we or our civilization will perish.

Nevertheless, no high devotion to the good of men bound together on this strange and beautiful planet by common destiny— or common doom—will absolve us of the necessity for planning and for organizing to carry out our social plans.

Planning is essential in modern society. It is a grim and bitter necessity in war; it is in peace an essential to prevent war and conquer poverty. But there are various kinds of planning. Much of the current objection to planning by government rests on the false analogy of blueprints for buildings. Society is a growing thing. It is not a static organism. It is made up of men with wills of their own. Planning must be in terms of life in which the planners are involved, not of man's controls over inert matter. Plans must be concerned with the directions in which we should go, the goals we should seek, and the roads toward them. It should never be based on a dogmatic acceptance of an abstraction like collectivism as a good in itself. Always the question should be how much collectivism and what sort will serve mankind in pursuit of plenty, peace, and freedom.

In this spirit let us start our discussion of planning by asking

SOURCE: Norman Thomas, *A Socialist's Faith* (Norton, New York, 1951), passim pp. 184–207.

what should be socially owned. That has always been a basic question in socialism. I believe it is still basic in spite of the facts (1) that social ownership is not of itself the panacea for all social ills, and (2) that a sufficient degree of overall planning by no means requires such a complete collectivization of capital goods as exists to-day in the Soviet Union. Other governments in war and even in peace have established a considerable degree of control without ownership. Nazi Germany went very far in that direction. In the process it illustrated one of the dangers of the method. If the state is not to be largely the tool of the great interests it nominally controls, it will be under grave temptation to develop extremely authoritarian attitudes and apparatus. For effective control over industries still legally owned by private individuals requires a more arbitrary exercise of political power than the state operation of these industries by public authorities under a system of social ownership.

Moreover, the bureaucracy which watches other people work is even more likely than any public authority which actually works to adopt those attitudes and habits which we associate with bureaucracy at its worst. This statement is supported by experience with bureaucratic controls even in wartime when the stimulus of danger was a spur to action.

Sound democratic socialism will seek public ownership under democratic control of the commanding heights of the modern economic order. It is neither necessary nor desirable, so long as there is unity of purpose in the main direction of our economy, that there should be a monolithic type of ownership and control. There is a wholesome stimulus in competition, or emulation, and in diversity of functional apparatus. There is large room for private ownership when the owners are serving a useful function, provided that their ownership does not give them undue control over our social life. Public ownership need not be of one type. Generally speaking, the state should be the agency of ownership, and public corporations or authorities of somewhat various types its administrators. But there will be a large place for cooperatives, especially consumers' cooperatives, in the good society.

Often it will be advantageous to combine different types of social ownership and sometimes of social and private ownership. Thus, we have already made a good beginning in setting up cooperatives to distribute electricity in rural areas. These could be linked to a publicly owned giant power system administered under public authority.

A way of combining public authority and planning with co-operatives and with private enterprise was found when the Tennessee Valley Authority was set up. It has been so successful that it is amazing that no more river-valley authorities have been created either by the federal government or by treaties between states such as that which established the successful Port of New York Authority. The constitution of these authorities we shall discuss after we have examined what we mean by the commanding heights of the economic order.

Broadly, they fall in three divisions: (1) natural resources; (2) the system of money, banking, and credit; and (3) the great monopolies or oligopolies in which already most ownership is absentee ownership, there is no effective competition, and the initiative of the engineer and manager has superseded the initiative of the owner or enterpriser. These three divisions require further comment.

Land, including the minerals in it and the forests on it, is, except for the fish in the sea, still the basis for the supply of our needs. On it and by it men must live. The defense of its ownership by individuals and corporations is (1) that men deeply crave land they can call their own, and (2) that collective ownership and use of land in Russia has been maintained by a continuing coercion of a sort that society should not afford.

If our American system of ownership of land and other natural resources was supposed to promote the state of Biblical bliss where every man lives under his own vine and fig tree, it has been a sorry failure. With few exceptions American farmers under free enterprise in all regions have ruthlessly mined out the topsoil and subjected it to erosion. A new country peopled by free settlers who acquired their own farms, often under the Homestead Act, is today, to a great extent, a country of tenant farmers. California is known for its "factories in the fields." The plantation system of the South is responsible for the lowest form of cultural and economic well-being in America and one of the lowest in the world. Even under our so-called system of free enterprise it is now generally agreed that soil conservation must be a concern of the state.

To be sure, agricultural poverty and waste in America, like the poverty of the city slums, has other roots than private landlordism.

That fact does not invalidate Henry George's classic criticism of allowing individual landlords to take to themselves values in the form of rent, which values are a social creation. His remedy of expropriating by a tax the economic rental value of land in behalf of the society which has created it is both just and useful. It is not, however, an adequate panacea either in town or in country. It is a basis for proper planning in cities and for the best use of the soil in the country, not a substitute for such planning. To apply Henry George's tax to mineral lands would encourage a rapid competitive exploitation of them which would be socially detrimental.

The extraction of mineral wealth involves something very different from the use of land for homes or farms. Mining exhausts the store of the mineral that is mined or the oil that is pumped. There is a sense in which we can speak of the conservation of coal by proper mining, but not in the sense that soil can be conserved or forests restored. Mining and oil production are large-scale industries in which the key man today is not the owner, the prospector, or the promoter. He is the geologist, the engineer, and the manager. Few things are more absurd than the American law that the man who owns the surface of the earth should also own the oil a mile below it. When Clare Boothe Luce voted for social control of the entire process of producing atomic energy, including ownership of uranium mines, she admitted it might mean letting socialism in "through the back door." She spoke more truly than she knew, for if society's good compels this socialization of atomic energy, it logically compels a similar process in the case of iron, petroleum, and other resources not as dangerous in private hands as uranium but as necessary for the social good. Democratic socialism, therefore, in America proposes the following principles for the ownership and administration of land, forests and minerals:

1. Where family farming is the way of life it should be recognized and protected, but title should depend on occupancy and use, and private landlordism should be abolished by a land-value tax. Farm cooperatives should be encouraged for ownership of machinery and marketing products, and standards of soil conservation should be enforced. Corporation farms and great plantations should be transformed into agricultural collectives, cooperatively run.

2. Land in cities should be controlled not only by a land-value tax but by zoning and large-scale planning. Until the wage struc-

ture is radically raised upwards there will have to be subsidized housing for low-income groups. The proper housing program involves more than the control of land. It involves the correct use of government credit; it requires drastic reform in taxation and in the building industry, including some of the practices of the labor unions as well as of the bosses.

3. Title to all mineral wealth should be vested in the government as the agent of society. This fact should be specified in all future deeds to land, and that mineral wealth which is now in private hands should be acquired by the government. The occupying owner of the surface of the land should, of course, be compensated for any loss of its value to him arising from the extraction of mineral wealth. The federal government is in far the best position to organize a socially owned coal, iron, copper, or oil industry and should be the principal agent of society rather than the state governments, but the latter must participate in working out a plan because of their ownership of much land where minerals exist and their present dependence on the taxation of the land for education and other functions of local government.

4. Large stands of forests and large acreages of reforested land should be socially owned and socially used, not only for supplies of lumber and wood products but for protection against floods. Under American conditions, federal, state and municipal governments must cooperate in a comprehensive plan for the development of the use of forests. Wood lots of any considerable size on family farms should be subject to regulation as to use and perpetuation by proper planting.

The second major essential to an economy of abundance is the proper management of money, or more accurately, of money, banking, and credit. The invention of money was one of man's major achievements, but like others of his other inventions, man has used money to his own hurt. Properly speaking, money has two and only two functions. The first is to facilitate the exchange of goods, and the second, to simplify cost accounting, on which any dynamic society must depend. The trouble is that men have considered money as in itself real wealth, and they have speculated on it in terms which make those who manipulate it masters of us all.

Politicians and bankers have been the principal manipulators. Often they have worked at cross purposes, neither group having in mind the real welfare of society. For a long time money manipulation was more or less restrained by the quantity of the precious metals, gold and silver, used for money. Shortage of this supply of hard money helped to bring down the Roman Empire. The increase of the supply of precious metals in the western world, as a result of the discovery of America and later of the British conquest of India, helped to finance modern capitalism and imperialism in their career of expansion.

The one thing that seems most vital in the regulation of money is the ending of the outrageous system under which generation after generation pays interest to private banks for no other service than what ought to be the social function of the creation of money in the form of credit. A large part of our staggering national debt represents a logically unnecessary payment of interest on bank-created credit, not backed by an actual savings of individuals or corporations. It is preposterous to believe that government is essentially incapable of creating money parallel to the creation of goods on terms that will not invite inflation. Yet to hold this defeatist conviction is the only excuse for turning over to private banks so large a share of the creation of credit, that is, money, in war and peace. No nation fights a war with men or goods not yet in being. Every war debt is essentially a bookkeeping transaction by which fortunate sections of a population and their children after them are able to draw interest from the general public. Privately owned banks of issue or those which virtually create money by setting up credit are chief instruments in this process.

Any modern monetary system is bound up with the whole business of investment, and upon wisely directed investment a dynamic economy emancipated from the recurrent cycle, boom-to-bust, must depend. Increasingly the control of investment must be directed toward social ends. Here in "free-enterprise" America we have seen the persistence and growth of the Reconstruction Finance Corporation, an instrumentality originally set up by that rugged individualist, Herbert Hoover, to save great corporations from the fate to which they were condemned under a *laissez-faire* economy. The very existence of RFC marks the surrender of a basic principle of private capitalism. Under better and more democratic controls RFC could become an instrument for achieving and operating a socialist economy.

The third category of commanding heights in the economic order includes the public utilities and the other monopolies and oligopolies so characteristic of the American economic order. There is today a strong movement to make private monopoly the scapegoat of our economic system and to seek salvation through a return to competition by means of deliberate imposition of limitations on size. All monopoly needs to be watched because bigness can be a disease, and monopoly, even under social control, may paralyze economic development. Private monopoly, especially in the era of finance capitalism, has permitted a concentration of control dangerous alike to true freedom and plenty. It is, however, absurd to argue that we shall be saved from these evils by an indiscriminate and, in view of the historical record, impossible return to competition. It was out of competition that monopolies grew. If they should be broken, they would probably grow again except for state intervention of a sort which the United States has conspicuously failed to develop satisfactorily under the Sherman Anti-Trust Act. Some of the worst conditions in respect to wages and prices exist in the textile and other industries in which there is the least monopoly. In the last two decades of the nineteenth century, J. P. Morgan and others thought, with some justice, that they did a public service by ending or policing cutthroat competition. The classical contention that monopoly would tend to stifle production as compared with competition has been refuted by the history of production in America, a fact of significance for a socialist-planned economy.

In such an economy, there will still be a role for competition of various sorts. But competition can never be the dominant principle for the organization of an economy directed to the conquest of poverty. That requires the ethical and practical sovereignty of the principle of cooperation. The size of operating agencies and the degree of monopoly will depend upon conditions. Most of what we now call public utilities are natural monopolies and direct public operation of them under proper control is preferable to the attempt to regulate them. Contrast, for example, even in capitalist America, the superiority of municipally owned water systems to privately owned companies, or the electric power rates under the Ontario Hydro-Electric system, or the Jamestown, New York, system, with similar rates in New York City, which is dependent on regulated private corporations. Rates under private ownership of electric power are about 40 per cent higher than under public ownership. Our public utilities—even the well-run telephone industry—would be able to give us cheaper service under public ownership if for no other reason than they could get new money cheaper. The recently increased rate for telephone service in New York State was justified partly by the plea that the company had to pay up to 10 per cent to get new capital. Government now pays far less.

There is a popular argument for capitalism that under it bad management can be punished and checked by bankruptcy as it cannot under public ownership. That is doubtfully true of big corporations such as those which President Hoover felt that he must save through the RFC in the early thirties. It is not true at all of public utilities which must be kept going. In the late forties, the remedy for the badly managed Long Island Railroad was not bankruptcy. Nor was receivership an answer to its problems in dealing with its workers or its passengers. As I write, conservatives are beginning to say that the road must be put under some sort of state authority. The state, it appears, is always useful for salvaging what isn't always profitable! Then if the state finds the job hard, it can always be alleged that its troubles prove the folly of public ownership! There is a field in which responsible private ownership permits easier change and adjustments to new conditions than public. But that field is not the field of public utilities or basic resources.

Look, for example, at the coal industry, to which I have previously referred. Bituminous coal is produced under competitive conditions very wastefully. The marvelous picture which *Fortune* once presented in detail of what could be done by proper management of coal to eliminate the smoke nuisance from cities, to utilize all by-products and to avoid present wastes of coal and the very lives of the men who mine it, requires a comprehensive control of the whole industry such as could be committed to no private group without great danger to democracy. It is only when engineers work for society in this field that we can reasonably hope to utilize for the common good their knowledge and their skill.

Just how far in this industrial field social ownership should go is not a matter which one generation can absolutely determine for the next. In the peaceful achievement of democratic socialism a happy medium must be found. Piecemeal nationalization or even socialization won't get very far in a society still dominated by private ownership and the psychological attitude it breeds. Successful operation of, let us say, socialized coal mines would be easier as part of a planned socialization of commanding heights than as individual experiment. On the other hand, wholesale socialization of almost all industry would impose a crushing burden on government and any apparatus it might set up. I suggest, therefore, that when a socialist government has decided what industries should be socialized and what left to private enterprise or cooperatives, the decision, while not immortal, should not be subject to capricious revision. The managers in every type of industry should have an assurance of reasonable time to show what they can do under whatever setup is adopted.

One advantage of the socialization of major and basic industries is that it will simplify the conquest of depression. In every dynamic society there will be changes in demand. No economic order can successfully continue for decades if it is frozen into a pattern, no matter how admirable that pattern was when it was set. Changes in population, changes in the relative growth of different geographic sections, changes in methods of production, and changes in the wants of men require a flexible system. That flexible system can be better guarded against depression if the great basic industries are in public hands and their output and investments in them can be varied according to the state of the economy as a whole. Control over the rate of interest which Keynesians consider so important can be more fairly exercised by public authority if such a dominant industry as steel is socially owned.

We Americans have already accepted in theory the idea that government spending in public works should be pushed in relatively dull times. There are severe limits to the usefulness of public works as checks on depression. Those limits would be greatly widened if the same principle could be used in the operation and development of public utilities as a whole and of such basic industries as steel and coal, under conditions of public ownership which would not involve the subsidization of private owners.

Two questions always arise in the discussion of socialization of industry: the first, "How will you pay for them?" and the second, "How will you run them?"

Socialists themselves, even democratic socialists, have been divided on the question of compensation. "Why," it is asked, "should special privilege be continued and income diverted to nonworkers on the basis of ownership through payment in bonds or otherwise for the great corporations that are taken over?"

There are several parts to the answer. A policy of compensation is worth its cost if it promotes peaceful and orderly transfer. Nothing would cost the people so much as bitter confusion. Compensation, moreover, is fair in equity when certain industries are socialized and others are not. There would be no particular justice in expropriating the owners of coal mines and steel mills while the owners of the cosmetic industry or of printing plants were untouched. It is a much fairer device to offer reasonable compensation and then to tax the wealth derived from such compensation and all other wealth on the same basis. Inheritance taxes, income taxes, and, if necessary, *a carefully graduated capital levy* can take care of our problem more equitably than expropriation.

The principle of compensation, of course, should never be interpreted so as to permit private owners to unload on the public. No compensation should carry with it any lingering control over the industry. If compensation is on the principle of the substitution of bonds for the outstanding securities, the rate of interest should be low and the bonds should be amortized within a reasonable period of years. Generally speaking, the bonds should be a charge upon the industry itself rather than directly upon the government. Under no circumstances must the owners of sick industries be allowed to profit by government bounty in fixing the purchase price.

Admitting that payment for the properties the state takes over represents a real problem, it is very naive to say, "How can any government anywhere at any time afford to buy out industry?" The public now pays, very often through the nose, a great reward to the owners of industry, a reward by no means to be explained as a mere payment for tools. The public would pay less, always provided the industries were efficiently operated, for the capital charges, including purchase price, of socialized industries. A proper substitution of bonds under public ownership could squeeze a good deal of water out of the capitalization of some private industries and the necessary replacement of tools or purchase of new tools could be more cheaply managed than through the manipulations of the stock market.

These financial manipulations, whether in the stock or in the commodity market, have more than an economic cost. Defenders of free enterprise can argue until they are blue in the face that gambling in commodities—wheat futures, for instance—at a time when children are starving for bread, really adds nothing to price. Ordinary men will never believe it. Grain should be sold by those who raise it to those who use it without intervention of any elaborate gambling apparatus. This is especially true at a time when the production and probable consumption of grain and other commodities can be as well estimated as it is today. President Truman's friend, Ed Pauley, holder of high governmental posts, may not have made any illegal use whatever of inside information in cleaning up nearly a million dollars in wheat "to protect his family" in a world where millions of families can't get enough bread for their children. In the process, in the eyes of the whole world, he dishonored democracy and bestowed upon the communists an illustration of inestimable value for their propaganda. Reasonable compensation emphatically does not mean the continuance of opportunities for lucky men to make vast fortunes by gambling on the basic necessities of life. The work of the world will be better done when men do not see its material rewards distributed to speculators who have made no single contribution to the creative work of the world.

In the administration of socialized industries, there should be considerable variety and flexibility. The general pattern should be the public authority of which TVA is a successful example, rather than the Post Office Department. I still prefer the latter to the American Railway Express, but it is not the type of democratic administration which socialists desire, and the Postmaster Generalship has too often been the reward for partisan political service. Every public authority, unlike TVA, should be organized on the principle of direct representation of consumers and of the workers, with hand and brain, in a particular industry. Whether there should also be representatives of the state or the government as such, I rather doubt.

By no means is social ownership the beginning and end of a socialist system. Proper planning for the common good will require as a fundamental basis an authority which, as need arises, can determine priorities in access to materials. It will also involve a constructive use of taxation and labor legislation. It will provide cradle-to-grave social security. It will set up special agencies to deal with the prevention of unemployment by guiding and directing new investment in those functional lines and those geographical areas where such investment will be useful in meeting human wants and needs.

The inescapable conclusion is this: social planning is not something to be loved for its own sake. It is desirable to keep as much individual initiative as possible and greatly to develop the responsibility of individuals in a democratic society. But planning we must have. We have forced it on ourselves by our inventions, our technology, our growth in population. It is for us to examine our democratic instrumentalities and to improve them.

E. CROSLAND'S REVISION OF DEMOCRATIC SOCIALISM

The ever-recurring redefinitions of socialism have been made necessary by the fact that socialists have been concerned with socialism as it should be, not as it is on the basis of available evidence and of experience. Convinced that failure could not be related to socialism itself but only to a certain concept of it and its practical application, socialists have followed each experience that fell short of expectations with a spate of new definitions. Great Britain probably has the highest percentage of convinced socialists of any major nation, a few supporting authoritarian tendencies, the overwhelming majority genuinely democratic. With the enthusiastic support of half the electorate and a benevolent wait-and-see attitude on the part of most of the other half, socialists guided the Labour Party in 1945 toward what was to have been the total progressive transformation of British life. There were important reforms: the nationalization of the coal and steel industries, of the Bank of England, of most transportation; comprehensive and generous social security and health service; expansion of public housing; improvement and expansion of the school system; partial planning. Compared with the pre-World War II situation, there was considerable improvement in many aspects of British life: lessening of economic and social inequality, ending of economic insecurity, full employment, more instruction available to more young people, important steps in speeding up the transformation of the British Empire into the Commonwealth of Nations. There were continuing economic difficulties, however, and little realization of the promises, implicit in the reforms, concerning the elimination of pathological social phenomena. Happiness still eluded the British people. In 1957 appeared Crosland's *The Future of Socialism*, of which excerpts from the 1963 revised editions are included here. The book was an explanation of the lack of fulfillment during the 1945 to 1951 Labour tenure of office, and also a guide to future action. Crosland revised his socialism in a liberal, anti-doctrinaire sense.

Charles Anthony Crosland was born in 1918. Having seen action in World War II, he returned to Oxford University, where he was elected president of the Oxford Union. He taught economics from 1947 to 1950. He was a member of the House of Commons from 1950 to 1955 and again after 1959. Minister of State for Economic Affairs when the Labour Party returned to power in 1964, he became Secretary of State for Education and Science in 1965.

The Meaning of Socialism

IT IS surely time, then, to stop searching for fresh inspiration in the old orthodoxies, and thumbing over the classic texts as though they could give oracular guidance for the future. . . .

The need for a restatement of a doctrine is hardly surprising. The old doctrines did not spring from a vacuum, or from acts of pure cerebration performed in a monastery cell. Each was the product of a particular kind of society, and of minds reacting to that society. Since this external factor was not constant and unchanging, the doctrines changed from time to time. And as society has changed again since before the war, so again a restatement of objectives is called for. The matter can be put quite simply. Traditional socialism was largely concerned with the evils of traditional capitalism, and with the need for its overthrow. But today traditional capitalism has been reformed and modified almost out of existence, and it is with a quite different form of society that socialists must now concern themselves. Pre-war anticapitalism will give us very little help.

The traditionalists may comfort themselves by reflecting that this will not be the first time that socialism has been restated; nothing is more traditional in the history of socialist thought than the violent rejection of past doctrines. Marx expended prodigious energy in flaying the Utopian and Owenite brands of socialism that held the field before him. The Fabians used less vitriolic pens, but were as vehement in rejecting Marx as Marx had been in rejecting Owen. Neither owed anything significant to previous doctrine. Thus even revisionism is hallowed by an appeal to the past; and the

SOURCE: C. A. R. Crosland, *The Future of Socialism* (Schocken, New York, 1963), passim pp. 61–78, 323–351.

common-sense view that the more is achieved, the less relevant traditional dogmas become, need not be thought heretical.

. . . M. Raymond Aron has correctly observed that "Socialism has ceased in the West to be a myth because it has become a part of reality"—not, of course, a complete reality, but sufficiently so to be no longer a myth. Labour governments have been in power, and have found responsibility harsher and quite different from anything they expected; while full employment and social security have destroyed the rationale of much of the old emotional enthusiasm.

Revisionism draws attention to this new reality. It is an explicit admission that many of the old dreams are either dead or realised; and this brutal admission is resented. It is resented, first, because it destroys the old simplicity, certainty, and unquestioning conviction. "The will to Socialism," wrote G. D. H. Cole before the war, "is based on a lively sense of wrongs crying for redress." And when the wrongs were so manifest, we all knew what to do, and where the enemy was, and what was the order of battle; it was exhilarating to fight for such clear-cut and obviously righteous aims. But now the certainty and simplicity are gone; and everything has become complicated and ambiguous. Instead of glaring and conspicuous evils, squalor and injustice and distressed areas, we have to fuss about the balance of payments, and incentives, and higher productivity; and the socialist finds himself pinioned by a new and unforeseen reality.

And the objective has become not only less clear-cut, but also . . . less urgent; hence it no longer excites the same crusading spirit. But people want something to crusade about; and even the partial fulfilment of a dream leaves a feeling of lassitude and anticlimax. "Oh, how I should like to begin all over again!" cries Olof in Strindberg's play at the moment when the Reformation triumphs; "it was not victory I wanted—it was the battle!"; and many socialists, deep down, feel much the same. A people enjoying full employment and social security has lost its dreams, and lost the need to struggle; and the activists in consequence feel restless and frustrated. That is why they resent revisionist thinkers who compel them to face the new reality, and try to delude themselves instead that all the old enemies—capitalist barons, Wall Street, exploiting profiteers—are still there, waiting to be attacked. Ninety per cent of resolutions at Annual Conference to-day are Quixotic tilts at objects still hopefully seen as "outrageous giants of that detested race"; unfortunately, there are too few Sancho Panças to point out that they are really only windmills.

If we are to formulate socialist doctrine, the first task is clearly to decide what precise meaning is to be attached to the word "socialism."

This is not an easy question to answer. The word does not describe any present or past society, which can be empirically observed, and so furnish unimpeachable evidence for what is or is not "socialism." Thus statements about socialism can never be definitely verified; and we cannot treat it as being an *exact* descriptive word at all. There is therefore no point in searching the encyclopaedias for a definitive meaning; it has none, and never could.

This can easily be seen by considering the numerous and . . . often inconsistent meanings attached to the word by people who have called themselves "socialists." Marx, defining it as the "nationalisation of the means of production, distribution, and exchange," meant something quite different from Proudhon, who defined it as consisting of "every aspiration towards the amelioration of our society." Sir William Harcourt, declaring in 1892 that "we are all socialists now," evidently had a different version from his contemporary Bradlaugh, to whom socialism meant that "the State should own all wealth, direct all labour, and compel the equal distribution of all produce." And any history of socialist thought will provide dozens of different definitions, some in terms of ownership, some of co-operation, some of planning, some of income distribution; and it soon becomes simply a matter of subjective personal preference which is chosen as the "correct" one. Many definitions, moreover, are so vague as to be virtually meaningless; one can read almost anything, for example, into Sidney Webb's definition: "the economic side of the democratic ideal."

The confusion has become worse inasmuch as the word is also charged with a high degree of emotional content, and so has acquired a range of purely persuasive meanings. It is either used to denote or win approval, as in Hitler's National "Socialism" and "Socialism" in Eastern Europe, or when Left-wing weeklies attack a policy which they dislike as not being "Socialist"; or pejoratively, as when Right-wing Americans speak of "creeping Socialism."

But the worst source of confusion is the tendency to use the word to describe, not a certain kind of society, or certain values which might be attributes of a society, but particular policies which are, or are thought to be, means to attaining this kind of society, or realising these attributes. To rescue the word from these confusions, and the debasement referred to above, one must begin by asking what, if anything, is common to the beliefs of all, or almost all, of those who have called themselves socialists. The only constant element, common to all the bewildering variety of different doctrines, consists of certain moral values and aspirations; and people have called themselves socialists because they shared these aspirations, which form the one connecting link between otherwise hopelessly divergent schools of thought.

Thus the word first came on the modern scene with the early nineteenth-century Owenites, whom Marx contemptuously termed "Utopian" socialists. They based their "socialism" explicitly on an ethical view of society, a belief in a certain way of life and certain moral values. The means by which they thought this "good society" could be attained are irrelevant to-day; and in fact they were quickly challenged by other socialist schools of thought since when a continuous debate has proceeded, with no agreement, about what constituted the most suitable means. This debate would have no particular interest to-day, but for the fact that all the protagonists tried to appropriate the word "socialism" to describe the particular means which they themselves favoured.

Thus Marx appropriated it for the collective ownership of the means of production on the false assumption . . . that the pattern of ownership determined the character of the whole society, and that collective ownership was a sufficient condition of fulfilling the basic aspirations. And generally the word came to be applied to policies for the economic or institutional transformation of society, instead of to the ultimate social purposes which that transformation was intended to achieve; so one often hears socialism equated not only with the nationalisation of industry, but with government planning, or redistribution, or state collectivism. This of course is quite unhelpful, for although people may agree on ends, they may legitimately disagree about means. Moreover, the means most suitable in one generation may be wholly irrelevant in the next, and in any case (still more significant) a given means may lead to more than one possible end, as indeed has happened with each of the policies just mentioned.

Thus if, for example, socialism is defined as the nationalisation of the means of production, distribution and exchange, we produce conclusions which are impossible to reconcile with what the early socialists had in mind when they used the word: such as, that Soviet Russia is a completely socialist country (much more so, for instance, than Sweden)—even though it denies almost all the values which Western socialists have normally read into the word. Similarly, if socialism is defined as economic collectivism or State control of economic life, then Nazi Germany would correctly have been called a socialist country. But in neither case would the end-result be described as socialism by most socialists; the means of nationalisation and planning have proved adaptable to more than one purpose, which shows how unwise it is to identify the means with the end.

. . . The one single element common to all the schools of thought has been the basic aspirations, the underlying moral values. It follows that these embody the only logically and historically permissible meaning of the word socialism; and to this meaning we must now revert.

These ethical and emotional ideals have been partly negative—a protest against the visible results of capitalism—and partly positive, and related to definite views about the nature of the good society; though of course negative and positive strands are often inter-twined.

Perhaps one can list them roughly as follows. First, a protest against the material poverty and physical squalor which capitalism produced. Secondly, a wider concern for "social welfare"—for the interests of those in need, or oppressed, or unfortunate, from whatever cause. Thirdly, a belief in equality and the "classless society," and especially a desire to give the worker his "just" rights and a responsible status at work. Fourthly, a rejection of competitive antagonism, and an ideal of fraternity and co-operation. Fifthly, a protest against the inefficiencies of capitalism as an economic system, and notably its tendency to mass unemployment. The first three formed the basis of socialism as "a broad, human movement

on behalf of the bottom dog." The first and last were censures on
the material results of capitalism; while the other three stemmed
from an idealistic desire for a just, co-operative and classless society.

How should we re-formulate these aspirations to-day in such a
way as to preserve their basic emotional and ethical content, yet
discarding what is clearly not germane to present-day conditions?
Of the original five, the first and last are rapidly losing their
relevance. . . . Such primary poverty as remains will disappear
within a decade, given our present rate of economic growth; and
the contemporary mixed economy is characterised by high levels
both of employment and productivity and by a reasonable degree
of stability. In other words, the aspirations relating to the economic
consequences of capitalism are fast losing their relevance as capitalism itself becomes transformed.

But the remaining three more positive ideals, described above as
stemming either from a concern with the "bottom dog," or from a
vision of a just, co-operative and classless society, have clearly not
been fully realised. No doubt we should phrase them differently to-
day, but their basic content is still perfectly relevant. We have
plenty of less fortunate citizens still requiring aid; and we certainly
have not got an equal or classless society, nor one characterised by
"co-operative" social relations.

I propose to discuss the co-operative aspiration first. . . .
Britain to-day is a markedly less competitive society than it was a
century ago. This is especially true of industry; and it was industrial competition which drew down the strongest strictures of
the early anti-competitive socialists. Such competition is now both
more limited in extent, and less fierce in character. . . .

But the change goes wider than this, and reflects a deep-seated
change in the accepted ideology—from an uncompromising faith
in individualism and self-help to a belief in group action and "participation," and collective responsibility for social welfare. The
consequence is a pronounced tightening of the conventional rules
of competitive behaviour. A century ago competition was virtually
unrestricted. It justified colonial aggression, child-labour, sweated
workshops, violence against labour leaders, a callous ruthlessnes
towards competitors, and even interference with personal liberty.
All these to-day would be excluded from the bounds of what was

conventionally, and often legally, permissible. The moral consensus of opinion has altered; and the aggressive instinct has been civilised and circumscribed.

There is now probably no country in the world where competition is less aggressive, or individual exertion more suspect. The worker who exceeds his norm or works too hard, the employer who embarks on a price-offensive, are thought guilty at the least of not playing the game, and probably of flouting the principle of fair shares and showing disloyalty to comrades. To a large extent, security has replaced competition as the guiding rule of economic conduct. At any rate, it could scarcely be denied that the intensity of competition was significantly less.

. . . matters look a good deal less clear-cut than when the co-operative ideal was first formulated over a century ago. On the one hand, the excesses of competitive individualism have been significantly moderated; on the other hand, competition is seen to have certain compensating advantages, not previously much discussed. However, let us consider the implications of endeavouring to realise the ideal more fully. There appear to be two spheres in which it might be relevant: personal motives and relations at work.

First, people should work not for private material gain, but for the social good—either because they will then find a greater self-fulfilment and so be more contented, or because they will work better and harder, or simply because it is held to be ethically good that self-regarding instincts should be suppressed, and other-regarding instincts encouraged.

This is partly a factual statement, that people *do* work harder and feel happier if certain incentives are present: and partly a normative statement, that people *should* work for certain motives and not for others. Unfortunately the first is difficult to prove or disprove, and the second hard to express in concrete, practical policies.

The second sphere in which the co-operative ideal is relevant . . . is that of relations at work. The early socialists wanted people to work, not as separate individuals, but communally and co-operatively, organised in groups (co-operative guilds or communes) inspired with an altruistic collective purpose. To-day, since self-governing guilds are now impracticable, we should no

doubt interpret this in terms of joint consultation or joint participation, that is, of groups within a large industrial unit (whether
public or private) identified with, and working co-operatively for,
the purposes of that unit.

But we now see that the difficulty is often not, as the early
socialists thought it would be, to resolve a clash between individual
and collective instincts, or to persuade people to form groups and
adopt group standards. The human instinct towards gregariousness
is so strong that groups form automatically, in industry as elsewhere, and quickly establish their own informal leaders and standards of behaviour.

The difficulty is that these natural, self-created groups may be
far from expressing the co-operative ideal. It is not merely that
groups may develop (as anyone with experience of small political
or religious or refugee groups will know) extremely disagreeable
characteristics—intolerance of dissent, excessive conformity, arbitrary cruelty in the exercise of their ultimate power to ostracise
(in modern language, send to Coventry): but even if they do not,
their purpose and function may be in no way communal or
altruistic so far as objectives and institutions *outside* the group are
concerned. On the contrary, their function and behaviour may be
wholly selfish, and the element of identification or co-operation
with the firm or industry entirely lacking. Thus they may, as
industrial research has demonstrated, serve to restrict output, not
to expand it: to worsen relations with management, not to improve
them: to foster resentment and discontent, instead of harmony and
a sense of common purpose.

The problem is to harness the group instinct in such a way as to
create the desired social and co-operative atmosphere—to cause the
natural groups to identify themselves with the larger unit in which
they work. Unfortunately we scarcely know in detail how this is
to be done. It does not follow automatically either from nationalisation, as the mines and railways show, or from setting up joint
consultation, which may simply impose a formal and rootless
group on top of, and at cross-purposes with, the real groups below.

The two remaining aspirations—the concern with social welfare,
and the desire for an equal and classless society—still have a
perfectly clear relevance. The first implies an acceptance of collective responsibility and an extremely high priority for the relief of

social distress or misfortune, in contrast to the much lower priority which it would receive in a "free" economy guided mainly by an individualistic philosophy. This is the contemporary version of the traditional welfare and social-service philosophy of the Labour movement, and of the instinct to side automatically with the less fortunate and those in need.

There is plenty of residual social distress in Britain. It is now caused less by primary poverty, though this can still be found, than by secondary poverty, natural misfortune, physical or mental illness, the decline in the size of the family, sudden fluctuations in income, and deficiencies in social capital. These last, for all the high level of average personal spending, are still appalling—ugly towns, mean streets, slum houses, overcrowded schools, inadequate hospitals, under-staffed mental institutions, too few homes for the aged, indeed a general, and often squalid, lack of social amenities.

The relief of this distress and the elimination of this squalor is the main object of social expenditure; and a socialist is identified as one who wishes to give this an exceptional priority over other claims on resources. This is not a matter of the overall vertical equality of incomes; the arguments are humanitarian and compassionate, not egalitarian. It is a matter of priorities in the distribution of the national output, and a belief that the first priority should always be given to the poor, the unfortunate, the "have-nots," and generally to those in need; from which follows a certain view about collective social responsibility, and thence about the role of the state and the level of taxation. This represents the first major difference between a socialist and a conservative.

The second distinctive socialist ideal is social equality and the "classless society." The socialist seeks a distribution of rewards, status, and privileges egalitarian enough to minimise social resentment, to secure justice between individuals, and to equalise opportunities; and he seeks to weaken the existing deep-seated class stratification, with its concomitant feelings of envy and inferiority, and its barriers to uninhibited mingling between the classes. This belief in social equality, which has been the strongest ethical inspiration of virtually every socialist doctrine, still remains the most characteristic feature of socialist thought to-day.

It is significant that these aspirations are not now primarily economic in character. The worst economic abuses and inefficiencies of modern society have been corrected; and this is no longer the sphere, as it has been for the greater part of the life of modern socialism, in which reforms are most urgently required. . . .

It is also obvious that these ideals are much less pertinent to Britain, than to Britain's relations with the outside world. It is in the backward nations that the real poverty exists; and the inequality between those nations and Great Britain is far more glaring than the inequality between rich and poor in Britain. That is why the most obvious fulfilment of socialist ideals lies in altering not the structure of society in our own country, but the balance of wealth and privilege between advanced and backward countries.

Nationalisation and Planning

The diminished importance of nationalisation on economic grounds is only one aspect of the diminished importance . . . of industrial ownership for social relations as a whole. Socialism, whether viewed in social or ethical or economic terms, will not be brought much nearer by nationalising the aircraft industry. A higher working-class standard of living, more effective joint consultation, better labour relations, a proper use of economic resources, a wider diffusion of power, a greater degree of co-operation, or more social and economic equality—none of these now primarily require a large-scale change in ownership for their fulfilment; still less is such a change a *sufficient* condition of their fulfilment.

In this new situation, probably most thoughtful socialists would agree on two points. First, any nationalisation proposals must be capable, given the present climate of public opinion, of being justified to the electorate as likely to lead to an economic improvement. The approach must therefore be precise and selective, concentrating not on the next industries in order of size, or on those which happen to be in the public eye, but on those where a genuine economic case can be made out. Secondly, in the light of the evident disadvantages, outside the public utility field, of state monopoly and enormous scale, the method should be to take over not whole industries, but individual firms, leaving others still in private hands: or to set up new government-owned plants to compete with existing private firms. This is the "competitive public enterprise" approach. It need not rule out occasionally nationalising whole industries where the arguments for doing so seem overwhelming; but it should have a preference wherever possible.

So far as economic efficiency is concerned, it will already be clear that no general statements about public versus private ownership can ever be justified. . . .

The basic fact is the large corporation, facing fundamentally similar problems and acting in fundamentally the same way whether publicly or privately owned. Its efficiency depends on the quality of its top management, and on whether the firm or industry is structurally well adapted from a technical point of view. There are, of course, exceptions—as when a dynamic and progressive top management (or an all-important research team) has a strongly marked private-enterprise outlook. . . ; or where the whole enterprise revolves round a refractory individual genius . . . or, in the opposite case, where the workers would refuse to co-operate with private owners (as they would in coal). But with these exceptions, ownership as such makes little difference; and a transfer to public ownership will improve efficiency only if either (1) the Government puts in a better management, or compels the existing management to take greater long-term risks, or (2) it is able to adapt the structure of the industry (e.g. by amalgamations) in a manner obviously required by productive efficiency. Conversely, it will make things worse if it does the opposite.

In certain cases it might easily do the opposite. Thus the imposition of centralised monopoly control on an efficient competitive industry would certainly lead to a fall in efficiency. This danger is now well understood. But a further danger is not—that nationalisation might actually lower the caliber of management. This will occur if we continue to pay such stingy salaries in the public sector. We have heard too much objection to the allegedly high, but in fact relatively low, level of salaries in nationalised industry; we can begin to worry about these when we have removed many far more glaring (and socially unjustified) sources of inequality. As it is, we simply place nationalised concerns under a hopeless handicap in competing with private enterprise.

The second condition is that we give the industry a more efficient structure than it had before. There are certainly cases where this is in theory possible—cases, that is, where larger scale would be a positive advantage: where the average existing scale is too small for maximum technical efficiency: where there are too many small, non-specialised firms each producing a wide range of output, and consequently gaining no advantages of scale: and where competition is too imperfect to compel a greater concentration. In such cases, the public acquisition and subsequent amalgamation of a number of separate firms might greatly improve the structural fitness of the industry.

. . . if we achieve the prime objective of successful planning, namely, to get the right distribution of resources between the main sectors of the economy within a framework of non-inflationary full employment, I doubt if we want too much detailed planning *within* each sector . . . the post-war attempts at detailed planning of production and investment decisions were not a great success; and in any case . . . the traditional socialist case for such planning, based on an assumed divergence between production for profit and production for use, has much less application at present levels of material welfare.

The price-mechanism is now a reasonably satisfactory method of distributing the great bulk of consumer-goods and industrial capital-goods, given the total amount of resources available for consumption and industrial investment. The consumer is the best judge of how to spend his money; and even if he were not, the principle of individual liberty would still require that he should be left free to spend it, subject only to . . . social service considerations. . . . This does not mean that the distribution of goods *between* individuals will be ideal: on the contrary, it will not, for purchasing power is still too unequally distributed. But that inequality must be corrected directly by attacking the distribution of wealth; and at any given distribution, save in periods of exceptional crisis or acute shortage, people should now be left free to spend their incomes as they choose. Production for use and production for profit may be taken as broadly coinciding now that working-class purchasing power is so high. What is profitable is what the consumer finds useful; and the firm and the consumer desire broadly the same allocation of resources. . . .

Nevertheless there will be cases where the government wishes to intervene to override the market allocation of resources within the total allotted to a particular sector: that is, where it decrees that there shall be less of this consumption-good and more of that, or (more commonly) less investment in this direction and more in that. One cannot list such cases by reference to general *a priori* principles. The only sensible approach is a strictly empirical one, which concedes on the one hand that the price-mechanism does not work in so marvellous a welfare-maximising way that we shall jeopardise some optimum conditions, or risk upsetting a delicate mechanism, by intervening: but that on the other hand it does work in a general way to produce those goods which the consumer or investor wants, so that intervention must be justified by evidence either that what is being produced is obviously against the public interest, or that the producer is not correctly interpreting the future course of demand.

Socialists often rely on the latter argument, maintaining that industrial investment should be planned from Whitehall (i.e. its distribution between industries determined) on the grounds that the government planners have better information, or a wider insight, about future demand than a private industry can have.

Now the planners, if not the politicians, may certainly be expected to have a better idea than private industry of the future rate of growth of the economy as a whole. It follows that in the case of commodities for which demand varies directly with incomes and output—commodities, that is, subject to little cross-elasticity of demand or possibility of substitution (e.g. fuel as a whole, or transport, or steel)—the Government will normally be able to take a sounder view.

. . . planning intervention on grounds of "superior knowledge" will be justified only if two conditions are fulfilled. (1) The Government must have an obviously clearer view of future demand than private industry; there is no reason why this should normally be true of the great bulk of industries producing ultimately for a free consumer and export market. (2) Even where this condition is fulfilled (that is, in the case of basic commodities whose required growth is broadly related to total growth), we need the further condition that Ministers should in fact accept the view of the central planners, and enforce it. . . .

But this second condition is much more relevant to the question of planning within the public sector, than to the question of extending planning further over the private sector; for the commodities or industries most obviously concerned—coal, gas, electricity, railways, and roads—are already fully under public ownership.

The case for further intervention in the private sector is normally different. It arises first when the government is willing, but private enterprise is not, to shoulder the risks of expansion: and secondly where divergences arise between private and social cost.

On the first point, there are certain industries which require an exceptionally large amount of capital (and managerial skill) per unit of output; and these are normally the basic industries, whose expansion is a prior condition of expansion in the rest of the economy. This high ratio of fixed capital to output means first that they find it difficult to expand production quickly to meet a sudden rise in demand: and secondly that the risks of long-term expansion, owing to the heavy cost of excess capacity, appear particularly heavy. Thus a fully integrated steel plant costs about 600 times as much to build as a medium-sized factory; and overheads cannot be covered unless the plant is continuously operated at very near full capacity. Businessmen will then want an unusually high degree of assurance about future demand before embarking on large new capital schemes; and they may tend, as the British steel masters have done, to be too cautious, and always lag one step behind the rise in demand. It pays them better to make mistakes in this direction; and the result is a constant tendency to insufficient capacity—even though government and industry may privately agree in their respective projections of future demand.

The other group of cases where intervention is often desirable is where private and social costs diverge—where, that is, the costs borne by, or gains accruing to, the community from a particular line of action are not fully reflected in the balance-sheet of the private (or nationalised) unit. This is the oldest of the economist's justifications for state intervention.

An obvious example of this divergence is the location of new factories. When a firm leaves one area and migrates to another, it involves the community in all sorts of costs and gains—in the one area, perhaps unemployment, or an unbalanced labour force, or wasted capital capacity (in social capital or public utilities): in the other, perhaps acute labour scarcity, traffic congestion, urban sprawl, and so on. There is a clear case here for vigorous planning

—indeed without it in the immediate post-war years we might well have had serious unemployment in the Development Areas; and the lack of it now is helping to ensure that traffic in London and Birmingham gradually grinds to a standstill.

Another case where private cost fails to reflect the national interest is where the anticipated profit from an "essential" investment is quantitatively insignificant to the individual firm, and scarcely worth the bother; yet, taking the whole of industry together, the total result of such investments would be of major importance. This is the case, for example, with coal economy. Fuel costs are usually a very small fraction of total costs, and the reduction in costs and increase in net profits to be expected from installing fuel-saving equipment seem insignificant to the individual business; and the investment is not made. Yet if the whole of industry installed such equipment, the resultant saving of coal would be of considerable significance to the national economy. Government intervention is fully justified in cases such as this.

Balance of payments factors may also cause private and social cost to diverge. The desirability or otherwise of particular categories or amounts of imports, exports or import-saving output may be affected by considerations of bilateral trade, or foreign policy, or colonial policy (as with synthetic rubber), or the prospect of holding a particular exchange-rate, or a scarcity of particular currencies. And, lastly, I say nothing of the traditional cases of "social costs," such as smog, river pollution, and the like; these are now on the whole non-controversial.

It will be seen how little can be said in general terms. Occasionally the divergence between private and social cost will be so glaring that everyone agrees. Occasionally expansion is obviously called for, which the industry itself is unwilling to undertake. Occasionally the Government can take a clearer or more enlightened view than private industry.

This certainly does not add up to an argument for a detailed, overall government plan embracing our industry. . . .

VI

Recent Variations of Socialism

In the freer environment created in nations of western Europe by the success of liberal revolutions were born both socialism and, somewhat earlier, nationalism. The two movements, dynamic and expanding, were bound to interact. For several generations, most socialists had, at least theoretically, few if any doubts. They rejected nationalism in its implications of absolute sovereignty and arrogant pride in any nation's uniqueness—the negation of all men's fundamental equality, a socialist article of faith. Most socialists advocated instead an internationalism compatible with a good deal of autonomy for national communities but not with total independence. Internationalism went together with pacifism. For socialists, nationalism was a manifestation of bourgeois middle-class interests and values, to be rejected with capitalism. The brotherhood of all workers ignored national boundaries and national interests. Equality as uniformity, not as equal rights for different groupings, meant the elimination not only of classes but also of everything making for differences that were bound to lead to antagonisms and tensions. Lassalle is considered an early spokesman for a socialist position in which nationalism played an important role. But the overwhelming majority of socialists, even when accepting Lassalle's expedient democraticism, rejected his nationalism.

This situation began to change even during World War I. Many socialists discovered then that they were nationalists more than socialists. From their ranks came, in Italy and in France for instance, some of the fascists of the 1920's and 1930's. Other socialists, like Lenin, made a distinction between nationalism in capitalistic countries and nationalism in colonial or semi-colonial areas, with which he advocated alliance. The position of large sectors of the socialist movement toward nationalism has changed even more since World War II. Most democratic socialists have remained loyal to the old values of internationalism and pacifism; not so the authoritarian socialists. The diffusion of nationalcommunism and of socialnationalism within the authoritarian majority wing of socialism has been facilitated by, among others, two factors: the world-wide diffusion of authoritarian socialism and the greater difficulty in maintaining ideological homogeneity and political cohesion; and the animosity, shared by socialists and nationalists in the emerging nations and the older nations of the underdeveloped area of the world, against what Marxist-Leninists label imperialistic nations.

In the post–World War II period, nationalism has meant different things to authoritarian socialists. For Marxist-Leninists it was at first simply a temporary compromise with the immediate realities of the national community. Of course, any temporary compromise that lasts long enough can become a permanent feature of a movement. Because the idea of the compromise was first rationalized by Marxist-Leninists, the new position was called nationalcommunism. The term can, however, be found in the writings, dating from the end of the 1920's, of the Italian revolutionary socialist Mario Bergamo. Others, non-Marxist-Leninist authoritarian socialists, went further; they incorporated in their ideology traditional concepts and values of their national community. This has been the case with the authoritarian socialists who have acquired control of Middle Eastern, south Asian, and Negro African countries. A socialist movement incorporating traditional elements should be called nationalsocialism, but to avoid identification with the German National Socialism of the 1920's and 1930's it has been called socialnationalism.

Nationalcommunism had little ideological and political impact at the time of the quarrel between the Soviet and Yugoslav Marxist-Leninist dictators in 1948. It grew in importance in later years. Socialnationalism made its appearance in the Middle East during World War II, when the conflicts between the European powers that had been paramount in the area led to a political vacuum favorable to the development of new ideas and new movements. The Latin-American movement known as Castroism is akin to nationalcommunism in countries where Marxist-Leninist influences are strong, to socialnationalism in countries where those influences are weak. It also has its own distinctive features because of the emphasis on agrarianism and of the role played by traditional caudillismo. In Negro Africa, nationalcommunism, socialnationalism, and democratic socialism exist side by side.

In this section, the first selection contains excerpts from the book by V. Dedijer, a Yugoslav who for a while strongly supported Titoism or Yugoslav nationalcommunism. The second contains excerpts from a pamphlet written by the Argentine revolutionary Ernesto "Ché" Guevara, active in the Cuban revolution of 1959 and later elsewhere in Latin America, including Bolivia, where he was killed in 1967. Excerpts in the third selection describe the position known as "Arab" socialism. In the fourth a Marxist-Leninist and two other socialists explain what they mean by socialism within the Negro African cultural context.

A.   NATIONAL COMMUNISM IN YUGOSLAVIA

Vladimir Dedijer, the author of *Tito* (1953) from which excerpts appear here, was born in 1914. He grew up under the dictatorship established in Yugoslavia in 1929 by King Alexander I and overthrown by German invaders in 1941. Dedijer was a graduate of the University of Belgrade. He joined the guerrillas organized—shortly after the German invasion of the Soviet Union—by the Marxist-Leninist Josip Broz (or Tito, 1892–19), a courageous and experienced organizer but not an ideologue. Close to Tito, Dedijer for a few years occupied important positions in postwar Yugoslavia. In 1948 the break between Stalin and Tito occurred, caused by the Yugoslav Communists' unwillingness to follow the Soviet economic pattern blindly and to obey the Soviet representatives' instructions. The break was facilitated by the fact that Tito commanded his own loyal troops and that, in the event of armed conflict with the Soviet Union, he could count on help from foreign powers (i.e., the United States). Yugoslav Marxist-Leninists, or Titoists, conscious of the role of ideas and needing the guidance of clearly formulated concepts, had to rationalize the break in terms of a new ideological formulation. This was the work of intellectuals, prominent among whom were Pijade, Kardelj, and Dedijer himself. Particularly important in the new formulation were the concepts of national autonomy (and its corollary, the national road to socialism) and of decentralization. The antithetical Stalinist concepts were Soviet leadership and democratic centralism. At the point where it became evident that in autonomy and decentralization were implicit ideological and political pluralism, Titoists, afraid (like all authoritarian socialists) of liberalism, balked. In the late 1960's the contradiction between Marxist-Leninist monism and a tendency toward pluralism had not yet been overcome, but the communists' debates on the tendency were enough to make Yugoslav nationalcommunism a movement at variance with Marxism-Leninism as applied in the Soviet and Chinese halves of communism. Dedijer had already broken with Tito. In 1954 he defended the right of Milovan Djilas—author of a book criticizing communist practices and particularly bureaucraticism—to express himself. (Dedijer and Djilas, like Trotsky before them, ignored the bureaucratic requirements of collectivism.) Expelled from the Central Committee of the Yugoslav League of Communists, Dedijer went abroad, and for a while taught in Great Britain.

Dedijer on Yugoslav Marxism-Leninism

. . . IT MIGHT be worth while to discuss . . . a few of the theories of the Yugoslav Communist Party. . . . I will deal particularly with the question of socialism and individual rights, the differences between the social order in the Soviet Union and that in Yugoslavia, "Titoism" and the possibility of the spread of "Titoist" movements.

I want to draw the reader's attention to one important matter. The theories I shall describe in this chapter are neither the official

SOURCE: V. Dedijer, *Tito* (Simon and Schuster, New York, 1953), pp. 421–433.

Yugoslav views nor the only Yugoslav views. In 1951 the Central Committee of the Communist Party of Yugoslavia stated, in a special resolution, the principle that the opinions of individual leaders of the CPY on theoretical questions are not obligatory for the Party membership. This resolution spurred in Yugoslavia the struggle of opinions without which there can be no development of thought.

If we ask ourselves today what Yugoslavia has gained since she came into open conflict with the Soviet Union, we can reply quite definitely that the Yugoslavs, by preventing the subjugation of their country, have defended their rights to an unhampered independent development. They have rejected the Moscow thesis that "imitation of the Russian icon is the only correct and possible road toward socialism."

Accordingly, the international significance of the Yugoslav resistance against Soviet expansion does not consist only in the fact that a small country maintained and successfully defended the principle of equality between states, and in particular equality among large and small countries. Beyond that, Yugoslavia's internal development, especially during the last four years, has shown clearly in practice all the absurdities of the Kremlin contention that their way must be the way of all other countries. Defending the right of each country to proceed freely in its own specific ways, the Yugoslavs rose even against a monopoly of their own.

The Yugoslavs do not consider their development to be the only development. It might be perhaps useful as an experience, but it is not the inevitable course others must follow. In Yugoslavia there is a belief that socialism in the world today is developing in various ways; that the elements of a new society are mingling with elements of the old society, that the elements of the socialist society emerge in a series of states, although they are not called by that name. In Yugoslavia there exists an opinion that a revolutionary way is not inevitable for all other countries, especially for the economically advanced countries. In principle, the view of the Yugoslav Communists is that no progressive movement should in advance renounce the philosophy of using the revolutionary way. But it is obvious that no one should make revolution for the sake of revolution. If the advancement of society, that is to say, the solution of economic, social and political problems, could be achieved without revolutionary means, so much the better.

It is clear to any serious student that classical capitalism has outlived its time, that the world marches in the direction of something new, in most different forms and on different roads. In the period of transition from feudalism to capitalism, there existed in the French Revolution a classical bourgeois-democratic revolution; nonetheless all other countries made their way to capitalism in their own particular way.

Yugoslavia is a small country; her experience, her internal development, are still not known to the world. The theoretical thought in Yugoslavia is only in the beginning of its development. It has not yet in a sufficient degree generalized the Yugoslav experience. No wonder then that the world looks at Yugoslavia in a one-sided and superficial manner. It looks, too, with a large body of prejudices, created by the knowledge of what has happened in the Soviet Union. No one in modern times has so much betrayed the noble ideas of socialism and communism, for the development of which all peoples of the world have contributed so much, as has the Soviet Union, a country which calls itself socialist.

One of the above-mentioned prejudices is that there is no difference between the Soviet and the Yugoslav development, that only since 1948 have the Yugoslavs sought to break away from Stalinism, that both countries entertain the same viewpoints on the development of society, on the problems of individual freedom and of socialism.

There is no doubt that the October Revolution in Russia in 1917 and the revolution in Yugoslavia in 1941 by their very character have much in common. In both countries, the working masses came into power through revolution. But, setting aside for the moment the differences in the development of these two revolutions, it is necessary to point out that the Yugoslav revolution was built on a far wider basis than that of the October Revolution in Russia.

The October Revolution rallied the people against the war, calling upon them to abandon the front lines; the Yugoslav revolution was carried out during the Second World War, calling people to the front to defend their fatherland. In the War for Liberation, patriotism and social discontent were allied, and as a direct result, the masses entered directly into the struggle. While, especially at the beginning, the Russian revolution embraced the working masses in but a few large centers, the Yugoslav revolution enlisted broad masses of peasantry, poor and even rich, under the leadership of the working class. Furthermore, the majority of the intelligentsia joined the ranks of the revolution, while in Russia they held back. In Yugoslavia, the revolution won the support of a part of the clergy, if only the lower clergymen of the Serbian-Orthodox and Moslem communities; the Russian clergy remained hostile.

By its national character also, the basis of the revolution was broader in Yugoslavia. While in the revolution in Yugoslavia (a multi-national state) all five Yugoslav peoples took part, the revolution in Russia (also a multi-national state) was carried out primarily in a few large proletarian centers, whose population consisted largely of Russian inhabitants.

Finally, the masses of Yugoslavia were further advanced, and enjoyed a higher cultural standard, than their equivalents in 1917 Russia.

In the spring of 1952, in one of his conversations with the Delegation of the Socialist Party of India, Tito pointed out that the Yugoslav revolution might have been almost bloodless had it not been carried out during the Second World War, and integrally associated with the war against the Germans, Italians and other enemies of Yugoslavia.

"Our revolution was not only a struggle for liberation from the occupier," Tito said, "but a revolt against an old social system. This gave our revolution its broad mass basis. If it had been only a proletarian revolution, it would not have succeeded in Yugoslavia, or perhaps it could have been successful only with the aid of Soviet bayonets, in which case it would not have been a revolution at all.

"The broader the mass basis of a revolution, the more bloodless it becomes. We had the mass basis, but our war was a bloody one because our land was occupied. If there had not been occupiers, there would have been neither Quislings, Pavelić, Nedić nor other traitors, and the revolution would have been even more bloodless. Once the war ended, we had a huge mass basis of the revolution, and the class enemies did not dare resist; we nationalized their property and they did not move a finger or fire a shot. The problem of the nationalization of industry in Yugoslavia in 1945 was relatively an easy one. The owners of factories and enterprises could not resist as they did during the October Revolution, because the vast majority of the Yugoslav population were fully aware that the order that existed in Yugoslavia before the war would have been a hindrance to the future existence of the nation. In Yugoslavia, because of its belated development, the bourgeoisie could not play such an objectively progressive role as it had played in individual developed countries in the West; i.e., the class of owners of means of production had not developed the productive forces of the country but represented only an apparatus by aid of which the economically developed countries held Yugoslavia in a semi-colonial status, in a status of a half-developed country, as a raw-material source for the developed countries.

"During the war a substantial part of the nation's industry was nationalized because the owners had voluntarily consented to their factories contributing to the war potential of the occupiers. After the war, nationalization was fully carried out with the approval of the huge majority of the population. Not uncommonly in Yugoslavia, the former owner of a nationalized factory works today as a manager, engineer or clerk in his old firm or in another similar enterprise. In Yugoslavia, for all these reasons, there was no need for the physical liquidation of individual class groups, such as took place in Russia after the revolution. There were no mass deportations of hundreds of thousands of rich peasants into Siberia."

Subsequent development of these two revolutions has been different. The basic questions on which Stalin failed were the problem of socialism and of the individual freedoms.

In every revolution, at the outset, it is necessary to create a centralized state apparatus so that the aims of the revolution may be protected and successfully defended against attempts at counter revolution. This is, in fact, inevitable and at first progressive, but at the same time it forms the principal source of bureaucracy. Therefore the functions of the state should wither away from the moment the working masses take power. But in backward countries, as Russia was, there is always the danger that the state apparatus will begin as the servant of the community and end as its master. During the first Five-Year Plan, when huge industrial undertakings were begun, the power of the state apparatus began to increase rapidly. The rights of the workers shrank, the rights of the directors broadened steadily, so that this apparatus turned in the end into the master of the society. The development of the revolution in Soviet Russia came to a halt; the workers' rights were entirely destroyed; and the state went the way of state capitalism. Stalin has created the most centralized state in history. The entire country of two hundred millions of people possesses only one brain—that of the Kremlin.

In Yugoslavia the development has been otherwise. The achievements of the revolution are being protected in that there shall never be permitted a return to old conditions, no return to the defeated and discredited classes, there shall never be allowed the exploitation of man by man. The French Revolution has proclaimed: No freedom for the enemies of freedom. But the development, on the other hand, proceeds in the direction of socialist democracy, toward the withering away of the state, toward debureaucratization and decentralization, toward ever less interference with the work and life of individuals. In this respect the basic thing is the direct rights of the producers; namely, whether they may freely decide about their surplus labor, or whether this is done by state officials. In Yugoslavia the factories are turned over to the workers, they decide themselves where the surplus value of their labor will go, and thus has been created the fundamental basis for the future development of socialist democracy, of such a social order where socialism will, in the end, mean full economic and political freedom for each individual.

For that reason, the Yugoslav experience should be studied most carefully, and not routinely condemned. It is true, this development is in its first steps, but its foundation has been set.

Before Yugoslavia lies still another huge problem to be reckoned with—the problem of the village. It is clear that it would result in a sheer economic catastrophe if the village were permitted to sustain small producers with their primitive agricultural equipment. A terrific disproportion between industry and agriculture is already emerging. For that reason, in Yugoslavia immediately after the war, measures were gradually taken to bring the individual farm producers into co-operatives which could rapidly increase the agricultural production. In this field blind Stalinism was perhaps the most damaging to Yugoslavia. Co-operatives were created after the pattern of the Soviet kolkhozes. Some Yugoslav leaders, in particular Edvard Kardelj, quickly sensed the error and insisted that co-operatives of a general type should first be created, and only later working co-operatives, but local officials, under the influence of Stalin's kolkhoz theories, raced into the creation of kolkhozes.

It should be pointed out, however, that the methods of organizing co-operatives were different from those in Russia. There was in Yugoslavia no physical liquidation of rich peasants as such. Neither was there the barbarism that took place in England at the beginning of the industrial revolution, when small village owners were wiped out overnight.

The problem of the village in socialism is the basic question with which the Yugoslavs must now reckon. They are fully aware that the solution lies in some form of co-operatives, but the proper form—one which would harmonize the interests of the peasant-producers with the interests of the community, which would stimulate the villages as the factories have been stimulated—such a form has not yet been found.

Here is how Tito enumerates the differences between the Yugoslav and Soviet social systems:

"The first difference, the principal one, is that we are building a genuine socialism, while in the Soviet Union the building up of socialism has degenerated into state capitalism under the leadership of a dictatorial bureaucratic caste.

"Second, socialist democracy in Yugoslavia is beginning to dominate the entire social life, and nothing impedes an even more rapid development except the lack of technology and a too-slow increase of tempo of socialist consciousness on the part of the citizens of our country. Yet, while in our country this democratic development is noticeable from day to day, in the Soviet Union there is no democracy at all. In the Soviet Union there is neither political nor cultural democracy, nor is there democracy in production; on the contrary, a real reign of terror dominates the scene. There, even after thirty-four years, the factories have not been given over to the workers. There is no freedom of thought and creative work in literature, science, music or anywhere else.

"Third, here in Yugoslavia the national question has been correctly solved, formally and in substance, and a federative state has been created out of six republics based on an equality in which the various people decide freely their lives and their futures. A national community has been created in which there is no leading nation to impose its will on the others, nor to suppress other peoples. In the Soviet Union, the national question has been solved on paper, but in substance nothing has been carried out except a formal creation of different republics governed by one nation—the Russian. By dictate of the bureaucratic leaders from Moscow, not only entire republics but whole nations are being forcibly moved and exposed to annihilation.

"In Yugoslavia the man means everything. Our aim is to create, as early as possible and in an utmost humane way, a better life for our people, for all individuals and for the whole community. We try, even under the hardest conditions, to take care of those people who labor for the materialization of socialism. In the USSR a man is a number, and the people a colorless mass which must docilely obey and fulfill all the orders of their leaders. There is in the Soviet Union no patient re-educating over to socialist consciousness, because there they do not build socialism but a superstate capitalism, which to the outside world shows all the qualities of imperialism and internally represents a strictly centralized bureaucratic absolutism. In Yugoslavia an ever-growing development toward decentralization of the economic, cultural and other life is noticeable, because only such a system is genuinely in accordance with the concept of power as resident in the people.

"In that consists the huge substantial difference between the Yugoslav system and that of the Soviet Union. There are many additional examples, many other differences springing out of either specific conditions in our country or out of the degeneration of further revolutionary development in Soviet Russia."

As we see, in Yugoslavia the state is withering away, and a socialist democracy is developing. But what of the Communist Party? What of the one-party system in Yugoslavia? For this I refer to a discussion held on this question between Tito, Kardelj, Djilas and Kidrič on one side and an outstanding socialist leader of Western Europe on the other. I attended this discussion. It is here described for the first time.

The Western socialist asked if the Communist Party in Yugoslavia were withering away.

"The Communist Party cannot continue to function in the same old way if at the same time the state is withering away," Tito replied. "If the state does not wither away, then the Party becomes, in a certain sense, an instrument of the state, a force outside of society. If the state really withers away, the Party necessarily withers away with it. Many of our own people do not realize this fact yet. We have to explain to them gradually of what this withering away consists, and we have begun to do so."

Visitor: "As far as we can see, the Yugoslav masses have very well understood two practical aspects of the withering away of the state: the decentralization and debureaucratization. They have well understood these specific steps, but have they truly understood the second theoretical part of the problem: the withering away of the Party?"

Tito: "This process will take a little longer."

Visitor: "In the West, where there exist labor, socialist and social-democratic movements and broad masses under their influence, they still may confuse the Yugoslav situation with that in Soviet Russia and its satellites. It may be they believe the state in Yugoslavia is an instrument of the Party, for you have a one-party system. It would be of great importance—not because of the bourgeoisie and the reactionaries, for they do not matter, but because of certain progressive people who do not see the difference —to clarify that.

"For these progressive people in the West it would be important if you could explain how you disassociate yourself from this Stalinist conception and how, to your mind, the one-party system and party dictatorship are a transitory means rather than an end."

Tito: "The fact is that our socialist revolution and proletarian dictatorship are different from their Russian counterparts in all their aspects. Our revolution had a different basis from that of the Russian, and our Party had different partners, for our revolution developed under its own particular conditions in the course of the War of Liberation. Our basis has been much broader than that of the Russians, despite the fact that Russia is a huge country.

"I would like to point out the unsoundness of objections based on our so-called one-party system. We do have one revolutionary party which leads the country and provides its entire theoretical and practical line. But united in our People's Front we have all the citizens of our country who are in accord with the final aim and program of the Communist Party. These are not, necessarily, Communists; these are people who desire a change, who want a socialist society. This is not a one-party system. Rather, it is a means of uniting the citizens of a country in one Front, of which the purpose is the materialization of the program of the Communist Party. Aided by that Front we carry through this program. In Yugoslavia the Communist Party has organized the revolution, brought to a successful end its period of armed struggle and now is carrying out the complete social transformation.

"But you must also consider that in a revolutionary period it is absurd to speak about a multi-party system. What does such a system mean? Several parties mean several programs, and here in our land, there is only one program: to create a socialist society. Around this program is joined the vast majority of the citizenry of our country. Those opposed to this program cannot be permitted to impede its materialization. Out of sixteen million people we have eight million enrolled in the People's Front, all these people united around one program. That is something specific; what we have today in Yugoslavia is perhaps unique in the world. And this phenomenon can be easily explained and understood if one realizes that the basis of our revolution is huge and broad.

"For that reason I have always said that Yugoslavia's recent past cannot be applied without reservation as a pattern for other countries. Let us consider, for example, India, where there are many progressive parties, each with its own nuances. All these parties might maintain their separate programs, but they might also be able to unite around a final goal for which they could strive in common. And as they began to approach that goal, all these parties would tend to unite in the form of a Front.

"We wonder why the West wants a multi-party system, why the West wants us to go backwards, to throw away what we have achieved. This would mean only a retrogression, a return to capitalism, the conversion of our country into a satellite of this or that great power. The first business of a revolution is the liquidation of the multi-party system, whether the Communist or the Socialist Party is in power. We do not claim that those only who call themselves Communists can create socialism. We do not consider it to be a monopoly of the Communists. It can be achieved by a revolutionary socialist party. Therein lies the very difference between our view and that of the Soviets.

"It is not a question of form or name, but of the practical implementation of an idea.

"Finally, I would like to add this: such a development is not necessarily applicable everywhere. For example, the size of the party depends upon the degree of social consciousness of the proletariat. It would be larger, but we think that in our situation, in our undeveloped country, too large a party would only represent a great danger. Naturally, this is true only in a backward country. In developed countries it might be quite different."

Visitor: "Up to this point we are in full accord. We believe it would be an error at present to grant freedom to various bourgeois parties which might drag you backwards. Up to this point I fully agree. But we must also know this: what will be the role of the party when the management of the economy is entirely in the hands of the producer?"

Tito: "I shall answer that briefly. The role of the party is historically limited to a certain period. How the society will then arrange its affairs remains to be determined, but one party will not be necessary. The party withers away gradually. That does not mean that a one-party system will be superseded by a multi-party system. It merely means that the one-party system, having superseded a multi-party system, will in turn vanish."

Kardelj: "This phase is not so far away. I think we shall perhaps live to see it in our time."

Visitor: "It would be of great importance for us to be able to take with us such a statement, which, in my opinion, is the essential thing which distinguishes you from the Russian Cominform countries. To them the one-party system is an eternal matter and the state a timeless conception . . . "

Tito (interrupting): "Any movement in history which attempts to perpetuate itself becomes reactionary."

Visitor: " . . . and by the very fact that the state would seek to last eternally it would cease to serve the masses and would put itself into its own service."

Tito: "We do not consider that we have achieved the culmination, nor do we wish to become a new Roman Catholic Church with a pope at the head of it."

Kardelj: "Tito, ten days ago, gave an interview for the press in which the inevitability of this withering away was discussed. I mention this here to show that we have begun to discuss these problems in public. What is more, a series of concrete measures has already been taken. For instance, the secretaries of the Party committees no longer represent authority in the districts, and a Party member no longer has privileges merely by reason of being a Party member. But, still, plenty of work is ahead of us, still!"

In the West it is often believed that since 1948 Yugoslavia has been creating a new ideological line, a so-called "Titoism." Some people even have gone so far as to compare Tito to Luther, with Stalin cast as the pope.

I once brought this matter up with Tito. "Titoism as a separate ideological line does not exist," he answered at once. "To put it as an ideology would be stupid. I do not say that out of modesty. It is simply that we have added nothing to Marxist-Leninist doctrine. We have only applied that doctrine in consonance with our situation. Since there is nothing new, there is no new ideology. Should 'Titoism' become an ideological line, we would become revisionist; we would have renounced Marxism. We are Marxists, I am a Marxist and therefore I cannot be a 'Titoist.' Stalin is the revisionist: it is he who has wandered from the Marxist road. 'Titoism' as a doctrine does not exist. We try to find the most correct, the most humane and the most appropriate way to develop Marxism in practice. What exists in our country is socialism and cannot be called 'Titoism.'

"We, the Communists of Yugoslavia, do not consider Marxism-Leninism as something which must go on determined tracks, but as a means to be employed according to circumstances. It may often seem that we are by-passing. But Marxism-Leninism serves us as a means to lead us in the direction of the goal toward which we strive. Our way is not necessarily everybody's way (nor should it necessarily be applied everywhere). Neither Marx nor Engels could have foreseen everything for thousands of years in advance; they gave the analysis and the method of Marxism but they could not prescribe the road from one epoch to another."

This is Tito's opinion. But, if "Titoism" as an ideology of its own does not exist, it is not entirely meaningless if this term is used to reflect the desire of individual countries to resist the expansion of the great powers. This expression is in particular much applied in the case of Eastern European countries which are exposed to the oppression of the Soviet Union. For the very fact that Yugoslavia exists as an independent socialist country after more than four years of open conflict with the USSR, that this Yugoslavia continues to find its own way to socialism—these facts are a nightmare to those in the Kremlin. Only this can explain the hysteria which overcomes the creators of the foreign policy of the Kremlin when relations with Yugoslavia are on their agenda. For four and one-half years, in her relations with Yugoslavia, the USSR has committed a series of gross mistakes, blunders and failures which can only be explained by Stalin's undisguised fury that this Yugoslavia continues to exist. There cannot be any doubt that Yugoslavia represents the hardest blow Stalin has been struck since he assumed power. . . .

B. LATIN AMERICAN CASTROISM

In 1953, an abortive coup against the long-established dictatorship of Fulgencio Batista took place in Cuba. The leader of the coup was the young lawyer Fidel Castro, born in 1927 of a land-owning family. Sentenced to fifteen years' imprisonment, Castro received an amnesty in 1956. He left Cuba, returned a few months later leading a guerrilla group, and early in 1959 was in complete control of the island. Success in the face of opposition from the United States made him an inspiring charismatic leader for the revolutionary sectors of the Latin-American intelligentsia, organizers of revolts and guerrilla activities in South and Central America; also for New Left adherents and Black Power advocates in the United States. Elimination of foreign and native economic privileges, emancipation, and the welfare of the working classes—especially of the downtrodden wretched peasantry—were the chief passions animating Castro and his collaborators. These goals and passions do not necessarily mean authoritarian socialism and dictatorial absolutism. Neither could be said to have been present in the movement that triumphed in 1959. Both became features of Castroism because, to reorganize the Cuban state and economy, Castro relied largely on Cuban and foreign Marxist-Leninists, and on help from the Soviet Union. Dictatorship and rigid state-enforced conformity combined with collectivism have made the Cuban régime a variation of authoritarian socialism. On the other hand a continuation of traditional Latin-American caudillismo together with more emphasis on agriculture than on industry, direct participation by workers and peasants in the political and economic process, and action largely divorced from ideological preoccupations—all these distinguish Castroism from Marxism-Leninism.

Because of the Cuban emphasis on action and on the use of guerrilla warfare the main excerpt in this section is on insurgency, from Ché Guevara's little book *Guerrilla Warfare*, published in 1961. Ernesto (Ché) Guevara, an Argentine intellectual, was born in 1920. He cooperated closely with Castro before and after the seizure of power in Cuba, and came as near to being an ideologue as is possible for a Castroite. In the middle 1960's he left Cuba to organize insurgencies elsewhere in Latin America. Little was known of his activities or whereabouts until he was identified as one of the victims in a clash in 1967 between a small band of guerrillas and governmental troops in southern Bolivia. Guevara's book, as much as Mao's "little red book," became a must for young revolutionaries everywhere in the world. There are Castroites in all countries of Latin America, in the United States, and in some countries of Negro Africa. Castroite guerrillas have operated with varying success in Bolivia, Colombia, Guatemala, Peru,

Venezuela, and other Latin-American republics. Insurgency activities are coordinated by LASO (the Latin American Solidarity Organization), created at the 1966 meeting of the Tri-Continent Solidarity Organization in Havana.

Ché Guevara on Castroism

. . . THIS NATIONAL Revolution, fundamentally agrarian, having the enthusiastic support of workers, of people from the middle class and today even of owners of industry, has acquired a continental and world-wide importance, enhanced by its peculiar characteristics and by the inflexible will of the people.

It will not be possible to present a synthesis, however brief, of all the laws passed, all of them undoubtedly of popular benefit. It will be enough to select a few for special emphasis and to show at the same time the logical chain that carries us forward, step by step, in a progressive and necessary order of concern for the problems of the Cuban people.

The first alarm for the parasitic classes of the country is sounded in the rent law, the reduction of electric rates, and government intervention of the telephone company followed by a reduction in rates, all decreed in rapid succession. Those who had thought Fidel Castro and the men who made this Revolution to be nothing more than politicians of the old style, manageable simpletons with beards their only distinction, now began to suspect that something deeper was emerging from the bosom of the Cuban people and that their privileges were in danger. The word "Communism" began to envelop the figures of the leaders and of the triumphant guerrilla fighters; consequently the word anti-Communism, as the position dialectically opposed, began to serve as a nucleus for all those who resented the loss of their unjust privileges.

The law on vacant lots and the law on installment sales aggravated this sensation of malaise among the usurious capitalists. But these were minor skirmishes with the reactionaries; everything was still all right and possible. "This crazy fellow," Fidel Castro, could be counseled and guided to good paths, to good "democratic" paths, by a Dubois or a Porter. It was necessary to place hope in the future.

The Agrarian Reform law was a tremendous jolt. Most of those

SOURCE: Ché (E.) Guevara, *Guerrilla Warfare* (Monthly Review Press, New York, 1961), passim pp. 109–127.

who had been hurt now saw clearly. One of the first was Gaston Baquero, the voice of reaction; he had accurately interpreted what was going to happen and had retired to quieter scenes under the Spanish dictatorship. There were still some who thought that "the law is the law," that other governments had already promulgated such laws, theoretically designed to help the people. Carrying out these laws was another thing. That brash and complex child that had the initials INRA for its familiar name was treated at the beginning with peevish and touching paternalism within the ivory towers of learning, pervaded with social doctrines and respectable theories of public finance, to which the uncultivated and absurd mentalities of the guerrilla fighters could not arrive. But INRA advanced like a tractor or a war tank, because it is tractor and tank at the same time, breaking down the walls of the great estates as it passed and creating new social relations in the ownership of land. This Cuban Agrarian Reform appeared with various characteristics important for America. It was anti-feudal in the sense that it eliminated the Cuban-style latifundia, annulled all contracts that called for payment of rent of land in crops, and liquidated the servile relations that existed principally in coffee and tobacco production, two important branches of our agriculture. But it also was an Agrarian Reform in a capitalist medium to destroy the pressure of monopoly on human beings, isolated or joined together, to help them work their land honorably and to produce without fear of the creditor or the master. It had the characteristic from the first moment of assuring to peasants and agricultural workers, those who give themselves to the soil, needed technical help from competent personnel; machinery; financial help provided through credits from INRA or para-state banks; and big help from the "Association of People's Stores" that has developed on a large scale in Oriente and is in process of development in other provinces. The state stores, replacing the old usurers, provide just financing and pay a just price for the harvest.

Compared with the other three great agrarian reforms in America (Mexico, Guatemala, and Bolivia) the most important distinctive characteristic is the decision to carry Cuban reform all the way, without concessions or exceptions of any kind. This total Agrarian Reform respects no rights that are not rights of the people nor singles out any class or nationality for discriminatory treatment: the force of the law falls equally on the United Fruit

Company and on the King Ranch, as on the big Cuban landowners.

Under these conditions land is being cleared, mainly for the production of crops which are very important to the country, rice, oil-producing grains and cotton; these are being intensively developed. But the nation is not satisfied and is going to recover all its stolen resources. Its rich sub-soil, which has been a field of monopolist voracity and struggle, is virtually recovered by the petroleum law. This law, like the Agrarian Reform and all the others promulgated by the Revolution, responds to Cuba's irresistible necessities, to urgent demands of a people that wishes to be free, that wishes to be master of its economy, that wishes to prosper and to reach ever higher goals of social development. But for this very reason it is an example for the continent and feared by the oil monopolies. It is not that Cuba directly hurts the petroleum monopoly substantially. There is no reason to believe the country to be rich in reserves of the prized fuel, even though there are reasonable hopes of obtaining a supply that will satisfy its internal needs. On the other hand, by its law Cuba gives a palpable example to the brother peoples of America, many of them foraged by these monopolies or pushed into internecine wars in order to satisfy the necessities or appetites of competing trusts. At the same time Cuba shows the possibility of acting in America and the exact hour when action ought to be considered. The great monopolies also cast their worried look upon Cuba; not only has someone in the little island of the Caribbean dared to liquidate the interests of the omnipotent United Fruit Company, legacy of Mr. Foster Dulles to his heirs; but also the empires of Mr. Rockefeller and the Deutsch group have suffered under the lash of intervention by the popular Cuban Revolution.

This law, like the mining law, is the response of the people to those who try to check them with threats of force, with aerial incursions, with punishments of whatever type. Some say that the mining law is as important as the Agrarian Reform. We do not consider that it has this importance for the economy of the country in general, but it introduces another new feature: a 25 per cent tax on the amount of product exported, to be paid by companies that sell our minerals abroad (leaving now something more than a hole in our territory). This not only contributes to our Cuban welfare; it also increases the relative strength of the Canadian monopolies in their struggle with the present exploiters of our nickel. Thus the

Cuban Revolution liquidates the latifundia, limits the profits of the foreign monopolies, limits the profits of the foreign intermediaries that dedicate themselves with parasitic capital to the commerce of importation, launches upon the world a new policy in America, dares to break the monopolist status of the giants of mining and leaves one of them in difficulty, to say the least. This signifies a powerful new message to the neighbors of the great stronghold of monopoly, and causes repercussions throughout America. The Cuban Revolution breaks all the barriers of the news syndicates and diffuses its truth like a shower of dust among the American masses anxious for a better life. Cuba is the symbol of nationality renewed and Fidel Castro the symbol of liberation.

By a simple law of gravity the little island of one hundred fourteen thousand square kilometers and six and one-half million inhabitants assumes the leadership in the anti-colonial struggle in America, in which serious handicaps in other countries permit Cuba to take the heroic, glorious and dangerous advanced post. The economically less weak nations of colonial America, the ones in which national capitalism develops haltingly in a continuous, relentless, and at times violent struggle against the foreign monopolies, now cede their place gradually to this small, new champion of liberty, since their governments do not have sufficient force to carry the fight forward. This is not a simple task, nor is it free from danger and difficulties. The backing of a whole people and an enormous charge of idealism and spirit of sacrifice are needed in the nearly solitary conditions in which we are carrying it out in America. Small countries have tried to maintain this post before. Guatemala, the Guatemala of Quetzal, that dies when it is imprisoned in a cage, the Guatemala of the Indian Tecum Umam, fell before the direct aggression of the colonialists. Bolivia, the country of Morillo, the proto-martyr of American independence, yielded to the terrible hardships of the struggle after setting three examples that served as the foundation of the Cuban Revolution: the suppression of the army, agrarian reform, and nationalization of mines —maximum source of riches and at the same time maximum source of tragedy.

Insurgency

Guerrilla warfare obeys laws, some derived from the general laws of war and others owing to its own special character. If there is a

real intention to begin the struggle from some foreign country or
from some distant and remote regions within the same country, it is
obvious that it must begin in small conspiratorial movements of
secret members acting without mass support or knowledge. If the
guerrilla movement is born spontaneously out of the reaction of a
group of individuals to some form of coercion, it is possible that
the later organization of this guerrilla nucleus to prevent its annihilation will be sufficient for a beginning. But generally guerrilla
warfare starts from a well considered act of will: some chief with
prestige starts an uprising for the salvation of his people, beginning
his work in difficult conditions in a foreign country.

Absolute secrecy, a total absence of information in the enemy's
hands, should be the primary base of the movement. Secondly and
also very important is selection of the human material. At times this
selection can be carried out easily, but at others it will be extremely
difficult, since it is necessary to rely on those elements that are
available, long-time exiles or persons who present themselves when
the call goes out simply because they understand that it is their
duty to enroll in the battle to liberate their country, etc. There
may not be the necessary facilities for making a complete investigation of these individuals. Nevertheless, even though elements of the
enemy regime introduce themselves, it is unpardonable that they
should later be able to pass information, because in the period just
prior to an action all those who are going to participate should be
concentrated in secret places known only to one or two persons;
they should be under the strict vigilance of their chiefs and
without the slightest contact with the outside world. Whenever
there are concentrations, whether as a preparation for departure or
in order to carry out preliminary training or simply to hide from
the police, it is necessary always to keep all new personnel about
whom there is no clear knowledge available away from the key
places.

In underground conditions no one, absolutely no one, should
know anything more than the strictly indispensable; and there
ought not to be talk in front of anyone. When certain types of
concentration have been carried out, it is necessary even to control
letters that leave and arrive in order to have a total knowledge of
the contacts that the individuals maintain; no one should be permitted to live alone, nor to go out alone; personal contacts of the
future member of the liberating army, contacts of any type, should

be prevented by every means. However positive the role of women in the struggle, it must be emphasized that they can also play a destructive part. The weakness for women that young men have when living apart from their habitual medium of life in special, even psychic conditions, is well known. As dictators are well aware of this weakness, they try to use it for infiltrating their spies. At times the relationship of these women with their superiors is clear and even notorious; at other times, it is extremely difficult to discover even the slightest evidence of contact; therefore, it is necessary also to prohibit relations with women.

The revolutionary in a clandestine situation preparing for war should be a complete ascetic; this also serves to test one of the qualities that later will be the basis of his authority, discipline. If an individual repeatedly disobeys orders of his superiors and makes contacts with women, contracts friendships that are not permitted, etc., he should be separated immediately, not merely because of the potential dangers in the contacts, but simply because of the violation of revolutionary discipline.

Unconditional help should not be expected from a government, whether friendly or simply negligent, that allows its territory to be used as a base of operations; one should regard the situation as if he were in a completely hostile camp. The few exceptions that of course can occur are really confirmations of the general rule.

. . . The minimum number with which it is possible to initiate a guerrilla war . . . should be a nucleus of 30 to 50 men; this figure is sufficient to initiate an armed fight in any country of the Americas with their conditions of favorable territory for operations, hunger for land, repeated attacks upon justice, etc.

Weapons, as has already been said, should be of the same type as those used by the enemy. Considering always that every government is in principle hostile to a guerrilla action being undertaken from its territory, the bands that prepare themselves should not be greater than approximately 50 to 100 men per unit. In other words, though there is no objection to 500 men initiating a war, all 500 should not be concentrated in one place. They are so numerous as to attract attention and in case of any betrayal of confidence or of any raid, the whole group falls; on the other hand, it is more difficult to raid various places simultaneously.

The central headquarters for meetings can be more or less known, and the exiled persons will go there to hold meetings of all types; but the leaders ought not to be present except very sporadically, and there should be no compromising documents. The leaders should use as many different houses as possible, those least likely to be under surveillance. Arms deposits should be distributed in several places, if possible; these should be an absolute secret, known to only one or two people.

Weapons should be delivered into the hands of those who are going to use them only when the war is about to be initiated. Thus a punitive action against persons who are training, while leading to their imprisonment, will not produce a loss of arms that are very difficult to procure. Popular forces are not in any condition to suffer such a loss.

Another important factor to which due attention must be given is preparation of the forces for the extremely hard fight that is going to follow. These forces should have a strict discipline, a high morale, and a clear comprehension of the task to be performed, without conceit, without illusions, without false hopes of an easy triumph. The struggle will be bitter and long, reverses will be suffered; they can be at the brink of annihilation; only high morale, discipline, faith in final victory, and exceptional leadership can save them. . . .

Besides ideological and moral preparations, careful physical training is necessary. The guerrillas will, of course, select a mountainous or very wild zone for their operations. At any rate, in whatever situation they find themselves, the basic tactic of the guerrilla army is the march, and neither slow men nor tired men can be tolerated. Adequate training therefore includes exhausting hikes day and night, day after day, increasing gradually, always continued to the brink of exhaustion, with emulation used to increase speed. Resistance and speed will be fundamental qualities of the first guerrilla nucleus. Also a series of theoretical principles can be taught, for example, direction finding, reading, and forms of sabotage. If possible there should be training with military rifles, frequent firing, above all at distant targets, and much instruction about the way to economize bullets.

To the guerrilla fighter, economy and utilization of ammunition down to the last bullet should be almost like religious tenets. If all these admonitions are followed, the guerrilla forces may well reach their goal.

Naturally victory cannot be considered as finally won until the army that sustained the former regime has been systematically and totally smashed. Further, all the institutions that sheltered the former regime should be wiped out. But since this is a manual for guerrilla bands we will confine ourselves to analyzing the problem of national defense in case of war or aggression against the new power.

The first development we meet is that world public opinion, "the respectable press," the "truthful" news agencies of the United States and of the other countries belonging to the monopolies will begin an attack on the liberated country, an attack as aggressive and systematic as the laws of popular reform. For this reason not even a skeleton of personnel from the former army can be retained. Militarism, mechanical obedience, traditional concepts of military duty, discipline and morale cannot be eradicated with one blow. Nor can the victors, who are good fighters, decent and kind-hearted, but at the same time generally lacking education, be allowed to remain in contact with the vanquished, who are proud of their specialized military knowledge in some combat arm—in mathematics, fortifications, logistics, etc.—and who hate the un-cultured guerrilla fighters with all their might.

There are, of course, individual cases of military men who break with the past and enter into the new organization with a spirit of complete cooperation. These persons are doubly useful, because they unite with their love of the people's cause the knowledge necessary for carrying forward the creation of the new popular army. A second step will be consequent upon the first: as the old army is smashed and dismembered as an institution and its former posts occupied by the new army, it will be necessary to reorganize the new force. Its former guerrilla character, operating under independent chiefs without planning, can be changed; but it is very important to emphasize that operational concepts of the guerrilla band should still serve as the guide to structure. These concepts will determine the organic formation and the equipment of the popular army. Care should be taken to avoid the error that we fell into during the first months of trying to put the new popular army into the old bottles of military discipline and ancient organization. This error can cause serious maladjustments and can lead to a complete lack of organization.

Preparation should begin immediately for the new defensive war that will have to be fought by the people's army, accustomed to independence of command within the common struggle and dy-namism in the management of each armed group. This army will have two immediate problems. One will be the incorporation of thousands of last-hour revolutionaries, good and bad, whom it is necessary to train for the rigors of guerrilla life and to give revolutionary indoctrination in accelerated and intensive courses. Revolutionary indoctrination that gives the necessary ideological unity to the army of the people is the basis of national security both in the long and short runs. The other problem is the difficulty of adaptation to the new organizational structure.

A corps to take charge of sowing the new truths of the Revolution among all the units of the army should immediately be created. It should explain to the soldiers, peasants, and workers, who have come out of the mass of the people, the justice and the truth of each revolutionary act, the aspirations of the Revolution, why there is a fight, why so many companions have died without seeing the victory. United to this intensive indoctrination, accelerated courses of primary instruction that will begin to overcome illiteracy should also be given, in order to improve the rebel army gradually until it has become an instrument of high technical qualifications, solid ideological structure, and magnificent combat power.

. . . It begins to appear as if a direct aggression on the part of the monopolies will be necessary: various possible forms are being shuffled and studied in the IBM machines with all processes calculated. It occurs to us at the moment that the Spanish variant could be used. The Spanish variant would be one in which some initial pretext is seized upon for an attack by exiles with the help of volunteers, volunteers who would be mercenaries of course, or simply the troops of a foreign power, well supported by navy and air, well enough supported, shall we say, to be successful. It could also begin as a direct aggression by some state such as the Dominican Republic, which would send some of its men, our brothers, and many mercenaries to die on these beaches in order to provoke war; this would prompt the pure-intentioned monopolists to say that they do not wish to intervene in this "disastrous" struggle between brothers; they will merely limit and confine and freeze the war within its present limits by maintaining vigilance over the skies and seas of this part of America with cruisers, battleships, destroyers, aircraft carriers, submarines, minesweepers, torpedo boats, and airplanes. And it could happen that while these zealous guardians of continental peace were not allowing a single boat to pass with things for Cuba, some, many, or all of the boats headed for the unhappy country of Trujillo would escape the iron vigilance. Also they might intervene through some "reputable" inter-American organ, to put an end to the "foolish war" that "Communism" had unleashed in our island; or, if this mechanism of the "reputable" American organ did not serve, they might intervene directly, as in Korea, using the name of the international organ in order to restore peace and protect the interests of all nations.

Perhaps the first step in the aggression will not be against us, but against the constitutional government of Venezuela, in order to liquidate our last point of support on the continent. If this happens, it is possible that the center of the struggle against colonialism will move from Cuba to the great country of Bolivar. The people of Venezuela will rise to defend their liberties with all the enthusiasm of those who know that they are fighting a decisive battle, that behind defeat lies the darkest tyranny and behind victory the certain future of America. A stream of popular struggles can disturb the peace of the monopolist cemeteries formed out of our subjugated sister republics.

Many reasons argue against the chance of enemy victory, but there are two fundamental ones. The first is external: this is the year 1960, the year that will finally hear the voices of the millions of beings who do not have the luck to be governed by the possessors of the means of death and payment. Further, and this is an even more powerful reason, an army of six million Cubans will grasp weapons as a single man in order to defend its territory and its Revolution. Cuba will be a battlefield where the army will be nothing other than part of the people in arms. After destruction in a frontal war, hundreds of guerrilla bands under a dynamic command and a single center of orientation, will fight the battle all over the country. In cities the workers will die in their factories or centers of work, and in the country the peasants will deal out death to the invader from behind every palm tree and from every furrow of the new mechanically plowed field that the Revolution has given them.

And around the world international solidarity will create a barrier of hundreds of millions of people protesting against aggression. Monopoly will see how its pillars are undermined and how the spiderweb curtain of its newspaper lies is swept away by a puff. But let us suppose that they dare to defy the popular indignation of the world; what will happen here within?

The first thing to be noted, given our position as an easily vulnerable island without heavy arms, with a very weak air force and navy, is the necessity of applying the guerrilla concept to fight with the fervor, decision, and enthusiasm of which the sons of the Cuban Revolution are capable in these glorious years of our history. But if the worst occurs, we are prepared to continue fighting even after the destruction of our army organization in a frontal combat. In other words, confronting large concentrations of enemy forces that succeed in destroying ours, we would change immediately into a guerrilla army with a good sense of mobility, with unlimited authority in our column commanders, though with a central command located somewhere in the country giving the necessary direction and fixing the general overall strategy.

The mountains would be the last line of defense of the organized armed vanguard of the people, which is the Rebel Army; but in every house of the people, on every road, in every forest, in every piece of national territory the struggle would be fought by the great army of the rearguard, the entire people trained and armed in the manner now to be described.

Since our infantry units will not have heavy arms, they will concentrate on anti-tank and anti-air defense. Mines in very large numbers, bazookas or anti-tank grenades, anti-aircraft cannon of great mobility and mortar batteries will be the only arms of any great power. The veteran infantry soldier, though equipped with automatic weapons, will know the value of ammunition. He will guard it with loving care. Special installations for re-loading shells will accompany each unit of the army, maintaining reserves of ammunition even though precariously.

The air force will probably be badly hurt in the first moments of an invasion of this type. We are basing our calculations upon an invasion by a first-class foreign power or by a mercenary army of some other power, helped either openly or surreptitiously by this great power of first magnitude. The national air force, as I said, will be destroyed, or almost destroyed; only reconnaissance or liaison planes will remain, especially helicopters for minor functions.

The navy will also be organized for this mobile strategy; small launches will give the smallest target to the enemy and maintain maximum mobility. The great desperation of the enemy army in this case as before will be to find something to receive his blows. Instead he will find a gelatinous mass, in movement, impenetrable, that retreats and never presents a solid front, though it inflicts wounds from every side.

It is not easy to overcome an army of the people that is prepared to continue being an army in spite of its defeat in a frontal battle. Two great masses of the people are united around it: the peasants and the workers. The peasants have already given evidence of their efficiency in detaining the small band that was marauding in Pinar del Rio. These peasants will be trained principally in their own regions; but the platoon commanders and the superior officers will be trained, as is now already being done, in our military bases. From there they will be distributed throughout the thirty zones of agrarian development that form the new geographical division of the country. This will constitute thirty more centers of peasant struggle, charged with defending to the maximum their lands, their social conquests, their new houses, their canals, their dams, their flowering harvests, their independence, in a word, their right to live.

At the beginning they will oppose also a firm resistance to any enemy advance, but if this proves too strong for them, they will disperse, each peasant becoming a peaceful cultivator of his soil during the day and a fearsome guerrilla fighter at night, scourge of the enemy forces. Something similar will take place among the workers; the best among them will be trained also to serve thereafter as chiefs of their companions, teaching them principles of defense. Each social class, however, will have different tasks. The peasant will fight a battle typical of the guerrilla fighter; he should learn to be a good shot, to take advantage of all the difficulties of the ground and to disappear without ever showing his face. The workers, on the other hand, have the advantage of being within a modern city, which is a large and efficient fortress; at the same time their lack of mobility is a drawback. The worker will learn first to block the streets with barricades of any available vehicle, furniture, or utensil; to use every block as a fortress with communications formed by holes made in interior walls; to use that terrible arm of defense, the "Molotov cocktail"; and to coordinate his fire from the innumerable loopholes provided by the houses of a modern city.

From the worker masses assisted by the national police and those armed forces charged with the defense of the city, a powerful block of the army will be formed; but it must expect to suffer great losses. The struggle in the cities in these conditions cannot achieve the facility and flexibility of the struggle in the countryside: many will fall, including many leaders, in this popular struggle. The enemy will use tanks that will be destroyed rapidly as soon as the people learn their weaknesses and not to fear them; but before that the tanks will leave their balance of victims.

There will also be other organizations related to those of workers and peasants: first, the student militias, which will contain the flower of the student youth, directed and coordinated by the Rebel Army; organizations of youth in general, who will participate in the same way; and organizations of women, who will provide an enormous encouragement by their presence and who will do such auxiliary tasks for their companions in the struggle as cooking, taking care of the wounded, giving final comfort to those who are dying, doing laundry, in a word, showing their companions-in-arms that they will never be absent in the difficult moments of the Revolution. All this is achieved by wide-scale organization of the masses supplemented with patient and careful education, an education that begins and is confirmed in knowledge acquired from their own experience; it should concentrate on reasoned and true explanations of the facts of the Revolution.

The revolutionary laws should be discussed, explained, studied in every meeting, in every assembly, wherever the leaders of the Revolution are present for any purpose. Also, the speeches of the leaders, and in our case particularly of the undisputed leader, should constantly be read, commented upon, and discussed. People should come together in the country to listen by radio, and where there are more advanced facilities, to watch by television these magnificent popular lessons that our Prime Minister gives.

The participation of the people in politics, that is to say, in the expression of their own desires made into laws, decrees, and resolutions, should be constant. Vigilance against any manifestations opposed to the Revolution should also be constant; and vigilance over morale within the revolutionary masses should be stricter, if this is possible, than vigilance against the non-revolutionary or the disaffected. It can never be permitted, lest the Revolution take the dangerous path of opportunism, that a revolutionary of any category should be excused for grave offenses against decorum or morality simply because he is a revolutionary. The record of his former services may provide extenuating circumstances and they can always be considered in deciding upon the punishment, but the act itself must always be punished.

Respect for work, above all for collective work for collective ends, ought to be cultivated. Volunteer brigades to construct roads, bridges, docks or dams . . . should receive a strong impulse; these serve to forge a unity among persons showing their love for the Revolution with works.

An army that is linked in such ways with the people, that feels this intimacy with the peasants and the workers from which it emerged, that knows besides all the special techniques of its warfare and is psychologically prepared for the worst contingencies, is invincible. . . .

C. "Arab" Socialism

Leaders and followers of "Arab" socialism use the adjective "Arab" to indicate a distinctive socialist ideology—something on a par with, for instance, Leninism, not with a general term like European socialism. This is the reason for the use of quotes. Elimination of wealthy classes and replacement of them by a bureaucracy of public officials, governmental guidance of a partly collectivized economy, steps toward industrialization, measures for raising the living standards of the working classes (particularly the peasantry), political absolutism described as a superior form of democracy, state-enforced ideological conformity, these together justify the inclusion of the "Arab" variation in the wider stream of authoritarian socialism. The emphasis on integral nationalism, the preservation of Islamic values and institutions, and the incorporation of other elements of the traditional way of life, distinguish "Arab" socialism from communism and nationalcommunism and make it a socialnationalist movement.

"Arab" socialism was the ideology of the Ba'th Party, founded by Syrian intellectuals and influenced before and during World War II by European fascist ideologies. Internal quarrels have been a feature of the party, whose main ideologue, Dr. Aflaq, was exiled by his own collaborators. Ba'thism has, nevertheless, remained a considerable force among the Arab intelligentsia, of Syria particularly but also of Iraq and, to a minor extent, Lebanon. Although Ba'thism is the older version, today's "Arab" socialism is mainly the ideological rationalization by intellectuals of the policies adopted by Egypt's charismatic leader. Gamal Abdel Nasser, born in 1918, was educated at the royal military academy of Cairo. Convinced that the Arabs lost the 1948 war against Israel because of the corruption and inefficiency of the existing Western-oriented régime, Nasser played a major role in the 1952 *coup-d'état* that ended the monarchy. Another coup made him Prime Minister in 1954, giving him total power. A distinctive socialnationalist position was formulated mainly in the 1960's, when Nasserism appealed to revolutionary sectors of the intelligentsia in all Arab nations. Egypt's intervention put "Arab" socialism in power in Yemen. In Algeria a military coup in 1965 replaced a government oriented toward Marxism by another closer to "Arab" socialism.

The excerpts here are from *The 'Arab' Ba'th Socialist Party* by Kamel S. Abu Jaber (1966) and "The Theoretical Structure of Nasser's Arab Socialism" by Fayez Sayegh, published in *Middle Eastern Affairs*, No. 4 (1965).

The Ideology of the Ba'th Socialist Party

. . . ARAB SOCIALISM has had to rely on the pragmatic approach. The Arabs suddenly awoke to find themselves in the twentieth century—a century not particularly pleasant for the weaker nations. They have had little time to produce theories; they are still learning. With the exception of Aflaq, there are few Arab intellectuals who command attention in the Arab world. Practice of socialism there has preceded doctrine. Manfred Halpern is perhaps correct in his conclusion that Arab socialism came out of necessity rather than reasoned conviction. On the other hand, the Arabs thus far have resisted the temptation of adopting a totalitarian regime to achieve their objectives.

Upon reviewing the available literature on Arab socialism, one comes to the conclusion that the movement was an alternative method of attack on the problems of modern society, a middle way between capitalism and communism. Such is the view of socialism in the Arab world. This, however, leaves the relation between Arab socialism and Western socialism rather ambiguous. . . . "History and circumstances have conspired to make Asiatic socialism a Third Force in the effort to find a path between capitalism and Stalinism." Arab Socialists, intent upon finding an ideology

SOURCE: Kamel S. Abu Jaber, *The Arab Ba'th Socialist Party: History, Ideology and Organization* (University of Syracuse Press, Syracuse, New York, 1966), pp. 100–109, 169, 171–172.

they could claim as their own and not associated with either of the two great power blocs, hit upon socialism. According to Ahmad I. Khalaf-Allah, "There was only one door by which the developing nations might save themselves from the capitalist or communist imperialist octopus. . . . This [door] is the human, democratic, cooperative socialist." . . . Socialism in the Arab world is nothing more than an expression of nationalism. The Ba'th party adopted "Unity, Liberty, and Socialism" as its slogan. Note the order of words: unity first, socialism last. Why?

In the Arab world socialism as an ideology remained a wing of the nationalist movement which would develop as soon as independence was won. Unlike Communist ideology, nurtured by Moscow, there was no outside help in the development of socialism in the Middle East. The nationalists, such as the Ba'th party, who fought for political independence from foreign rule, subjected their Socialist ideas to a secondary role until that independence was won. Socialism evolved as part of the nationalist revolution.

Ba'th ideology explicitly emphasizes nationalist goals over Socialist ones. In justification of such a view, Gebran Majdalany, a prominent leader of the Ba'th in Lebanon, maintains that British or French Socialists have no problem of national unity and thus are able to concentrate their efforts on social ideas. But Arab Socialists must solve nationalist problems, such as unity, first. Aflaq agrees with such a view, writing that "unity takes precedence [in our principles] over socialism." In another passage he adds that Arab Ba'th nationalism is a guarantee "of its humanity [that it is a humanitarian movement]. . . . Our Socialism thus is a means . . . through which our Arab nation enters history anew." Socialism thus, as seen by Aflaq, is a means by which Arab glory can be regained.

In linking socialism to nationalism and unity, Ba'th intellectuals have found a way of accomplishing two aims at the same time. They can fight a revolution on two fronts. They can combat their "colonial" adversaries in the international sphere who do not wish to see the Arabs unite, and the domestic problems of an underdeveloped society. Bitar identifies the enemies of Arab unity as colonialism and Israel. Later he adds Communists, capitalists, and reactionaries. Thus the struggle for Arab unity is a struggle for progress and against colonialism.

Unity is necessary before socialism can be achieved. The Arab countries individually are considered too poor to achieve any real economic advancement. Bitar states it is obvious that individual Arab countries are unable to achieve "real economic and social progress without unity." Elias Murkos, another Ba'thist intellectual, adds that "socialism cannot be achieved except in a large country with huge complementary resources," while Aflaq concludes that "neither the liberation nor the Socialist struggle can succeed as long as the one nation is divided."

That socialism is an expression of nationalistic aspirations in Ba'th ideology cannot be denied. Ba'th intellectuals stress this point. They take pride in their so-called ideological neutrality. They reject both approaches: capitalist and Communist. They do not admit that capitalism in the classic sense is no longer in existence.

Aflaq says Arab socialism is "independent . . . does not follow a particular doctrine . . . but benefits from all theories and experiments of other people while it attempts to condition itself to the circumstances and desires of the Arab nation." Bitar was more explicit in his doctrine of a neutral ideology between capitalism and communism. Capitalism entails injustice, the exploitation of the majority of the people by a minority. It cannot secure social justice for Arab society. On the other hand, communism with its repressive methods prevents the exercising of individual initiative.

In the internal sphere, the local capitalist system has failed to secure any social or economic advancement for Arab society. Moreover, local capitalists allied with "imperialist" powers in exploiting Arab lands. Murkos states that while Arab capitalism has failed to partake of the first "industrial revolution," the world today is on the verge of a second industrial revolution brought about through automation. Since a capitalist system has failed to benefit from the first, then only in a Socialist system is there hope for real progress. Socialism is the only hope for salvation from poverty and the only means to social justice.

Imperialism, a synonym for capitalism in the parlance of the Ba'th party, cooperated with communism to crush the nationalist aspirations of the Arabs. The imperialist powers also cooperated with reactionary local capitalists to retard social progress. Often the most influential private enterprises in the Arab world were controlled by foreigners. Local capitalists were closely allied with and/or dependent upon these enterprises and the foreign powers behind them. "Hence," as Manfred Halpern writes, "acts of na-

tionalization are above all declarations of national independence."
Since the Ba'th calls for complete independence, economic as well
as political, it has often demanded nationalization of all foreign
companies in Syria.

In the international sphere, the Arabs were disillusioned with
their maltreatment by the West, which culminated in the creation
of the State of Israel in 1948. Since they sided with the West in
two world wars, they see as unjust the division of their lands into
mandates and protectorates after the First World War and
Western creation and sustenance of the State of Israel. "Arab
liberalism," according to Morroe Berger, "never more than a
tender shoot . . . finally withered just after World War II in the
white heat of the West's insistence upon maintaining its special
position in the Near East and the creation of the State of Israel in
1948 and the ensuing War."

To this may be added that the humiliating Arab defeat by Israel
explains why Ba'th Socialist doctrine stresses national strength. It
also helps explain the rejection of Western ideas and thought.
Clovis Maqsud clearly points out that the "Arab Left was not a
political force of import until the Arab defeat in Palestine when the
traditional leadership failed." The implication is obvious. The
creation of the state of Israel was blamed on the West, and
thereafter the Ba'th party, intensely nationalistic, could not accept
anything Western.

As strongly as Ba'th ideology claims independence of Western
influence, it also claims independence of Marxist doctrine. Perhaps
its rejection of Marxist doctrine rests on more solid ground than its
rejection of Western influences. Taking Marxist doctrine at its
word, Sa'dun Hamadi, minister of agricultural reform in Iraq
during the Ba'th regime in 1963, writes that communism in the
West came as a result of industrial capitalist advancement and as a
reaction to the socioeconomic and political conditions brought by
the Industrial Revolution. In the Arab world, he states, socialism
came as a result of socioeconomic and political retardation. The
Arab world was still under the agricultural, feudal order of the
Middle Ages. Thus, Hamadi concludes, the Arab world is not yet
ready to accept Communist doctrine. Hamadi here is obviously
ignoring the fact that Communist accession to power in many parts
of the world did not follow classic Marxist doctrine.

Just as the West was equated with colonialism, so Marxism was equated with the Soviet Union and its activities. The distinction between the Soviet Union and Marxist ideology was not made until much later in Ba'th history. The Soviet Union was anti-Arab nationalism; in the United Nations it voted for partition of Palestine. It was considered just as wicked as the West. The charge that Communist parties in both the Arab world and the Soviet Union were and continue to be opposed to Arab unity and nationalism has appeared in Ba'th literature since the creation of the party.

In addition to the idea of nonalignment in world affairs, an idea the party has expounded since 1948—perhaps the first Arab party to do so—the Ba'th charges the Communist doctrine is too cruel. Communism "treats disease with disease." Atasi, another important Ba'th writer, denies that the Soviet Union has a Socialist system. Soviet postponement of Socialist aims during the period of the "dictatorship of the proletariat" has created the worst kind of cruel and bureaucratic police state. Socialism, avowedly an ideology aimed at the economic and political liberation of man, has been distorted to fit the Soviet regime. Furthermore, the Soviets by postponing the idea of "the withering away of the state" have created a new directing class, a new bureaucracy that is ever more efficient in its totalitarian police methods. What the Arabs want is not only nationalization of the means of production but the means to rule as well.

Communist doctrine was also rejected on ideological grounds. Primary among these is the desire for an indigenous ideology. Aflaq wrote that "communism is the daughter of European thought." "The Arabs are not like any other nation of secondary importance." Thus they cannot accept an alien doctrine; they cannot imitate: they must create. Aflaq objects to Marxism as a "materialistic internationalistic message," which denies the existence of nationalities as well as of spiritual values. Communism is destructive, he says, because it comes as a "revelation" that promises "Heaven on Earth"—a Heaven that follows the destruction of the present society. It is also destructive because of its desire to bind Arab destiny to that of the Soviet Union.

Ba'th socialism objects to the Marxist doctrine of economic determinism, arguing that to explain history in terms of economics alone is a denial of the spiritual values cherished by the Arabs. To attribute everything to one factor is to distort the meaning of life and progress. While Marxists believe socialism to be the inevitable result of dialectical materialism, Ba'th ideology preaches that social-ism will come about as a result of the conviction of the majority of the people, that socialism answers the need for a moral and just order in society.

Ba'th insistence on a brand of socialism resulting from the conviction of the majority of the people amounts to denial of the Marxist principle of class struggle. Aflaq rejects the idea of repre-senting any one class. "In the West," he says, "injustice touches only some classes [in the society]. . . . [All] the East represents nothing but an oppressed people." Ba'th socialism as a "cooperative movement believes that the majority of the people—not one class" —has an interest in changing the existing order. While Ba'th socialism recognizes that throughout history there has been class friction, it believes that this principle has been exaggerated and that history, so far, has proved its invalidity. It clearly rejects the international labor movement. Rather than champion the interests of one class against the rest, the Ba'th wishes to level the differences between classes and to narrow the gap between wealth and poverty.

Communist insistence on economic determinism has caused dis-regard of the individual and his liberty. It has permitted the rise of a totalitarian regime that "suffocates the liberty of man." It also ignores the wish of men to own and to inherit private property. Further, while the Ba'th party claims to be secular, it objects to the Marxist's total denial of religion as an essential factor in society.

Rejection by the Ba'th party of many Communist party princi-ples has not prevented it from cooperating with the Communists when such cooperation was propitious. In Jordan the Ba'th party worked with the Communists after 1954 for the purpose of ridding that country of British influence, and of Glubb, the commander of the Jordanian army. In Iraq the Ba'th cooperated with the Com-munists until the time of, and during the fall of, the monarchical regime in 1958, in an effort to embarrass the regime and bring about its downfall. Only after the Qasim regime came to depend too heavily on the Communist party did the Ba'th break away from it. In Syria cooperation between the Ba'th and Communist parties commenced after the Shishakli takeover. Because of the cooperation between the two parties in Syria, Khalid Bakdash, secretary general of the Syrian Communist party, became the first Communist to be elected to Parliament in the Arab world. The Ba'th used its cooperation with the Communists to discredit and destroy its rival political parties in Syria. Thus it reduced the power of the Syrian National Socialist party (PPS); and by so doing, was able to dominate the Syrian political arena from 1954 to 1958, when unity with Egypt was accomplished. The Ba'th call for union with Egypt in 1957 was partly due to its fear of rising Communist influence.

Just as vehemently as it rejects Communist ideology, the Ba'th also rejects Fascist and Nazi socialism. These two movements permit colonialism in the name of superiority of certain races over others. Internally, they rest on the superiority of one individual over another and because of this they permit the rise of an autocratic regime. Ba'th socialism does not seek imperialist expansion, nor does it preach the racial superiority of Arabs. It only calls for the erection of a "just economic order" in the Arab world alone and demands an end to the exploitation of certain nations by others.

Arab socialism and Western socialism have several similarities. Both movements refute the Marxist claim of the inevitability of scientific socialism, the theories of class struggle, and the dictatorship of the proletariat. Both movements have similar economic programs, placing special emphasis on the degree of nationalization they advocate. Since most Arab Socialist intellectuals either received their education in the West, or received a Western-oriented education, a trace of liberal democracy lingers in Arab socialism. Both movements emphasize improving the conditions of the working class. Arab socialism, however, gives more emphasis to the problems of the peasantry and is more nationalistic than Western socialism.

The difference between the two movements lies in the kinds of problems they face in domestic and foreign affairs. Internally, Western Socialist theories emerged in the wake of the industrial advances made in the nineteenth century. They emerged as a reaction to economic class stratification following the Industrial Revolution. Emphasizing the element of class struggle that transcends national boundaries, they aimed at improving conditions of the working class the world over. In economically underdeveloped countries, socialism emerged as a result of the social consciousness of nationalists, clamoring for independence, and, in the Arab world, for unity. Since Western industrialization hardly spread to the Arab world, there was no large proletariat there that a Socialist movement might defend. Socialism thus remained merely a wing of nationalism. In essence, it might be considered the social content of nationalism. In this light, Arab nationalism may be considered a constructive force.

In the Arab world, where problems of industrialization are not so acute, socialism is less class conscious than in the West. Furthermore, owing to the presence of a large peasant population, Arab socialism naturally pays more attention to peasants' problems. It places great emphasis on land reform and on the problems of agricultural workers.

The strong link between nationalism and socialism in Ba'th ideology is justified in terms of the problems the Arabs have to face. Aflaq thus advances the theory of "battle on two fronts": externally to "struggle against imperialism" and for unity; internally to "struggle against internal maladies." Lack of unity, blamed on the West, and internal maladies have permitted "imperialism" to penetrate the Arab world. Western Socialists are not confronted with problems of national unity. Their independence and dignity are secure. Western influence, Socialist and otherwise, "was contaminated with political domination and with military occupation, suppressing those Arabs who found hope for the building of a new society in Western ideas." Aflaq states that Western Socialists were just as imperialistic as anyone else when they assumed power in their own countries. The Léon Blum government in the 1930's did not give Syria and Lebanon independence. Israel was created while the Labor party was in power in Britain in the 1940's. Moreover, French Socialists have supported the suppression of the nationalist movement for the liberation of Algeria. "Such action is not only anti-socialist but inhuman," states Khalil, the prominent Lebanese Ba'thist. Western socialism is "too materialistic" and has "stood beside exploitation, injustice, reaction, expansion, and colonialism." Maqsud states that Western socialism is at best a "progressive wing in a colonialist, capitalistic frame." The connections between the capitalist colonial interests and the Socialist parties in the West, he continues, have caused the latter to support the State of Israel. Thus the Ba'th party approaches its understanding of socialism. In its eyes, and indeed in the eyes of most nationalists in the Arab world, the West is morally discredited.

The final point to be made concerning Arab *vis-à-vis* Western socialism is in terms of the evolution of these movements. In Asia socialism evolved after, rather than before, the formation of Communist parties. Therefore, unlike Europe, where communism emerged as a reaction to the slow progress of socialism, in Asia socialism emerged as a reaction to Communist doctrine. This is of the utmost importance in understanding the implications of social development. Examination of the ideological differences between Ba'th and Communist theories reveals the complete rejection by Ba'th socialism of the "cruelty," "inhumanity," and "dogmatism" of Communist doctrine. This also indicates that Ba'th socialism might be a reaction to the infiltration of Communist ideology in the Arab world.

The Ba'th party's attitude toward the major ideological movements in the twentieth century manifests a series of negative attitudes. Frustrated nationalists that they are, the Ba'th intellectuals cannot bring themselves to associate with a West they consider imperialistic. Thus even in terms of ideology they insist not only on being neutral but on embracing only "Arab" Socialism.

From the Constitution of the Arab Ba'th Socialist Party:

Article 4. The Party of the Arab Ba'th is a Socialist party. It believes that socialism is a necessity which emanates from the depth of Arab nationalism itself. Socialism constitutes, in fact, the ideal social order which will allow the Arab people to realize its possibilities and to enable its genius to flourish, and which will ensure for the nation constant progress in its material and moral output. It makes possible a trustful brotherhood among its members.

Article 26. The Party of the Arab Ba'th is a Socialist party. It believes that the economic wealth of the fatherland belongs to the nation.

Article 27. The present distribution of wealth in the Arab fatherland is unjust. Therefore a review and a just redistribution will become necessary.

Article 28. The equality of all the citizens is founded on human values. This is why the party forbids the exploitation of the work of others.

Article 29. Public utilities, extensive natural resources, big industry, and the means of transport are the property of the nation.

The state will manage them directly and will abolish private companies and foreign concessions.

Article 30. Ownership of agricultural land will be so limited as to be in proportion to the means of the proprietor to exploit all his lands without exploitation of the efforts of others. This will be under the control of the state and in conformity with its over-all economic plan.

Article 31. Small industrial ownership will be so limited as to be related to the standard of living of the citizens of the state as a whole.

Article 32. Workers will participate in the management of their factory. In addition to their wages—fixed by the state—they will receive a proportion of the profits, also fixed by the state.

Article 33. Ownership of immovable property is allowed to all the citizens so long as they do not exploit it to the harm of others, and so long as the state ensures for all citizens a minimum of immovable property.

Article 34. Property and inheritance are two natural rights. They are protected within the limits of the national interest.

Article 35. Usurious loans are prohibited between citizens. One state bank is to be founded to issue currency, which the national output will back. This bank will finance the vital agricultural and industrial plans of the nation.

Article 36. The state will control directly internal and external trade in order to abolish the exploitation of the consumer by the producer. The state will protect them both, as it will protect the national output against the competition of foreign goods and will ensure equilibrium between exports and imports.

Article 37. General planning, inspired by the most modern economic ideas, will be organized so that the Arab fatherland will be industrialized, national production developed, new outlets opened for it, and the industrial economy of each region directed according to its potential and to the raw material it contains.

Nasserite Socialism

Of the diverse components of "Nasserism," socialism is the most recent. It was on the ninth anniversary of the Egyptian Revolu-

SOURCE: Fayez Sayegh, *The Theoretical Structure of Nasser's Arab Socialism* (in A. Hourani, ed., *Middle Eastern Affairs*, No. 4, Oxford University Press, London, 1965), passim pp. 10–30.

tion, in July 1961, that a programme of socialization was formally launched; and it was not until the following May that the theoretical framework of Nasser's socialism was constructed and announced.

. . . Nasser's socialism now has its own *theory*. It is the kind of theory that suits a man like Nasser, who scorns abstract speculation and pure theory. Theories are meaningful to him only in their practical application. As such, they must follow application, not precede it. Extracted from past experience in order to guide future action, theories are a legitimate exercise which can also be helpful; constructed in advance of experience, or in detachment from practice, they are worthless; indeed, they may deceptively appear to be useful, and thereby become actually harmful. The antipathy of some "doctrinaire socialists" towards Nasser is clearly mutual.

Nasser's theory of socialism partakes of his antitheoretical bias. It was constructed after the comprehensive socialization programme of July 1961 had been launched. It was designed to do no more than provide the post-1961 phase of the systematic socialization of the U.A.R. with the programme which the pre-1961 stages of the social revolution had lacked. It was no more and no less than a blueprint of the socialist society that would be built, and a programme and time-table for the construction process.

Socialism is the pursuit of "sufficiency," "justice," and "freedom." By "sufficiency," Nasser means the expansion of the nation's total wealth. "Justice" connotes freedom from exploitation and the enjoyment of an equal opportunity to develop one's abilities and to receive a fair share of the national wealth according to one's efforts. "Freedom" is the participation in the shaping of the nation's destiny.

The attainment of each of these three ideals requires certain readjustments in the existing system of social, economic and political organization, and the creation of a new system by appropriate means and devices. It is these changes, systems and means that primarily concern Nasser. Further analysis of his views on the goals, however, is necessary for fuller understanding of his choice of specific measures of social change as well as his selection of the socialist pattern as a whole.

Emphasis on *sufficiency* as an integral element of socialism is inescapable in an underdeveloped society, where poverty is endemic and the standard of living below the level demanded by the dignity of man. In an already developed society, sufficiency need not occupy as prominent a position in the scheme of socialist objectives.

Sufficiency entails not only the increase of production but the expansion of services as well. The true object of production is to provide the greatest amount of services. According to the *Charter* [of National Action, Nasser's socialist manifesto], the principal services which socialism must provide include medical care (treatment and medicament), education, employment, and insurance against old age and sickness.

Sufficiency, in production and services, is a relative term. Its minimum magnitude may be determinable in a given socio-economic situation; but there can be no maximum, no outer limit to the socialist aspiration to attain sufficiency. Sufficiency merges imperceptibly into abundance and prosperity, as its true end. If his sights are set on mere sufficiency as the economic ingredient of the socialist objective, it is because Nasser is realistically aware of the difficulties and time involved in the thoroughgoing development of his country; and because, by virtue of his step-by-step approach to the monumental enterprise of "socialist conversion," he must for the time being focus on the task immediately ahead. Of his visions of the more distant horizons, he must allow himself at present to indulge in only passing glimpses. Besides, to encourage the people at this stage to entertain hopes which cannot in the near future be realized, is to indulge in deception and is unworthy of true leaders.

Sufficiency (and prosperity, to which it is a prelude) is justified in its own right; but it is also justified by the fact that, without it, social justice and equality of opportunity, the second goal of socialism, cannot be attained. "In proportion to the expansion of the base of production . . . new hopes are opened, affording equal opportunities to all citizens." To focus on social justice and on equal opportunities for a fair share of the nation's wealth, without in the meantime expanding the wealth of the nation, is in the final analysis tantamount to spreading poverty to all. Only in a more productive society can the equalization of opportunities mean their enlargement as well; and, unless in its striving for equal opportunities, socialism aims also at their enlargement as an indivisible part of the same goal, the prize is scarcely worth the price. Tirelessly, Nasser strives in his public speeches to bring this point home to his audiences. The frequency of his reiteration of this idea, the simple terms in which he expresses it, and the imagery and the passion he brings to his elaboration of its theme and implications, indicate clearly that Nasser has a genuine fear lest the masses, long deprived, should now seek quick relief: waiting passively for the redistribution of national wealth instead of vigorously contributing to its enlargement. This is not the way of socialism, he keeps telling them in endlessly varied ways; rights entail corresponding duties, and the chief beneficiaries of socialism can actually come to enjoy its promised benefits only if they apply themselves loyally to its tasks. Nasser ridicules the lazy man's socialist manual, which counsels nationalization of existing enterprises without simultaneous efforts to expand production. Nationalization without vigorous development plans neither leads to genuine socialism through sufficiency nor advances socialism through the establishment of social justice: it replaces class exploitation by state exploitation; it punishes a few, where it should aim at rewarding the many.

Only the vigorous, methodical pursuit of sufficiency, then, can make possible the establishment of social justice and meaningful equality of opportunity. But these, in turn, are a prerequisite of sufficiency: they are necessary for invigorating the pursuit of sufficiency and giving it a chance to reach its destination. A happier, healthier, better educated or more skilled farmer or worker, liberated from the oppression of the feudal master or purged of the debilitating estrangement caused by the exploitation of his employer, can apply himself with greater dedication and usefulness to the productive enterprise, to which his enjoyment of social justice gives him a sense of belonging.

> Sufficiency, i.e. increased production, without justice, means a fuller monopolization of wealth. Justice, i.e. the equitable distribution of national income, without increased production, is tantamount to the distribution of poverty and misery. But, hand in hand, they reach their objective . . .

To aim at both sufficiency and justice at the same time, however, is not without its strains and problems. Three difficulties in particular frequently engage Nasser's attention.

To make goods and services available more abundantly to a

larger number of formerly deprived citizens, as social justice demands, is appreciably to increase consumption; but the increase of
production, in pursuit of sufficiency, requires the expansion of
investments and savings and a commensurate curtailment of consumption. The means militate against one another, although the
purposes are mutually complementary. True socialism cannot con-
template ignoring, or even temporarily suspending, either purpose
in order to serve the other; yet the paucity of resources is such as
to forbid the pious hope that both purposes might be adequately
satisfied at the same time. To temper this sobering influence of
economic reality upon his socialist idealism, Nasser resorts to
planning, in the magic efficacy of which he has well-nigh unlimited faith. (In fact, his faith in planning antedated his faith in
socialism, as his pre-socialist economic policies show.)

Planning comes readily to the rescue of socialism in another
difficulty, akin to the first: the conflict between the satisfaction of
the needs of today's generation, and the expansion of the productive base of the economy in order that sufficiency and prosperity may be ensured for future generations. This dilemma adds the
dimension of time—the sequence of the generations—to the first. It
does not revolve, as does the first, around the apportionment of the
country's limited resources between consumption by the present
generation and savings and investments for later consumption by
the same generation; rather, it raises the more fundamental question
of whether the well-being of one generation should be sacrificed
for the happiness of another. The choice raises questions of principle. He would—Nasser intimates—be untrue to his concept of the
centrality of man in society, or to his belief that man is the end of
social action, if he were to opt for the well-being of unborn
generations and thereby sacrifice the happiness of the real, suffering, long-deprived men and women who compose today's generation. His choice is therefore clear. He would not countenance
"sacrificing the living generation of citizens for the sake of those
still unborn." So important is this decision in his view, that Nasser
considers it a distinguishing feature of his socialism, setting it apart
from other systems: "Other experiments of progress have realized
their objectives at the expense of increasing the misery of the
working people, either to serve the interests of capital or under the
pressure of ideological applications which went to the extent of
sacrificing whole living generations for the sake of others still

unborn." In those experiments, "extremely cruel pressure was exerted on living generations, who were deprived of all the fruit of their labour for the sake of a promised tomorrow which they could neither see nor reach."

Closely related to these two problems is the possible conflict between the economic and the social aspects of socialism. The establishment of social justice may at times demand readjustments in the economic relationships which tend, in the short run at any rate, to diminish economic productivity and retard progress towards sufficiency. The breaking-up of large estates may be one such instance. Some of the privileges given to workers in the socialist laws of July 1961, which may seem somewhat lavish in the context of the present economy of the U.A.R., are another illustration. Once more, then, essentially harmonious objectives may be found in practice to work at cross-purposes. Choices have to be made, which, in their consequences if not in the intentions behind them, involve the priority of either the economic or the social aspect of socialism over the other. The factors governing the practical decisions called for in a given instance cannot be evaluated from the perspective of economic efficiency alone or social imperativeness alone; they can be properly seen, in relation to one another and to socialist aims as a whole, only from a transcendent socialist vantage point which encompasses in its vision the whole range of social action, including primarily economic and essentially social considerations. No *a priori* formula, determining the relative value of the economic or the social ingredients within the structure of socialism which embraces them equally, and producing a social-ist yardstick by which the socialist significance of the diverse components of socialism can be measured, is possible—even as-suming that Nasser's pragmatic approach to socialism permitted the search for such a formula and the employment of such a hypotheti-cal standard of measurement. The problems raised in this context call for practical judgments passed in each instance on the merits of the case at hand—judgments in which purely technical considera-tions of an economic or a social character, however important in themselves, must be supplemented by the insight of the statesman. Examination of the individual choices made by Nasser thus far, however, does reveal a general trend which may be indicative of the orientation and pattern of his social thought: on the whole, social values tend to receive priority over purely economic considerations, at the present stage of the period of "socialist conversion."

Social justice demands the eradication of exploitation: the exploitation of farmers by feudal masters, of labourers by capitalist employers, and of society as a whole by the "alliance of feudalism and capitalism."

Exploitation is at its worst when it is a lasting and continuous condition, and when the victim is powerless to escape from its clutches. It is in this form that it perpetuates itself, extending from one generation to the next. Such "hereditary exploitation" commits the gravest sin against the dignity of man: it inculcates in some of its victims hopelessness, resignation, and perhaps acceptance. Nasser waxes indignant whenever he speaks of such "hereditary exploitation," with its twin components: hereditary privilege and hereditary privation.

> Neither the law of justice nor divine law allows that wealth should be hereditary and that poverty should be hereditary; that health should be hereditary and that illness should be hereditary; that learning should be hereditary and that illiteracy should be hereditary; that human dignity should be hereditary and that human degradation should be hereditary.

Social justice is the enjoyment of equal opportunities: an equal opportunity for a share of the national wealth, proportionate to one's work and ability; an equal opportunity for a share of the essential services necessary for decent living; an equal opportunity for self-realization and dignity.

To strive for making the opportunities open to all citizens equal is not to assume equality among the citizens, Nasser emphasizes. As human beings and as citizens, they are entitled to equal chances to actualize their respective potentialities and to make those contributions to society of which they are capable; they must not be barred from education, or medical care, or appropriate employment, by the rigid barriers imposed by an exploitative social order or by the great disparities in fortune bequeathed by one generation to another. But, beyond the opening-up of equal opportunities for fulfilment to all citizens, socialism cannot and does not endeavour to equalize human beings who are essentially unequal in their abilities.

Equality of opportunity, and the eradication of hereditary and other circumstantial barriers obstructing the enjoyment of such equality mean that man, every man, shall have the chance under socialism to "determine his place in society by his own work and his own effort." Moreover, "every individual should feel that his own exertion entitles him to progress and advancement."

In the final analysis, social justice means the "dissolution of class distinctions." In the pre-socialist era, "the son of a pasha became a pasha at birth; he was born with a golden spoon in his mouth, and grew up to find the country wide open to him," while "the son of the overseer became a hired farmer on the land." Under socialism, "every individual shall have a chance and an opportunity. This is what I mean when I talk about dissolving class barriers: there shall be no pashas, no beys, no masters. . . . Instead, there shall be equality and freedom for each individual in this nation." "I want a society in which class distinctions are dissolved through equality of opportunities to all citizens. I want a society in which the free individual can determine his own position by himself, on the basis of his efficiency, capacity and character."

Just as equality of opportunity does not signify equality of abilities, so too "the dissolution of class distinctions" does not mean the dissolution of classes as such. The object of socialism is not a classless society; it is the creation of conditions in which diverse classes, each performing a valid social function, and all free from domination and exploitation, can coexist within a framework of national unity and in harmony. It is the vertical stratification of classes, so to speak, in accordance with which some are subordinate and exploited while others are dominant and exploitative, that Nasser's socialism rejects. The continued existence of classes as such (although Nasser prefers to call them "popular powers," "working powers," or "powers of the working people") is implicit in the very nature of Nasser's socialist ideal. For that ideal, to which the dissolution of class distinctions leads, is a social order in which both the *diversity* and the *harmony* of the "working powers" obtain; it is an order based on "the *alliance* of the working powers of the people," not on their fusion. Socialism, according to Nasser, rejects the colourless vision of classless uniformity just as forcefully as it rebels against the actuality of the hierarchical class structure of non-socialist societies. It is this feature that primarily distinguishes socialist democracy, the only "true" and "sound" democracy, from the "false" and "counterfeit" democracy which obtains under conditions of class-domination.

The "alliance of all popular powers" is the socio-political ideal of Nasser's socialism, the basis of socialist democracy. The opening words of the 1964 Constitution describe the United Arab Republic as "a democratic, socialist State based on the alliance of the working powers of the people." These working powers are defined as "the farmers, workers, soldiers, intellectuals and national capital."

Misunderstandings and conflicts among these classes or "powers" cannot be excluded, even after the domination of the former exploitative classes has been brought to an end and class distinctions have been dissolved. Such misunderstandings and conflicts do not constitute class struggle or generate class warfare, however, for they can be resolved peacefully and within the framework of national unity.

The alliance of the working powers of the people is possible, despite differences among them. The alliance of the exploitative classes, feudalists and capitalists, is also possible; it is actual in pre-socialist society. But the two groups cannot coexist peacefully and on the basis of mutual respect, for by nature the alliance of feudalism and capitalism rests on domination and exploitation of the working powers of the people. Divided, these working powers submit, however resentfully, to the dominance of the exploitative classes. But the submission is always potentially explosive; and, unless political revolution rids society of the control of the alliance of feudalism and capitalism over the government and over the nation as a whole, the restiveness of the subdued classes must sooner or later express itself in class struggle and class warfare. The ominous threat of civil war and bloodshed is ever present. It is lifted only when the social revolution, made possible by the destruction of the dominance of the exploitative alliance by political revolution, proceeds to create social justice and construct an alliance of all the working powers of the people. Social peace, then, as well as social justice, is the promise of socialism: actual injustice and potential civil war are what the social system based on the exploitation and domination of the alliance of feudalism and capitalism offers. Socialism, through the justice and peace it provides, makes true democracy possible and prepares the ground for it; the alliance of capitalism and feudalism makes democracy impossible, notwithstanding the facade of quasi-democratic institutions and processes which it maintains. "He who monopolizes and controls the fortunes of farmers and workers can, in consequence, monopolize and control their votes as well, and impose his will upon them. The freedom of the loaf of bread is an indispensable guarantee of the freedom of the vote." "Political democracy cannot be separated from social democracy. . . . Political democracy cannot exist under the domination of any one class."

But socialism, Nasser insists, does not aim at replacing the exploitative alliance of capitalism and feudalism by the exploitative domination of any other class or alliance of classes. It is not the purpose of socialism to substitute one exploitation for another. The domination of any one class—be it capital or labour, feudalism or the farmers—is incompatible with socialism and true democracy. The domination of one class, or one alliance of classes, is *class dictatorship*, whatever the identity of the dominant group. For wherever one class or some classes lord it over the rest, there is dictatorship, which Nasser defines as the rule of some over all, in the interest of the rulers. Only where all working powers jointly participate in the councils of the nation and determine its policies within a framework of all-embracing national unity does democracy, the rule of all the people, obtain.

> We are pledged to the establishment of a new socialist experience in our country, based on love and brotherhood and not on the domination of any one class, whatever name it may take. . . . If we declare that we will not allow capitalism or feudalism to return, because they represent the rule of a minority, the rule of one class, we also declare that we will not allow the dictatorship of the proletariat, as envisaged by communism, because that too means the domination of a particular group over all. . . . Our socialism, which rejects the rule of one class, shall not fall under the domination of any class. . . . A small group of people cannot be allowed to monopolize the political scene, whether in the present or in the future: political action belongs to all the people.

Nor does socialism aim at liquidating those *individuals* whose domination, as a *class* or an *alliance of classes*, it feels constrained to destroy. Describing the measures taken at the final stage of "liquidating the alliance of reaction and imperialism as well as liquidating their inherited privileges" (beginning in the autumn of 1961), and reporting the end of that phase of internal policy, Nasser told the new National Assembly at its first meeting:

> There was no enmity towards any individual or family. I sincerely say to you that I hesitated for a long time before signing the decree imposing sequestration upon a number of individuals from this class . . . I was fully alive to the fact that they were human beings, in addition to their being a class. My aim was to liquidate the class but in such a way that the dignity of every member and his right to live would be safeguarded, as long as he performed his national duty. I tried my best to mitigate the effects of this change upon them. But I rightly considered that the law of justice must take its course. . . .
>
> We were not against individuals. We were opposed to class distinction. It was our right to eliminate its effects. But it was not our right to eliminate the dignity and humanity of individuals.

D.   AFRICAN SOCIALISM

Negro African intellectuals and political leaders in many of the nearly thirty Negro African states that have achieved independence since 1957 use the term African socialism to indicate a distinctive movement. Theoretically, the main components of African socialism, besides communalism (priority of the group over the individual) and partial or total collectivism, are the values and institutions of the traditional (i.e., precolonial) way of life. The socialist society of Negro African emerging nations would be not so much a new as an improved traditional society, freed from the elements introduced during the colonial period (seven or eight decades for most of Negro Africa) and incorporating modern knowledge and modern technology. Actually, because of the variety of Negro traditional cultures, differences in the Western impact, and the varying approaches to institutional changes since independence, African socialism is a general more than a specific expression, indicative less of a distinctive movement than of attempts at modernization that have taken different forms. Advocates of a distinctive African socialism have not overcome the contradiction deriving from the fact that the traditional way of life is related to tribal structures, while socialnationalist leaders of the new Negro African states aim at replacing tribalism with nationalism. In practice, socialism in Negro Africa has meant anti-capitalism and anti-parliamentarianism and, positively, a system aimed at the transformation of traditional societies through the centralized institutions of the one-party state and governmental guidance of economic activities, to be financed in large part by foreign aid and by the nationalization of enterprises owned by foreigners and by non-Negro minorities.

This selection contains excerpts from writings published in *African*

Socialism (W. H. Friedland and C. G. Roseberg, eds., 1964). George Padmore (1903–1960), a West Indian Negro from Trinidad, became a Marxist-Leninist in the 1920's, but later broke with the organized communist movement. He was the author of several books dealing with British colonial policies, chiefly in relation to Africa. Before and after independence for Ghana he acted for several years as mentor to Kwame Nkrumah (1909–   ), Ghana's constitutional Prime Minister and later dictator, who was overthrown by a military coup in 1966. Before the establishment of the dictatorship the main opposition to Padmore's and Nkrumah's authoritarian socialism had come from Ghanaian democratic socialists. Julius Kambarage Nyerere, born in 1922 in Tanganyika, was educated at Makerere College and the University of Edinburgh. In 1954 he founded the Tanganyika African National Union, and in 1960 was appointed Prime Minister by the British authorities. After independence he was elected President of Tanganyika (known as Tanzania after union with Zanzibar in 1964). Nyerere is one of the most distinguished statesmen in Negro Africa. Equally distinguished is Leopold Sidar Senghor, poet and statesman, born in 1906, educated at the University of Paris, a teacher in France from 1935 to 1948, member of the French Constituent Assembly in 1945 and 1946, member of the French government in 1955 and 1956. He became President of Senegal when the country achieved independence in 1960.

Socialism for Ghana (George Padmore)

THE REVOLUTION taking place in Africa is threefold. First, there is the struggle for national independence. The second is the social revolution, which follows the achievement of independence and self-determination. And third, Africans are seeking some form of regional unity as the forerunner of a United States of Africa. However, until the first is achieved, the energies of the people cannot be mobilized for the attainment of the second and third stages, which are even more difficult than the first. For it means the total elimination of the economic and social heritage of colonialism, such as bribery and corruption, ignorance, poverty, disease, and the construction of a society in consonance with the aspirations of the people for a welfare state with their well-being at heart.

The socialist objective is not, as certain of its opponents have made out, the leveling down of living standards, but rather their raising

SOURCE: G. Padmore, *Socialism for Ghana* (in W. H. Friedland and C. G. Roseberg, eds., *African Socialism*, Stanford University Press, Stanford, California, 1964), pp. 228–236.

up, so that the majority, rather than just a minority as at present, will enjoy the benefits of the abundance which machine techniques and modern science have made possible.

Nor does socialism, as has also been contended, mean merely taking from the rich to give to the poor, for a mere redivision of the present available wealth in the hands of individuals will not satisfy to any appreciable extent the gap which now exists between the "haves" and the "have nots." The socialist objective means the scientific planning of production and distribution, through the common ownership of the basic means of production and services, so that ultimately all people regardless of race, color, creed, or social origin will be able to enjoy exactly what they want to fill their needs. But this stage, according to Marx, will not be reached until socialism evolves into full-fledged communism, which will correspond to the attainment of the classless society. At such a stage there is no privileged class which exploits others by exercising exclusive ownership over the means of production.

[Although there are many forms of socialism, there is a general philosophy that can be summarized as follows:]

1. From each citizen according to his ability.
2. To each citizen according to his needs.
3. Equal opportunity for all citizens to give of their best to their country.
4. Democratically elected government of the people, by the people, for the people.

. . . we must evolve our own form of African Socialism, suited to our own conditions and historical background, so as to serve best the needs of the people of Ghana. . . . the African approach to socialism must be based on a policy of adaptation, while keeping constantly in mind our goal—the peaceful advance to African Socialism, which should have the following principal aims and objectives:

1. *Politically*, African Socialism shall strive to promote and safeguard popular democracy based upon universal adult suffrage (one individual, one vote, regardless of race, color, creed, or sex), fundamental human rights, social justice, and the rule of law.

2. *Economically*, African Socialism shall seek to promote and safeguard the people's well-being through the common ownership and control of the essential means of production and distribution,

and ultimately the abolition of power to live by rent, interest, and profit.

3. *Socially*, African Socialism shall seek to promote and safeguard full employment by the state and performance by all citizens of work of social value according to their ability, while all citizens will share in the common resources of the nation according to their needs. Equal opportunity shall be given to all, regardless of race, tribe, color, class, or creed. Talent and character shall be the only criteria of merit in public life.

In Ghana, unlike Russia, the Convention People's Party (CPP) government have already laid the solid foundation of political democracy based upon parliamentary government, universal adult suffrage, freedom of assembly, speech, and press, as well as the rule of law. It is now up to the Ghana government to reinforce political democracy with economic democracy. This calls for planning, as it is only through planning that the CPP will be able to fulfill its election promises to the people and eradicate the main social evils facing the country—unemployment, disease, poverty, illiteracy.

But to carry out our plans in order to attain the objective of the welfare state means not only a change in the economic structure of society. The approach to planning and the carrying out of that planning call for fundamental changes in the customs, habits, and institutions of the people as well as an overhauling of their mode of thinking. All the planning in the world will not carry us forward to the "New Jerusalem" as long as those responsible for the implementation of those plans do not have a socialist approach. Thus, it is only with changes in thought and customs and approach that it will be possible to create the social mechanisms and human means which socialism and its building call for. In other words, you cannot build socialism without socialists.

It cannot be too firmly stressed that socialism is more than an economic system. It is a social arrangement whereby the people hold in common the means of production and share according to their needs in the fruits of their collective labor, that is, the goods and services which they together fashion from the productive means. In contradistinction to the capitalist system, in which each individual is out for himself only, the socialist system demands the maximum cooperation between all the members of the society, because it is this cooperation alone which will bring that abundance which will make the good life available for all in Ghana.

Our starting point in economic reconstruction must be the *land*, with its communal ownership and production and its element of cooperative self-help. This is the foundation stone on which we must build the new socialist pattern of society in Ghana. We may borrow ideas from America, China, India, Yugoslavia, Israel, Sudan, and elsewhere, but the actual pattern must be founded upon the African base. The agricultural sector, which is already largely in the hands of the Africans, must be raised to such a level that the condition of the farmer not only is advanced from its present subsistence level, but must be made to produce a surplus of wealth to provide the accumulation of capital necessary to pay for the importation of the machinery and technical "know-how" required for the industrial sector.

The primary aim of agriculture must be diversification to relieve the country's reliance upon its present single-crop economy— cocoa. Emphasis must first of all be upon food production, with a greater variety of foods for home consumption, so as to do away with the considerable importation of foodstuffs, which are at present such a drain on our foreign exchange resources, which could otherwise be employed for development purposes. Animal husbandry and dairy farming must be included in our agricultural planning. Increased availability of foodstuffs from our land will be effective in holding down the cost of living, which reflects positively upon the general cost of our development. For we shall not have to meet constant demands for increased wages to meet inflationary living costs.

As far as the farmer himself is concerned, he must be assured of markets for his product at agreed price levels; otherwise he will have no incentive in increasing his output. In addition to taking care of domestic needs, agricultural production must sustain our industrial development. Market research should show the way to increase our agricultural exports.

To meet these objectives, we may find that the existing agricultural and rural pattern can be adapted to more than one productive form. There is, for instance, large-scale cooperative farming like the Gezira scheme, which has been so successful in the Sudan. The United Ghana Farmers Council could here take the initiative in getting villages to clear stool lands and put them under cultivation, while the Agricultural Development Corporation

(ADC) would assist with loans and technical management until the farmers are able to take over and run the enterprise themselves.

Producers' cooperatives should also enter upon the scene as the marketing entrepreneur. Another form could be that of individual farm production linked to the cooperative village center, which will be the point of collection for farm products and their subsequent distribution by the cooperative societies in the towns and other urban communities.

But whatever form is adopted, it is necessary that the village shall be the focal point of the surrounding farming community, and shall provide the social and cultural amenities which will bring town life to the countryside and thereby save the drift away from the land and the rural areas, since our industrial development must, at least for the time being, be toward small-scale rather than large-scale enterprises.

Industries must first aim at meeting domestic requirements to save importations. Where it is possible, surpluses can be provided for export to pay for welfare necessities. Ancillary industries should be linked to the products of agriculture and mining.

Because of lack of capital resources by Ghanaians and the deficiencies in technical and managerial experience, it will be necessary for government or semipublic institutions like the Industrial Development Corporation (IDC) and ADC in many cases to initiate and carry out singly or jointly with private enterprise and the cooperatives the major industrialization projects and the modernization of large-scale agricultural and husbandry schemes where these will be advantageous.

The whole aim of our economic program, agricultural and industrial, must be to move away from a trading economy to an industrial economy. African businessmen today are too tied up with merchandising; they are too concerned with distributing foreign importations instead of busying themselves with the production of consumer goods in Ghana. We want to encourage manufacturing capitalists and not wholesale and retail trading capitalists. For as long as African businessmen continue to think only in terms of selling other people's goods we shall not be able to alter the old imperialist pattern of our economy. Only to the extent that we are able to transform the present economic structure from trade to manufacture shall we be able to progress along the socialist road to self-sufficiency and prosperity. Therefore, while government should give every encouragement to Ghanaians to enter the fields of producing essential goods and adopt positive measures to protect them from unfair competition by foreign imports, no assistance should be given to them for purely shopkeeping and trading operations.

Apart from economic planning as such, there must be technical planning. And for this, it is necessary to have a whole new educational system which, apart from the traditional educational subjects having an African perspective, will provide the human instruments for the carrying through of socialist planning. The educational system must provide more statisticians, bookkeepers, accountants, auditors, commercial legal experts, technical experts at all levels and in all branches, scientists, engineers, managers, administrators, and the rest. In this respect, we can learn much from the Russians, who have revolutionized their educational system to meet the demands of our scientific and technological age.

Moreover, the new education must be geared to producing a different kind of citizen from the one we know: one who will know his history, his background and his socialist future; his need to live in cooperation with his neighbors and to give unselfish service to his country; and the need for his country to live in unity and amity with other countries. The new citizen must be made aware of the new socialist planning and understand his part and place in the new scheme of things.

There must be capital. Nothing is possible without capital. Socialists are, in effect, the manipulators of capital free of capitalist aims; that is, they want to invest capital for social ends rather than for private profit and the exploitation of man by man. Society cannot be built without capital, but capital can be accumulated without capitalists. Ghana is rich in capital.

Ghana is rich in capital which consists of her natural resources plus her labor power. Yet we cannot escape a period of austerity in order to harness this capital for constructing our socialist pattern of society. But how to attain this austerity? We must forgo those things which are not essential by imposing heavy taxation on luxury goods. Let those who want them pay for their ostentation.

The government must use all the powers invested in it to accelerate this process of industrialization. This calls for bold planning on all fronts of our national life. It involves the complete reorganization not only of the basic foundations of our society, but of the ideas, the mental outlook, and the social habits of the people. Many prejudices and social attitudes will have to be abandoned, wasteful expenditure on funerals and weddings, and the giving and taking of "dash." The youth will have to be taught the dignity of labor. Older people will have to be taught thrift—the need to save and invest their savings in productive undertakings. Idleness will have to be condemned as a social evil. The spirit of self-help and cooperation will have to be encouraged. Bribery and corruption must be harshly punished and examples made of the most important transgressors by long terms of imprisonment and the confiscation of their property, especially in cases involving theft of state funds and property. For these are crimes against society as a whole and not just an individual.

As the first independent African nation to embark upon a program of economic planning, we must make a conscious effort to evolve new forms of socialist techniques applicable to our African environment and historical background, which may serve as a guide to other African countries when they, too, attain independence. It is, therefore, important to have convinced and dedicated socialists responsible for our socialist planning. Only through such a realistic approach will we be able to achieve our social objectives and make socialism a reality for the people of Ghana and an example to the rest of Africa.

Since the government and public corporations will have to shoulder the major responsibility for industrialization, they will need the active support and cooperation of the Ghana Trades Union Congress, the United Ghana Farmers Council, and the Cooperative Movement, representing the two most important social classes in Ghana—the industrial workers and the peasant farmers. This alliance between the real producers of the nation's wealth will enable the government, through the political guidance of the socialist committed CPP, to mobilize the enthusiasm and dynamism of the whole people in the carrying out of the Five-Year Plan.

On the other hand, national planning must be flexible enough to draw in the participation of local as well as foreign capital interests. But these antisocialist elements must not control or direct our march toward Pan-African Socialism. Accordingly, the following sectors will have their definite functions within the Plan:

1. *State and semipublic sector*, i.e. rail, road, sea and air trans-

port, electricity, port authorities, etc., will represent the main socialist sector.

2. *Cooperative sector.* This will represent the semisocialist sector and should receive special assistance in order to broaden and strengthen the cooperative character of the national economy. The cooperative movement must become the main economic instrument to combat and contain the expansion of private capitalists and middlemen seeking to monopolize trade and commerce.

3. *African business sector* will aim to assist Africans in promoting industrial, agricultural, and commercial undertakings that will benefit the general national economy.

4. *Free enterprise sector.* While foreign capitalists should be encouraged to participate in productive undertakings or in providing essential services of a socioeconomic nature as will benefit the general national economy, they must be rigidly controlled and kept strictly within their allotted sector. All business dealings in usury and stock market speculation must be forbidden.

5. *Mixed state and private sector.* This mixed state-capitalist economic sector will cover joint enterprise of government subsidized corporations and private capital (local and foreign) under such conditions as will ultimately strengthen and broaden the socialist sector of the national economy. (The Puerto Rican government has used this form of mixed economy most successfully.)

It is only out of the wealth derived from industrialization and increased agricultural productivity that we shall be able to pay for the social services and other amenities which the CPP and the CPP government have pledged to the people. These amenities—water, electricity, roads, telecommunications, houses, hospitals and health centers, and schools—must take top priority in our next Five-Year Plan. For politics cannot be divorced from economics; as a socialist political party we must, if we want to retain the support of the masses and thereby political power, meet the immediate basic needs of the voters before the next general election.

The CPP has not only to explain the government's policy and plan to the masses. It has the task, above all, to mobilize the support of its main allies, the Trade Union Congress and the United Ghana Farmers Council, the youth, and the working women to back the economic revolution at which we are aiming, just as it did in carrying through the national revolution which has brought us independence. Both revolutions—the national revolution and the economic revolution—are interrelated, the second being dependent upon the first.

Political power has given us the possibility of planning the country's economic emancipation. Without political power, no planning would have been possible, as we know from our period of colonial dependence. But to have achieved political independence and to fail to carry the national revolution into the economic revolution would be to betray the interests of the common people and the trust which they have placed in our party. Our failure in this connection would, moreover, leave our political independence open to perpetual threat from outside imperialist pressures.

Ujamaa: The Basis of African Socialism (J. K. Nyerere)

. . . When a society is so organized that it cares about its individuals, then, provided he is willing to work, no individual within that society should worry about what will happen to him tomorrow if he does not hoard wealth today. Society itself should look after him, or his widow, or his orphans. This is exactly what traditional African society succeeded in doing. Both the "rich" and the "poor" individual were completely secure in African society. Natural catastrophe brought famine, but it brought famine to everybody—"poor" or "rich." Nobody starved, either of food or of human dignity, because he lacked personal wealth; he could depend on the wealth possessed by the community of which he was a member. That was socialism. That is socialism. There can be no such thing as acquisitive socialism, for that would be another contradiction in terms. Socialism is essentially distributive. Its concern is to see that those who sow reap a fair share of what they sow.

The production of wealth, whether by primitive or modern methods, requires three things. First, land. God has given us the land, and it is from the land that we get the raw materials which we reshape to meet our needs. Second, tools. We have found by simple experience that tools do help! So we make the hoe, the axe, or the modern factory or tractor, to help us produce wealth—the goods we need. And, third, human exertion—or labor. We don't need to

SOURCE: J. K. Nyerere, *Ujamaa: The Basis of African Socialism* (in W. H. Friedland and C. G. Roseberg, eds., *African Socialism*, Stanford University Press, Stanford, California, 1964), pp. 239–246.

read Karl Marx or Adam Smith to find out that neither the land nor the hoe actually produces wealth.

And we don't need to take degrees in economics to know that neither the worker nor the landlord produces land. Land is God's gift to man—it is always there. But we do know, still without degrees in economics, that the axe and the plow were produced by the laborer. Some of our more sophisticated friends apparently have to undergo the most rigorous intellectual training simply in order to discover that stone axes were produced by that ancient gentleman "Early Man" to make it easier for him to skin the impala he had just killed with a club, which he had also made for himself!

In traditional African society everybody was a worker. There was no other way of earning a living for the community. Even the Elder, who appeared to be enjoying himself without doing any work and for whom everybody else appeared to be working, had, in fact, worked hard all his younger days. The wealth he now appeared to possess was not his, personally; it was only "his" as the Elder of the group which had produced it. He was its guardian. The wealth itself gave him neither power nor prestige. The respect paid to him by the young was his because he was older than they, and had served his community longer; and the "poor" Elder enjoyed as much respect in our society as the "rich" Elder.

When I say that in traditional African society everybody was a worker, I do not use the word "worker" simply as opposed to "employer" but also as opposed to "loiterer" or "idler." One of the most socialistic achievements of our society was the sense of security it gave to its members, and the universal hospitality on which they could rely. But it is too often forgotten, nowadays, that the basis of this great socialistic achievement was this: that it was taken for granted that every member of society—barring only the children and the infirm—contributed his fair share of effort toward the production of its wealth. Not only was the capitalist, or the landed exploiter, unknown to traditional African society, but we did not have that other form of modern parasite—the loiterer, or idler, who accepts the hospitality of society as his "right" but gives nothing in return! Capitalistic exploitation was impossible. Loitering was an unthinkable disgrace.

Those of us who talk about the African Way of Life, and, quite rightly, take a pride in maintaining the tradition of hospitality which is so great a part of it, might do well to remember the

Swahili saying, *Mgeni siku mbili; siku ya tatu mpe jembe*—or in English, "Treat your guest as a guest for two days; on the third day give him a hoe!" In actual fact, the guest was likely to ask for the hoe even before his host had to give him one—for he knew what was expected of him, and would have been ashamed to remain idle any longer. Thus, working was part and parcel, was indeed the very basis and justification, of this socialist achievement of which we are so justly proud.

There is no such thing as socialism without work. A society which fails to give its individuals the means to work, or, having given them the means to work, prevents them from getting a fair share of the products of their own sweat and toil, needs putting right. Similarly, an individual who can work—and is provided by society with the means to work—but does not do so, is equally wrong. He has no right to expect anything from society because he contributes nothing to society.

The other use of the word "worker," in its specialized sense of "employee" as opposed to "employer," reflects a capitalist attitude of mind which was introduced into Africa with the coming of colonialism and is totally foreign to our own way of thinking. In the old days the African had never aspired to the possession of personal wealth for the purpose of dominating any of his fellows. He had never had laborers or "factory hands" to do his work for him. But then came the foreign capitalists. They were wealthy. They were powerful. And the African naturally started wanting to be wealthy too. There is nothing wrong in our wanting to be wealthy; nor is it a bad thing for us to want to acquire the power which wealth brings with it. But it most certainly is wrong if we want the wealth and the power so that we can dominate somebody else. Unfortunately there are some of us who have already learned to covet wealth for that purpose—and who would like to use the methods which the capitalist uses in acquiring it. That is to say, some of us would like to use, or exploit, our brothers for the purpose of building up our own personal power and prestige. This is completely foreign to us, and it is incompatible with the socialist society we want to build here.

Our first step, therefore, must be to re-educate ourselves; to regain our former attitude of mind. In our traditional African society we were individuals within a community. We took care of the community, and the community took care of us. We neither needed nor wished to exploit our fellow men.

And in rejecting the capitalist attitude of mind which colonialism brought into Africa, we must reject also the capitalist methods which go with it. One of these is the individual ownership of land. To us in Africa, land was always recognized as belonging to the community. Each individual within our society had a right to the use of land, because otherwise he could not earn his living, and one cannot have the right to life without also having the right to some means of maintaining life. But the African's right to land was simply the right to use it; he had no other right to it, nor did it occur to him to try and claim one.

The foreigner introduced a completely different concept—the concept of land as a marketable commodity. According to this system, a person could claim a piece of land as his own private property whether he intended to use it or not. I could take a few square miles of land, call them "mine," and then go off to the moon. All I had to do to gain a living from "my" land was to charge a rent to the people who wanted to use it. If this piece of land was in an urban area I had no need to develop it at all; I could leave it to the fools who were prepared to develop all the other pieces of land surrounding "my" piece, and in doing so automatically to raise the market value of mine. Then I could come down from the moon and demand that these fools pay me through their noses for the high value of "my" land: a value which they themselves had created for me while I was enjoying myself on the moon! Such a system is not only foreign to us, it is completely wrong. Landlords, in a society which recognizes individual ownership of land, can be—and they usually are—in the same class as the loiterers I was talking about: the class of parasites.

We must not allow the growth of parasites here in Tanganyika. The TANU government must go back to the traditional African custom of landholding. That is to say, a member of society will be entitled to a piece of land on condition that he uses it. Unconditional, or "freehold," ownership of land (which leads to speculation and parasitism) must be abolished. We must, as I have said, regain our former attitude of mind—our traditional African Socialism—and apply it to the new societies we are building today. TANU has pledged itself to make socialism the basis of its policy

mea

in every field. The people of Tanganyika have given us their mandate to carry out that policy, by electing a TANU government to lead them. So the government can be relied upon to introduce only legislation which is in harmony with socialist principles.

. . . true socialism is an attitude of mind. It is, therefore, up to the people of Tanganyika—the peasants, the wage earners, the students, the leaders, all of us—to make sure that this socialist attitude of mind is not lost through the temptations to personal gain (or to the abuse of positions of authority) which may come our way as individuals, or through the temptation to look on the good of the whole community as of secondary importance to the interests of our own particular group.

Just as the Elder, in our former society, was respected for his age and his service to the community, so, in our modern society, this respect for age and service will be preserved. And in the same way as the "rich" Elder's apparent wealth was really only held by him in trust for his people, so, today, the apparent extra wealth which certain positions of leadership may bring to the individuals who fill them can be theirs only insofar as it is a necessary aid to the carrying out of their duties. It is a "tool" entrusted to them for the benefit of the people they serve. It is not "theirs" personally; and they may not use any part of it as a means of accumulating more for their own benefit, or as an insurance against the day when they no longer hold the same positions. That would be to betray the people who entrusted it to them. If they serve the community while they can, the community must look after them when they are no longer able to do so.

In tribal society, the individuals or the families within a tribe were "rich" or "poor" according to whether the whole tribe was rich or poor. If the tribe prospered, all the members of the tribe shared in its prosperity. Tanganyika, today, is a poor country. The standard of living of the masses of our people is shamefully low. But if every man and woman in the country takes up the challenge and works to the limit of his or her ability for the good of the whole society, Tanganyika will prosper; and that prosperity will be shared by all her people.

But it must be shared. The true socialist may not exploit his fellows. So that if the members of any group within our society are going to argue that, because they happen to be contributing more to the national income than some other groups, they must therefore take for themselves a greater share of the profits of their own industry than they actually need; and if they insist on this in spite of the fact that it would mean reducing their group's contribution to the general income and thus slowing down the rate at which the whole community can benefit, then that group is exploiting (or trying to exploit) its fellow human beings. It is displaying a capitalist attitude of mind.

There are bound to be certain groups which, by virtue of the "market value" of their particular industry's products, will contribute more to the nation's income than others. But the others may actually be producing goods and services which are of equal, or greater, intrinsic value although they do not happen to command such a high artificial value. For example, the food produced by the peasant farmer is of greater social value than the diamonds mined at Mwadui. But the mineworkers of Mwadui could claim, quite correctly, that their labor was yielding greater financial profits to the community than that of the farmers. If, however, they went on to demand that they should therefore be given most of that extra profit for themselves, and that no share of it should be spent on helping the farmers, they would be potential capitalists!

This is exactly where the attitude of mind comes in. It is one of the purposes of trade unions to ensure for the workers a fair share of the profits of their labor. But a "fair" share must be fair in relation to the whole society. If it is greater than the country can afford without having to penalize some other section of society, then it is not a fair share. Trade union leaders and their followers, as long as they are true socialists, will not need to be coerced by the government into keeping their demands within the limits imposed by the needs of society as a whole. Only if there are potential capitalists among them will the socialist government have to step in and prevent them from putting their capitalist ideas into practice!

As with groups, so with individuals. There are certain skills, certain qualifications, which, for good reasons, command a higher rate of salary for their possessors than others. But here again, the true socialist will demand only that return for his skilled work which he knows to be a fair one in proportion to the wealth or poverty of the whole society to which he belongs. He will not, unless he is a would-be capitalist, attempt to blackmail the community by demanding a salary equal to that paid to his counterpart in some far wealthier society.

European socialism was born of the Agrarian Revolution and the Industrial Revolution which followed it. The former created the "landed" and the "landless" classes in society; the latter produced the modern capitalist and the industrial proletariat.

These two revolutions planted the seeds of conflict within society, and not only was European socialism born of that conflict, but its apostles sanctified the conflict itself into a philosophy. Civil war was no longer looked upon as something evil, or something unfortunate, but as something good and necessary. As prayer is to Christianity or to Islam, so civil war (which they call "class war") is to the European version of socialism—a means inseparable from the end. Each becomes the basis for a whole way of life. The European socialist cannot think of his socialism without its father —capitalism!

Brought up in tribal socialism, I must say I find this contradiction quite intolerable. It gives capitalism a philosophical status which capitalism neither claims nor deserves. For it virtually says, "Without capitalism, and the conflict which capitalism creates within society, there can be no socialism"! This glorification of capitalism by the doctrinaire European socialists, I repeat, I find intolerable.

African Socialism, on the other hand, did not have the "benefit" of the Agrarian Revolution or the Industrial Revolution. It did not start from the existence of conflicting "classes" in society. Indeed, I doubt if the equivalent for the word "class" exists in any indigenous African language; for language describes the ideas of those who speak it, and the idea of "class" or "caste" was non-existent in African society.

The foundation, and the objective, of African Socialism is the extended family. The true African Socialist does not look on one class of men as his brethren and another as his natural enemies. He does not form an alliance with the "brethren" for the extermination of the "non-brethren." He rather regards all men as his brethren—as members of his ever extending family. That is why the first article of TANU's creed is: *Binadamu wote ni ndugu zangu. Na Afrika ni moja.* If this had been originally put in

English, it would have been: "I believe in human brotherhood and the unity of Africa."

"*Ujamaa*," then, or "familyhood," describes our Socialism. It is opposed to capitalism, which seeks to build a happy society on the basis of the exploitation of man by man; and it is equally opposed to doctrinaire socialism which seeks to build its happy society on a philosophy of inevitable conflict between man and man.

The African Mode of Socialism (Leopold Senghor)

Among the values of Europe, we have no intention of retaining capitalism, not in its nineteenth-century form at least. Of course, private capitalism was, in its early days, one of the factors of progress, just as feudalism was in its time, and even colonization. . . .

Today it is an out-of-date social and economic system—like feudalism, like colonization. And, I would add, like the imperialism in which it found its expression. Why? Because if, with its specializations, the collectivization of work constitutes a critical step toward socialization, the defense or, more exactly, the extension of private property does not lead in this direction. Just as serious is the alienation, in the material realm and the realm of the spirit, of which capitalism is guilty. Because capitalism works only for the well-being of a minority. Because, whenever state intervention and working-class pressure have forced it to reform itself, it has conceded only the minimum standard of living, when no less than the maximum would do. Because it holds out no prospect of a fuller being beyond material well-being. . . .

But our socialism is not that of Europe. It is neither atheistic communism nor, quite, the democratic socialism of the Second International. We have modestly called it the *African Mode of Socialism* . . . Mr. Potekhin, the Director of the African Institute in Moscow, in his book entitled *Africa Looks Ahead*, gives the following definition of the fundamental traits of the socialist society: the state's power is vested in the workers. All means of production are collective property, there are no exploiting classes, nor does one man exploit his fellow; the economy is planned, and

SOURCE: L. Senghor, *The African Mode of Socialism* (in W. H. Friedland and C. G. Roseberg, eds., *African Socialism*, Stanford University Press, Stanford, California, 1964), pp. 264–266.

its essential aim is to afford the maximum satisfaction of man's material and spiritual needs. Obviously we cannot withhold our support from this ideal society, this earthly paradise. But it still has to come about; the exploitation of man by his fellow has yet to be stamped out in reality; the satisfaction of his spiritual needs which transcend our material needs has to be achieved. This has not yet happened in any European or American form of civilization, neither in the West nor in the East. For this reason we are forced to seek our own original mode, a Negro-African mode, of attaining these objectives, paying special attention to the two elements I have just stressed: *economic democracy and spiritual freedom.*

With this prospect before us, we have decided to borrow from the socialist experiments—both theoretical and practical—only certain elements, certain scientific and technical values, which we have grafted like scions onto the wild stock of Negritude. For this latter, as a complex of civilized values, is traditionally *socialist* in character in this sense; that our Negro-African society is a classless society, which is not the same as saying that it has no hierarchy or division of labor. It is a *community-based society*, in which the hierarchy—and therefore power—is founded on spiritual and democratic values: on the law of primogeniture and election; in which decisions of all kinds are deliberated in a Palaver, after the ancestral gods have been consulted; in which work is shared out among the sexes and among technico-professional groups, based on religion. . . .

Thus, in the working out of our African Mode of Socialism, the problem is not how to put an end to the exploitation of man by his fellow, but to prevent it ever happening, by bringing political and economic democracy back to life; our problem is not how to satisfy spiritual, that is cultural needs, but how to keep the fervor of the black soul alive. . . .

Scientific research, planning, and cooperation sum up exactly the program which my country, Senegal, has just put into action, the moving force being Monsieur Mamadou Dia, the Prime Minister. Our first four-year plan is under way with its research institutes, its state banks, its state enterprises, its produce marketing boards, its cooperatives, which now comprise 80 per cent of the peasants, who themselves form 70 per cent of the total population. All this was preceded by a social and economic survey, which took more than 18 months to complete.

And yet we have not legally suppressed private capitalism which is foreign to our country; we have not even nationalized anything. Above all, we have not shed a single drop of blood. Why? Because we began by analyzing our situation as an underdeveloped and colonized country. The essential task was to win back our national independence. Next we had to eliminate the flaws of colonial rule while preserving its positive contributions, such as the economic and technical infrastructure and the French education system. Finally, these positive contributions had to be rooted in Negritude, and fertilized at the same time by the socialist spirit to make them bear fruit. They had to be rooted in Negritude by a series of comparisons between existing systems. Where private capitalism comes into peaceful competition with socialism, the latter must, I feel sure, emerge triumphant, provided that it transcends the goal of mere well-being, and does not secrete hatred. In the meantime, we need capital, even from private sources. Our aim is to fit it into the development plan, by controlling its use.

At this point we part company with the socialist experiments of Eastern Europe, with Communist experiments, while taking over their positive achievements. I spoke earlier of the living experience of a re-won freedom. To the list of needs which the plan must satisfy, I might have added leisure. This is how research, planning, and cooperation transcend, in their essence, the objective of material well-being. Science, by which I mean the quest for truth, is already a spiritual need. As is that rapture of the heart, of the soul, which art expresses, art which itself is only the expression of love. These spiritual needs, which weigh so heavy in Negro-African hearts, were touched on by Marx, as by Mr. Potekhin; but Marx did not stress them, nor did he fully define them.

Sources and Acknowledgments

II. THE CONTINUING THREAD

The Republic, Plato, trans. A. D. Lindsay (Dent, London 1935).

Utopia, Thomas More, trans. Paul Turner (Penguin Books, London 1965).

The Defense of Gracchus Babeuf, François-Noël Babeuf (Gehenna Press, Northampton, Mass. 1964).

III. SOME NINETEENTH-CENTURY SOCIALIST THINKERS

A New View of Society and Other Writings, Robert Owen (Everyman's Library Text, J. M. Dent & Sons Ltd., London, and E. P. Dutton & Co., Inc., New York 1949).

Socialist Thought, edited by Albert Fried and Ronald Sanders (Doubleday & Company, Inc., New York 1964, and The University of Edinburgh Press, Edinburgh).

Selections from the Works of Fourier, F.M.C. Fourier, trans. Julia Franklin (Swan Sonnenschein, London 1901).

What is Property? An Inquiry into the Principle of Right and Government, P.-J. Proudhon, trans B. R. Tucker (Reeves, London).

Communist Manifesto, K. Marx and F. Engels (F. Engels ed., authorized translation, London 1888).

Engels on Capital, F. Engels (International Publishers, New York 1937).

Socialism, Utopian and Scientific, F. Engels (Swan Sonnenschein, London 1892).

The Political Philosophy of Bakunin: Scientific Anarchism, Mikhail A. Bakunin (G. P. Maximoff, ed., The Free Press of Glencoe, New York).

Reflections on Violence, G. Sorel, trans. T. E. Hulme and J. Roth (Collier Books, New York 1961).

IV. MARXISM

The ABC of Communism, Bukharin and Preobrazensky (University of Michigan Press, Ann Arbor 1966).

What is to be Done?, V. I. Lenin (International Publishers, New York).

The State and Revolution, V. I. Lenin (The International Publishers, New York).

The Defense of Terrorism, L. D. Trotsky (The Labour Publishing Co., London 1920).

The New Course, L. D. Trotsky, trans. and ed. Max Schachtman (University of Michigan Press, Ann Arbor 1965).

The Permanent Revolution, L. D. Trotsky, trans. Max Schachtman (Pioneer Publications, New York 1931).

Foundations of Leninism, J. V. Stalin (International Publishers, New York 1937).

Quotations from Chairman Mao Tse-tung, Mao Tse-tung (Bantam Books, New York 1967).

Selected Works of Mao Tse-tung, Mao Tse-tung (Foreign Language Press, Peking 1965).

V. DEMOCRATIC SOCIALISM

Fabian Essays, George Bernard Shaw (George Allen & Unwin, London 1948, and Humanities Press, Inc., New York).

Evolutionary Socialism: A Criticism and Affirmation, Eduard Bernstein, trans. Edith C. Harvey (Schocken, New York 1963).

Aims and Tasks of Democratic Socialism (Socialist International, London 1951).

The World Today . . . The Socialist Perspective (Socialist International, London 1962).

A Socialist's Faith, Norman Thomas (Norton, New York 1951).

The Future of Socialism, C.A.R. Crosland (Schocken, New York 1963 , and Jonathan Cape, London).

VI. RECENT VARIATIONS OF SOCIALISM

Tito, V. Dedijer (Simon and Schuster, Inc., New York 1953).

Guerilla Warfare, Ché Guevara (Monthly Review Press, New York 1961).

The Arab Ba'th Socialist Party: History, Ideology, and Organization, Kamel S. Abu Jaber (Syracuse University Press, New York 1966).

The Theoretical Structure of Nasser's Arab Socialism, Fayez Sayegh (in A. Hourani, ed., *Middle Eastern Affairs*, No. 4, Oxford University Press, London 1965).

African Socialism, ed. William H. Friedland and Carl C. Rosberg (Stanford University Press, California 1964).

Freedom and Unity—Uhuru Na Umoja, Julius K. Nyerere (Oxford University Press, London).

Index

DOCUMENTARY HISTORY OF WESTERN CIVILIZATION
edited by Eugene C. Black and Leonard W. Levy

ANCIENT AND MEDIEVAL HISTORY OF THE WEST

Morton Smith: ANCIENT GREECE

A. H. M. Jones: A HISTORY OF ROME THROUGH THE FIFTH CENTURY
Vol. I: The Republic
Vol. II: The Empire

Deno Geanakopolos: BYZANTINE EMPIRE

Marshall W. Baldwin: CHRISTIANITY THROUGH THE CRUSADES

Bernard Lewis: ISLAM THROUGH SULEIMAN THE MAGNIFICENT

David Herlihy: HISTORY OF FEUDALISM

William M. Bowsky: RISE OF COMMERCE AND TOWNS

David Herlihy: MEDIEVAL CULTURE AND SOCIETY

EARLY MODERN HISTORY

Hannah Gray: CULTURAL HISTORY OF THE RENAISSANCE

Florence Edler De Roover: MONEY, BANKING & COMMERCE, 13TH-16TH CENTURIES

V. J. Parry: THE OTTOMAN EMPIRE

Ralph E. Giesey: EVOLUTION OF THE DYNASTIC STATE

J. H. Parry: THE EUROPEAN RECONNAISSANCE

Hans J. Hillerbrand: THE PROTESTANT REFORMATION

John C. Olin: THE CATHOLIC COUNTER-REFORMATION

Orest Ranum: THE CENTURY OF LOUIS XIV

Thomas Hegarty: RUSSIAN HISTORY THROUGH PETER THE GREAT

Marie Boas-Hall: THE SCIENTIFIC REVOLUTION

Barry E. Supple: HISTORY OF MERCANTILISM

_____: IMPERIALISM, WAR & DIPLOMACY,1550-1763

Herbert H. Rowen: THE LOW COUNTRIES

C. A. Macartney: THE EVOLUTION OF THE HABSBURG & HOHENZOLLERN DYNASTIES

Lester G. Crocker: THE ENLIGHTENMENT

Robert Forster: EIGHTEENTH CENTURY EUROPEAN SOCIETY